Hiking America's Wilderness

600 Destinations in the Natural World

STEPHEN BRUMBACH

Disclaimer

This book describes hiking and backpacking in wilderness areas. These activities involve inherent, unavoidable risks of death or injury. This book is not intended to be an exhaustive authority on hiking and backpacking, nor is it intended to be your only source of information on this subject. The reader accepts all risks, dangers, and liabilities that may result from these activities. The author and publisher of this book disclaim any and all liability for any injury, loss, or damage that the reader may incur.

ISBN: 978-1-59152-272-0

Published by Stephen Brumbach
© 2021 by Stephen Brumbach

For more information, or to order extra copies of this book
call Farcountry Press toll-free at (800) 821-3874.

Produced by Sweetgrass Books;
PO Box 5630, Helena, MT 59604;
(800) 821-3874; www.sweetgrassbooks.com.

The views expressed by the author/publisher in this book do not necessarily
represent the views of, nor should be attributed to, Sweetgrass Books.

Sweetgrass Books is not responsible for the content of the author/publisher's work.

Produced in the United States of America. Printed in China.

24 23 22 21 1 2 3 4

Contents

Introduction

Purpose

This book is intended to provide hikers and others who love the natural world with descriptions of six hundred of the congressionally designated wilderness areas of the United States. These descriptions are based on more than forty years of hiking some of the most fabulous examples of the nation's remaining natural lands.

There are a lot of federally designated wilderness areas in the United States: about 769 as of December 2018. I have been to just over 600 of them. They have included almost every landscape and ecosystem found in the country. Some I found more appealing or interesting than others. My opinions of the aesthetic charms of different areas are incorporated here into a rating system. The purpose is to provide hikers with some idea of what to expect when visiting an area and to suggest the most rewarding areas to visit depending on their tastes, interests, and hiking abilities.

Because I give at least some coverage to about 600 wilderness areas, this is not a short work. In an attempt to control length, I do not provide as much introductory material as one often finds in hiking guides. For example, I do not give lectures on safety, water purification, waste disposal, food storage, or minimum-impact practices. I assume that my readers are prepared to behave responsibly in the outdoors. I do not give detailed driving directions to specific wilderness areas, although I do give general location information. Also missing are detailed hiking directions, although I do describe my hikes with trailheads and trails or routes where there were no trails.

About the Author

I am a native of rural Pennsylvania, born in 1944. Rural areas were still pretty rural then. Access to the outdoors was easy; walk out the back door. Behind our house was a derelict orchard, overrun with weeds, vines, and bushes. I spent a lot of time there. Not very far away were tracts of forest, farm fields, and cultivated orchards. When I was too young to go to these more distant places alone, I would beg, cajole, and wheedle any nearby adult to accompany me. I just loved being out and seeing the natural world. When I was old enough to go out by myself, I always looked for the quietest, most remote spots. This inclination has remained with me and persists to this day.

Young adulthood was focused on college and graduate school. My nose was almost always in books or laboratories. There was little time for hiking or many other outdoor activities. I did end up becoming a practicing scientist, earning a PhD in chemistry. An early research job in the Chicago suburbs did not lend itself to much outdoor recreation. Things changed significantly in 1979 when I found a job with my Illinois employer at a branch facility in Idaho. Here outdoor activities started to become a serious part of my life. Many coworkers were longtime hands at hiking, climbing, and skiing. They proved to be great mentors. Here is where I started to spend serious time in the West's designated wilderness areas. Access was easy with the Wind River, Teton, Sawtooth, Gros Ventre, Absaroka, Beartooth, and Uinta ranges within a day's drive. Also helpful was my employer's generous allowance of vacation time.

But after almost twenty years with my employer, I grew disillusioned and just said, "I'm out of here."

I moved to Wyoming and built an off-the-grid house on the western edge of the Wind River Mountains. I had more time for hiking and more opportunities for going farther afield, to the Pacific Northwest, California, Colorado, Arizona, and New Mexico. Now almost all my trips were in designated wilderness areas. I became convinced that if one really wanted to experience the best nature has to offer, wilderness areas were the place to go.

Somehow, life seemed incomplete, so I looked for some sort of job to reconnect with the rest of the world. I started teaching part-time for a community college. This turned out to be a very positive experience, so I moved to the "big town" of Rock Springs. After a few years as an adjunct, I was offered a full-time job teaching chemistry. With no summer commitments there were still many opportunities for exploring wilderness areas.

It was while a part-time faculty member that I started thinking about visiting wilderness areas systematically. Not just the old familiar territory in the West, but also relatively unexplored (by me) areas in the East. At this time, almost all of the areas I had visited were administered by the United States Forest Service (USFS). I looked at lots of maps and researched on the internet to generate a list of these areas. There were around 400, and I had been to fewer than half. I made it a conscious goal to visit all of them.

Somewhere around the year 2002 or 2003 I realized that I could not reach my goal and teach full-time, so I decided to retire and become a full-time hiker. This was in 2004. I still taught a little bit part time, but the bulk of my time was spent exploring in the woods.

The result of all this is that I have visited and done at least some hiking in just over 600 designated wilderness areas, including 446 of the 447 USFS areas and 57 of the 61 areas administered by the National Park Service (US-NPS) as of the end of 2018. My records tell me that I have spent 1,614 days with my feet on the ground in some designated wilderness area.

I am often asked who accompanied me to these sometimes-obscure destinations. The short answer is nobody. In the early days on long trips I often did go with one or a few other folks. After getting familiar with backcountry travel, I increasingly went alone. Now, I am completely comfortable going just about anywhere alone.

I presently live in Green River, Wyoming. I still hike, but a lot more slowly and with a lot less agility.

The United States Wilderness System

The 1960s in the United States was a time of great conflict and upheaval. Among several high-profile issues were those associated with the environment. After many decades of industrial, agricultural, and urban expansion, some observers became concerned that lands retaining any characteristics of their original natural states were disappearing and something ought to be done to retain some of these remaining places and protect them from development. One result was the Wilderness Act of 1964. I do not intend to attempt to retell the tale of this act except to say that the lands designated as wilderness should be:

> "… an area where the earth and its community of life are untrammeled by man …"

> "… an area of undeveloped federal land retaining its primeval character and influence, without permanent improvement or habitation …"

> "… generally appears to have been affected primarily by the forces of nature, with the imprint of man's work substantially unnoticeable …"

> "… has outstanding opportunities for solitude or a primitive and unconfined type of recreation …"

> "… shall be devoted to the public purpose of recreation, scenic, scientific, educational, conservation and historic use."

The Wilderness Act passed the US Senate in 1963 by a vote of 73 to 12. It passed the US House of Representatives on July 30, 1964, by a vote of 373 to 1. At the time of writing this in 2018, I hate to think of what the outcome of this vote would be today.

Following the act, 54 areas were designated covering 9.1 million acres. Many more areas were added in the following years (especially in 1984), and as of early 2018 there were 769 areas encompassing 109,142,230 acres. These acres amount to about 5 percent of the area of the United States. However, about half of these acres are in Alaska, with only about 2.7 percent of the contiguous United States designated.

Additional Sources of Information

Good, so you want to go visit some wilderness areas. I hope this book has provided enough information for you to select some destinations. However, my descriptions are not especially detailed, and you may need some more information. Where might you go to learn more about a specific wilderness area? One good source is the website wilderness.net. This site is managed by the Wilderness Institute at the University of Montana's College of Forestry and Conservation and was founded by the university in 1996. The site lists wilderness areas by name and by location. Location is by state with an alphabetical list of areas for each state. Zoom-in maps are also provided for each area. Addresses and phone numbers are provided for the nearest land management agency responsible for each wilderness area.

Maps are very handy, probably essential for exploring the backcountry. I have spent an inordinate part of my life looking at maps. As a child, I drew maps or copied maps from books. I still rely on paper maps. In most of my hiking years the gold standard was the 7.5-minute United States Geologic Survey (USGS) topographic map with a scale of 1:24,000. At this scale, 1 mile is about 2.625 inches on the map. Contour intervals are typically 40 feet, which provides enough detail to evaluate off-trail hiking. Also common and still standard in Alaska are USGS topographic maps with a scale of 1:63,360 and contour interval of 100 feet. These contour intervals can hide a lot of obstacles, so be careful in route selection.

Today, USGS maps are available online for download. Digital maps are also available with GPS (global positioning system) devices. Even without downloaded maps, I consider a GPS to be an essential piece of equipment.

The Bear's Tooth, Fitzpatrick Wilderness, Wyoming

I was given my first GPS by friends in 2004 and now I always carry one. It has often kept me from getting lost in areas without trails or with dense forest and few visible landmarks.

Land management agencies also provide maps and information about specific wilderness areas. The US Forest Service publishes physical maps for individual national forests that mostly include roads, wilderness boundaries, and maintained trails. If you are hiking on trails, these Forest Service maps may be all you need. Some national forests, especially in the east, have one- or two-page writeups for individual wilderness areas that include directions to trailheads and suggested hikes. The Bureau of Land Management publishes paper topographic maps with a 1:100,000 scale that show "surface management status" that includes roads and wilderness boundaries. The National Park Service publishes maps of various sorts that often identify designated wilderness areas within their respective parks.

The National Geographic Society also publishes maps of national parks and other areas of interest to hikers. These can be quite detailed including wilderness boundaries, trails, and sometimes even trail mileage. For large parks like those in Alaska, the scale can be rather large so a lot of detail is lost.

Another often-helpful guide for me has been the state-by-state Atlas & Gazetteer published by DeLorme. Many, but not all, wilderness areas are shown. These maps are best for identifying roads to provide wilderness access. Be warned, however, that there are some roads on the ground not on these maps and some roads shown on the maps that are not on the ground.

There are also books out there that provide information and detailed directions for finding and navigating within specific wilderness areas, often by state. Some of the larger, better-known wilderness areas such as Wyoming's Wind River Range, Utah's High Uinta, Colorado's Weminuche, and new Mexico's Gila have whole guidebooks dedicated to trails, trailheads, and destinations including driving directions.

A final source of information, especially if one is having difficulty finding a particular destination, is the live human. The Forest Service and Bureau of Land Management (BLM) have ranger stations or district offices that house people responsible for wilderness management. Some offices have a designated wilderness ranger. Often some person in these offices knows about your destination and can give pretty good information. I have on a few occasions needed a person to draw me a map or find me a map to get me where I wanted to go. On at least two occasions the person with whom I spoke said, "Unless I draw you a map you will never find this place." Note, however, these offices are only open for limited hours, typically 8:00 am to 4:30 pm and *weekdays only*. National Park Service ranger stations keep more visitor-friendly hours.

Some wilderness areas require permits for overnight trips and, in a few instances, even for day trips. Permits are normally available in ranger stations or visitor centers that often (but not always) have more liberal office hours. Sometimes permits can be obtained at trailheads. Permit requirements are most common in high visitor density areas like the Sierra Nevada in California and a few very popular BLM desert areas.

The Wilderness Area Rating System

I have hiked a lot of wilderness areas. More than 600 of them. Some of them have just blown me away with spectacular scenery or the sights and sounds of wildlife and the opportunity to experience the natural world in an intimate setting. Some areas have done this to a greater or lesser extent than others. One of the goals of this book is to give hikers some idea of the best areas to visit. Providing a rating system is a way to achieve this goal. Identifying an area as "best" is, of course, a subjective judgment.

Never shy about having opinions, I have a five-star (best) through one-star (least good) system. This is based on my sense of aesthetics, interests, and values associated with natural settings.

I am a hiker. The ratings are *from a hiker's perspective.* Areas with a large fraction of water might get a low rating even if they are very wild and beautiful. Some areas are, without doubt, best seen from a boat. This is particularly true for states like Florida and other states of the Southeast. The ability of a hiker to navigate an area is one component of its rating.

Ratings are based on my perhaps very limited experience. Ratings of many areas, especially in the East, are based on a single day hike. If I was there on a rainy day with poor visibility, my rating might be lower than if I had been there on a sunny day. Also, for many eastern areas where I might not be especially knowledgeable, my choice of routes may not have taken me to the best spots.

Some specific criteria are:

1. **Is it wild?** Hearing Interstate 75 traffic noise through much of the Horseshoe Bay Wilderness in Michigan did not help its rating. There are other areas near big cities that are overrun by folks as well as being noisy, full of signs, and big parking lots charging fees (Sandia Mountain, New Mexico), all of which make me hurry away. A factor related to wildness is the impact of domestic livestock grazing. Overgrazed desert areas or hiking behind 2,000 sheep will not improve any area's rating.

2. **Does it have scenic value?** This is, of course, subjective, but I find some landscapes a lot more appealing than others.

3. **Does it have unique biological or geological features; i.e., is it interesting?** Here I think about Coronation Island's eroded shore, Russell Fiord's birds and brown bears, or Chuck River's whales playing offshore in contrast to some eastern areas that in my perhaps unfair view are almost indistinguishable. In fact, I have a generic problem with many eastern areas. As I hike along, my thought often is "Didn't I just do this hike yesterday?"

4. **Which brings us to the criterion "Is it at least pleasant?"** Small, trailless areas of swamp filled with walls of vegetation knitted together with greenbrier are not pleasant in my view. Coastal North Carolina areas left me muttering under my breath. There may have been interesting frogs or wetland plants in there, but after a while I was looking for the exit.

My translation of the ratings is:

★ ★ ★ ★ ★ Five-star (31 areas) This is the best. Go. Go out of your way to visit.

★ ★ ★ ★ Four-star (51 areas) Go. This may not be the best but it is close; really nice areas.

★ ★ ★ Three-star (203 areas) These are nice destinations. I recommend them. They have most of what you would want in a wilderness hiking destination. Maybe not as spectacular as some, but worth a visit. I would gladly go back. Nobody should be offended if their favorite area got "only" three stars.

★ ★ Two-star (287 areas) No features of special interest, not spectacular, but still pleasant. It's just that I would not travel far out of my way to go back. If you are in the neighborhood, go for it.

★ One-star (28 areas) These are areas I found neither particularly interesting nor pleasant.

There are 285 five-, four-, and three-star areas. That should keep many hikers busy for a while.

I provide a summary list at the end of the book with wilderness areas organized by star rating, and a second list organized by state.

As a final comment about the rating system, let me emphasize that every wilderness area I visited, regardless of rating, did indeed help preserve some remnant of the natural world.

A Note on Photographs

All the photographs in this book were taken by the author. Many of them were taken a long time ago using that antiquated medium called film. Many wilderness photos from long ago no longer survive due to editing, periodic house cleaning, or digital incompetence. I have tried to digitize old slides and prints with varying degrees of success. I have tried to include here only better-quality images that represent the landscapes found in a particular wilderness area or a collection of similar areas. No images remain from several areas that I visited.

Selecting which photos to include here was a difficult task. It would be easy for me to find dozens of images from my favorite areas, but that would demand too much space when covering hundreds of areas. Most five-star and four-star areas got at least one photo each. Some three-star and two-star areas got photos representative of their area or landscape types, or just because I had a photo that I really liked.

Organization

I have organized wilderness areas by region of the United States. These regions are roughly described by the major biomes present in that region. Biomes are regions with various sets of climate conditions, growth patterns, vegetation types, and animal species. Within a particular region, the areas are listed according to number of ranking stars, five stars first. Within star rankings, areas are presented by state. The sequence of regions is approximately north to south and west to east. California, with a large variety of biomes and ecosystems, is covered as a unique region. Likewise, Hawaii is considered by itself.

For each area visited I give the size in acres, the year it received congressional designation, the federal agency responsible for managing the area, the approximate location of the area, the dates of my visit, and where I went in that area. For areas visited many times I only mention my favorite trips. For most areas I have tried to keep descriptions concise. Sometimes a tale may be told of things seen and heard during a visit. Because I am a semi-enthusiastic birder, I may also mention sightings that I found interesting. Descriptions of two-star and one-star areas are more compact than those of higher-ranked areas.

Some Commonly Used Acronyms

AT	Appalachian Trail
BLM	Bureau of Land Management
CDT	Continental Divide Trail
GPS	Global Positioning System
PCT	Pacific Crest Trail
USFS	United States Forest Service
USFWS	United States Fish and Wildlife Service
USGS	United States Geological Survey
USNPS	United States National Park Service

A Final Note on Safety

This book does not include "difficulty" ratings when hikes are described. I decided such a rating was too subjective and levels too hard to define. While I have said earlier that I assume readers are competent, responsible hikers, I should probably mention some cautionary points about hiking in US wilderness areas. Hikers should first of all be self-reliant. Most wilderness areas are remote. Visitor services are normally *not* provided. If hikers encounter a problem, they should not expect someone else to solve it for them. Also, many, probably most, wilderness areas do not have cell phone service.

Many wilderness areas described in this book have no trails. Hikers need to know whether or not they have the skills and mentality to travel without a trail. Even if an area has trails, signage can be sparse. Some national forests deliberately minimize signage.

Hikers should always have a sense of the terrain they will be visiting. Be prepared. What temperatures should be expected? Will you be able to find water? *Many* wilderness areas have limited or no water availability. Will it be necessary to ford rivers or streams (a big issue for me)? Most wilderness areas do *not* have bridges for water crossings.

A very important consideration for a wilderness hiker is to know your own limits. How many miles can you realistically cover in a day, especially in a day with no trail? Can you really carry a backpack with a week's worth of food and clothes appropriate for your destination? Some of the hikes described here would be perfect for beginners. Many would most certainly not be. Be adventurous, but also be objective. Never be afraid to turn around if you are out of your depth.

The wilderness is out there. Go if you are ready.

Mount Blackburn, Wrangell-Saint Elias Wilderness, Alaska

Mount Rainier from Spray Park,
Mount Rainier Wilderness, Washington

The Pacific Northwest

The Pacific Northwest is the region of the United States defined by the biomes of tundra, rock and ice, boreal forest, and temperate coniferous forest. I put the states of Alaska, Washington, and Oregon into this region. The eastern parts of Washington and Oregon also have areas better represented by the biome of dry shrubland.

Because travel in general and hiking in particular in Alaska are unlike that for the rest of the United States, I begin discussion of this region with an introduction just for Alaska.

An Introduction to Alaska

Alaska is a very beautiful place. Much of it remains wild. There are more acres of designated wilderness than in any other state. Many of these areas are large. There are nineteen US Forest Service (USFS)-managed areas, all in the Tongass National Forest, eight National Park Service (USNPS) areas scattered throughout the state, and twenty-one US Fish and Wildlife Service (USFWS) areas. I have been to all the USFS areas, seven of the NPS areas, and only one of the USFWS areas.

Hiking and backpacking in Alaska offer challenges not often encountered in the lower forty-eight. First of all, only five areas have road access, and two of these still require a trip on an airplane. Getting to your starting point for a hiking trip will require a boat or, more likely, an airplane. *This is how people get around in Alaska.* Fortunately, there are plenty of expert bush pilots to get you where you want to go (and boat operators where landing an airplane is problematical). A nontrivial problem with airplanes and boats is that they are expensive. For my Alaska wilderness areas visits I used my own pickup truck for exactly one, two with rental cars, one with a tour boat, one with both a charter boat *and* a bush plane, and the others with twenty-four round-trip bush plane flights (twenty-three of these with a float plane, one with a wheeled plane).

Not only are the bush planes the best way to get around, the pilots are excellent sources of information about various destinations, often including the best places for hiking. They see their territory every day and have pretty much *memorized* the terrain.

Another challenge for Alaska wilderness hikers is that there are almost no trails. There are some old maps that show trails, but on the ground, you will probably not see them, or even consider them to be trails if you do see them. Well, OK, so one hikes cross country. This brings up what I consider the biggest Alaska challenge, dense vegetation. The hiker's enemies are willow, blueberry, devil's club, and, worst of all, alder. If sufficiently dense, alder can become a virtual wall. Up to twenty feet tall with interlocking branches, one can simultaneously be held by the ankle, knee, waist, chest, and neck. I have more than once been stopped dead by alder. These conditions are called "Green Hell." The photo shows my campsite in the Endicott River Wilderness surrounded by alder. Hikers must realize that the time it takes to travel a mile in Alaska can be *much* longer than in the lower forty-eight. An additional problem with dense vegetation is that the hiker sometimes cannot see his feet, resulting in stumbling over rocks and deadfall debris. In terrain that has never had trails, deadfall is another obstacle.

If you want to avoid many of these vegetation-related problems, study your maps and talk to your pilot, because the best way to avoid the problems is by starting out at relatively high elevation. Above about 2,000 feet dense vegetation is a lot less common than at lower elevations. My favorite hiking routes are along ridges above tree line, but one must still be careful in selecting starting points.

Southeast Alaska, home to the Tongass National Forest, is wet. Even when it is not raining, low clouds and fog are common. The high rainfall results in lots of steep-sided gullies that also slow down the hiker. In flatter terrain, much of the land is covered with shallow water, another impediment. Real Alaskans often wear tall rubber boots called "Alaska sneakers." They are good at keeping feet relatively dry, but provide little support. I personally do not like to backpack in rubber boots, but sometimes it is the best way to go.

Bush planes almost always operate on visual flight rules. This means the pilot must be able to see well enough to avoid flying into terrain. Because of the wet weather, there are lots of days when the visual criteria cannot be met. This means that the hiker does not fly that day (or part of a day). If this occurs on the day the hiker is supposed to be picked up, that means the hiker spends an extra day in the wilderness. This happens. Because of this possibility, the hiker needs to take extra food in case of delays. The longest I was ever weathered in was three days because of a pretty big storm.

I also experienced a few one-day delays, mostly due to fog, but on at least one occasion by high wind. Float planes do not do well in windy conditions; they can be blown onto the shore, or be blown away from shore after landing. The hiker should always talk to his pilot to see how much extra food should be carried for any specific destination.

Lots of rainfall also produces big creeks and rivers. In many cases, a hiker faces potentially dangerous water crossings. I must confess here that I am a chicken when it comes to fast, cold water and have more than once been turned back rather than take the risk of a crossing (I have *always* hiked alone in Alaska).

Other potential hazards that may be more important in Alaska than in the lower forty-eight are bugs and bears. Alaska is famous for its clouds of mosquitoes. In all my Alaska travels I have rarely had a serious mosquito problem. Part of this is timing. I often schedule trips after the middle of July if I think I will be in mosquito country. Coastal areas are less mosquito prone and I have done earlier trips there. What has been a problem are little gnat-like bugs called "white sox" because of tiny white stripes on their legs. These guys are persistent and have a nasty bite. They love to get into your eyes. Another bug, a surprise to me, was horse flies. I have seen lots of horse flies in the lower forty-eight, but never expected to see them in Alaska. I did one August trip in the Misty Fiords Wilderness when the land temperature was over 80 degrees F. There were clouds of horse flies latching onto any exposed skin. I covered up as best I could and camped in the middle of the biggest snowfield I could find.

Camp surrounded by the enemy alder, Endicott River Wilderness

Bears. If you go to Alaska you will see bears. Period. Guaranteed. *They* own the place. *You* are the visitor. If you are in a high-use bear area you will probably know from tracks and scat, both unmistakable. What should you do? First, if possible, do not camp in any space where you see lots of tracks and scat. Second, make noise. This is especially important in dense vegetation. Bears do not like surprises. Third, keep a clean camp. Do not carry odiferous food. What food you do carry should be in a "bear-proof" container. (The National Park Service *requires* bear-proof food storage.)

I have seen lots of bears both black and brown in Alaska. Mostly they just ignored me. Most other times I only knew they were there because I saw them running away from me. Only once have I encountered a bear that frightened me. It was a black that, upon seeing me, kept coming closer until it was really too close, and I made a lot of noise and waved my hands and it finally left me alone. I do always carry pepper spray, and it was in my hand, pointed at the bear on that occasion.

If a hiker wants to experience nature undisturbed by other humans, Alaska is your place. Outside of the heavily visited Denali, I have spent 132 days in Alaska wilderness areas. The total number of other hikers I have encountered is exactly four.

Finally, Alaska might not be a great place for beginners. All hikers must be completely self-reliant, knowledgeable about navigation (and *always* carry a GPS), and willing to live within the constraints of the terrain.

Wrangell-Saint Elias

★ ★ ★ ★ ★

Size: 9,078,675 acres   **Year Designated:** 1980   **Responsible Agency:** USNPS

Most of Wrangell-Saint Elias National Park is designated wilderness. It is the largest wilderness area in the country. It is located along the Gulf of Alaska east of State Highway 4, east of the town of Valdez, and north of the town of Yakutat. The eastern wilderness boundary is the US-Canada border.

MY VISIT: August 3–5, 2008 plus a few days around the edges

This was my first time ever in Alaska. I drove. From Wyoming. The drive, while long, was interesting as so much of the territory was new to me. The hike started in the little community of McCarthy, accessed by an unpaved road ending at the old Kennecott copper mine and mill. Now there is a lodge, and the mill is being restored by the Park Service. In the not-too-distant past this road was famous for destroying tires. The road mostly follows the route of an old railroad that served the mill. After the mill closed, the track was removed. The rail spikes were *not* removed and caused the tire problems. The spikes were pretty much gone when I drove the road. Today private vehicles are not allowed in the lodge and mill area, so one parks just outside. This parking requires a fee. The fee collector wandered over to my truck.

On one hip he carried a canister of bear spray. On the other hip he carried a very large revolver. Yes, the density of bears in greater McCarthy was high.

For my backpacking trip, my route was from the Kennecott Mill along the Root Glacier to a small summit called The Knoll. Day one was mostly gray but dry. Occasional gaps in the clouds gave tantalizing views of serious peaks nearby. The first day's hike was along, not on, the glacier. Day two took me to the top of The Knoll. Much of this day was on the glacier. The Park Service folks assured me that this was a safe glacier without need for special equipment. About the time I arrived at The Knoll, the clouds parted and the view was spectacular. The photo shows the Stairway Icefall, taken from the summit of The Knoll. I spent the rest of the day exploring around the immediate area. Day three started (and ended) with rain. Not just drizzle, but real rain. I could have stayed another day, but given the rain and not eager to test my skill on the Icefall, I decided to go back to McCarthy. On my way up, I had to negotiate a modest willow thicket. It was not a big deal going up, but going down I got seriously drenched as the willows were a lot taller than I was. The rain persisted all day, and by the time I got close to Kennecott I was starting

to get cold. While descending the glacier, a black bear came into view. I was on the ice and the bear was on the moraine. I figured "this is cool." However, upon seeing me the bear came down onto the ice and approached. Because the ice was not particularly flat, he disappeared and reappeared, each time closer. I finally had enough and got out my bear spray and proceeded to make a lot of noise with a lot of waving of arms. He finally left.

At this point I was really getting cold, and when I got to the mill I was in early hypothermia. Once in my truck I was able to warm up fairly quickly.

The next few days I wandered around the edges of the wilderness part of the park, mostly day hikes along the Nabesna Road. I may have made it past the wilderness boundary, but I doubt it.

The year 2008 was not a good year to visit Wrangell-Saint Elias. Many locals said it was one of the wettest summers they had ever seen. This continued to be the case and I was only able to get short glimpses of the interior parts of the wilderness. It was enough, however, to convince me that this was some very serious, spectacular country. It seems out of place to say I truly saw this area in only a few days given the enormous size, but this was all I could do. I have no doubt that this area rates five stars.

Gates of the Arctic

★ ★ ★ ★ ★

Size: 7,245,600 acres **Year designated:** 1980 **Responsible Agency:** USNPS

Most of Gates of the Arctic National Park is designated wilderness. The park is located north of the Arctic Circle west of State Highway 11 (the Dalton Highway) and west of the Alaska Pipeline. The two gateway communities for the park are Bettles to the south and Anaktuvuk Pass to the north, each with USNPS ranger stations. Access to these communities is only by air. There is no road access to the park itself.

MY VISITS: July 23–30, 2015 and July 17–22, 2019

The 2015 trip was wonderful. I flew commercial air to Fairbanks, then a local carrier to Bettles, a standard jumping-off point for the park. The National Park Service has a small ranger station in Bettles, and they like visitors to come in and get an orientation.

From Bettles I took a float plane to the Gaedeke Lakes at the headwaters of the Alatna River and very close to the Continental Divide. This is also close to the headwaters of the Killik and Nigu Rivers. My route was covered by the USGS maps Survey Pass D-4 and D-5. For an old man I was carrying way too much weight, partly because of *two* food canisters with food for ten days, eight days planned and two in case of pickup delays. The terrain near the drop off point was mostly dry hummocks with a little low brush. Hummock terrain is pretty slow and a trekking pole was essential. My first destination was the headwaters of the Weyahok River. The higher I climbed, the easier the walking as the hummocks gave way to pretty even tundra and broken rock. I made it to the Divide ridge and the walking became easier still, presenting wonderful views of nearby peaks and almost infinite tundra. My nominal goal was the summit of Cravens Peak. I did not quite get to the summit due to rotten rock.

My next destination was the upper Nigu River. This was gentle terrain, very open with some lakes. I made a camp nearly on the Continental Divide and near a lake featuring a very vocal solitary loon and constant entertainment provided by a pair of Arctic terns. The final destination was the upper Killik River. Here I was surprised to see about seventy caribou. I had been told that it would be too early for them to be here, but there they were. The hike back to my drop-off point took me past the only sign of human activity that I saw. It was an old homestead consisting of a house and a few outbuildings. While nobody was present it was clear that the place was well cared for.

It is hard for me to imagine a better introduction to true Arctic ecosystems. This place was about as pristine as one could imagine. While hard to get to, hiking once here was not difficult. My destination was not as well known as the Arrigetch Peaks area to the south. On one of my flights my pilot took me skimming over these truly spectacular mountains.

The 2019 trip began with a float plane flight from Bettles to Lake 3520 (on the USGS Chandler Lake A-1 map) just a few meters west of the Continental Divide in the eastern part of the wilderness. My route from the lake was west up the North Fork of the Koyukuk River, then north over what some maps call Peregrine Pass, then dropping into the Grizzly Creek valley. This was a very rugged, scenically dense route. The Grizzly Creek area was the highlight of the trip. The weather was not the best with a lot of cloud cover and smoke from fires off to the south, but I did have a little sun one morning and was able to get a photo of Limestack Mountain, which I thought would make a good cover photo for this book. After losing a day to steady rain I retraced my steps to Lake 3520. While sitting near the lakeshore waiting for my pickup flight, what should stroll down the shore but a wolverine, my first and only sighting of one of these beasts. There were also caribou in the neighborhood.

View south from the Continental Divide, Gates of the Arctic Wilderness

Misty Fiords National Monument

★ ★ ★ ★ ★

Size: 2,142,434 acres   **Year Designated:** 1980   **Responsible Agency:** USFS

Most of the Misty Fiords National Monument in the Tongass National Forest is designated wilderness. The area is just west of the Canadian border with most of the wilderness on the mainland, but the eastern portion is on Revillagigedo Island. The city of Ketchikan is west of the wilderness.

MY VISITS: July 6–7, 2011 and July 29–August 1, 2013 and August 5–7, 2013

Most of the Tongass National Forest wilderness areas are in the string of islands in the Alaska Panhandle called the Alexander Archipelago. The gateway to Misty Fiords and other nearby wilderness areas is the city of Ketchikan. Ketchikan is also a stop for many large cruise ships. The main source of revenue for bush pilots is taking cruise ship passengers flightseeing over the spectacular nearby terrain.

The 2011 trip was my first with a bush pilot. I searched the internet for flight services. Most advertised fishing, hunting, and flightseeing. Only one mentioned hiking, and that is the one I chose. It was a wise choice. I was told my original destination was a poor choice because while I could be dropped off at my selected lake, I would not be able to do any hiking because of thick vegetation. We agreed on an alternative, "Sundial Lake." Like many locations in Alaska, this name has been assigned by locals to a feature not named on official USGS maps. On the Ketchikan B-3 map this lake is just Lake 1890, its elevation, in feet, above sea level. On drop-off day the weather was, well, misty with lots of low clouds, but we were able to land on the lake. Hiking around the lake was tricky because there was still brush. It was, however, possible to go higher into the more open terrain and get good views of the area.

Upon returning from my first hike to an open ridgetop I could see my tent below me. Strolling right by my campsite was a rather large bear (probably black). The bear paid absolutely no attention to my tent or food canister.

For my first 2013 trip my pilot suggested going to "Helicopter Lake," so called because it "can only be accessed by a helicopter," although the float plane had no problem landing (or later taking off). On this occasion, access to ridges was pretty straightforward and I had a couple of days of nice hiking.

In addition to the famous bears, there were also mountain goats. There may have been several, and there may also have been only one that I saw multiple times. One of those times was quite close.

Valley above Leduc Lake, Misty Fiords Wilderness

Punchbowl Lake, Misty Fiords Wilderness

It was also warm, temperatures over 80 degrees F. This brought out swarms of insects, most notably horse flies. I always wore long sleeves and sometimes a head net. I moved my campsite to the middle of as big a snow-field as I could find near the lake.

My third Misty trip was a few days later. This time, with the same pilot, the destination was Leduc Lake, north of my two previous destinations. This lake and surrounding valley were very beautiful and I had excellent weather during this short trip. There were lots of steep, smooth granite walls surrounding a lush green valley.

For someone new to Alaska hiking, Misty can be an excellent introduction. It is relatively easy to get to and there are lots of local pilots who know the country. Large lakes are plentiful and, depending on elevation, can make good starting points for hiking. I highly recommend this area to other hikers.

ALASKA

South Etolin

★ ★ ★ ★ ★

Size: 82,619 acres | **Year Designated:** 1990 | **Responsible Agency:** USFS

The South Etolin Wilderness is located in the Tongass National Forest on the southern portion of Etolin Island between Ernest Sound on the east and Clarence Strait on the west. The city of Ketchikan is to the south and the town of Wrangell is to the north.

MY VISIT: July 25–August 1, 2012

The winter of 2011/2012 was very snowy in southeast Alaska. There was still ice on the higher lakes in late July. My plan was to fly into an unnamed lake at 1,900 feet elevation. My pilot (in Ketchikan) demanded that I have an alternative, lower destination in case the first-choice lake was frozen. As it turned out, the first destination lake was just barely open, and there was significant snow around the lake as shown in the photo. (Note the departing airplane in the center of the photo.)

As it turned out, this snow was a blessing. It was a lot easier to hike on consolidated snow than to scramble through brush and over rocks. Access to high ridges was painless. The terrain was marvelous with cliffs, peaks, lakes, and forest and views of salt water. I did not see much wildlife on my visit but did see bear tracks on the snow, just enough to make a hiker pay attention.

I had a few days of excellent weather. Then, the day before I was scheduled for pickup, it started raining. Seriously. It rained all day on the day I was

supposed to be picked up, and the visibility made flying impossible. The next day looked a lot like the previous day except the wind was worse. The day after that was no better. I had left a metal coffee cup outside with my food and stove during this storm. The cup is 3.5 inches deep and I emptied it more than once; I think I received about 6 inches of rain during the storm.

The original plan was for me to be on the island for five days. I was finally picked up on day eight. This was the longest pickup delay I ever experienced.

While not large and not easy to get to, the wilderness scenery is spectacular and is easily worth five stars.

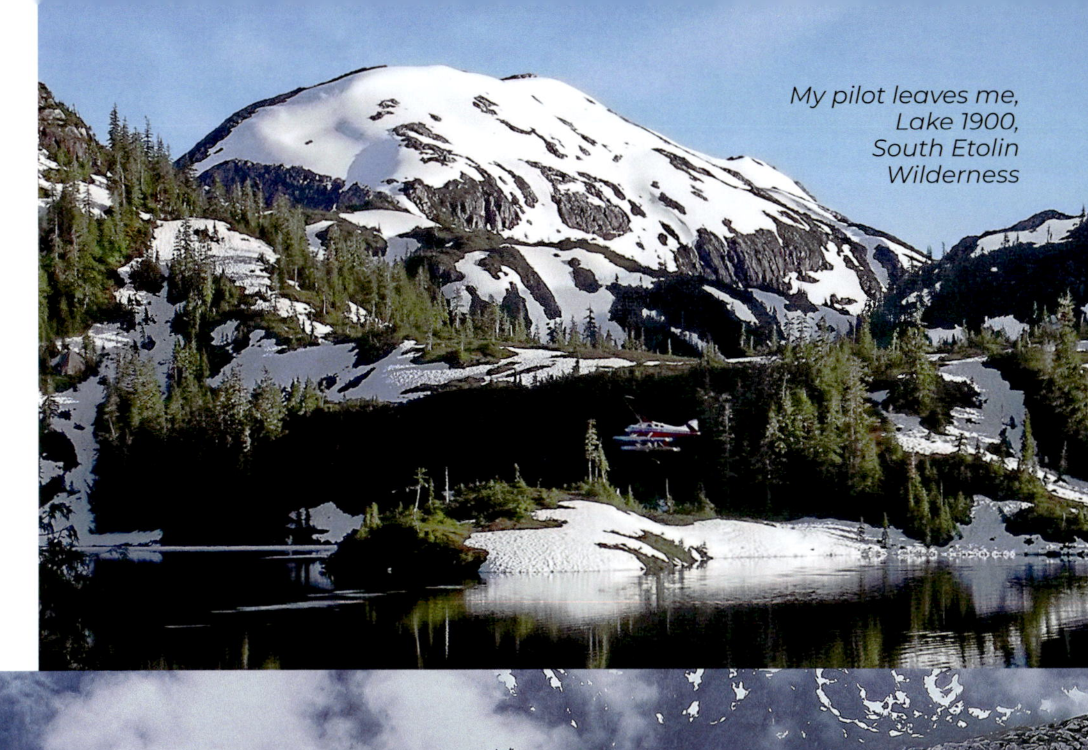

My pilot leaves me, Lake 1900, South Etolin Wilderness

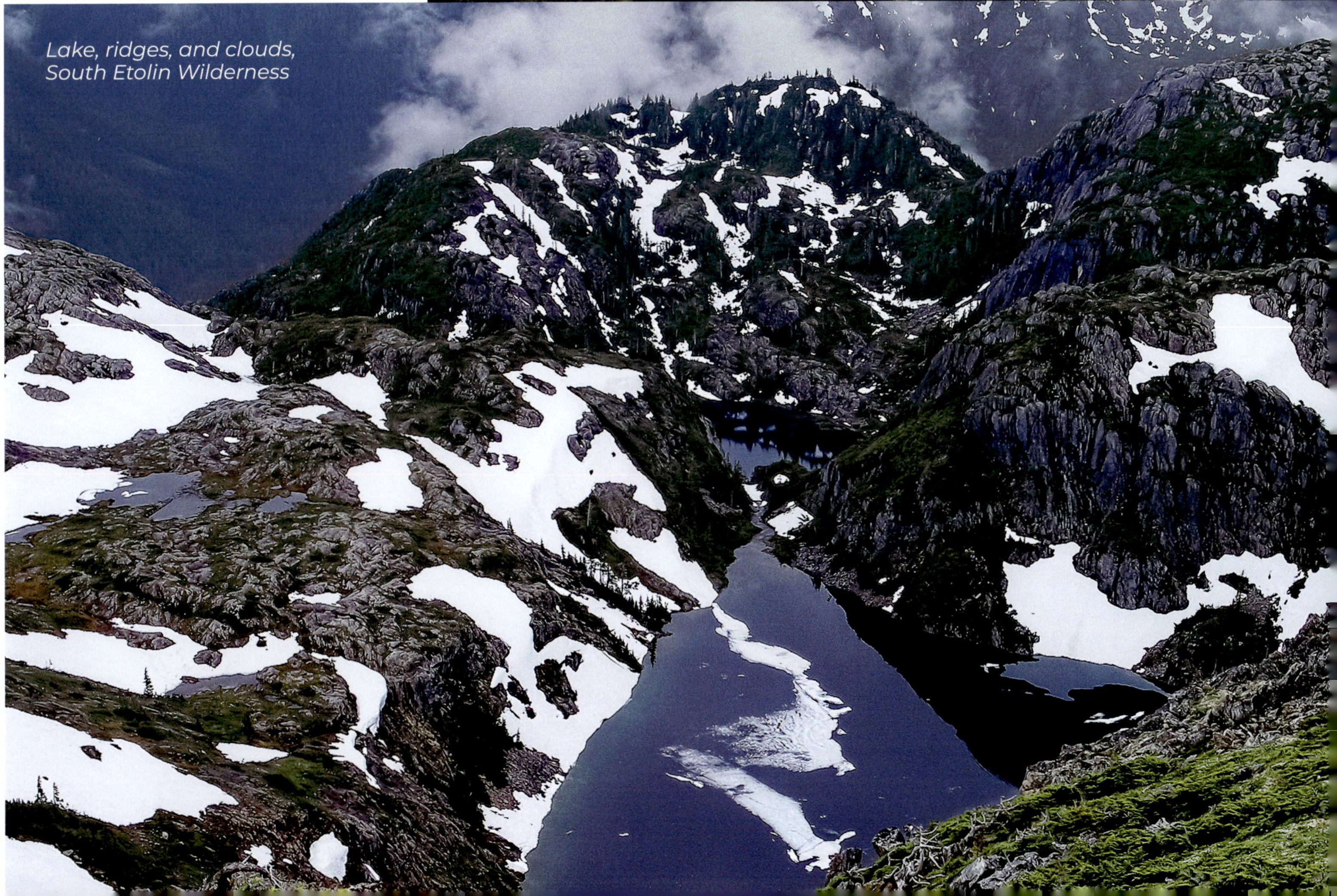

Lake, ridges, and clouds, South Etolin Wilderness

West Chichagov-Yakobi

★ ★ ★ ★ ★

Size: 265,286 acres | **Year Designated:** 1980 | **Responsible Agency:** USFS

The West Chichagov-Yakobi Wilderness is located in the Tongass National Forest north of the town of Sitka. The Pacific Ocean is to the west, the Icy Strait is to the north, and the Chatham Strait is to the east. Yakobi Island and part of Chichagov Island make up the wilderness.

MY VISIT: July 2–7, 2012

My trip was a four-day, fly-in backpacking trip starting in Sitka. It was a clear example of the value of a good pilot. My original intention was to do some day hikes from a base camp on one of the low-elevation Goulding Lakes. The attempt to get me to Goulding Lakes failed because of fog over the lakes and we had to return to Sitka. Given the conditions, another pilot suggested that I come back the next morning and go to a different destination that he had visited himself with a few others on an exploratory trip some years earlier. I happily agreed. I was dropped off at "Goon Dip Lake," yet another unnamed lake just northeast of Goon Dip Mountain. The mountain is shown in the photo.

The day after my arrival the weather turned gorgeous, and once again I had been dropped off at sufficiently high elevation that I had access to some open terrain. This was one spectacular hiking day. As is visible in the photo, there was a large layer of limestone running through Goon Dip Mountain and across a valley to White Stripe Mountain, named for this limestone.

Unfortunately, I got only one nice weather day. Pickup day had light rain and dense fog, and the next day did not look too great either, but my pilot was able to weave through the mountains and clouds to get in and get me out.

Another area of spectacular scenery. Yes, hard to get to, but once there the hiking was good. Definitely worth five stars.

Goon Dip Mountain and the Pacific Ocean, West Chichagov-Yakobi Wilderness

Tracy Arm-Fords Terror

★ ★ ★ ★ ★

Size: 653,179 | **Year Designated:** 1980 | **Responsible Agency:** USFS

The Tracy Arm-Fords Terror Wilderness area is located in the Tongass National Forest east and a bit north of Sitka, and includes the fiords Tracy Arm, Endicott Arm, and Fords Terror. Mr. Ford was on an early surveying mission and decided to visit his fiord in a kayak. This little fiord had fierce tidal currents and Mr. Ford got caught and had to fight (successfully) for his life. Hence the name. The eastern wilderness boundary is the Canadian border. Stephens Passage is to the west.

MY VISIT: June 27–July 2, 2014

My six-day fly-in backpack began with a float plane flight from Sitka. We landed on Lake 1673 in the northeast corner of the USGS Sumdum B-4 map. None of the Sitka pilots had ever been there, but were confident that they could land. There was quite a bit of brush and bear scat by the lake and I wanted to hike some high ridges, so I toted my gear up to a small, higher lake. The clearest route up was along and in the upper lake's outlet stream. I was forced

to pull myself up while holding on to alder branches. Once at the upper lake, the terrain opened almost completely. This upper lake camp acted as a base camp for day hikes to higher ridges and minor summits. My best hike was to an unnamed small summit southeast of my camp. There was still a lot of snow at these elevations, so travel was pretty easy. Views were magnificent: east to the border peaks with British Columbia, down to Endicott Arm and the North Dawes Glacier, and an almost infinite array of gnarly rock, glaciers, and vast snowfields.

Wildlife was not abundant, but I was quite impressed to see at my highest point in this somewhat forbidding terrain a trail of very large bear prints. I remain curious to know what tempted a bear to this spot.

Yes, I give this area five stars. Again, access is not easy, but the area provides many rewards. Hiking was pretty easy, and only having one rainy day probably helped the positive rating.

Coronation Island

★ ★ ★ ★ ★

Size: 19,232 acres   **Year Designated:** 1980   **Responsible Agency:** USFS

The Coronation Island Wilderness is located in the Tongass National Forest west of Prince of Wales Island, northwest of the town of Craig. All of the island is designated wilderness. The USGS map Craig D-7 includes the island.

MY VISIT: May 28–31, 2013

This is one of the more difficult Alaska wilderness areas to access. The island is completely open to the Pacific Ocean and float plane pilots do not like to fly there because of wind and water conditions. For my trip I took a float plane from Sitka to the tiny village of Port Alexander on Baranof Island. Here I hired a charter fishing boat to take me to Coronation Island. Because of the boat's draft, we used a small rubber dinghy, rowed by the boatman's teenage daughter, to get me the last few yards to the shore. My landing spot was the southernmost end of Egg Harbor.

Coronation Island is a uniquely beautiful place. It is made mostly of karst, eroded limestone formations famous for making caves. The shore is dominated by such erosional features as caves and arches. An arch along the Egg Harbor shore is pictured below. One of the caves I explored is known for its long, vertical passages with remnants of old wooden ladders left over from early investigators. I have seen reports of people finding the very old remains of animals that had fallen into sinkholes. There were also lots of tide pools and interesting vegetation. However, the interesting vegetation was quite dense and my attempt at exploring the island's interior was frustrated. I spent most of my time walking the shoreline.

Locals in Port Alexander asked me to look for signs of wolves, bears, and Sitka deer. In the past the island had an overabundance of deer. Alaska Game and Fish tried to fix the problem by introducing wolves. It sort of succeeded; the wolves killed all the deer and then the wolves all starved. I saw no sign of wolves or bears, and evidence for deer was marginal. I only had one wildlife encounter. While walking near the shore on an obvious game trail, a river otter came toward me on the trail (getting quite close) and, upon seeing me gave a look of horror and ran away as fast as it could go.

Sea arch, Coronation Island Wilderness

Daniel J. Evans

★ ★ ★ ★ ★

Size: 876,669 acres   **Year Designated:** 1988   **Responsible Agency:** USNPS

Most of Olympic National Park is designated wilderness. The wilderness is named for a former governor and US senator from Washington state. The wilderness is bounded on three sides by US Highway 101 west of Seattle and south of the town of Port Angeles.

MY VISIT: September 1983

My notes do not give me exact dates of this visit, but it was in September of 1983 and it included both day hikes and a backpacking trip. I have a memory of being here a few years earlier and doing some day hikes in late spring/early summer and in steady rain, but 1983 is the trip I remember best so is what I will relate here.

It was one of my early experiences in the true (non-California) Pacific Northwest. In the 1980s my photographs were almost all 35 mm slides. My memory is guided by cryptic notes on the cardboard surrounding the transparent film. I did a loop backpack from the Soleduck Trailhead up to Heart Lake. At this time, I had little experience with bears. On my way up, I passed a group of backpackers descending. Behind the last woman in the group was a bear. I mentioned the bear to this hiker and her response was "There are so many bears up there that I have stopped paying attention." My response was "Oh." As I approached Heart Lake and tree line, I realized the situation; the open ground above tree line was covered with huckleberry bushes. Big patches of berries were filled with little black bears stuffing themselves. I camped in these open areas that night. I did not sleep well. Every rustle during the night (mostly by deer) had me convinced that there was a bear outside my tent. I got over that fear.

From Heart Lake I did a day hike along the High Divide toward Cat Peak and saw for the first time a wall of fog trying to spill over a pass into a valley.

Up to this day the weather had been wonderful. There were great views of Mount Olympus. On my last clear night, I remember standing outside my tent watching the stars as fog and clouds came up from over the ocean. It was still just possible for me to see a few stars as the rain began to fall.

Descending back to the Soleduck Trailhead the next morning I saw my very first Roosevelt elk running down ahead of me. It was also somewhere near Mount Carrie and Cat Peak that I saw my first ever mountain goats.

Other hikes that I know I have done in this wilderness include a day hike from the Elwah Trailhead to Hurricane Ridge with great views, a day hike up the Hoh River from the Hoh Rain Forest Visitor Center (yes, it rained), and a day hike from the Dosewallips Trailhead to the foot of the Anderson Glacier.

Mount Olympus from the north, Daniel J. Evans Wilderness

Stephen Mather

★ ★ ★ ★ ★

Size: 634,614 acres   **Year Designated:** 1988   **Responsible Agency:** USNPS

Most of North Cascades National Park is designated wilderness. The northern wilderness boundary is the Canadian border. Access from the west is by State Highway 542, and State Highway 20 divides the wilderness into north and south portions. Multiple USFS wilderness areas surround the park. Stephen Mather was an early conservationist and the first director of the National Park Service.

MY VISITS: September 12–15, 2011 and September 17, 2013

September is often an excellent time for backpacking in the Pacific Northwest. That was certainly true for me in 2011. The trip began by wandering around looking for the right place to obtain a required overnight permit. Hiking started at the Hannegan Trailhead at the western boundary of the Mount Baker Wilderness (USFS). The first route segment was a 2,000-foot climb through the Mount Baker Wilderness and just over Hannegan Pass and then down into North Cascades National Park and the Stephen Mather Wilderness. Because of a late start I camped just inside the park at a suggestively named campsite called Boundary (wilderness camping must be in designated sites). The trail was pretty busy and there were other tents.

Day two was on the Copper Ridge Trail on a gorgeous day with wonderful views of the large glaciated peaks of Mount Shuksan, Ruth Mountain, Mineral Mountain, Mount Challenger, and the whole Picket Range. There were still segments of trail that were snow covered. Not all of it would melt. I camped near Copper Lake. Day three began with fog, but it soon burned off and I did a little day hike to the end of Copper Ridge, then went back to my camp, packed up, and returned to Hannegan Pass for the night. The reverse hike along Copper Ridge was just as spectacular as the previous day. This route will remain in my mind as one of the nicest I have ever taken. Easy five stars.

The day hike in 2013 was from the Roads End Trailhead through the Lake Chelan-Sawtooth Wilderness (USFS) through Twisp Pass and to Dagger Lake. Another nice hike. I highly recommend this wilderness for just about any hikers.

Fog spill on Challenger Glacier, Stephen Mather Wilderness

Mount Rainier

★ ★ ★ ★ ★

Size: 228,480 acres   **Year Designated:** 1988   **Responsible Agency:** USNPS

Most of Mount Rainier National Park is designated wilderness. The park is located southeast of Tacoma, and State Highway 123 provides access from the east.

MY VISIT: September 11–14, 2013

Many hikers come to this area and never see the namesake mountain because of weather. A friend and I came here in September of 2013 for four days of hiking and never saw a cloud. We did two overnight backpacks. The first was the Palisades Lakes Trail from the Sunrise Point Trailhead camping at Upper Palisades Lake (with mountain goat). This was a pretty interesting volcanic area with nice if not jaw-dropping views. A very pleasant and pretty easy hike.

The second hike was the Spray Park Trail from the Mowich Lake Trailhead. Now, on a clear day, *this* is a jaw-dropping hike. We were blown away. We camped at the Eagles Roost campsite. We were here only four days, but I have no problem giving the area five stars.

Glacier Peak

★ ★ ★ ★ ★

Size: 576,865 acres   **Year Designated:** 1964   **Responsible Agency:** USFS

The Glacier Peak Wilderness is located in the Mount Baker-Snoqualmie and Wenatchee National Forests north of US Highway 2, east of State Highway 530, and east of the town of Darrington.

MY VISITS: August 27–September 2, 1990 and September 2011

The first visit was with a friend who was a serious climber. I was not. Our intention was to summit Glacier Peak. We had ice axes and rope, but no other technical equipment. It was not a difficult mountain. I do not have detailed notes from this trip, but I think we started at Little Wenatchee Ford Campground, went up Cady Creek to Cady Pass and then north on the Pacific Crest Trail (PCT) to the base of the mountain. I do remember that our first two days were overcast with at least intermittent rain. We had no views, but we did hear what sounded like low-flying aircraft. I also remember that at one of the PCT passes the sky cleared, and as we were eating our evening meal, over our campsite came a US Navy A-6 aircraft one hundred or so feet above our heads. This was what we had been hearing, and it was quite the sight.

Looking at the maps after so many years, I cannot remember our climbing route; only that we left the PCT and dodged crevasses over continuous snowfields to the summit (10,541 feet). Fog played with the summit as we approached, but we basically had excellent conditions the whole way. This is the *only* big Cascades summit I have done, and it was a perfect trip.

The 2011 backpacking trip started on the North Fork of the Skykomish River in the Henry Jackson Wilderness. Indeed, most of the time on this trip was in the Henry Jackson, but parts of days one and two were in the Glacier Peak. My notes from this trip make multiple mentions about insect problems, both for me and other hikers that I encountered. There was still snow around and little meltwater ponds were keeping bugs numerous. I went up to Dishpan Gap on the PCT, then quickly over to Blue Lake in the Glacier Peak and camped there for the night. The next day I did a side trip to the top of Johnson Mountain (there was a trail) with good views of Glacier Peak. I then descended to June Mountain with more good views and continued to drop down the Bald Eagle Trail until it came to Quartz Creek, where I camped. The next day I went back to my truck. All this last day was in the Henry Jackson. Everything I saw on this trip convinced me that the Glacier Peak Wilderness is worth five stars. I recommend it to any hikers willing to invest a few days.

WASHINGTON

Pasayten

★ ★ ★ ★ ★

Size: 505,524 acres | **Year Designated:** 1968 | **Responsible Agency:** USFS

The Pasayten Wilderness is located in the Okanogan and Mount Baker-Snoqualmie National Forests south of the Canadian border, north of State Highway 20, west of US Highway 97, east of Ross Lake, and west of the town of Oroville.

MY VISITS: Six backpacking trips from 1989 to 2019 covering thirty-two days

Six backpacking trips totaling thirty-two days on (and off) the trail. Do I like this place? Yes, it is one of my favorites. Unfortunately, I do not have detailed notes from all of these trips, but I do have some sketchy recollections based on old maps and photograph labels as to routes and destinations.

The first trip was a solo backpack starting at the Billy Goat Corral, then up to the long, skinny valley with the Hidden Lakes. From there, I continued north to almost the Canadian border, but cut a bit to the west and then south up the Middle Fork of the Pasayten River. From the river, my route was a trail over Point Defiance then south to Fred's Lake and Shellrock Pass, then down Ptarmigan Creek and a return to the Hidden Lakes and then back to the trailhead. The segment from Fred's Lake to Ptarmigan Creek featured wonderful views of Osceola Peak, Mount Carru, and Mount Lago. The area around the Hidden lakes was also very pretty, dark water in dense, dark forest.

The second trip was with two friends from Idaho. We started at a popular trailhead for the PCT at Slate Peak, then went north on the PCT to Castle Pass. All along this trail segment we were truly on the crest and had great views of nearby peaks, dominated by Jack's Peak. From Castle Pass we went west on the Three Fools Trail, again with great views, all the way to Ross Lake. As soon as we lost enough elevation we were swarmed by mosquitoes. Fortunately, I had thought to bring repellent even though it was late in the season. Before we got to Ross Lake itself, and being without a map for this part of the trip, we were overtaken by darkness. We were in dense forest. We decided to make a hasty camp with a poor tent site; the only place for a stove was the trail. The next morning as we started out, we saw that we were really quite close to a developed, boat-in campground. We just shook our heads, went south along the lake, then east on a trail over the Devil's Dome and Devil's Pass, Deception Pass, and on to Holman Pass on the PCT and back south to Slate Peak. This was an enjoyable trip with good weather and superb scenery.

Trip three was a solo backpack from the Andrews Creek Trailhead. The route was up Andrews Creek to the Cathedral Lakes where I made a base camp with a day hike to Bald Mountain and the Border Ridge and another to Wol-framite Mountain. The area around the Cathedral Lakes was quite beautiful.

Trip four was another solo trip, this one starting at the Lake Creek Trailhead, going past Black Lake, through Ashnola Pass and down into the Ashnola River valley, then up to the Ramon Lakes and Sheep Mountain. I made a base camp at the Ramon Lakes with day trips to the summits of Sheep Mountain and Quartz Mountain and the very pretty Whistler Basin, shown in the photo.

The fifth and final trip was a short backpack to show my friend Maya just how nice the Pasayten Wilderness was. We started at the Thirtymile Trailhead and went up the Chewuch River to Tungsten Creek and made camp. The next day we hiked up across Apex Pass, by an old, abandoned tungsten mine and just east of Cathedral Peak. We retraced our steps back to the trailhead. The area around Thirtymile had been the scene of an intense fire a few years earlier that took the lives of multiple firefighters. There is a memorial and account of events at the trailhead.

The sixth and final trip was a solo trip from the Irongate Trailhead into Horseshoe Basin. The basin was at its peak of flowers. The area had seen some pretty severe fire damage in recent years.

Alpine Lakes

★ ★ ★ ★ ★

Size: 306,000 acres   **Year Designated:** 1976   **Responsible Agency:** USFS

The Alpine Lakes Wilderness is located in the Mount Baker-Snoqualmie and Wenatchee National Forests east of the city of Seattle, south of US Highway 2, north of Interstate Highway 90, and west of the town of Leavenworth.

MY VISITS: August 28–30, 2003 and October 12, 14, 15, 2008

My first trip into this area was to the Necklace Valley. It was a three-day solo backpack. I went from US Highway 2 to Forest Road 68 to a trailhead for the East Fork of the Foss River. Strung out along the trail are Jade, Locket, Emerald, Cloudy, and Opal Lakes. I think I camped near Opal Lake and then did a day hike the next day to a major divide to the south for a good look at the area. Day three was just retracing my steps back to the trailhead. I have two distinct memories from this very warm trip (temperatures over ninety degrees in Seattle). One is that the area was very beautiful and the other is that the density of biting insects was large.

The first day hike in 2008 was close to the Necklace Valley trip, but a different trailhead at the end of Forest Road 68 at Trout Lake. The trail went through dense, lovely forest to a series of large lakes: Malachite, Copper, Little Heart, and Big Heart.

The second day hike was just a bit west of the previous day, beginning at a trailhead at the end of a road up the East Fork of the Miller River. This trail went past the large Lake Dorothy, then climbed to Bear Lake, Deer Lake, and Snoqualmie Lake. Both these day hikes were in perfect fall weather with considerable color in the understory vegetation.

The third day hike was to a spot I will remember for a long time. It was to a famous set of peaks and valleys called The Enchantments. The area is easy to get to and famous for its scenery. It is so popular that the nearby USFS ranger station in Leavenworth holds a lottery every morning to allow in a very limited number of people. When I arrived, the lottery was finished, but I could still go to a different spot and get close to the area. I hiked to Lake Stuart on a marvelous fall day with good light on the peaks and just enough color from some tamarack trees to present the peaks at their best. This was one of the most beautiful day hikes I have ever done.

Autumn sunlight on The Enchantments, Alpine Lakes Wilderness

Three Sisters

★ ★ ★ ★ ★

| **Size:** 286,708 acres | **Year Designated:** 1964 | **Responsible Agency:** USFS |

The Three Sisters Wilderness is located in the Deschutes and Willamette National Forests south of State Highway 242, west of US Highway 97, west of the city of Bend, and southwest of the town of Sisters. At the time of my visit there was a Geo-Graphics recreation map dedicated to this area.

MY VISITS: August 1–5, 2000 and September 28, 2004 and October 17–18, 2008

The Cascade Range in Oregon is pretty much a continuation of the Cascades in Washington. It is classic volcanic terrain with dense forest low down and glaciated peaks higher up. The Three Sisters—North (Faith), Middle (Hope), and South (Charity)—are volcanic peaks. There is also a Little Brother and a Husband.

The year 2000 backpack (solo) started at the Pole Creek Trailhead located at the end of Forest Road 15, which takes off south from State Highway 242. I first went to Camp Lake near the crest of the Cascades with a side trip to the top of the crest. Very nice. I retraced some of my steps to a trail south toward Green Lake. I camped near Golden Lake and did a day hike cross country below Broken Top and Broken Hand. The Golden Lake neighborhood was very nice and avoided the crowds. The Three Sisters sees a lot of traffic. This was my first visit and I was favorably impressed.

The day hike in 2004 was directly off State Highway 242, and I went south on the PCT just past South Mattheu Lake. It was a nice day with good views.

The 2008 trip was a solo backpack into a very popular area, the Obsidian Cliffs. It is so popular that a permit is required for all entry, including day trips. It being the middle of October, I was able to get a permit. It was an easy trail and I had lots of time and took a side trip up the PCT to Opie Dilldock Pass for some good views. I found a spectacular campsite near Obsidian Falls. It was then just about sunset, and the low-angle sun was reflecting off the smooth obsidian stones so completely that one was almost blinded. It was an easy next day back to the trailhead. My favorite Three Sisters photo is of the North Sister and the Little Brother.

I recommend this area to just about any hiker who does not mind encountering other hikers.

North Sister and Little Brother, Three Sisters Wilderness

★ ★ ★ ★ ★ The Pacific Northwest

Stikine-LeConte

★ ★ ★ ★

Size: 448,926 acres | **Year Designated:** 1980 | **Responsible Agency:** USFS

The Stikine-LeConte Wilderness is located in the Tongass National Forest west of the Canadian border, east of Fredrick Sound, east of the town of Petersburg, and north of the town of Wrangell. The Stikine River flows through the wilderness. There are no trails.

MY VISIT: August 24–28, 2013

It was hard to select a destination. This area does not get much visitation. I relied on phone conversations with a couple of USFS folks who had at least a little experience in this area. First of all, I needed a place where a float plane could land. I flipped a mental coin and chose a lake at the head of Goat Creek. This is "Goat Lake" to me, but just Lake 1240 on the USGS Bradfield Canal C-6 topo.

I began this five-day fly-in with my Ketchikan pilot. Upon landing it was clear that I was in a very beautiful place. I was also concerned that at 1,240 feet there was still a lot of brush. Going far would be difficult. My goal was to go up the main inlet valley, perhaps to a glacier south of the lake. I made a real effort, but was frustrated by the dense vegetation, very rough terrain, and rain. I gave up. On the fourth day I did succeed in getting to a higher lake (Lake 1668) on what was a pretty hike, sometimes just walking in the outlet stream bed from the upper lake. Pickup day dawned brilliantly clear and I finally got good views of the surroundings. The flight back to Ketchikan was very scenic.

While this is a fabulously scenic area, I would caution potential visitors that foot travel is very difficult. Not a beginner's trip.

Lake 1240 at the head of Goat Creek, Stikine-LeConte Wilderness

Chuck River

★ ★ ★ ★

Size: 74,298 acres | **Year Designated:** 1990 | **Responsible Agency:** USFS

The Chuck River Wilderness is located in the Tongass National Forest on the mainland west of the Canadian border and on the southwest shore of the Endicott Arm just south of the Tracy Arm-Fords Terror Wilderness. The closest town is Petersburg to the south. Most of the wilderness is on the USGS Sumdum C-5 topo map.

MY VISIT: July 3–6, 2014

This four-day trip began with a float plane flight from Sitka on a gray, overcast day. The Endicott Arm is sufficiently sheltered that pilots don't mind landing here. Our landing spot was on the shore of Sanford Cove. There were two kayaks pulled up on the shore a bit east of where we landed. The Dawes Glacier is at the end of the Endicott Arm and there were chunks of ice floating by our landing spot. After dropping me off, the pilot stopped, climbed out on one of the plane's floats, and picked up some chunks of glacial ice to show his children.

I set up camp several yards from the shore along a modest stream entering the cove. It was pretty clear that there was a lot of activity on the Arm. Boats were going up and down, including one large tourist boat.

Here at sea level the vegetation was very thick and the terrain behind the shore was quite steep. It was clear that hiking would be mostly right on the shore. The next two days I did just that. Hiking was easy to the northwest and for a little way to the east. The biggest issue was tides. Tide swings were large and, as I discovered, being forced away from the unvegetated shore made for much more difficult hiking. There were some good views across the Arm into the Tracy Arm-Fords Terror Wilderness.

The most noteworthy feature of this spot, however, was the wildlife. In addition to humans and boats, the Arm had lots of humpback whales. On one of my hiking days whales were almost constantly near the surface. Once I saw a big chunk of ice float by with a seal hitching a ride. Sea otters were common. One evening, I was sitting on the bank of my little stream and noticed motion to my right. I looked over and not thirty feet away was a bear about to cross the stream. We looked at each other for about two seconds and the bear quickly went back into the forest. Later that evening as dusk was getting deep, I took a final stroll down to the beach.

There was something large and dark floating just off-shore. It was a humpback whale, sleeping.

On my pickup day I was sitting on some rocks above the beach. Again, I saw some motion. It was a wolf ambling along, then ducking into the forest. He appeared not to see me. Then after a few more seconds he reappeared and stared right at me before returning to the forest. Cool.

While not a great hiking destination, this area would probably be a rewarding spot for wildlife viewing.

Humpback whales in Endicott Arm, Chuck River Wilderness

Glacier Bay

★ ★ ★ ★

Size: 2,664,876 acres   **Year Designated:** 1980   **Responsible Agency:** USNPS

Most of Glacier Bay National Park is designated wilderness. It is located on the mainland south of the Canadian border and north of the Icy Strait. The area has a long stretch facing the Pacific Ocean. The city of Juneau is to the east and the village of Gustavus is on the southern shore.

MY VISIT: June 19–26, 2016

Between Memorial Day and Labor Day, Alaska Airlines provides service to the little town of Gustavus. From the airport one can take a bus to Bartlett Cove where there is a lodge, a visitor center, a ranger station, and a walk-in campground. Backcountry travelers are required to get a permit from the ranger station with a required orientation session.

My trip had three components: a day hike, a four-day backpack, and a three-day backpack. The day hike was first. This was just a plain beach walk from Bartlett Cove almost to Gustavus Point in a stand-alone segment of the wilderness area. It was a pleasant day and a pleasant hike with lots of birds, especially black oystercatchers, which I find hilarious. I also scared up one very large black bear.

The second trip was the main event. There is a famous boat tour that departs every day from Bartlett Cove. It is the one thing that most tourists do. Lesser known is that hikers and kayakers can also take this boat tour and be dropped off at one of two locations select-ed by the Park Service. Not all drop-off points are hiker friendly, but the one I chose was. It was close to Scidmore Bay and an easy backpack from the drop-off point. Scidmore Bay was a very nice place. I set up camp near where the meltwater from Scidmore Glacier flows into the bay. I spent my two whole days here doing day hikes, one to the base of the Scidmore Glacier and one south along the bay shore. Both were very enjoyable. There was some rain on my drop-off day, but the other three days were clear.

The bay was full of life. There were more sea otters than I could count plus humpback whales plus lots of shorebirds, especially scoters. On the beaches, plovers were fledging their chicks. There were also lots of moose tracks and some *very* big bear tracks.

One always is told to look for bear sign before setting up a camp. I did; there was no bear sign. One afternoon after a day hike I walked around my tent and not twenty feet away was a big pile of bear scat. My camp had had a visitor.

The third trip was less enjoyable. I hiked from Bartlett Cove on a trail (!) to Bartlett Lake. It basically rained all three days. The terrain was mostly flat and rather wet with moderate vegetation. I walked most of the way around the lake, which seemed almost lifeless.

This is an area with a lot to offer visitors. However, opportunities are limited for hikers. The best way to see this wilderness would be by watercraft.

Looking south along Scidmore Bay, Glacier Bay Wilderness

Lake Clark

★ ★ ★ ★

Size: 2,619,550 acres   **Year Designated:** 1980   **Responsible Agency:** USNPS

Most of Lake Clark National Park is designated wilderness. The park is located on the western shore of the Cook Inlet southwest of the city of Anchorage and northwest of the town of Homer.

MY VISIT: July 31–August 4, 2017

The terrain in Lake Clark is dominated by large volcanoes near Cook Inlet, with big lakes and big peaks farther west. My visit was by float plane from Homer to Upper Twin Lake, well away from the coast at an elevation of 1,982 feet. Our landing spot was at the famous Proenneke Cabin. In 2017 there was a Park Service ranger stationed there who gave guided tours to anyone who showed up. There was also a rustic campground. A rather heavy forest with some brush surrounded the lake, but more open country was not much higher.

The destination for my planned four-day backpack was Low Pass and then down into the Kijik River drainage to try to get a view of the tall peaks at the head of the Kijik. My route up to Low Pass was slow because of poor route selection. I climbed away from the lake too soon and ended up in brush and scree. But I got there and set up camp in a nice spot. The weather was good on my way up. My intention was to go to the Kijik the next day. That night it started to rain. The next morning was heavily socked in with poor visibility. I stayed in my tent awhile but decided to try for the Kijik. I tried to stay high for better views, but the visibility was so poor that I had to give up and go back to my camp. The next day was still pretty gray and the visibility not great, so I decided to go up a drainage not far from my camp in some potentially interesting terrain.

Up I went, slow and watching my feet so as not to slip or trip in the wet conditions. Here I had one of my more memorable "the one that got away" moments. As I slogged up, I suddenly realized that something was just off to my right looking at me. About fifty feet away was a Dall ewe (Dall sheep are the pure white bighorns). She was gorgeous. I asked her if it would be OK if I took her picture. No response. I took off my pack and unzipped the compartment with my camera. As soon as my hand touched the camera she bolted. I saw her again a minute or two later, about 400 yards away. Later I saw about another dozen ewes, a few with lambs.

The next day I went back down to the lake. It was a lot easier to see a good route from above than from below. The following day I returned to the Proenneke Cabin. I checked in with the ranger. She was completely occupied trying to shoo off a black bear that was making a nuisance of itself. I waited somewhat nervously for my pilot to pick me up, but did not see the bear.

The flight back to Homer was on a clear day, and we flew over the famous volcanic peaks, including the Redoubt.

This is another beautiful place where hiking is possible, but there are no trails and visitors should be careful when selecting destinations.

Noatak

★ ★ ★ ★

Size: 5,765,427 acres   **Year Designated:** 1980   **Responsible Agency:** USNPS

Most of the Noatak National Preserve is designated wilderness. The reserve is west of Gates of the Arctic National Park and south of the Alaska Petroleum Reserve. All of it is above the Arctic Circle. Kotzebue is probably the closest town, although my starting point was Bettles.

MY VISIT: July 31–August 4, 2015

I visited the Noatak after Gates of the Arctic. The destination was "Polly Lake," an unnamed lake in the eastern part of the wilderness near the southern bank of the Noatak River. My impression is that people come here for two main reasons: hunting and river floating. The hunting is for caribou. Before my trip I had a phone conversation with the chief ranger in Kotzebue, who told me the Noatak sees about 450,000 caribou come through on their migration.

After the float plane from Bettles dropped me off I saw nobody until the float plane picked me up five days later. Not only did I not see anybody, there was no sight nor sound of human activity. There was no trash, no boot prints, no sound of aircraft and not even any aircraft contrails. It was the wildest place I have ever been. The area of my visit (shown on USGS topo map Ambler River D-3) was dominated by tundra. There were some willows, but otherwise the terrain was completely open. Relief was provided by rounded limestone hills. There were numerous lakes near the river and, of course, the river itself.

The elevation at my drop-off point was about 1,500 feet and I went to one limestone summit of 3,253 feet. The words I would use to describe this area are stark and spare but somehow enchanting. There were lots of flowers, caribou antlers, and dwarf huckleberries, many of which I ate. There were lots of trails on the gray hills, all made by the caribou. The only large wildlife I saw was a very large bear running away from me. There was plenty of bear scat around.

I wandered the south bank of the river one day. It was brilliant blue, deep and majestic. The scenery was not as dramatic as Gates of the Arctic, but still a very nice area. Once here the hiking was relatively easy. One could go a long way. If you seek solitude, this is your destination.

Peak in fog, Noatak Wilderness

Denali

★ ★ ★ ★

Size: 2,146,580 acres   **Year Designated:** 1980   **Responsible Agency:** USNPS

Most of Denali National Park is designated wilderness. The park is located southwest of the city of Fairbanks, north of the city of Anchorage, and west of State Highway 3. The town of Healy serves as a visitor gateway.

Denali is unique among the Alaska national park wilderness areas in that it is easy to get to. One can arrive by a paved highway, by passenger train, by air, or by road or rail from cruise ships. It was almost a shock when I arrived by rental car from Anchorage to see just how dense the visitors were—real crowds. Denali is also unique because backcountry visitation is tightly controlled. All overnight trips require permits, and permits may only be obtained no more than twenty-four hours in advance of a trip. The backcountry is divided into units and each unit is assigned a maximum number of humans. A visitor cannot know in advance of their arrival at the park where they can go in the backcountry.

MY VISIT: July 26–31, 2018

My visit began at the backcountry desk at the park visitor center. I watched a required video of general park safety, especially bear safety. After that I obtained a permit for a five-day backpack in the zones for the upper Savage River and the upper Sanctuary River. I chose these areas because they had potential for good scenery and good wildlife, and little requirement for scary river crossings. My backpack began on July 26 near the Savage River Campground after a short bus ride from the visitor center. The route was simply south along the river. There were, of course, no trails other than a few game trails, and there was a fair amount of brush that made progress slow. I had seen enough brush in southeast Alaska to realize that with patience one could get through. I camped on a gravel bar by the river that first night, having made it through most of the brush. Day two was marvelous. I got out of the brush into mostly open tundra and the hiking was easy near the river. My intention was to cross into the Sanctuary River drainage so

I looked for an easy pass. I went too far upstream, and instead of a nice grassy route I ended up on steep scree, which is just what the Park Service tells you to avoid. I did get across though, and as a reward I ended up right at the foot of Fang Mountain. This was a wonderful camp spot. On the morning of the third day I made a day hike to the upper Sanctuary River to a nice overlook of where the Sanctuary River flowed out of the Refuge Valley. After returning to my campsite I packed up and hiked back to the Savage River drainage, this time on a much nicer tundra route.

The morning of day four was interesting. While having breakfast, I noticed above the river a blond grizzly sow heading away from me with two tiny brown dots working hard to keep up with her. About two minutes later, on the opposite hillside and much closer, came another blond grizzly sow, this time with one small cub. They were approaching me so I decided to make some noise and the bear disappeared into some brush and I did not see her again. About two more minutes after the bear, into

Fang Mountain, Denali Wilderness

my camp walked a caribou, probably a female. She stopped to take a drink about thirty feet away from me, and just as her nose got to the water, she realized I was standing there watching her. She immediately jumped up, pranced around a bit, decided I was way too scary, and trotted away. Too bad my camera was back at my tent (away from my food stash). Still, not bad wildlife viewing for one morning's breakfast. The rest of the trip was just going back to the park road.

The last day of my visit was devoted to a day hike of the Triple Lakes Trail, one of the very few trails in the wilderness. Because it was so easy to get to, there were a lot of other hikers.

For many, perhaps most hikers, Denali might be their best way to see some of Alaska. The scenery and wildlife are great and access is not difficult. One can discuss destinations with knowledgeable rangers. It is not as "wild" as other parks, but still a beautiful place.

Mount Baker

★ ★ ★ ★

Size: 117,900 acres　　　　**Year Designated:** 1984　　　　**Responsible Agency:** USFS

The Mount Baker Wilderness is located in the Mount Baker-Snoqualmie National Forest on the west slope of the Cascade Range just south of the Canadian border and northeast of the city of Bellingham. The easiest access is by State Highway 542 from the west.

MY VISITS: July 22–23, 2003 and September 14-15, 2011 and September 14-15, 2013

The day hikes in 2003 were both spectacular, one reason being perfect weather. The first hike began at the end of State Highway 542 at Artist Point. Here began the Ptarmigan Ridge Trail to the Portals. This was the standard entry point for climbers seeking the Mount Baker summit. I hiked along behind a group of climbers. A great day in an interesting volcanic area, the peak always in view.

The second day hike started off the road to Twin Lakes on a trail for Yellow Aster Butte. I hiked past Yellow Aster and on to Tomyhoi Peak. There were great views on a fabulous day.

Looking west from the summit of Hannegan Peak, Mount Baker Wilderness

In 2011 I went through the Mount Baker Wilderness to enter the Stephen Mather Wilderness in North Cascades National Park. On the return trip I spent the night of September 14 and 15 on the Mount Baker side of Hannegan Pass.

In 2013 I wanted to show my friend Maya how nice the Mount Baker area was and we took the Hannegan Pass Trail to the pass, then the trail to the summit of Hannegan Peak. Wonderful views on a nice day. The photo is looking toward the west from the summit.

I heartily recommend this area to other hikers.

Goat Rocks

★ ★ ★ ★

Size: 105,633 acres　　　　**Year Designated:** 1964　　　　**Responsible Agency:** USFS

The Goat Rocks Wilderness is located in the Gifford Pinchot and Wenatchee National Forests south of US Highway 12 and west of the city of Yakima. The Pacific Crest Trail (PCT) runs through the area. At the time of my visit there was a USFS map dedicated to this wilderness.

MY VISIT: August 6–9, 2001

This four-day backpack began at a trailhead for the PCT at White Pass on US Highway 12. I did not get an early start but was able to go south on the PCT around Hogback Mountain and past Shoe Lake to a campsite at Hidden Spring. Day two had great weather and I continued south on the PCT through volcanic terrain with great views to a campsite at the upper end of McCall Basin. A common sight throughout this trip was of Mount Rainier in the near distance.

Day three was another magnificent day and I just did a day hike south on the PCT right on the spine of the Cascade Range. The trail here was genuinely exciting. It was a narrow traverse only a few feet wide with steep drops onto snow and glaciers on both sides. The narrow route for the trail had resulted in the USFS posting signs asking hikers not to begin the traverse if they saw horses anywhere on the narrow trail. While my memory is now a bit fuzzy, I do remember this day as one of my finest trail days ever. The photo shows the Goat Rocks themselves from the PCT near Old Snowy Mountain.

I heartily recommend this stretch of the PCT to just about anybody who likes to hike.

Early morning sun on the Goat Rocks, Goat Rocks Wilderness

Eagle Cap

★ ★ ★ ★

Size: 358,461 acres   **Year Designated:** 1964   **Responsible Agency:** USFS

The Eagle Cap Wilderness is located in the Wallowa-Whitman National Forest in northeast Oregon west of State Highway 82 and just west of the quaint town of Enterprise. It includes most of the Wallowa Mountains.

MY VISITS: August 28–September 1, 1991 and July 29–August 1, 1999

The first of these trips has been wiped from my memory. I know I went and did a five-day solo backpack in the southwest portion of the wilderness. My 1991 appointment calendar has these days noted that I was in the Eagle Cap, but no notes on exactly where I went. It appears that I also have no photos. I don't remember photos so it is possible that I did not even take a camera (this has been true on a few other trips).

For the second trip I have photographs and a USFS map of the wilderness marked with my route. I went up the East Fork of the Lostine River to Mirror Lake where I camped. From here I did a day hike to Glacier Lake and the summit of the Eagle Cap (pictured, 9,595 feet). On the third day I went west to Minam Lake and then on the fourth day out by the main fork of the Lostine River. My recollections are that this was a very nice area with forest, lakes, and pale gray, nonvolcanic rock—and one that did not get a lot of visitation. I recommend the area.

Russell Fiord

★ ★ ★

Size: 348,701 acres   **Year Designated:** 1980
Responsible Agency: USFS

The Russell Fiord Wilderness is located in the Tongass National Forest south of Wrangell-Saint Elias National Park, north of Glacier Bay National Park, and northeast of the town of Yakutat. The eastern wilderness boundary is the Canadian border and the western boundary is the shore of Yakutat Bay off the Gulf of Alaska. Russell Fiord is one of the very few Alaska wilderness areas where you can drive to a trailhead. Having said that, the only way to get to the access road is by airplane.

The Eagle Cap, Eagle Cap Wilderness

Upon arrival on Alaska Airlines in Yakutat I rented an old Chevy Suburban (1987 if I remember) so that I could get to nearby hiking destinations. It was in this wilderness that I made my first use of a USFS fishing cabin. These cabins are placed along major lakes throughout southeast Alaska. They provide shelter from the weather and from the bears. They can be reserved online and require a small fee.

My first foray into the Russell Fiord was on a *trail* to Situk Lake and its cabin. I drove to the trailhead and backpacked to the cabin. It was a gray day with showers, and the low clouds prevented any views. From the cabin I did a day hike to Mountain Lake a few miles away. The terrain was wet and almost flat with heavy forest. I went back to the cabin. There was a lot of bear scat (I was warned) but I saw no bears. It was nice being in the cabin as it rained all night. The next morning was perfectly clear. There were won-

derful views of Mount Saint Elias (18,008 feet) off to the north in Wrangell-Saint Elias National Park and of Mount Mallott, also to the north. Given the better weather I made a second day hike to Mountain Lake. This day there were lots more views. The lake was pretty but completely surrounded by dense forest. I went back to the cabin and then back to the trailhead. Along the way I found and ate wild blueberries, salmonberries, and strawberries. At the trailhead were two brown bears. They appeared to be young, in their first year away from their mother. They were truly cute—oversized stuffed animals cavorting along the road. They seemed to take no notice of me, but they did quickly go off into the forest.

I camped in the Suburban that night. The next day was nasty with wind-driven rain. I did not even try to do much until pretty late when the rain eased. I went down to the end of the road just after it crosses the Dangerous River. There was a sign for a trail around Harlequin Lake. The lake is

Harlequin Lake, Russell Fiord Wilderness

just inside the wilderness boundary. Dense alder surrounded the lakeshore and I could not find any way around or through so I gave up. The lake is large and was filled with icebergs. The ice comes from the Yakutat Glacier at the northeast (inlet) end of the lake.

The next day I did a day hike on a trail to the shore of Russell Fiord itself. Beyond the end of the trail the forest was just about impenetrable, but the shoreline was an easy and rewarding walk. I enjoy birding and saw here for the first time Arctic tern, marbled murrelet, parasitic jaeger, Pacific loon, and white-winged scoter. In the late afternoon clouds gathered and a light rain be-gan, so I headed back to the trailhead. It was a worthwhile day in a nice setting.

My map showed another trail taking off from the Dangerous River Road and following a ridge into the wilderness. I looked multiple times for this other trail but failed to find it. Upon returning to Yakutat I learned from the Forest Service that the trailhead had been overgrown and they needed to fix it.

I recommend this area to hikers who are looking for a way to explore wild Alaska without the expense of a bush pilot. The terrain is quite varied, but I suspect much of it is hard to get to.

Karta River

Size: 39,889 acres **Year Designated:** 1990 **Responsible Agency:** USFS

The Karta River Wilderness is a gentle place in the Tongass National Forest northwest of Ketchikan near the center of Prince of Wales Island. The area is dominated by two lakes, Salmon and Karta.

MY VISIT: July 10–12, 2011

Salmon Lake has USFS fishing cabins and I had reserved one. My Ketchikan pilot did not have time to take me there until 7:00 pm, so I did not do much this first day. Describing my cabin as rustic is an understatement. It was falling to pieces and completely overrun by mice. The location, however, was superb. It was set among large cedar trees and had good views of lake and forest. The weather was about perfect: calm, sunny, and 70 degrees.

The maps, USGS Craig C-2 and Craig C-3, showed trails both upstream and downstream from the cabin. The morning of day two was very nice and I tried the upstream trail. This was a "Cheshire Cat" trail. With every step it got fainter and fainter until it completely disappeared in the forest. So, I turned around, went back to the cabin, then took the downstream trail. This trail was clear, probably from use by fishermen. It went to Karta Lake, then all the way out to salt water over pleasant, level terrain through forest and meadow. Day three also had perfect weather, and I went back to Karta Lake and hung out with numerous Sitka deer until it was time to go back to Salmon Lake for pickup back to Ketchikan.

This was certainly a pleasant and relaxing destination, perhaps a perfect introduction to Alaska for someone looking for a low-stress trip. I recommend it to just about anybody who wants to see something of Alaska and does not mind paying for a short bush plane flight. The terrain was pleasant if never spectacular.

Warren Island

★ ★ ★

Size: 11,181 acres | **Year Designated:** 1980 | **Responsible Agency:** USFS

Warren Island sits in the Pacific Ocean just east of Coronation Island between the towns of Craig and Port Alexander. It is part of the Tongass National Forest.

MY VISIT: June 24–26, 2014

None of the Sitka pilots I knew had ever been here, but they were willing to try to get me in. Getting there was something of an adventure. The weather in Sitka was bad again and the float planes were not getting out. Later that afternoon there was a plan to fly north, go around to the east side of Baranof Island and then to Port Alexander. This worked. We dropped two passengers off in Port Alexander and the pilot and I went to Warren Island. As we approached the island, we agreed that it was not a hospitable-looking place. My impression was that I would never want to try to cross the little island from one side to the other. It would take days. The forest was dense and the terrain steep. We flew a couple of loops and landed in Warren Cove on the southeast of the island. The problem was that there were some minor swells and float planes don't like swells because they can push the plane onto the beach. One part of the cove looked to have flat water and so we went there. The only problem was that the water was pretty deep, but I just got out on the float and slid into the waist-deep water. The rocks were slippery, but I staggered with my load to the beach, keeping my balance with a trekking pole. I was now on the beach in the rain and started looking for a campsite close to fresh water. I found a spot and set up my tent in a mossy opening. A night of early to bed.

Day two was sunny with a few clouds and warm. Perfect for day hikes north and south to explore the island. The forest was very dense. My first hiking attempt was north. Things were still wet. The rocks and deadfall were slippery. The going was slow but the beach was nice. The biggest problem was steep limestone ridges that extended from the forest over the beach and into the water. A hiker had to climb over each one of these ridges, which made the going slow. I turned around and headed south. The same problem with limestone ridges was here. Going inland was no help because the forest was dense and there were steep gullies between ridges. The terrain just in from the beach was very steep as I expected from the topo map, USGS Craig D-6. There was at least one fairly large cave. The photo was taken from just north of my campsite. I basically saw no wildlife.

Later a small boat pulled into the cove. A couple rowed onto the beach in a rubber dingy. They landed close to me and the man said they were from Ketchikan and when he was a child his father used to take him to this beach.

My pickup was scheduled for 11:00 am on day four. It was a nice day so I knew flying should be good. I was at the rocky shore waiting for my pilot, but because there were no swells he landed on the gentle, sandy part of shore. There may not have been any swells, but there was a modest onshore breeze. As I hustled as fast as I could, I saw my pilot standing in his waders pushing with both arms against the tail of the airplane to prevent it from blowing onto the shore. It was a sight I will remember as long as I live. I clambered aboard and we took off as quickly as we could.

Beach, Warren Island Wilderness

Kenai

★ ★ ★

Size: 1,345,247 acres   **Year Designated:** 1980   **Responsible Agency:** USFWS

Most of the Kenai National Wildlife Refuge is designated wilderness. The refuge is south of Anchorage and State Highway 1 cuts through the refuge and provides rare, easy road access to backcountry destinations. The wilderness is large and diverse. Some parts are relatively flat at low elevation with dense forest and lakes. Other parts include high-elevation environments with sizeable glaciers falling away from the Harding Ice Field.

MY VISITS: August 5–7, 2017

My 2017 Alaska trips included a rental car, so I was able to get to some trails taking off from State Highway 1. Two of these day hikes were on a weekend and the number of people in the refuge was large. The locals told me that they had a long, gray, wet winter and early summer, and they were taking the opportunity offered by these good-weather days. Finding camping space in designated campgrounds was difficult.

My first day hike began at the Skyline Trailhead along State Highway 1. There was an ant-parade of people coming up and down. The trail was very steep. The formal trail ended at timberline, but many people were continuing on up to some minor summits. On my summit there was a mountain goat wandering around, and other hikers said they had seen a bear. There were nice views of the refuge from this summit. It was on this trail that I encountered, for the first and only time, people carrying assault rifles. I just shook my head.

The second day hike was on the Fuller Lakes Trail. This trail was longer, but still moderately busy. Like the day before, there was a steep early part of the trail, breaking out into the open near the top. The lakes and the surrounding Mystery Hills were pretty.

The last day hike was short, starting at a trailhead from the Swanson River Road going to Drake and Skookum Lakes. The terrain here was just about flat and the forest was dense but not impenetrable. There was only a little meadow separating the lakes from the forest. The only people I encountered this day were two fishermen. They said the lakes in this area were good fishing.

My summary conclusion for this wilderness is that if a hiker is anywhere close to Anchorage this would be a good place to explore. My hikes were not as spectacular as some other areas, but still quite nice and a lot cheaper to visit.

Katmai

★ ★ ★

Size: 3,384,358 acres   **Year Designated:** 1980
Responsible Agency: USNPS

Most of Katmai National Park is designated wilderness. The park is located on the northeast portion of the Alaska Peninsula southwest of the town of Homer and east of the town of King Salmon.

MY VISIT: July 26–30, 2017

Katmai National Park is probably best known for its bear viewing at Brooks Camp and its big volcanoes near the Cook Inlet, especially the Valley of Ten Thousand Smokes. My destination, reached by a float plane from Homer, was Hammersly Lake (1,599 feet), best known as the starting point for fishing trips down American Creek. Instead of going to American Creek I went up an eastern tributary and into the Walatka Mountains. This was classic hiking in open tundra. The only brush was down close to the lake. One could go a long way over relatively gentle terrain. There were lots of lakes of varying sizes and the summits were below 5,000 feet. Other than a red fox that walked through one of my camps I saw little wildlife. The trip was quite enjoyable, although the weather included a lot of low clouds and I was not able to get views of the big volcanoes. The photo is a good representation of the terrain.

When my pilot picked me up, I mentioned to him that I had not seen any of the big, famous volcanoes. He fixed that by flying over all of them on our way back to Homer.

The terrain around these volcanoes would present a serious challenge to any hiker.

WASHINGTON

Henry Jackson

★ ★ ★

Size: 103,591 acres   **Year Designated:** 1984
Responsible Agency: USFS

The Henry Jackson Wilderness is located in the Mount Baker-Snoqualmie and Wenatchee National Forests north of US Highway 2 near Stevens Pass and northwest of the town of Leavenworth. At the time of my visit there was a USFS map devoted to the wilderness. From a map, the wilderness area boundary looks like that of a jerrymandered congressional district. The Pacific Crest Trail (PCT) runs through the area.

MY VISITS: Four day hikes and one three-day backpack between 2003 and 2011

My first visit began at the old mining settlement of Monte Cristo. The last part of the road was closed to vehicles. This was a day hike on the trail up to Silver Lake, over Poodle Dog Pass and then to Twin Lakes where it ends. There were good views of the impressive Monte Cristo Peak and its neighbors. This peak is often seen from many points in the wilderness. My recollection is that the terrain here was not volcanic.

The second trip was on a very painful day. I had hurt my back picking up my cooler the previous day, but I was eventually able to do a day hike to Heather Lake on the east side of the wilderness. The route was through heavy timber to a lake in a pretty setting. On the way to Heather lake I encountered a man carrying a bucket and a shovel and some other gear. He was a rock hound and had been hunting garnets. He showed me his not-insignificant haul.

Trip three was another day hike following trip two. My back was still tender but better than the previous day. I went to a different nearby trailhead for Top Lake. It was a cold but sunny morning with fresh snow on the ground. The trail climbed a ridge through timber with occasional views. There were bear tracks in the snow. Top Lake sits in a scenic spot. It was not much farther to Pear Lake and the PCT, but it was late and I preferred to walk back with some daylight and so turned around. Top Lake is shown in the photo.

The 2011 backpacking trip was mentioned earlier with the Glacier Peak Wilderness. In fact, most of that trip was in the Henry Jackson. I started up the North Fork of the Skykomish River. I had been warned that the bugs were still bad. They were. I made it to Blue Lake (Glacier

The first red maple leaves, Henry Jackson Wilderness

Peak Wilderness) and camped for the night. The next day I hiked part of the way in the Glacier Peak, but returned to the Henry Jackson after going past June Mountain. The trail descended around Bald Eagle Mountain, then dropped into Quartz Creek where I spent my only night in the Henry Jackson. Day three was spent hiking back to trailhead. This was a nice trip in a pretty neighborhood.

The next day was my last in the Henry Jackson. From the same trailhead as the previous hike, I went up the West Cady Ridge Trail through the newly designated (2008) Wild Sky Wilderness. The ridge was nice and the views were good, but the air quality was poor due to smoke and haze and the bugs were still bad. Continuing upward, the trail entered the Henry Jackson, then went to the summit of Benchmark Mountain (5,816 feet) where I turned around. It was now very warm. On the way down I passed an occasional, unofficial campsite. Rummaging around the campsite was a bear. After seeing me he headed for the forest, but as he ambled off, I swear he was panting.

This is a very nice area with an extensive trail system and I recommend it for both day hikers and backpackers.

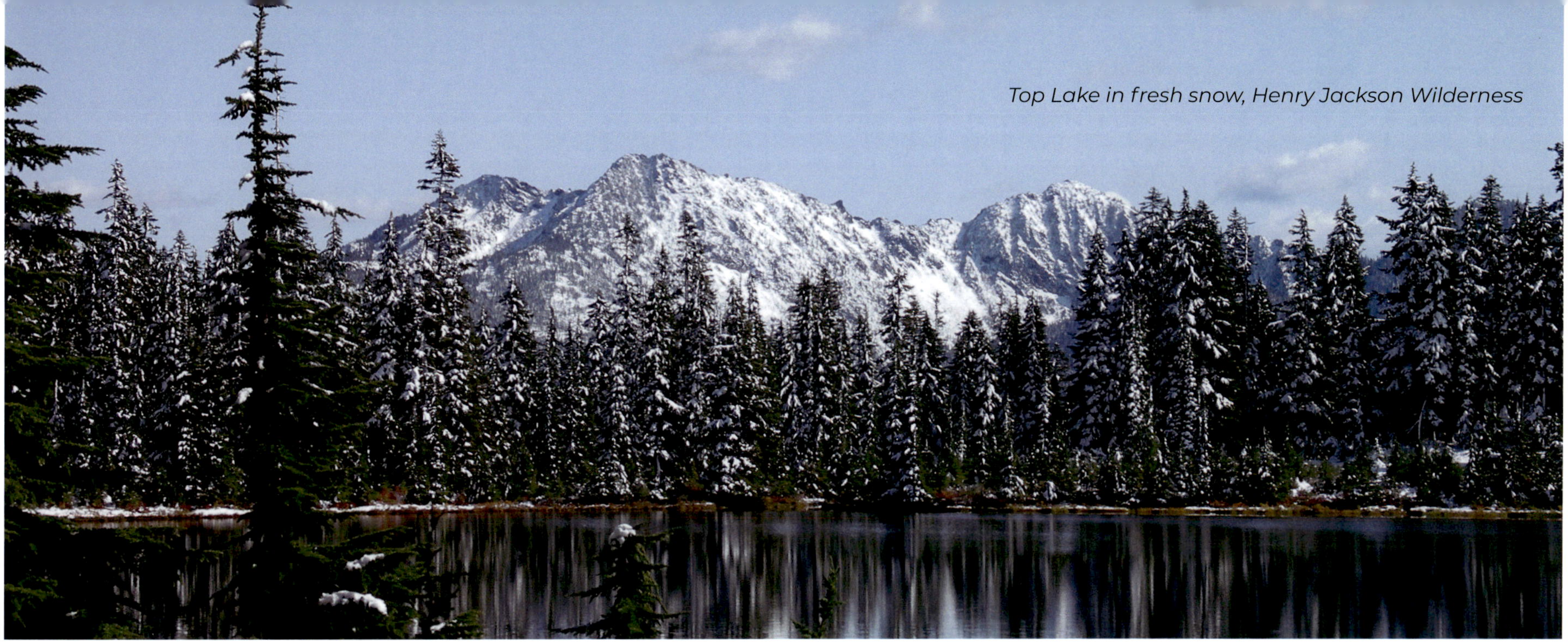

Top Lake in fresh snow, Henry Jackson Wilderness

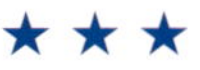

WASHINGTON

Lake Chelan-Sawtooth

★ ★ ★

Size: 145,667 acres **Year Designated:** 1984 **Responsible Agency:** USFS

The Lake Chelan-Sawtooth Wilderness is located in the Okanogan and Wenatchee National Forests south and west of State Highway 20 and southwest of the town of Twisp.

MY VISITS: July 22–23, 2002 and July 24, 2002 and September 17, 2013

The overnight backpack was up South Creek to South Pass on the border with the Stephen Mather Wilderness. It was very warm and smoky and the mosquitoes were about at their peak. The route was not especially interesting, although I did see a male blue grouse drumming. The following day hike was from the Road's End Trailhead up to Twisp Pass, then back down partway and up to Copper Pass, both passes leading into the Stephen Mather Wilderness. This was a nicer and more interesting day. Copper Pass had good views, especially of Stiletto Peak.

The day hike in 2013 was to show my friend Maya the sights of Washington. Again, we hiked from Road's End over Twisp Pass and on into the Stephen Mather Wilderness to Dagger Lake. This was a nice day and a scenic destination. The photo is from Twisp Pass. The terrain was hard rock with dense forest down low. I think most hikers would likely enjoy this area.

Mount Adams

★ ★ ★

Size: 46,800 acres   **Year Designated:** 1964   **Responsible Agency:** USFS

MY VISITS: October 5–6, 2008

This was supposed to be an overnight backpack. My day started at the Shorthorn Trailhead on the southern boundary of the wilderness. It rained most of the previous night in the adjacent Morrison Creek Campground where I had camped. After about two minutes on the trail it began to snow. It snowed persistently as I climbed. At about 6,000 feet, at a junction with the "Round the Mountain" Trail, there was significant snow on the ground. I kept going up until I got to the PCT. It was still snowing. I was concerned about my ability to find the trail back down if I went much farther up and camped overnight, so I turned around and went back to the trailhead. It was completely socked in. I took one photo, but it was worthless. I spent a wet night camped near the trailhead.

The next day it was still raining, but I didn't want to give up, so I drove to a western trailhead at Divide Camp. My route this day was up the Divide Camp Trail to the PCT, then south on the PCT to Sheep Lake. When it was time to turn around, I was about three miles north of where I had turned around the day before. It was drier and I could get a few views and even photos of Mount Adams.

The author enters the Lake Chelan-Sawtooth Wilderness

Wild Sky

★ ★ ★

Size: 106,577 acres | **Year Designated:** 2008 | **Responsible Agency:** USFS

The Wild Sky Wilderness is located in the Mount Baker-Snoqualmie National Forest north of US Highway 2, west of Stevens Pass, and east of the town of Gold Bar. The wilderness is contiguous with the western and southern boundaries of the Henry Jackson Wilderness.

MY VISITS: October 11, 2008 and October 13, 2008 and September 11, 2011

The Wild Sky Wilderness was only freshly designated when I first visited in October of 2008. My access was from US Highway 2 to Forest Road 65, then on Forest Road 6520 to a trailhead for Johnson Ridge. There were a lot of cars at the trailhead, for a good reason: it was a beautiful, clear morning and there had been a little recent snow so views were fabulous. I counted about twenty-two other hikers on this day. The trail ended at Scorpion Peak at 5,400 feet with complete snow cover. Setting all of this off were brilliant red huckleberry bushes, as seen in the photo. If conditions are good, I would recommend this hike to anybody.

On October 13, I made another day hike, this time up Meadow Creek from Forest Road 6530. It was raining or drizzling all day with heavy overcast, socked-in conditions. This hike in heavy timber was probably as good a choice as any. There were no wilderness signs at the trailhead, but the map showed the trail entering the Henry Jackson and there was a sign at that boundary. I went into the Henry Jackson a way, had lunch, turned around, and went back to the trailhead.

The September 2011 day hike went through the Wild Sky to get to the Henry Jackson. That hike was described for the Henry Jackson, but I'll summarize briefly here. This was a hot, buggy day with smoke and haze. My route began at the West Cady Ridge Trailhead off Forest Road 63, then followed the ridge through the Wild Sky and into the Henry Jackson and on to the summit of Benchmark Mountain (5,816 feet). I had lunch on the summit, then turned around and retraced my steps to the trailhead. This is the hike where I scared the bear that was so hot, he was panting. The terrain here was just like that in the Henry Jackson, consistently nice.

Huckleberry bushes on Scorpion Peak after the first snow, Wild Sky Wilderness

Mount Hood

★ ★ ★

Size: 63,177 acres   **Year Designated:** 1964
Responsible Agency: USFS

The Mount Hood Wilderness is located in the Mount Hood National Forest north of US Highway 26 and southeast of the town of Estacada.

MY VISIT: July 13–14, 2005

Mount Hood dominates the skyline around greater Portland, Oregon. It pops up all the time as you drive about. It is yet another in the long string of Cascades volcanoes.

My trip was short but memorable. I stopped in at a USFS ranger station near Hood River and got some maps. I was advised that, since it was a Wednesday in July, if I wanted to visit the Mount Hood Wilderness, today would be the time to go. I took the advice and drove to the Cloud Cap Trailhead to begin a solo overnight backpack. It was a fabulously clear day and the wildflowers were at their peak. I found a great campsite at Elk Cove. Views from my camp were wonderful. The next day was just as nice, and upon leaving my tent I was struck by the heavy and heavenly scent of lupine. I turned around and went back to the trailhead the same way. Even for weekdays, there were lots of folks along the trail both days. Still, a nice hiking destination.

Strawberry Mountain

★ ★ ★

Size: 68,700 acres   **Year Designated:** 1964
Responsible Agency: USFS

The Strawberry Mountain Wilderness is located in the Malheur National Forest south of US Highway 26 and southeast of the town of John Day. When I visited there was a USFS map dedicated to this wilderness.

MY VISITS: August 2–3, 1999

The first day hike here was from the Strawberry Campground to Slide Lake. The terrain was quite lovely. The second day's hike also started at Strawberry Campground and went past Strawberry Lake and Strawberry Falls and on to the summit of Strawberry Mountain. I know I took photographs, but none survive. I recommend these easy hikes in gentle, always scenic terrain to anybody who likes to hike.

Sky Lakes

★ ★ ★

Size: 116,300 acres   **Year Designated:** 1984
Responsible Agency: USFS

The Sky Lakes Wilderness is located in the Winema and Rogue River National Forests south of Crater Lake National Park and west of the town of Chiloquin. When I visited there was a USFS map dedicated to the wilderness.

This was supposed to be a backpack into Mount Jefferson Wilderness, but the winter of 1998-1999 was a heavy snow season and the Cascades high country still held a lot of snow, so I decided to go to Sky Lakes instead. It was a good choice.

My three-day backpacking route started at the Nannie Creek Trailhead, joined the northbound PCT, and then made a loop through the Seven Lakes Basin. This was very nice country, fairly gentle with lots of lakes and enough rock to be picturesque. Nothing too hard core or dramatic, just pleasant scenery. I recommend this area to just about any hiker.

OREGON

Gearhart Mountain

★ ★ ★

Size: 22,809 acres   **Year Designated:** 1964
Responsible Agency: USFS

The Gearhart Mountain Wilderness is located in the Fremont National Forest west of US Highway 395 and northwest of the town of Lakeview. At the time of my visit there was a USFS map devoted to this wilderness.

MY VISIT: June 28, 2002

My route for this day hike began at the trailhead near Lookout Rock, just past the Corral Creek Campground, entered the wilderness at the Palisades Rocks, then worked along the base of Gearhart Mountain and returned the same way. To me, this area was a little gem. For my visit it was lush and green, rather open, and the Palisades Rocks were very cool. This is another area that I would recommend to just about anybody who likes hiking. I doubt that the area sees many visitors.

OREGON

Diamond Peak

★ ★ ★

Size: 54,185 acres   **Year Designated:** 1964
Responsible Agency: USFS

The Diamond Peak Wilderness is located in the Willamette and Deschutes National Forests southeast of the town of Oakridge, with Odell Lake, the Union Pacific Railroad, and Crescent Lake on the east side. At the time of my visit there was a USFS map dedicated to the wilderness.

MY VISIT: October 3–4, 2004

My overnight backpack began near the Trapper Creek Campground at the railroad tracks. There was a sign there saying that one had permission to trespass and I did so by crossing the tracks. I took a trail going up Trapper Creek through dense forest south to Diamond View Lake where the terrain became mostly open. My route continued southwest across the PCT to Marie Lake for the night. The next day began in open terrain with great views of Diamond Peak. This day's route went back to the PCT, then north on the PCT to Lils Lake, then a short, easy cross-country segment to Karen Lake and a trail back to my truck.

Both days had perfect weather and the views were fabulous. The terrain was classic Cascades volcanic. I was and remain quite impressed with this area. Hikers would probably want to take two days to really see it. This is another area that I recommend to just about any hiker.

*Moon over Diamond Peak,
Diamond Peak Wilderness*

Mount Jefferson

★ ★ ★

Size: 107,008 acres   **Year Designated:** 1968
Responsible Agency: USFS

The Mount Jefferson Wilderness is located in the Willamette, Deschutes, and Mount Hood National Forests north of US Highway 20 and northwest of the town of Sisters.

MY VISIT: July 29–31, 2001

My three-day backpack began at a trailhead on the east side of the wilderness. My notes for this trip are just a few words on a calendar and I do not remember the name of the trailhead. I do know that I went to the PCT, set up camp, and made a day hike to the south. My best guess is that the trailhead was Jack Lake. I remember very clearly that the mosquitoes were numerous and I camped in as much snow as I could find. Day two I made a day hike north on the PCT and got pretty close to Mount Jefferson, at least to North Cinder Peak. Day three was spent going back to the trailhead.

This was classic Cascades volcanic terrain. The scenery was always good, as was the trail system, and I recommend the area to just about anybody. The area does see a lot of hikers.

Mount Washington

★ ★ ★

Size: 52,738 acres   **Year Designated:** 1964
Responsible Agency: USFS

The Mount Washington Wilderness is located in the Willamette and Deschutes National Forests just north of State Highway 242 (the McKenzie

Highway) and west of the town of Sisters. At the time of my visit there was map dedicated to this wilderness.

MY VISIT: September 29, 2004

My day started in overcast conditions at the PCT north trailhead near McKenzie Pass on State Highway 242. I went to the base of Mount Washington and turned around. By then the sky had cleared and there were good views of Mount Washington and the Three Sisters. On the return trip, I took the side trail to the summit of Little Belknap (6,305 feet), then went back to the trailhead. A nice day with good views. This is a classic Oregon Cascades hike. I recommend it.

Mount Thielsen

★ ★ ★

Size: 54,267 acres   **Year Designated:** 1984
Responsible Agency: USFS

The Mount Thielsen Wilderness is located in the Umpqua, Winema, and Deschutes National Forests east of Diamond lake and State Highway 138.

Mount Jefferson, Mount Jefferson Wilderness

My day hike started from the Howluck Trailhead off State Highway 138 east of Diamond Lake. The trail went up to the PCT, and I went south on the Thielsen Creek Trail to just north of Mount Thielsen. It was a dry day, but with clouds rolling in. At the PCT junction there were some great views of a partially obscured Mount Thielsen. My route next went north on the PCT making a loop to the Howluck Trail and back to my trailhead. This was a very rewarding day with classic Oregon Cascades scenes in nice conditions and nobody else around. I had good weather until a little drizzle when I was almost back to the trailhead. This is another hike I recommend to almost any hiker who wants to see some of the Oregon Cascades.

OREGON

Badger Creek

★ ★ ★

Size: 29,057 acres   **Year Designated:** 1984
Responsible Agency: USFS

The Badger Creek Wilderness is located in the Mount Hood National Forest southeast of the Mount Hood Wilderness and west of US Highway 197.

MY VISIT: July 16, 2005

My access point was the Fifteenmile Trailhead at the northern wilderness boundary. My route was past Oval Lake, then to the summit of Lookout Mountain. It was a very nice day and the views were outstanding, plus lots of flowers. Mount Hood was often in view. On my way back, I made a side trip toward Flag Point where there were still more views of dramatic basalt cliffs with brilliant fuchsia penstemon in the foreground and Oval Lake in the background, as shown in the photograph. This is another easy, scenic hike I recommend to anybody who likes hiking.

Azaleas and Forest,
Bull of the Woods Wilderness

OREGON

Bull of the Woods

★ ★ ★

Size: 36,731 acres   **Year Designated:** 1984
Responsible Agency: USFS

OREGON

Opal Creek

★ ★ ★

Size: 20,733 acres   **Year Designated:** 1996
Responsible Agency: USFS

The Bull of the Woods and Opal Creek Wilderness areas are in the Mount Hood National Forest northeast of the town of Mill City. These two areas are described together because I visited both on a single overnight backpack. The two areas share a long common boundary.

My access was at a trailhead for Whetstone Mountain. The route went to the summit of Whetstone Mountain (4,969 feet), then east along a ridge with the trail weaving between the two wilderness areas. My destination was the scenic Twin Lakes in Bull of the Woods, where I spent the night. It was a nice route to a scenic destination. Once again, volcanic terrain predominated, with some of the route in dense forest and some open slopes with good views. This is an easy hike and I recommend it to anyone looking for a nice destination away from crowds.

OREGON

Kalmiopsis

★ ★ ★

Size: 2179,700 acres   **Year Designated:** 1964
Responsible Agency: USFS

The Illinois Wild and Scenic River, Kalmiopsis Wilderness

The Kalmiopsis Wilderness is located in southwest Oregon in the Siskiyou National Forest some twenty miles east of the Pacific Ocean and northeast of the town of Brookings. The terrain is very steep with densely forested ridges cut by the Chetco Wild and Scenic River and the Illinois Wild and Scenic River. River running is a common pursuit of visitors.

MY VISITS: July 25, 2005 and October 19–20, 2008

Sometime before my 2005 visit the wilderness had suffered the severe Biscuit Fire. Before hiking I visited the USFS ranger station in Brookings and asked for recommendations on hiking destinations. Their advice was to do rather short hikes along the western edge of the wilderness. I took their advice and did a day hike from a trailhead close to Vulcan Peak. My route went past Vulcan Peak, Vulcan Lake, and the Gardner Mine with its open tunnel, then along a ridge trail toward Johnson Butte. Views were good. It appeared that a large portion of the wilderness had burned, but along this west side the fire was spotty and vegetation was greening up nicely. As is often the case after fire, wildflowers were blooming in profusion, and I was most impressed with the lilies.

The first day hike in 2008 was from the Game Lake Trailhead with the intention of descending to the Illinois River. The fire had burned in a mosaic pattern along most of the trail, but toward the bottom there were almost no intact, full-grown trees. There were, however, new young trees starting the succession process. The forest floor cover was very green. I ran out of time before getting all the way to the river, but stopped and had lunch at a nice overlook before turning around and going back to the trailhead.

The second day hike started in light rain and heavy overcast at the Chetco Lake Trailhead. There were no views, and as I descended, deadfall of burned trees became a serious problem. I did not quite get to Chetco Lake, and considering the steady rain and deadfall I decided to return to the trailhead.

While the Kalmiopsis is a nice area deserving three stars, my enthusiasm for this area is limited. In my opinion there are nicer, more agreeable hiking areas in western Oregon. River travelers may be more likely to find it attractive.

Table Rock

★ ★ ★

Size: 5,500 acres **Year Designated:** 1964
Responsible Agency: BLM

The Table Rock Wilderness lies east of Salem and northwest of Bull of the Woods Wilderness not far from the town of Molalla.

MY VISIT : October 9, 2017

My first attempts at finding the area failed and I needed to get directions. Knowing how to get out of Molalla was key. There was a big recreation area along the Molalla River and signs started to appear for Table Rock. I arrived at the Table Rock Trailhead pretty late and camped there in my truck for the night. The next morning started mostly sunny, but it did not take long to change to lots of clouds as I started up the trail. Like most areas in this part of Oregon, the terrain was volcanic rock and heavy, moist forest. The major feature was an impressive block of volcanic rock with sheer walls. Before I was halfway up to the top it began to rain, and it rained for the rest of the day. Signs at the trailhead told visitors what distant peaks they would see from the summit, but by the time I was on the summit visibility was less than 100 yards. Still, it was a neat spot with some fall color. This is another easy day hike that I recommend to just about any hiker.

Looking at the summit of Table Rock in fog, Table Rock Wilderness

Shoreline by my camp, Pleasant-Lemesurier-Inian Islands Wilderness

Two-Star Areas

★ ★

ALASKA

Pleasant-Lemesurier-Inian Islands 23,098 acres, designated 1990, located in the Tongass National Forest in the Icy Strait between Glacier Bay National Park and Chichagov Island. The city of Juneau is to the east. My visit from June 20 to June 23, 2014 began with a float plane trip from Sitka that deposited me at a sheltered cove on Inian Island. There were two human inhabitants living in a small inholding not far from my camp. Their property was perhaps semi-famous and was called the Hobbit Hole. I hiked over there and had a nice visit with them. Their property was beautiful: nice buildings, some lawn, flowers, and a vegetable garden, and a boat dock. They told me that they had a resident brown bear, but had not seen it that year. On my second day I did a day hike north up to Inian Cove. It was a nice day with some sun. One needed to be very careful about tides. Some of the early part of the hike required going into the forest to avoid cliffs. There was a lot of wildlife around. I saw what I am certain was a red knot (a shorebird) well outside of its normal range. And, from farther north came the sound and site of orcas, my first. I also saw seals, sea otters, and river otters. I was briefly convinced I saw the Loch Ness Monster undulating through the strait, but it was just three seals moving together in a line, probably avoiding the orcas. Day three was supposed to be pickup day, but there was a storm and my pickup was delayed. I did get back to Sitka on the 23rd. Again, a nice place, but not a great hiking destination.

Petersburg Creek-Duncan Salt Chuck 46,849 acres, designated 1980, located in the Tongass National Forest on Kuperanof Island just across the Wrangell Narrows from the town of Petersburg. My trip from June 5 to June 7, 2013 started with a float plane flight from Sitka. We landed near a USFS cabin on Petersburg Lake (elevation 103 feet) that I had reserved. The terrain was rather flat and very wet with some open marshes and dense forest. The topo map (USGS Petersburg D-4) showed a trail going from the northwest wilderness boundary to the cabin and then continuing down Petersburg Creek to salt water. After arriving I explored the northwestern arm of this trail. It was another "Cheshire Cat" trail, visible close to the cabin and then gradually disappearing. The lakeshore could be hiked, but past the lake the vegetation was too dense, so I turned around. This was perfect moose habitat and there were plenty. My second day was devoted to hiking from the cabin down to salt water. There was a good trail to begin with, even some boardwalk. This soon degraded into the normal mess of brush, beaver ponds, and deadfall. The path was slippery and slow, but at least marked. I got close to salt water. I knew because I could hear boat motors. But it was getting late and I needed to turn around. Day three was pickup day.

This was another area that was not especially interesting and certainly not a great hiking destination. It can, however, be accessed from Petersburg without using a bush plane. For some hikers this may be a reasonable introductory destination.

Kootznoowoo 956,051 acres, designated 1980, located in the Tongass National Forest, occupying almost all of Admiralty Island just south of Juneau and across the Stephens Passage. The name comes from a word in the local native language that means "fortress of the bear." I was told that there were about 2,000 brown bears for the 2,000 square miles of the island. That is one big bear for each square mile.

The best way to experience this wilderness is by watercraft. Unfortunately, I did not have a watercraft, so my trip from June 2 to June 4 began with a float plane from Sitka to a USFS fishing cabin on Distin Lake (elevation 312 feet). I attempted to do some hiking. It did not go well. According to my map, USGS Sitka C-2, there were portage trails near both the inlet and outlet ends of the lake. My plan was to bushwhack from the cabin on the middle of the lake to one or both trails. (I wanted to stay in a cabin because of the bear density.) On day one I tried to go to the outlet but had to give up because of the very dense vegetation, large, boggy areas, and tangles of deadfall, devil's club, and alder. Day two was devoted to attempting to go to the inlet end of the lake and the portage trail to Thayer Lake. This was extremely slow going with the same obstacles as yesterday. I could not do even half a mile per hour. I ran out of time and had to turn around. Day three was cloudy with rain and I got picked up and went back to Sitka.

While on Admiralty Island I did not see a single bear—not a track, not a hint of scat. There was a note in the cabin saying there was not likely to be any bears around Distin Lake. In fact, I saw no wildlife at all. Rare for a destination in Alaska. This was one of my least favorite Alaska destinations.

Maurille Islands 4,937 acres, designated 1980, located in the Tongass National Forest. The Maurille Islands lie in the Pacific Ocean west of Prince of Wales Island and northwest of the town of Craig. Most of the islands are shown on the USGS map Craig C-5. There are at least fifteen named islands. This trip from August 2 to August 4, 2013 began with a float plane flight out of Ketchikan. We had some problems finding the islands and once there had trouble deciding where to land. Fortunately, my pilot had been here before to drop off and pick up shellfish harvesters. We landed at San Lorenzo Island where there was an old dock. A derelict boat was tied up to the dock, but there was no way to get from the dock to the shore because the end that had been attached to land was no longer attached. Maneuvering the plane so that I could get to shore was very tricky, but my pilot came through. The island was about one mile long and about five-eighths mile wide. Not much room for hiking. It was a pretty place, rising to a height of about 300 feet. There were big trees and some brush, but not too difficult to get around. The mostly rocky shore was attractive with lots of little creatures in tide pools. This was clearly not a hiking destination, but I was trying to visit all the national forest wilderness areas, so here I was. After a day to wander around, day three was pickup day and we returned to Ketchikan.

South Baranof 319,568 acres, designated 1980, located in the Tongass National Forest. The western wilderness boundary is the Pacific Ocean. The eastern boundary is the Chatham Strait. The closest main town is Sitka, the capital of Alaska in the days of Russian control. The terrain was very rugged and there were lots of large lakes and fiords. Most of the wilderness is on the USGS topo map Port Alexander C-3. My visit from June 27 to June 30, 2012 began with a float plane flight from Sitka to Davidof Lake where I had reserved a USFS fishing cabin near the inlet end of the lake. Davidof Lake sits at 687 feet elevation and is surrounded by heavy forest. Maps show a trail from the outlet of Davidof to the next lake down, Plotnikof Lake. Upon arrival I looked for a route from my cabin to the outlet. This was a complete failure as the terrain was *much* too steep. A journal in the cabin had an entry from a party who had come up from Plotnikof, and they indicated that they were in fear for their lives during their adventure. The number of entries in the journal were few, and none were recent.

The inlet end of the lake looked like some hiking might be possible. There were large trees, which is good because they prevent brush from getting too dense. There were lots of Sitka deer that just stood and stared at me. There were a few open areas of muskeg. The snow level was about 1,000 feet and everything was wet. I made decent progress and got to some open meadows with shallow lakes. I was hoping to access the ridge northwest of the lake, but the terrain was again too steep. Overall, this was not much of a hiking trip. The terrain was difficult, views were limited, and the weather unfriendly. Visitors need to know that hiking will be a challenge.

South Prince of Wales 90,968 acres, designated 1980, located in the Tongass National Forest near the southern tip of South Prince of Wales Island across the Clarence Strait southwest of Ketchikan. Most of the area is shown on the USGS topo map Dixon Entrance C-1. My visit from August 3 to August 5, 2012 began when I was dropped off late in the afternoon at Nichols Lake (elevation 32 feet) just outside the wilderness boundary. I was warned that the terrain here would be very wet so I was hiking in my "Alaska sneakers," high-top rubber boots. I don't like these boots for backpacking, but in this case, they were the best way to go. Once in the wilderness area, the ground was mostly muskeg. I slowly headed southwest maybe two miles and looked for a place to camp. This was difficult in muskeg with rock outcroppings, but I finally found a spot.

My second day began in fog that eventually burned off revealing a warm sunny day. I went west to Brownson Bay, a very pretty place with a pristine beach. I could not linger as it was getting late and I needed to get back to camp. On the way there were lots of Sitka deer and lots of bear tracks and scat. Day three was pickup day. While sitting above Nichols Lake a large black bear appeared from the forest, saw me, and returned to the forest.

While pleasant with at least one nice beach, this is probably not a great hiking destination.

Kuiu 60,581 acres, designated 1990
Tebenkov Bay 66,812 acres, designated 1980

The Kuiu and Tebenkov Bay Wilderness areas are contiguous and are in the middle of Kuiu Island across the Chatham Strait from the southern end of South Baranof Island. The closest town is Sitka. They are managed by the Tongass National Forest. I discuss both areas together because I visited both on the same trip.

My visit from May 22 to May 26, 2013 was by float plane from Sitka. On a very nice spring afternoon we landed at the northern end of the Affleck Canal, a fiord, in the Kuiu Wilderness. The first thing that struck both me and my pilot was the enormous amount of trash lining the shore. I have never seen such a concentration of trash anywhere in the wilderness system, or, indeed, anywhere on public land. And, no, there was no duck present to try and sell me insurance. The trash was essentially all plastic: nets, rope, hard hats, floats, buckets, barrels, clothes, and every imaginable container for food and beverages. There was a freshwater stream entering the canal near our landing spot. I was wearing my "Alaska sneakers" and carrying my regular hiking boots in one hand as I wandered around the area looking for an ideal camping spot. I found one and while setting up camp I realized that my hiking boots were missing. I retraced my steps as best I could, then traced them again. I searched for an hour, then gave up. How could I be so clueless?

Before coming on this trip, I had a phone conversation with a USFS employee who had some experience on this island. I was told that there were no brown bears, only black bears. As a consequence, and given the availability of fish here at salt water, the black bears get *really big*. One reason people come here is to hunt the monsters. In the early evening of my first day, not far from my camp, a black bear emerged from the forest to forage along the tidal zone. He was big. He disappeared into the forest before I could get a good photo.

I was also told that there was an old trail between Kuiu and Tebenkof Bay that had been for portaging canoes in the old days. I was also warned that this trail might be in some disrepair. Exploring a bit from my camp I found an old sign nailed to a big Sitka spruce indicating the presence of a portage route.

On day two I decided to backpack over to the Tebenkof Bay Wilderness. My map (USGS topo Port Alexander B-1) showed this being only a little over three miles. There really was a trail for maybe a quarter of a mile. After that it was heavy forest with lots of brush and deadfall and, especially, water hazards. This was low elevation at salt water in an area that gets a lot of rain. There were puddles, beaver dams, a creek, and an almost infinite array of ponds. It took me five hours to cover the three miles to Petrof Bay in the Tebenkof Bay Wilderness. I knew I was on the correct route because there was another portage sign at the Petrof Bay end. There was also another nice campsite there close to a freshwater stream and near the shore. Not so much as a postage stamp-size piece of trash was on this shore.

Day three was devoted to a day hike along the shore of Petrof Bay. It was another nice day and the shore walking was easy as the tide was out. I saw some harlequin ducks, always a joy. I returned to camp at high tide. Back in camp, early in the evening another *really big* black bear came out of the forest to forage along the shore. He was coming toward me and I saw that he was so huge he almost had trouble walking. He looked like a sumo wrestler. I wanted to get a photo, but he saw me and dodged into the forest.

On day four I packed up and backpacked to the Kuiu Wilderness and my previous camp. Upon arrival at my previous camp there was a huge surprise waiting for me. My hiking boots had washed up on the shore. Yes, they had spent about three days in salt water and did not look their best, but they appeared to be serviceable. I had put them down on a log below the high tide line when I was trying to identify a bird on the water. Day five was spent waiting for my pilot for my return to Sitka.

While this is a pleasant place, I do not recommend it as an interesting hiking destination.

Portage sign, Affleck Canal, Kuiu Wilderness

Mount Snokomish 15,686 acres, designated 1984, located in the Olympic National Forest west of US Highway 101 and south of the village of Duckabush, contiguous with the southwest corner of Olympic National Park. My visit was a day hike on July 14, 2007 beginning at the Mildred Lakes Trailhead off Forest Road 25. There were a lot of cars parked at the trailhead. The trail was steep and full of roots. At 4.5 miles from the trailhead there was a high spot with great views of Mount Cruiser, Mount Skokomish, Mount Ellinor, Mount Pershing, and Mount Lincoln. I continued on along the trail to its end at The Mildred Lakes, a spot filled with people and mosquitoes. I did not linger, but retraced my steps back through this pleasant area with standard Cascade Range volcanic features.

Buckhorn 45,601 acres, designated 1984, located in the Olympic National Forest, contiguous with Olympic National Park's eastern boundary. The nearest town is Quilcene. This day hike on July 15, 2007 began at a trailhead for the Big Quilcene Trail. I could tell from the number of vehicles parked here that this was a popular trail. It was a nice day and there were lots of folks on the trail. I went to Marmot Pass, also very popular, with nice views into the park and north into Puget Sound. From Marmot Pass I went partway along the Tubal Mine Trail for more views. While I have no desire to return, this area could be a good introduction to Cascades volcanic terrain.

The Brothers 17,239 acres, designated 1984, located in the Olympic National Forest, contiguous with Olympic National Park on the park's east side just west of Bellingham across the Hood Canal. My visit was a day hike on July 13, 2007 on the Duckabush Trail along the Duckabush River to the park boundary, then return. The trail was through heavy forest with few views. The Brothers Wilderness and a few other Olympic National Forest wilderness areas (Wonder Mountain, Colonel Bob, Glacier View and Clearwater) basically act as buffer areas around Olympic National Park. It was

classical Olympic terrain: steep and heavily forested with big, fast water in streams and rivers.

Wonder Mountain 2,349 acres, designated 1984, located in the Olympic National Forest, contiguous with the southern boundary of Olympic National Park. This little wilderness area was very hard to find and to access. There were no trails. My visit on July 16, 2007 was a day hike from Forest Road 2451, then a bushwhack up a steep, densely forested ridge to the southern wilderness boundary and a bit beyond. There were a few views from the ridgetop. This was a difficult hike with minimal reward. A GPS was mandatory.

Colonel Bob 12,120 acres, designated 1984, located in the Olympic National Forest, contiguous with the southern boundary of Olympic National Park. My visit on July 17, 2007 was a day hike on a trail from Forest Road 2204 to the summit of Colonel Bob. The day featured light rain and fog, and the terrain was steep and densely forested. I turned around before the summit because of rotten snow.

Glacier View 3,050 acres, designated 1984, located in the Gifford Pinchot National Forest, contiguous with the western boundary of Mount Rainier National Park. My visit on July 21, 2007 was a day hike that began at the Christine Lake Trailhead, went past Christine Lake and Goat Lake, and ended at the summit of Gobbler's Knob and a partially dismantled fire lookout (5,485 feet). The day was foggy with light rain and hordes of mosquitoes. There was a view of a glacier on the west side of Mount Rainier.

Clearwater 14,300 acres, designated 1984, located in the Snoqualmie National Forest, contiguous with the northern boundary of Mount Rainier National Park. I needed help finding a way to this area, but did manage a day hike on July 22, 2007. The hike was a bushwhack to Coundly Lake in a steady rain. At the lake was a group of loggers with the day off, fishing and tending a roaring fire they kept going with dry wood they had backpacked in. Other, better starting points existed, but were unavailable because of flood-induced road closures.

Noisy-Diobsud 14,300 acres, designated 1984, located in the Mount Baker-Snoqualmie National Forest west of State Highway 20 and east of the town of Concrete. The wilderness is contiguous with the western boundary of North Cascades National Park. My day hike on July 24, 2003 started at a trailhead just east of Baker Lake and quickly led me to the Watson Lakes nestled nicely below Mount Watson. I continued on up to almost the summit of Mount Watson with good views into the park, especially of Mount Shuksan. This area was very similar to others in this neighborhood.

Boulder River 49,444 acres, designated 1984, located in the Mount Baker-Snoqualmie National Forest south of State Highway 530, west of the Glacier Peak Wilderness, and southwest of the town of Darrington. My overnight backpack started on July 25, 2003 at a trailhead at the end of Forest Road 41 off the Mountain Loop Highway. My goal was to get to the summit of the Three Fingers. I remember good weather and a scenic route. My summit effort failed because there was too much steep snow for a solo attempt. The terrain looked a lot like that in the nearby Glacier Peak and Henry M. Jackson Wilderness areas.

Tatoosh 15,720 acres, designated 1984, located in the Gifford Pinchot National Forest west of State Highway 123, northwest of US Highway 12, and east of the town of Longmire. Its northern boundary is contiguous with the southern boundary of Mount Rainier National Park. This day hike on July 20, 2007 began at a trailhead for the Tatoosh Trail that goes to the Tatoosh Lakes. The terrain along the trail was quite rugged with volcanic outcroppings, some open slopes, and some remaining snow. The scenery was nice, but it rained the entire day, sometimes heavily. I have no photos and probably did not take any.

Norse Peak 50,923 acres, designated 1984, located in the Mount Baker-Snoqualmie National Forest and Wenatchee National Forest east of State Highway 410 and north of US Highway 12. It is a bit northeast of Mount Rainier National Park. My overnight backpack began on July 23, 2007. It

Wildflowers on Oregon Butte, Wenaha-Tucannon Wilderness

was a loop from the Raven's Roost to the PCT, south on the PCT to Little Crow Basin, then down Crow Creek. The terrain was almost exactly like that of Mount Rainier National Park itself: green meadows, a few lakes, and lots of volcanic cliffs and outcroppings. It rained much of the trip, although there were some nice views the second day.

William O Douglas 167,195 acres, designated 1984, located in the Gifford Pinchot and Wenatchee National Forests south of State Highway 410, north of US Highway 12, east of State Highway 123 and northeast of the town of Packwood. The wilderness is contiguous with the Mount Rainier National Park east boundary. My overnight backpack began on July 25, 2007 beside the Mather Memorial Highway at the East Entrance of Mount Rainier National park. My route was south on the PCT past Dewey Lake and Anderson Lake to Two Lakes, then retrace steps back to the trailhead. The problem with this trip was evident as soon as I opened the door of my pickup truck. Swarms of mosquitoes. The weather was sunny and the views were good, but there was no peace from the mosquitoes outside the tent. The route was busy with lots of other backpackers. The terrain was scenic, much the same as that in the park.

Trapper Creek 6,250 acres, designated 1984, located in the Gifford Pinchot National Forest close to the Mount Adams and Indian Heaven Wilderness areas in southwest Washington north of the Columbia River and east of Interstate 5, northeast of the city of Vancouver. At the time of my visit there was a 2005 USFS map dedicated to these three areas. My Trapper Creek day hike on October 2, 2008 was from a trailhead for the Soda Peaks. The trailhead was in a classic Cascades west slope terrain of dense forest with big trees. The day was gray, dark, and occasionally drippy. The trail climbed steeply through mostly closed-in forest but with occasional views. There was some understory with maple leaves already beginning to turn. The trail first went to Soda Lake in a pretty setting, then up to the Soda Peaks where it exited the wilderness. I think most hikers would like this destination.

Indian Heaven 20,600 acres, designated 1984, located in the Gifford-Pinchot National Forest in southwest Washington not far from the Trapper Creek Wilderness. My long day hike began at the Cultus Creek Trailhead, then went to the PCT. I took the PCT south past Bear Lake and Junction Lake to Blue Lake. At Blue Lake I turned around, took the PCT back to Junction Lake, then took a different trail to Lemei Lake and Cultus Lake and back to the trailhead. It rained all day after getting to the PCT. There was a lot of color from huckleberries, maples, and mountain ash. Conditions did not allow for any photos. I could recommend this area to anyone on a sunny day.

Wenaha-Tucannon 177,423 acres, designated 1978, located in the Umatilla National forest in the northeast corner of Oregon and the southeast corner of Washington in the Blue Mountains south and east of US Highway 12. The nearest town is Dayton to the northwest. It is drier here than in most of Washington and Oregon. The terrain is rugged if not very high. It is mainly river-carved volcanic rock covered with heavy forest.

A day hike on July 26, 2002 began at the Teepee Campground and Trailhead and went to the summit of Oregon Butte. The trail up to the butte was quite pleasant and the views from the summit were good. There was a fire lookout here and I had a chat with the man staffing the lookout. The flowers were spectacular. The photo is not the sharpest but gives one a sense of the density of the flowers.

An overnight backpacking trip in September of 2008 was from the Elk Flat Trailhead in Oregon and went down to the Wenaha River. My route dropped through layers of volcanic deposits to the river, which I forded. I went along the north bank and set up camp near the water. It was quiet here with only a few white-tailed deer. The area appeared to be quite wild and not heavily used.

Salmo-Priest 41,335 acres, designated 1984, located in the Colville National Forest in extreme northeast Washington. This corner of Washington was home to the very last inland caribou in the United States. They were called "The Gray Ghosts of the Selkirks" because of their rarity and coloration and the nearby Selkirk Mountains. As I write this in 2019, it is thought that the caribou are no longer in the area. My day hike on August 1, 2006 began at the Hughes Meadow Trailhead in Idaho, went up Thunder Mountain, then on the Shedroof Trail, Shedroof Cutoff Trail, and back to the trailhead. There was a lot of smoke in the air and little in the way of scenery.

OREGON

Monument Rock 19,650 acres, designated 1984, located in the Wallowa-Whitman National Forest southwest of the town of Unity. My September 27, 2004 day hike began at the Alicia Creek Trailhead and proceeded south to Bullrun Rock and Monument Rock. The terrain was grassland with volcanic outcrops. Cows and sheep were very much in evidence.

Menagerie 4,962 acres, designated 1984, located in the Willamette National Forest just north of US Highway 20 and east of the town of Sweet Home. My visit was a day hike on September 30, 2004. I began at the Rooster Rock Trailhead and went to the summit of Rooster Rock. The terrain was steep ridges and dense forest with some exposed, vertical rock. The area is reputed to be a destination for technical climbers and the only other person I saw was a climber. The rock features are supposed to resemble animals, but I never saw anything that looked like any beast.

Waldo Lake 36,868 acres, designated 1984, located in the Willamette National Forest, contiguous with the Three Sisters Wilderness. At the time of my visit there was a USFS map dedicated to this wilderness. My overnight backpacking trip from October 1, 2004 to October 2, 2004 began at the Winchester Trailhead, then went east to the Six Lakes Trail, then south past the Six Lakes to Lake Chetlo, then returned to the trailhead by the Winchester Ridge Trail. My camp was at Eddeeleo Lake. The terrain was fairly level with dense forest and rhododendron. The heavy vegetation concealed some of the numerous lakes. Total number of other people seen was one fisherman. Fall colors were probably the most noteworthy feature.

Mountain Lakes 23,071 acres, designated 1964, located in the Winema National Forest west of the city of Klamath Falls. I have no written records of this trip in the late Spring of, probably, 1978. My only souvenir is the USGS topo map Lake of the Woods, Oregon. I was on a business trip to Washington, and some friends in Portland invited me to go with them on a three-day backpacking trip to this area. What I do remember is that we were early, there was still a lot of snow around, and hiking was sometimes difficult because of post holing. My recollection is of a loop trip to multiple lakes in rather gentle terrain and a mix of forest and open mountainsides. I have no photos and almost certainly did not have a camera with me.

North Fork of the John Day 121,352 acres, designated 1984, located in the Umatilla and Wallowa-Whitman National Forests west of the city of Baker. There are several pieces to this wilderness and my only visit on July 27, 2002 was to the most northeast piece, just northwest of Baker City. I hiked the Elkhorn Crest Trail south from the Elkhorn Crest Trailhead off the Elkhorn Drive Scenic Byway. The trail entered, left, and reentered the wilderness area a few times. I have photographs from the trail at Lost Lake Saddle looking down into Lost Lake. I went a bit farther south past Mount Ruth. I have memories of big crowds at and near the trailhead and many gunshots as I hiked along with no idea who was shooting or at what. I did not find the area especially attractive.

Copper Salmon 13,700 acres, designated 2009, located in the Rogue River and Siskiyou National Forests southwest of the community of Powers and just east of the Grassy Knob Wilderness. For my visit in September 2011, I needed human help in order to find this recently designated area. I found the help in the Powers USFS ranger station. They had a map with wilderness boundaries drawn by hand. I got good directions and set off. My hike began at an abandoned USFS road that led into the wilderness. This old road was now part of the wilderness. The terrain was basically rainforest, very steep, and the "trail" contoured around Copper Mountain. (There is also a Salmon Mountain in the northern part of the wilderness.) The country had been logged and was now mostly second growth, but there remained sections of old growth with *huge* Douglas fir trees. Open areas had some deciduous trees and rhododendron. After a couple of miles, I just turned around and went back. The next day I drove to the Barklow Mountain Trailhead and hiked on a real trail into the wilderness through a mix of old- and second-growth trees to the site of an old fire lookout. In my opinion, a hiker could find better or more easily accessible forest destinations with at least some old-growth timber.

Drift Creek 5,798 acres, designated 1984, located in the Siuslaw National Forest about eight miles from the Pacific Ocean and a bit northeast of the town of Waldport. I did a day hike on July 21, 2005 beginning at the Harris Ranch Trailhead. I and two other hikers descended a short way through old-growth cedar and fir to the creek. The map showed the trail crossing the creek but we did not see it. I just went back to the trailhead. This was an easy hike through nice forest to a nice creek.

Rogue-Umpqua Divide 35,749 acres, designated 1984, located in the Umpqua National Forest northwest of Crater Lake National Park. My day hike on October 7, 2004 began at the Whitehorse Meadow Trailhead and went south through the meadow where I turned around. My notes call this a "day hike to nowhere." I did, however, see my first pileated woodpecker.

Bridge Creek 5,337 acres, designated 1984, located in the Ochoco National Forest south of US Highway 26. There were no trails. My day hike on October 8, 2004 began on an old two-track near a USFS road and I walked through rather open terrain to what my map called North Point, where there was a rim and some views. The area had seen heavy use by cattle.

North Fork Umatilla 20,435 acres, designated 1984, located in the Umatilla National Forest east of Pendleton. My day hike on July 12, 2005 began at a trailhead near the Umatilla Forks Campground and went up to and along Ninemile Ridge. I do not recall seeing anything of particular interest.

Mark Hatfield 65,822 acres, designated 1984, located south of Interstate Highway 84 and east of Portland. This wilderness area used to be called the Columbia, but is now the Mark Hatfield, for an Oregonian who served thirty years in the US Senate. My day hike on July 15, 2005 began at the Wahtum Lake Trailhead for the PCT. My route was north on the PCT along a ridge to the Benson Table where I made a small loop and rejoined the PCT to return south to the trailhead. The terrain was typical western Oregon dense forest.

Salmon Huckleberry 62,061 acres, designated 1984, located in the Mount Hood National Forest. My day hike on July 16, 2005 went up the Salmon River Trail a rather long way hoping to see waterfalls shown on my map. I never saw any falls. The terrain was very similar to that in other nearby areas.

Middle Santiam 8,844 acres, designated 1984, located in the Willamette National Forest east of Sweet Home. My day hike on July 20, 2006 began at a trailhead near Knob Rock. My route was basically to hike from the eastern wilderness boundary to the western boundary in the northern part of the wilderness on what may well have been the only trail. The terrain was steep and the forest was dense. The trail had lots of ups and downs, and when I got close to (maybe to?) Chimney Peak I had lunch, turned around, and went back to the trailhead.

Cummins Creek 9,443 acres, designated 1984, located in the Siuslaw National Forest just east of US Highway 101, quite close to the Pacific Ocean. My starting point on July 22, 2005 was a little trailhead parking area just off US Highway 101. There were signs at the trailhead warning visitors that this was a "high crime" area and not to leave any valuables in a vehicle. Next to my parking spot was a pile of broken automotive window glass. At one of the warning signs someone had scrawled over the sign in red crayon "believe it." This did not give me a warm feeling as mine was now the only vehicle here. I said, "Oh, well" and went up the trail anyway. The farther I walked, the less comfortable I felt about leaving my truck, so after only a mile or two I decided to turn around. Upon my return, the truck was fine. My route this short day was east from the trailhead through dense, wet forest with moss and ferns and, to my surprise, huge, blooming foxglove. I decided right then that I would try and come back again to this area.

The second opportunity was on August 22, 2011. I went to the *eastern* trailhead for the ridge trail. There were no worrying signs. The next morning was gray and drippy, and I hiked west down the ridge trail until I got to where I think I turned around in 2005, then retraced my steps to my truck. It was a ridgetop trail in dense timber with some deciduous understory, much like the western end.

Rock Creek 7,348 acres, designated 1984, located in the Siuslaw National Forest just south of the Cummins Creek Wilderness. There were no trails. My attempted day hike on July 22, 2005 began near a USFS campground off US Highway 101 where Rock Creek exited the wilderness. It was a slog through thick vegetation, deadfall, and devil's club, walking sometimes next to the creek and sometimes in the creek. Conditions were very wet whether in or out of the creek. I spent a few hours going at most two miles, decided I had enough fun, turned around, and went back to my starting point. I do not recommend this area for hiking.

Wild Rogue 25,658 acres, designated 1978, located in the Siskiyou National Forest east of US Highway 101. Some of the wilderness is on BLM lands. The main attraction is the Rogue River itself, very popular with floaters. My day hike on July 23, 2005 started at the Rogue River Trailhead and the trail followed the river upstream. There were lots of boats on the river, including jet boats, some hauling gobs of tourists. There were some cabins and even a lodge along the river. My favorite feature of the area was the blackberries. I happen to be quite fond of blackberries. They were here in profusion and I took my share. It should not have come as any surprise, but one big blackberry patch contained a bear, about 30 feet away from me. The beast totally ignored me. Late in the morning came a rush of excitement. Somewhere upstream was a fire, almost certainly just discovered. Now the jet boats were speeding up the river carrying firefighting crews. There was a roar overhead as a C-130 (four-engine turboprop) with Coast Guard paint circled the river some distance ahead of me. The area seemed to get a lot of use and campsites for floaters were scattered along the shore, each site equipped with food storage containers, presumably so that the bears stick to eating blackberries.

Grassy Knob 17,159 acres, designated 1984 located in the Siskiyou National Forest east of Port Orford. My day hike on July 24, 2005 began along Poverty Ridge on the western wilderness boundary. The beginning of the "trail" may have been an overgrown cherry-stem road. I took this "trail" to the site of an old, abandoned, dismantled fire lookout on what my USFS map said was Anvil Mountain and in the wilderness. I continued past this little summit along one of its ridges, but the route was severely overgrown and soon became impossible to get through.

I made a second visit on September 21, 2011. This hike was a short bushwhack from the Butler Bar Campground on the southeast side of the wilderness. I was able to access the area along a small stream, but the ravine became too steep with too much deadfall and I had to turn around. I do not recommend this area for hiking.

Roaring River 36,550 acres, designated 2009, located in the Mount Hood National Forest just south of the Salmon-Huckleberry Wilderness and south of the town of Estacada. This wilderness was recently (2009) designated when I made my 2011 visit. I stopped in the USFS ranger station in Sandy where they had a map showing the new boundaries. I penciled in the new area on my old Mount Hood National Forest map and went looking for trailheads. My starting point for a day hike on September 17, 2011 was the Frazier Turnaround Campground. This was clearly a popular spot as there were lots of folks and vehicles (including a small bus). It was a completely socked-in day but dry while hiking. My route was the "Lakes Loop" trail, going first to Lower Rock Lake (three tents), then Serene Lake (eight tents), then Cache Meadow and back to the trailhead. The terrain was closed-in dense forest, probably old growth with a few uninteresting lakes. The next day I hiked the Shining Lake Trail, which followed Indian Ridge with the Roaring River off to the northeast. It was another socked-in day and rained most of the day. I hiked this trail until it ended and turned around. Hikers can find much nicer destinations in Oregon.

Clackamas 9,470 acres, designated 2009, located in the Mount Hood National Forest just west of the Roaring River Wilderness. My September 19, 2011 day hike began at a trailhead along USFS Road 45 providing trail access to the wilderness and Memaloose Lake. My trip began after leaving Roaring River. There was plenty of time because none of the hikes are long and the two areas are close. The trail to Memaloose Lake was short, about one mile, climbing through nice old-growth forest. My guess is that this area was designated wilderness to preserve the forest. The lake was nothing special. The most interesting part of this hike was encountering a couple who had been harvesting "chicken of the woods" mushrooms. I was impressed but refrained from picking.

Lower White River 2,870 acres, designated 2009, no trails
Richard L. Kohnstamm Size unknown, designated 2009

I describe these two wilderness areas together because they are close together and because, I think, they were designated at the same time and I hiked them both on the same day. In truth, I don't know if the Richard L. Kohnstamm is really a wilderness area or not. The USFS Mount Hood National Forest map calls it a wilderness area as do the signs on the ground at the trailheads. However, the Wilderness.net website does not include it. Both areas are just south of the Mount Hood Wilderness. The Richard L. Kohnstamm area is accessible from the Timberline Lodge at Mount Hood. The Lower White River Wilderness is a bit farther south and east and is accessible from the Keeps Mill Campground off US Highway 26, State Highway 216, and Forest Road 2021. My day hikes on September 19, 2011 began with a bushwhack along the Lower White River from the Keeps Mills Campground. I did not go far, at least a mile but probably not much more. The river had high flow and velocity, but was nothing special. After getting back to the campground I drove to the Timberline Lodge and went to the northern boundary of the Richard L. Kohnstamm Wilderness and hiked the PCT south to the southern wilderness boundary, turned around, and retraced my steps. Here the PCT parallels the White River as it flows in a deep gully from the snow and ice of Mount Hood. There are more interesting hikes to be done in this neighborhood.

Oregon Badlands 29,301 acres, designated 2009, located on BLM lands southeast of the city of Bend. Access is easy as the southern wilderness boundary is just north of US Highway 20. My day hike on October 9, 2017 began at a developed trailhead just off US Highway 20. I took the Badlands Rock Trail to Badlands Rock and somewhat beyond, then retraced my steps back to my truck. The terrain along this trail was nearly flat with grass, shrubs and junipers growing on an old lava flow. While I only encountered one other hiker, I had the impression that the area was quite popular.

Soda Mountain 24,100 acres, designated 2009, located on BLM lands within the Cascade-Siskiyou National Monument, currently under attack by anti-conservation forces for being "too big." It is southeast of the city of Ashland off State Highway 66, the Green Springs Highway. There was a sign on the highway for a road to Soda Mountain. I took it to a Soda Mountain Trailhead, then a bit beyond for a quiet but very cold camp. There was even a little overnight snow. The next morning was brilliantly clear and I went back to the trailhead where a group of schoolteachers was setting up material for a student field trip. Here I began my day hike on October 12, 2017.

My hike was first up a gated road to the summit of Soda Mountain. The summit was filled with an impressive array of communications equipment including some big antennae. There was also a fire lookout. On my way back down the mountain I took a trail to the east into the wilderness proper and then to the PCT north to the northern wilderness boundary. The trail went through pleasant, mostly open forest with some nice, large trees. I turned around at the wilderness boundary and took a slightly different route back to the trailhead. I saw nothing of particular interest.

Spring Basin 6,382 acres, designated 2009, located on BLM public lands south of State Highway 218 and bounded on the west by the John Day River. I did a day hike here on October 8, 2017 from the southern wilderness boundary to the northern boundary through dry juniper and grasses along volcanic cliffs. While a pleasant hike, I did not see anything interesting.

Steens Mountains 170,025 acres, designated 2000, located on BLM public lands in southeast Oregon, west of State Highway 205 and east of US Highway 95. The closest town is Burns. The country is dominated by volcanic features. My friend Maya and I did a day hike on September 9, 2014 from the Wildhorse Canyon rim to Wildhorse Lake and upper Wildhorse Canyon, worn by glacial ice through the layers of volcanic rock. It was a pretty area and was green around the lake and upper canyon. This was a nice enough place, but I doubt that I would return.

One-Star Areas

ALASKA

Endicott River 98,729 acres, designated 1980, located in the Tongass National Forest on the mainland between Glacier Bay National Park on the west and the Lynn Canal (another fiord) on the east. The closest town is Haines. This area was very difficult to access. There are no lakes that can accommodate float planes. It may be possible to gain access from the Lynn Canal with an aircraft making a beach landing, but a pilot who could do this did not recommend it because the terrain is very difficult upstream of the mouth of the river. I spoke via phone with a USFS employee who had been there. He started with a kayak in Glacier Bay, then backpacked cross country to the Endicott River Wilderness. He acknowledged that it was a difficult trip. He informed me that sometimes people (mostly moose hunters) fly wheeled aircraft in to a gravel bar not far from the western boundary. I found a pilot who had made this trip. He was probably the only pilot who could take a paying passenger there.

My trip began in Haines with a flight in a Cessna 180 with fat, lightly inflated tires. We checked out the landing area and it was tiny, but we got down in good shape. The area was surrounded by tall alder, some big trees, and a few open areas. My goal was to bushwhack west into Glacier Bay National Park. From the air it was obvious that this would be difficult given the density of vegetation. A test hike was stopped cold by walls of alder. Then it began to rain. It rained for 96 consecutive hours. I had to get out. I called my pilot, and when there was a break in the weather, he was able to get me back to Haines. Basically, this trip was a bust. At least I got in and out in one piece. I do not recommend it to other hikers.

OREGON

Black Canyon 13,400 acres, designated 1984, located in the Ochoco National Forest south of US Highway 26 and east of the town of Dayville. My day hike on August 1, 2003 began at a trailhead for the Black Canyon Trail. The terrain was mostly burned timber with lots of cows and nothing interesting.

Mill Creek 17,400 acres, designated 1984, located in the Ochoco National Forest north of US Highway 26 and northeast of the city of Prineville. My day hike on July 31, 2003 began at the Twin Pillars South Trailhead and went north to the Twin Pillars. Much of the forest was burned and there were lots of cows, but I did get to see my first mountain quail. The Twin Pillars were just two volcanic pinnacles and not the least bit scenic.

Boulder Creek 19,100 acres, designated 1984, located in the Umpqua National Forest north of State Highway 138. My day hike on October 5, 2004 began at the Soda Springs Trailhead. The forest was heavily burned and deadfall was an obstacle. I encountered two men on horseback who had also given up because of deadfall. We walked out together.

Granite in Kerrick Meadow, Yosemite Wilderness

California

California is a very diverse place. From a nature perspective, it may be the most diverse in North America. One or two or even three biomes do not give a complete description. Back in my teaching days I occasionally taught a basic course in environmental science. Our textbook was Cunningham and Cunningham's *Environmental Science, a Global Concern.* The authors devoted a chapter to biomes. In one of their examples they cited a 100-kilometer transect (straight line) from the summit of Mount Whitney in the east to the city of Fresno in the west. They stated that "…transect crosses vegetation zones similar to about seven different biome types." From my own hiking experience in California I can attest to this diversity. The Red Buttes Wilderness on the Oregon border in the north is pretty much a rainforest. Portions of the Sequoia and Kings Canyon Wilderness include substantial areas of alpine tundra. The Mojave Wilderness in the south qualifies as genuine desert.

Given this diversity, I treat California as a stand-alone region. The organization is still by number of stars, but within each rating, the sequence will be from the moist and cool north to the dry and hot south.

A guidebook I found useful for my explorations was George Wuerthner's *California's Wilderness Areas, Volume 1, Mountains and Coastal Ranges* from Westcliffe Publishers.

TRINITY ALPS

★ ★ ★ ★ ★

Size: 537,363 acres | **Year Designated:** 1984 | **Responsible Agency:** USFS

The Trinity Alps Wilderness covers a big chunk of northcentral California west of the Whiskeytown Shasta-Trinity National Recreation Area and north of the Town of Weaverville. The area includes parts of the Six Rivers, Klamath, and Shasta-Trinity National Forests. At the time of my visits there was a USFS map dedicated to the area.

MY VISITS: July 16–19, 2004 and June 11–12, 2009 and June 13, 2009 and September 18–19, 2012

The four-day backpack in 2004 was my first experience in the Trinity Alps. The area had been recommended to me by some old friends in Idaho, so I went and was very impressed. This trip began at the Swift Creek Trailhead. It was an ambitious trip into the rugged, rocky eastern part of the wilderness. The first day went up Swift Creek, then up the Granite Lake Trail, then to the Four Lakes Loop Trail to Luella Lake for the night. The next day went past Deer Creek Camp to Morris Meadows and then to Emerald Lake, just on the south side of the Sawtooth Ridge. On day three I went back to the Four Lakes Loop and camped at Deer Lake. Day four was a hike back to my truck. Just about every minute of every day was filled with great views of lakes and peaks in rugged alpine terrain with some forest, a wonderful area. Some of the terrain was volcanic, some pale, harder rock.

Sawtooth Ridge above Caribou Lake, Trinity Alps Wilderness

My second trip was an overnight backpack from the Salmon Summit Trailhead in the lower-elevation, more heavily, forested, and greener western portion of the wilderness. This area appeared to have much less human traffic than the better-known eastern part. The trail was steep and in poor condition. My camp was at Rock Lake. The next day I tried to keep going southeast on the Salmon Summit Trail, but I completely lost the trail in an old burn and had to turn around. This route was less spectacular than the previous trip, but still quite nice. That evening I drove a little way back to Forest Road 93 and then east to the Hotelling Campground for a gray, drippy night.

The next day was again wet and drippy, but good enough to begin a day hike from the Long Gulch Trailhead up to Long Gulch Lake. There were a lot of fishermen on the trail and backpackers fishing at the lake. I continued up the trail to a ridge still covered in snow. I followed the ridge a way toward and above Trail Gulch Lake, then sat on a small summit for lunch with intermittent views of many distant ridges. This was steep, rugged terrain in heavy forest. I could have made a loop from this point, but decided instead to just return the way I came. The weather was not the best, but still a nice hike in a nice area.

My next visit was in 2012 for an overnight backpack to the famous Caribou Lake on the north side of the equally famous Sawtooth Ridge. The weather was perfect.

There were other hikers about, including some deer hunters. My trip began at the Big Flat Trailhead. The trail made a lot of switchbacks climbing through dense forest. Finally, the terrain opened with rough, serrated granite all around and beautiful lakes in the low spots, a magnificent spot to set up camp and spend the night. The next day I simply retraced my steps back to my truck. A great trip to a great destination in ideal conditions. I recommend this area to just about any hiker.

Ansel Adams

★ ★ ★ ★ ★

Size: 228,528 acres   **Year Designated:** 1964
Responsible Agency: USFS

The Ansel Adams Wilderness is located east of Yosemite National Park, south of State Highway 120, and west of US Highway 395. Several roads take off from US Highway 395 for trailheads into the wilderness. The wilderness is in the Inyo and Sierra National Forests. There was a USFS map dedicated to the area when I visited.

MY VISIT: September 27–30, 2005

My four-day backpack began at the Rush Creek Trailhead at Silver Lake. A late September start was deliberate because this area gets a lot of traffic. The weather was cool but sunny. The trail began along a cable tramway to Agnew Lake and Gem Lake, both hydroelectric dams, which explained the tramway. From Gem Lake I took the trail to the Alger Lakes and set up camp. This was a fabulous spot, right at timberline and just east of Yosemite. Great alpine terrain and I had it all to myself. The night here was pretty cold, and the next day was a day hike to the summit of Parker Peak (12,861 feet) with wonderful views, then I went back to my camp, packed up, and returned to Gem Lake and camped for the night. Day three was to Waugh Lake, then to the PCT and south to the famous Thousand Island Lake. The weather was perfect and there were great views every foot of the way. I camped near the Thousand Island Lake outlet and wandered around a bit to Emerald and Ruby Lakes. There were other backpackers around, but not many. Day four was just retracing my steps back to my truck. This remains one of the nicest backpacking trips I have ever done. The photo shows Mounts Banner and Ritter on the eastern boundary of Yosemite.

Eastern Ansel Adams Wilderness from the Owens River Headwaters Wilderness

Hoover

★ ★ ★ ★ ★

Size: 128,421 acres **Year Designated:** 1964 **Responsible Agency:** USFS

The Hoover Wilderness wraps around the eastern boundary of Yosemite National Park west of US Highway 395 and southwest of the town of Bridgeport. The wilderness is in the Toiyabe National Forest. There was a USFS map dedicated to this wilderness at the time of my visits.

MY VISITS: October 1–2, 2005 and October 3, 2005 and September 16–20, 2010

My first visit was an overnight backpack from the Virginia Lakes Trailhead to Summit Lake on the Yosemite boundary. I was probably pushing it by doing this in October, but the weather forecast was favorable. I had to cross one 11,000-foot pass and there was a heavy, cold wind up there. I got to Summit Lake early enough to set up camp and still do a day hike into Yosemite. I went down into the lovely Virginia Canyon, then almost up to Virginia Pass with very good views of the Shepherd Crest. The second day was just walking back to my truck. The next day I went south a bit to the Saddlebag Lake Trailhead and made a day hike loop including Steelhead Lake and Helen Lake. I was very impressed with the area and vowed to come back.

The 2010 trip was a five-day backpack starting at the Mono Village Trailhead. The trail was steep with never-ending switchbacks until I got to Peeler Lake and set up camp. There were lots of other hikers on the trail including one large group. On the 17th I crossed over into Yosemite and went south into Kerrick Meadow, camping at Arndt Lake. There was some nice fall color and a gentle, picturesque valley. On day three I went back north, then east over Rock Island Pass and back into the Hoover. The view of Snow Lake from my lunch spot in the pass was magnificent. After Snow Lake I took a trail to the southeast and over Mule Pass back into Yosemite. I continued east on this trail to Burro Pass and made a camp for the night under the Sawtooth Ridge. Day four started with a day hike to the top of Burro Pass for views of the neighborhood. I met a group of hikers headed for the summit of Matterhorn Peak. I turned around, went back to my camp, packed up, and grunted up Mule Pass, then went down into the Hoover past Crown Lake to Robinson Lake and made camp. Day five was spent in the Hoover going back to my trailhead. There were lots of folks coming up the trail. This was a truly wonderful trip spent in two outstanding wilderness areas. Any hiker who likes magnificent granite needs to come here.

Blue sky, blue water, and pale granite at Snow Lake, Hoover Wilderness

Yosemite

★ ★ ★ ★ ★

Size: 704,624 acres   **Year Designated:** 1984
Responsible Agency: USNPS

Most of Yosemite National Park is designated wilderness. The eastern wilderness boundary is shared with the Hoover Wilderness and some of the western boundary is shared with the Emigrant Wilderness.

MY VISITS: September 16, 2008 and September 16–20, 2010

My hikes have all started from outside the park: two from the Hoover and one from the Emigrant. The 2008 hike began at my Snow Lake camp in the Emigrant Wilderness (not the same Snow Lake near the Hoover). I went up to Summit Meadow, crossed into the park at Bond Pass, then went north on the PCT to Dorothy Lake. This was a very nice little hike in what seemed to be a lightly visited spot.

The 2010 backpack was described above with the Hoover Wilderness. Briefly, my Yosemite portion began when I crossed into the park from Peeler Lake and descended intro Kerrick Meadow (see the photo on page 56). I continued south to Arndt Lake, then farther south until the trail entered dense forest. I returned to Arndt Lake and made camp. The next day I went back north and left the park at Rock Island Pass, reentered the park at Mule Pass, and camped along the trail to Burro Pass. The following day I did a day hike to Burro Pass for great views of the Sawtooth Ridge and Matterhorn Peak. I went back to my camp, packed up, and left the park. This was another trip where essentially every minute was spent among magnificent scenery.

I also did a short visit in 2005 when I made a day hike from Summit Lake in the Hoover down into Virginia Canyon and partway up to Virginia Pass. There were great views of the Shepherd Crest and Virginia Canyon.

The Finger Peaks, Yosemite Wilderness

John Muir

★ ★ ★ ★ ★

Size: 650,734 acres   **Year Designated:** 1964
Responsible Agency: USFS

The John Muir Wilderness wraps around the Sequoia-Kings Canyon Wilderness on the north and east sides. It shares a boundary with the Golden Trout Wilderness on the south and with the Ansel Adams Wilderness on the north and west.

MY VISITS: September 7–12, 2004 and October 20 and October 21, 2009 plus other pass-through visits on trips to Sequoia-Kings Canyon

All my visits accessed the John Muir via side roads from US Highway 395 on the east, particularly from the towns of Bishop, Independence, and Lone Pine.

My first visit was a six-day backpack from the North Lake Trailhead off State Highway 168 out of Bishop. My notes from this trip are short on detail, but I marked my map indicating my route. On day one I went from the trailhead on the Piute Canyon Trail over Piute Pass and camped near Summit Lake. This was scenic, open, granite terrain. Day two was a short section on the Piute Canyon Trail, then cross country to and around Desolation Lake and to "L" Lake. Then I took the "L" Lake Trail toward Pine Creek Pass, camping off-trail near the Royce Lakes. By this time, I had done enough off-trail hiking in Wyoming to be comfortable in this easy, open granite of the Sierra Nevada. On day three I went southeast to the French Canyon Trail, then on the Piute Canyon Trail to the PCT. I camped near this trail junction.

I was intrigued by the nearby Evolution Canyon in the Sequoia-Kings Canyon Wilderness and decided to dedicate a day to exploring this side canyon. It was a good decision. I made a long day hike into the beautiful Evolution Canyon past Goddard Canyon, through Evolution Meadow, through McClure Meadow, and just past a backcountry ranger station. I remember a small wildfire burning at the meadow's edge. This was a truly wonderful day and I decided I wanted to see the other "evolution" features in Kings Canyon. (I ultimately did.) Day five was spent going up the Piute Canyon Trail, camping near Muriel Lake. Day six was spent walking back to the trailhead. This was another example of a place where every step takes the hiker through magnificent scenery of rock, meadow, and open forest.

The October 20, 2009 day hike was after a fairly serious snowstorm had come through the Sierra, but the weather was now crystal clear if cold. The starting point was the Onion Valley Trailhead, taking a little-used trail to the Golden Trout Lakes. There was a fair bit of snow and the trail was easy to lose, but I did get to the lakes. The Octobert 21, 2009 day hike used the same trailhead as the day before, but went up the main trail to Kearsarge Pass and about a mile down into the Sequoia-Kings Canyon Wilderness. This was a magnificent hike on a magnificent day. There was firm, crusty snow for a good portion of the trip, but hiking was always easy. I had a great lunch spot with views of Bullfrog and Kearsarge Lakes. The photo is from this day at Gilbert Lake on the way to Kearsarge Pass.

The 2010 "pass-through" hikes were on trips to the Sequoia-Kings Canyon Wilderness starting at the Cottonwood Lakes Trailhead, going first through the Golden Trout Wilderness, then through the John Muir past Long Lake and High Lake to New Army Pass. The 2012 "pass-through" hikes were between the South Lake Trailhead and Bishop Pass, going past Long Lake and Saddleback Lake.

Sequoia-Kings Canyon

★ ★ ★ ★ ★

Size: 768,222 acres   **Year Designated:** 1984
Responsible Agency: USNPS

The Sequoia-Kings Canyon wilderness is the heart of the Sierra Nevada. Several national forest wilderness areas share boundaries with it: the John Muir on the north and east, the Golden Trout on the south, and the Jennie Lakes and Monarch on the west.

MY VISITS: September 10, 2004 and October 21, 2009 and September 21–24, 2010 and September 21–25, 2012 and October 18, 2012

My first two visits were day hikes already described in the John Muir Wilderness. Briefly, the first was a hike up Evolution Canyon from the PCT as part of a John Muir backpacking trip. It was a fabulous day. The second was just a short continuation of a John Muir hike over Kearsarge Pass on another fabulous day.

The first backpacking trip in 2010 began at the Cottonwood Lakes Trailhead at the northeastern corner of the Golden Trout Wilderness. My route took me through the John Muir Wilderness past Long Lake and High Lake and then through New Army Pass into the Rock Creek drainage of the Sequoia-Kings Canyon Wilderness. It was cold and windy on the pass, and there were lots of other hikers. I set up a base camp here. The next day I went off-trail and up Rock Creek to the Soldier Lakes, Sky Blue Lake, and Iridescent Lake. This was a lovely if somewhat stark basin with big peaks all around. It seemed to have little visitation. I think I saw sheep scat and looked around for bighorns but no luck. Later I encountered a Game and Fish person who told me he saw nine rams by Iridescent Lake. I must have just missed them. Day three saw another day hike, this time up to the Siberian Pass, then along the park boundary above the Siberian Outpost with views of the Rocky Basin Lakes, around the head of Forgotten Canyon to an overview of Funston Lake. This was stark, spare,

almost hostile terrain, including large open meadows dark in brown/gold fall color. Day four I simply retraced my steps over New Army Pass and back to my truck. This day there were a lot of other hikers. All in all, a pretty neat trip.

I long had a goal of visiting LeConte Canyon and Evolution Basin. I finally accomplished that goal in 2012. This was a five-day backpack starting at the South Lake Trailhead, going through the John Muir Wilderness, across Bishop Pass and into Dusy Basin, then descending into LeConte Canyon to a campsite above the backcountry ranger station. This was a long, hard day for an old man. The weather, however, was perfect and the scenery magnificent. There were lots of other folks around. Day two was mostly overcast as I went north over Muir Pass (11,955 feet), past Bertha Lake, and found a campsite near an unnamed lake. Another day when every minute was in

Evolution Lake, Sequoia-Kings Canyon Wilderness

awesome scenery. Day three was a day hike to Evolution Lake, my main goal (see the photo). The lake was beautiful and surrounded by peaks named after scientists who were early participants in the discussion of evolution. A great day. I had enough time to pack up my camp and go back over Muir Pass for that night's camp. Day four took me back to Dusy Basin on another day with good weather and good views. Day five was spent going back over Bishop Pass to the trailhead. This will be another trip that I remember and cherish for a long time. It was hard work, but worth every minute.

The October 2012 visit was a side trip on a visit to the John Krebs Wilderness. The trip began at the end of the road to Mineral King. My day began in the Franklin Lakes area of the John Krebs. I went over Franklin Pass into the Sequoia-Kings Canyon Wilderness, then took a very obscure trail to Shotgun Pass. The pass had good views of Silver Lake in the Golden Trout Wilderness.

CALIFORNIA

Phillip Burton

★ ★ ★ ★ ★

Size: 25,952 acres   **Year Designated:** 1976
Responsible Agency: USNPS

California has a lot of coastline. The very best is in the Phillip Burton Wilderness. This area is west of State Highway 1 and northwest of the town of Bolinas, not far north of San Francisco. Phillip Burton represented California in the US House of Representatives from 1964 to 1983.

MY VISITS: There were many visits, mostly day hikes, in 1973 and 1974

I moved to California in late 1972 to be a postdoctoral fellow at UC Berkeley. After settling in, I began to explore this completely new territory. I had never lived close to an ocean, so exploring the coast was where I started. The area had been declared the Point Reyes National Seashore shortly before 1973. There was little infrastructure or even signage, but there it was, nearly pristine and with little visitation. I could drive up to some parking area near a beach and be the first vehicle there that day. When I left, I would often leave an empty parking lot. That gradually changed during my time in California as people became aware of the area's charms. Wilderness designation came in 1976, although I have not returned.

It remains the bit of coast that I know best. It was my first exposure to tide pools. I would poke around them for hours. There were wild beaches. Nobody would swim there because the riptides were fierce. There were rugged headlands, tall dunes, ice plant, grassy areas, and some forest. I don't remember how many days I spent there, but it was quite a few. I remember dragging friends there to let them in on the secret. I have heard that as of this writing the area has become seriously overrun by visitors.

I took many photographs here, but none of good quality survive. I will, however, remember it as a place of great beauty and fascination.

CALIFORNIA

Siskiyou

★ ★ ★ ★

Size: 153,000 acres   **Year Designated:** 1984
Responsible Agency: USFS

The Siskiyou Wilderness is located in northwest California southeast of US Highway 199 and west of State Highway 96 in the Siskiyou and Six Rivers National Forests. The nearest town is Crescent City. The area is in the same biome as nearby western Oregon. It is probably best known for its rare plants. There was a USFS map dedicated to this wilderness when I visited.

Azaleas and incense cedar,
Siskiyou Wilderness

famous flowers: Bolander's lilies, fawn lilies, and azaleas. Along the way was an old copper mine. Well, OK, the map did show a Copper Mountain and a Copper Creek. The end of this day was spent at the very pleasant Raspberry Lake where I camped. There was a lot of bear scat around. Day three I went back to Young's Valley, then to an obscure trailhead near Young's Peak, then back south for a camp near Trout Camp. The last day was just back to the trailhead. There were a few other hikers that day.

I recommend this wilderness to any hiker. A trip dedicated to the Siskiyou and nearby Marble Mountain and Russian Wilderness areas would be an excellent introduction to this part of the country. All three of these areas are nice, but the Siskiyou is my favorite.

CALIFORNIA

Lassen Volcanic

★ ★ ★ ★

Size: 78,982 acres   **Year Designated:** 1972
Responsible Agency: USNPS

The Lassen Volcanic Wilderness is within Lassen Volcanic National Park in northcentral California. There is good access (but not in winter!) via State Highways 44 and 89.

MY VISITS: September 28, 2007 and September 24–25, 2012

My 2007 trip was an 11-mile day hike from a trailhead at Summit Lake and went around the Lakes Loop Trail. The route included Echo, Upper and Lower Twin, Feather, Silver, Big, and Little Bear Lakes. This was mostly closed-in forest through volcanic cinders. The lakes were mostly shallow, perhaps just ponds. The terrain here was not especially interesting, but I do remember encountering on the trail a pine marten with a golden-mantled ground squirrel in its jaws. I stopped and watched, and the

MY VISITS: June 26–27, 2002 and June 6–10, 2009

My first trip was an overnight backpack from the Poker Flat Trailhead through Twin Valley and to the Lieutenants, small peaks surrounding a larger peak called The Captain. This is lush country—dense forest with scattered lakes and meadows and modestly tall, rocky peaks. My notes from this trip are pretty cryptic, but I remember being favorably impressed by, in part, the large number of bears and the small number of people. Wildflowers were numerous and gorgeous. When I returned to the trailhead, the only things in the parking area were my truck and a bear.

The second backpack covered more ground, beginning at the Doe Flat Trailhead, going to Trout Camp and then to Wilderness Falls on Clear Creek, then returning to Trout Camp for the night. I saw only two other hikers. The second day was to Young's Valley and Cracker Meadow through some of the

Mokelumne

★ ★ ★ ★

Size: 105,165 acres   **Year Designated:** 1964
Responsible Agency: USFS

The Mokelumne Wilderness is located in the Toiyabe, Eldorado, and Stanislaus National Forests south of the Desolation Wilderness. Access is by State Highway 88 on the north and west and by State Highway 4 on the south.

MY VISIT: September 24–25, 2007 and September 26, 2007

My overnight backpack began at the Grouse Creek Trailhead near the end of the Blue Lakes Road near some hydroelectric facilities. I hiked west through high, open forest with good views of granite and volcanic terrain. My intention was to camp at Grouse Lake, but a late start and confusion about the real trailhead meant that I camped at the head of Snow Canyon. My campsite was really neat—surrounded by what looked like giant eggs partially buried in soft earth. I called them dragon's eggs. They were probably hard glacial erratics buried in volcanic ash. The next morning, I did a day hike to Grouse Lake. All along the trail were nice views to the west and south. On the way back to camp I made a side trip to the summit of Deadwood Peak (9,846 feet) for even better views. Back at my camp I packed up and returned to the trailhead.

The next day I made a day hike from the Woods Lake Trailhead to Winnemucca Lake, then to Round Top Lake and most of the way to Fourth of July Lake, but instead of going down to the lake I went to the summit of Fourth of July Peak (9,536 feet). This was another day of beautiful weather and great views every step of the way. The terrain was very open with both dramatic volcanic cliffs and standard Sierra Nevada granite. Mokelumne has been discovered and there were lots of other hikers.

pine marten scooted around me and continued down the trail. Later I saw a badger on the trail.

What I saw on the 2012 backpack is why I call this a four-star area. The trip began at the Butte Lake Trailhead in the northeast corner of the park. I got an overnight camping permit and went south past the Cinder Cone to Snag Lake. This route went through some very nice volcanic terrain including colorful ash dunes and the Fantastic Lava Beds. I made my camp at Snag Lake as it was the only water source in the immediate area. The next day I retraced my steps. Both days saw other hikers.

I recommend this wilderness to anyone interested in volcanic terrain. The trails are good and the hiking pretty easy.

MY VISIT: May 5, 2006

The day before my hike I spent a lot of time driving around in an upscale residential neighborhood looking for a trailhead for this wilderness. I was hopelessly lost because of a common problem—the road names on my map had nothing in common with the names on the street signs. I found a patient man walking his dog who at first could not make sense of my map, then said, "Eureka" and told me how to find my destination. By now it was too late to hike. I spent the night at my truck at the trailhead since there were no signs saying not to. Early the next morning I began my hike from the Tenaja Trailhead down the Tenaja Trail to the San Mateo Trail, past the Bluewater Trail to a turnaround near the western wilderness boundary. This was a beautiful place. Yes, there was my less-than-favorite chaparral, but also scenic mountain views, oak trees full of birds and great riparian areas. One oak tree contained a whole flock of hermit warblers, my first. This was without doubt the nicest chaparral I have seen. I would go back in a heartbeat and recommend this hike to everybody. The area has been discovered and there were quite a few other hikers plus two people on horseback. Fortunately, there were no signs of overuse.

CALIFORNIA

San Mateo Canyon

★ ★ ★ ★

Size: 39,540 acres   **Year Designated:** 1984
Responsible Agency: USFS

The San Mateo Canyon Wilderness is located in the Cleveland National Forest west of Interstate Highway 5, southwest of the town of Elsinore. The wilderness shares its southern boundary with the Camp Pendleton Marine Corps Base.

CALIFORNIA

Joshua Tree

★ ★ ★ ★

Size: 594,502 acres   **Year Designated:** 1976
Responsible Agency: USNPS

Most of Joshua Tree National Park is designated wilderness. However, when you look at a map of the wilderness it looks like the pattern of broken-up ice on a melting puddle. There are eight separate pieces with roads between pieces. The park is located north of Interstate Highway 10 and south of State Highway 62, the Twenty-nine Palms Highway. The western side of the park and wilderness are very close to rather intense development. There was a

National Geographic Trails Illustrated map for Joshua Tree National Park that showed wilderness boundaries when I visited.

The first day hike was from the Indian Cove Trailhead at the northern edge of the wilderness. My route was the Boy Scout Trail to the Big Pine Trail and then on a spur trail north to a dense grove of large Joshua trees. This hike was on a very nice, warm day and the entire way was through a fascinating landscape of eroded granite. I returned the way I came, did a short hike to some technical rock-climbing routes, and camped in my truck in the Jumbo Rocks Campground.

The second day was spent on a hike from the Lost Palm Oasis Trailhead to that oasis and the Victory Palms oasis. For someone new to the area it was another fascinating day. I was not accustomed to palm trees. Other hikers told me of seeing a bighorn ram near the oasis, but I only saw scat. My notes say I also went to the Elton Mine, but now I cannot find it on my map. I spent the night in the White Tank Campground.

While I did not spend much time here, I was very favorably impressed. Great desert scenery with exotic plants and wonderful rock formations. A hiker could spend a lot of interesting days here and I recommend it.

Palm trees and eroded granite, Joshua Tree Wilderness

Red Buttes

★ ★ ★

Size: 20,323 acres   **Year Designated:** 1984
Responsible Agency: USFS

The Red Buttes Wilderness in located in the Rogue River National Forest in both Oregon and California northwest of the town of Yreka, California. There is good access from State Highway 96. There was a USFS map dedicated to this wilderness when I visited.

My day hike started at a trailhead for the "Shoo Fly" Trail, which quickly led me to a trail to the west along the Butte Fork of the Applegate River. There were low clouds that parted just enough to see tall volcanic peaks. The route was through nice forest with big trees. The trail took me through Cedar Basin with *really* big cedars, one of my favorite tree species. I went a bit farther west to Azalea Lake and a bit beyond that for better views. Here I turned around and retraced my steps. This was a pleasant day in a pleasant place. I think most hikers would enjoy coming here, although I saw nobody else this day. I know I took photographs, but they have been somehow lost.

Marble Mountain

★ ★ ★

Size: 214,500 acres   **Year Designated:** 1964
Responsible Agency: USFS

The Marble Mountain Wilderness is in the Klamath National Forest in northwestern California. It is east of the Siskiyou Wilderness and west of the town of Yreka and Interstate Highway 5.

My visit began with a six-day backpack from the Canyon Creek Trailhead near Love's Camp on the east side of the wilderness. I began in rain and the farther I went the harder it rained. I made a wet camp near the Marble Valley. The weather cleared for day two and I hiked west to the PCT, then north to the Box Camp Trail where I was blocked by deep but soft snow. This bit of the PCT was very scenic, especially going around the Black Marble. There was a lot of exposed, glacial-carved metamorphic rock including marble, schist, and quartzite. I turned around at the Box Camp Trail and went back south on the PCT to a different campsite in the Marble Valley. Day three I hiked to the top of the Marble Rim (6,880 feet), then continued south on the PCT to a trail to Summit Lake and made my camp at Campbell Lake. It was a very scenic day. On day four I went back to the PCT, then on the Marble Rim Trail to Big Elk Lake and camped there. On day five I did a day hike to the Cuddihy Lakes, and day six was spent going back to my trailhead.

On June 23 I went to a nearby trailhead for a day hike to Paradise Basin, a very beautiful spot. From Paradise Basin I continued south on the PCT to the Box Camp Trail where I had previously been blocked by snow. There was still a lot of snow, but I was chagrined to see two people coming north on the PCT carrying heavy packs and wearing sandals in the snow. Those hikers were tougher than I was. I simply turned around and went back to the trailhead.

These seven days were very worthwhile. The area was a little drier and more open than the Siskiyou, but still lots of flowers, nice forest, and interesting rock. I recommend this area to any hiker.

Sky High Lake, Marble Mountain Wilderness

Russian

★ ★ ★

Size: 12,521 acres   **Year Designated:** 1984
Responsible Agency: USFS

The Russian Wilderness is located in the Klamath National Forest southeast of the Marble Mountain Wilderness, the two areas separated by the Sawyers Bar Road. There was a USFS map for both the Marble Mountain and Russian Wilderness areas at the time I visited.

The first of my two hikes was from the Taylor Lake Trailhead and went to Taylor Lake and then on to Hogan Lake. The Russian and Marble Mountain areas are very similar—pleasant forest, numerous lakes, and steep, rough, metamorphic rock terrain. What I remember clearly from this hike was watching an osprey working Taylor Lake for fish as I began my hike. On my way back to the trailhead, again passing Taylor Lake, the osprey was perched on a fallen log near the lakeshore. The bird did not fly when I approached and, on a closer look, had clearly broken a wing. A tough way to go for a magnificent bird.

The second hike was from a trailhead on a ridge above Payne's Lake Creek. I went west past Payne's Lake and ended at Albert Lake. Both of these hikes were pleasant. Once again, I recommend the Siskiyou, Marble Mountain, and Russian Wilderness areas to any hiker.

My Marble Mountain and Russian photos are not the best. They are digitized from old slides, but I wanted to include at least one to provide a sense of the terrain.

CALIFORNIA

Caribou

★ ★ ★

Size: 20,625 acres   **Year Designated:** 1964
Responsible Agency: USFS

The Caribou Wilderness is located in the Lassen National Forest just east of Lassen Volcanic National Park. The easiest access is from State Highway 44. At the time of my visit there was a USFS map dedicated to the Caribou, Thousand Lakes, and Ishi Wilderness areas.

My overnight backpack began at the Indian Meadow Trailhead at the southern wilderness boundary. I hiked north and made camp at Long Lake. This was relatively flat, forested terrain with some meadows and a few old volcanic cones sticking up. On my second day I did a day hike north until I could see the North Caribou volcanic summit off to the east. I remember this hike because it was the first time I ever used a GPS (a Garmin Gecko). The device was necessary because the forest was pretty featureless. I got to the North Caribou summit (7,784 feet) in good time, had lunch, and allowed my GPS to guide me back to my camp. It was a flawless process. It was a good-weather day with scenic views of the area from the summit. At Long Lake I packed up and went back to the trailhead. This was a nice destination and the hiking was easy. It looked like it got little visitation.

CALIFORNIA

Thousand Lakes

★ ★ ★

Size: 16,355 acres   **Year Designated:** 1964
Responsible Agency: USFS

The Thousand Lakes Wilderness is located in the Lassen National Forest northwest of Lassen Volcanic National Park. Access is by roads from State Highway 89. At the time of my visit there was a USFS map dedicated to the Thousand Lakes, Caribou, and Ishi Wilderness areas.

My visit was a long day hike from the Tamarack Trailhead. The route was simple and pleasant, past Lake Eiler, Everett Lake, Magee Lake, and then to the summit of Magee Peak (8,945 feet). This area is a lot like the Caribou, but with more open terrain around Magee Peak. The return route differed from the inbound route only by going past Barrett Lake rather than Eiler Lake. This was a long but worthwhile day in an area I would recommend to almost all hikers. The terrain is softer and less dramatic than in the Lassen Volcanic, but still very nice.

North Fork

★ ★ ★

Size: 8158 acres   **Year Designated:** 1984
Responsible Agency: USFS

The North Fork Wilderness is located in the Six Rivers National Forest south of State Highway 36 and south of the community of Mad River. It is in the middle of nowhere by California standards.

MY VISIT: April 20, 2007

This wilderness area was hard to find. I stopped in at the Mad River Ranger Station for directions and had a long chat with one of their employees who was very helpful. Still, I got confused on the back roads, and even when on the right road had a hard time finding where to begin the area's only hiking trail. The problem was lack of signs. Finally, I saw what looked like a parking place and started walking. After blundering around a while, I eventually found an ancient two-track that was, in fact, the trail. At least there was a wilderness boundary sign. According to my map I began at the Packwood Flat Trailhead. The route was through forest with big trees: Douglas fir, pine, madrone, and oak. Flowers were everywhere and included shooting stars, poppies, and even orchids. The highlight of the day came when I exited an oak forest and there was a great view of the North Fork of the Eel River. There were old volcanic spires and open, green meadows. A magnificent spot. Because I had wasted a lot of time finding the trailhead,

Oak forest in spring, North Fork Wilderness

it was late and I decided against trying to cross the river. Instead I just sat at my viewing spot, had lunch, and then returned to my truck. A very worthwhile day.

Yolla Bolly-Middle Eel

★ ★ ★

Size: 162,824 acres   **Year Designated:** 1964
Responsible Agency: USFS and BLM

The Yolla Bolly-Middle Eel Wilderness is located in the Shasta-Trinity and Mendocino National Forests and some BLM land south of State Highway 36 and west of the city of Red Bluff. I did not have a map of the area with me for my first trip, but did subsequently purchase a USFS map dedicated to this wilderness. The name comes from a Native American language and means "snow-covered high peaks."

*North Yolla Bolly Mountain from Black Rock Mountain,
Yolla Bolly-Middle Eel Wilderness*

MY VISITS: April 23–25, 2007 and September 15–17, 2012

My first backpack began at the Boundary Trailhead. I had intended to go farther east along this ridge road, but was turned back by snow (it really was early for this area). I went south on the Boundary Trail past Ant Point where I lost the trail. I blundered on, eventually finding the Morrison Trail, then continued south until I got surprised by a "Private Property" sign and a dim road. I was now totally confused but made a camp in an obviously pre-used spot near a good-flowing stream. This day had good views of the higher and very snowy peaks to the north. The weather was good and the forest pleasant. Being this far south might have been a good choice. On day two I did a day hike on the old two-track "trail" to the Henthorne Lakes. It was a brilliantly clear day and along the way to the lakes I scared up a cinnamon bear that, in the sun, seemed to glow like a signal flare. Neat. Beyond the lakes I went to the Moxie Crossing of the Middle Eel River where I had my lunch, then turned around and went back to my camp. Again, along the way I saw the cinnamon bear. Deer were numerous and I also saw a coyote. Day three was just going back to my truck. Given the conditions (snow), this is probably as good a trip as I could have done.

The second backpacking trip started at the Stuart Gap Trailhead at the northern wilderness boundary. My timing was again not the best. The day turned out to be the first day of deer hunting season. There were a lot of hunters along the road. (Some hunters seem to have no problem letting their trucks sit in the middle of the road as they go off to do their thing.) Parking at the trailhead was tight. This day I hiked south on the Pettijohn Trail to the Yolla Bolly Lake Trail to North Yolla Bolly Lake. This was not much more than a big puddle, but it is where I made my camp. Day two was an ambitious day hike. I first went back to the Pettijohn Trail, then south to the Black Rock Mountain Trail and on to the summit (7,755 feet). This was a nice ridge walk to a derelict fire lookout tower. I had lunch there, then went back and took the North Yolla Bolly Mountain Trail to the summit of that mountain. The photo is North Yolla Bolly Mountain from Black Rock. On my way I walked past a camp of hunters who had pack goats to help carry their gear. I had seen pack goats in Wyoming, but was surprised to see them here. They bleated as I went by. It was late by now so I turned around and went back to my camp. Day three I returned to my truck. Overall, a trip with great weather and good views. Recent fires to the south had not reached this far north into the wilderness. I recommend this area to most hikers. There is a good trail system, and the hiking is pretty easy through open forest, meadow, and some exposed rock.

Note: Upon looking at a better map of the Yolla Bolly I saw that there are "allowed by permit" roads into the wilderness as well as private property inholdings. I saw no evidence that the roads were being used.

CALIFORNIA

Desolation

★ ★ ★

Size: 63,475 acres   **Year Designated:** 1969
Responsible Agency: USFS

The Desolation Wilderness is located in the Eldorado National Forest southwest of Lake Tahoe and west of the town of South Lake Tahoe. Access to the east side of the wilderness is from State Highway 89 and from US Highway 50 to the south. There was a USFS map dedicated to this wilderness when I visited.

My visit was two consecutive long day hikes. The first began at the Bayview Trailhead on the east side of the wilderness. My route went west on the Velma Lakes Trail past Granite Lake to Upper and Middle Velma Lakes, then to Dick's Lake with a side trip to Dick's Pass, then back to the trailhead. This was a beautiful day in an area of high scenic density, as in really nice country every step of the way. The terrain was open forest with many lakes large and small and lots of open granite. The views from Dick's Pass were spectacular.

The second day hike was from the Ralston Trailhead to the summit of Ralston Peak (9,235 feet) then down into Desolation Valley on the PCT and along the shore of Lake Aloha. The terrain here was like the previous day: nice forest, lots of granite, and great views.

While I only spent two days here, I think I got a good sense of the area—quintessential Sierra Nevada. I recommend these trails to anyone who likes to hike. As a side note, the area has been discovered. I saw lots of other hikers both days. Solitude was not a feature.

CALIFORNIA

John Krebs

★ ★ ★

Size: 39,740 acres   **Year Designated:** 2009
Responsible Agency: USNPS

The John Krebs Wilderness is wedged between the Sequoia-Kings Canyon Wilderness to the north and the Golden Trout Wilderness to the south. Access is from the road to Mineral King from the west side of the Sierra Nevada. The Mineral King was very controversial in my younger days, with powerful California developers fighting conservationists over a major development here. The conservationists ultimately prevailed, gaining maximum protection by wilderness designation in 2009.

My three-day backpack began at the Mineral King Trailhead and went up to Farewell Canyon close to Farewell Gap, but I turned around after becoming concerned about a lack of water near the gap. I backtracked to a junction with a trail to Franklin Lakes and went up to the lakes and set up my camp. This area was an extension of the Sequoia National Park high country in most ways. There were lots of big, high lakes, open and sometimes dramatic granite, and fascinating old trees hanging on for dear life. The area around Franklin Lakes and Pass was stark and lovely. On my second day I went over Franklin Pass and followed an obscure trail to Shotgun Pass for views into the Golden Trout Wilderness. Day three was just going back to the trailhead. This was classic southern Sierra Nevada and I recommend it.

As a side note, when I was ready to begin hiking, I noticed that all the other vehicles had their hoods up. There was someone else in the parking area so I asked the reason. The answer was that it was supposed to keep marmots out of the engine space so they would not chew on belts or, especially, radiator hoses. I declined to imitate these folks and my truck was fine when I returned. Maybe I was just lucky.

White Mountains

Size: 252,597 acres   **Year Designated:** 2009
Responsible Agency: USFS

The White Mountain Wilderness is located east of US Highway 395 and north of State Highway 168 in the Inyo National Forest. The best access is via Forest Road 1 from State Highway 168. Forest Road 1 is the Ancient Bristlecone Scenic Byway through the Ancient Bristlecone Pine Forest. The road ends at a University of California research station, but a locked gate stops visitors at a trailhead south of the research station.

MY VISITS: October 12, 2009 and October 19, 2009 and September 15, 2010 and May 17–19, 2012

My first day hike in 2009 was just after designation and the wilderness area boundaries were not shown on any maps. I stopped in the USFS ranger station in Bishop and was able to look at a map with hand-drawn lines for boundaries. I noted these on my Inyo National Forest map and went to the locked-gate trailhead on Forest Road 1. The road was a "cherry stem" through the wilderness, ending at the research station. The trailhead elevation was 11,700 feet. It was windy and cold, but I hiked past the end of the road and then east to a distinct saddle at 13,100 feet where there were great views. Everything here was above tree line with high flat areas cut by steep-walled canyons. This was stark, spare, and somewhat forbidding terrain, the sort of terrain I find attractive. These are called the White Mountains for a reason—they are *very* white, mostly dolomite with some non-white volcanic features mixed in. I ran out of daylight and had to go back to the trailhead vowing to return.

The time gap between my first and second White Mountains day hikes was because a major snowstorm came through the Sierra Nevada and I escaped to the south. The second hike began about one mile from the Patriarch Grove in the Ancient Bristlecone Pine Forest (the last bit of road to

the grove was blocked by snow). The map suggested I could get to the wilderness from here, so I blundered around looking for a route. I found one by following an obscure two-track and then ridgetops through bristlecone pine trees down into Cottonwood Basin (no trail). The basin was mostly snow free. The first item that caught my attention was a sign high up in a tree that said "No Fishing." (It turned out that Cottonwood Creek was a protected stream for cutthroat trout.) This was a nice little valley with areas of aspen, sagebrush, grass, and big chunks of fractured granite. There was a dim trail indicating that the area saw some human activity. Another day of being impressed with this area.

The day hike in 2010 started from the locked gate south of the research station. I left the trail just north of the station's telescope and hiked to an escarpment above a deep canyon, then north along this rim. The rim was stark and bare, but there were some green and probably wet areas in the east-sloping side canyons. I was ultimately blocked from going farther north by a very steep canyon wall, so I just turned around and went back to the trailhead.

For the 2012 backpack I returned to Patriarch Grove, hiked back to Cottonwood Basin, and set up camp in a previously used site near the creek. Then I did a day hike downstream through a nice narrows and granite jumbles but turned around when the brush got too thick. There were a lot of fish in the creek. The second day was a hike upstream, then to some ridges for views, mostly of granite jumbles. Day three was spent retracing my steps back to the Patriarch Grove. Again, a very nice trip.

I don't know how many hikers would have as much enthusiasm for this area as I do, but it appealed to me. If nothing else, I encourage everyone to see the ancient bristlecone pine trees. These little groves are home to the oldest living organisms on Earth, up to 5,000 years old, if my memory is correct. The setting among the brilliant white dolomite hillsides is worth a trip.

King Range

★ ★ ★

Size: 42,585 acres   **Year Designated:** 2006
Responsible Agency: BLM

Carson-Iceberg

★ ★ ★

Size: 158,670 acres   **Year Designated:** 1984
Responsible Agency: USFS

The King Range Wilderness is located on BLM land along the Pacific Coast north of the town of Shelter Cove and west of US Highway 101. The wilderness is within the King Range National Conservation Area. At the time of designation, it was one of the few remaining undeveloped stretches of coast.

MY VISIT: April 22, 2007

My visit began at the northern edge of the town of Shelter Cove on the Pacific Coast. There was a trailhead there for the Black Sand Trail. I was very confident that this trail would take me into this newly designated wilderness. The hike was a pure and simple beach walk north from the trailhead. As is often the case during the spring, the sun was shining over the ocean, but the beach and nearby land was covered with low clouds. While dry, it was not a good day for photographs. The surf was definitely up after a recent storm. There was lots of wildlife: seals, sea lions, herring gulls, brown pelicans, double-crested cormorants, a pair of black turnstones, and a giant squid corpse washed up on shore. There were *very* fresh bear tracks in the wet sand.

In addition to the wildlife, there were lots of other hikers. I saw at least nine backpackers and one other day hiker. There were trails leading away from the coast and into the adjacent hills. One of the backpackers was a young man who to me was the quintessential Californian—walking along with a backpack, his dog, and a surfboard tucked under one arm.

This was a worthwhile day, a nice hike in a nice area. I recommend this area to anyone looking to spend some time in a pristine bit of the Pacific Coast.

The Carson-Iceberg Wilderness is located in the Toiyabe and Stanislaus National Forests. Access is easy from State Highway 108 along the southern boundary and from State Highway 4 along the northwestern boundary. At the time of my visits there was a USFS map dedicated to this wilderness. The name Iceberg was given to an almost-white cliff at the wilderness boundary.

MY VISITS: September 21, 2007 and September 22, 2007 and September 13, 2008 and September 14, 2008

The first day hike began at the County Line Trailhead. I went north to Sword Lake. There were some good views. Some hunters suggested I hike up a trail to the northeast to the Dardanelle Cone. I did and it was excellent advice. This was a scenic destination with dramatic volcanic cliffs and peaks. The dim trail ended in a cirque with more good views. The area was heavily grazed and cows were all around. *The cows were wearing bells!* Was it to protect them from hunters? Despite the cows it was a worthwhile day.

The next (second) day hike was in poor weather: socked-in, drizzly, and cold. I was hoping to begin a backpack, but given the weather I decided to just do another day hike. I began at the Arnot Trailhead. My route went north to the Woods Gulch Trail, then to the Jenkins Canyon Trail. At this point I was just north and east of the Dardanelles, but was only able to catch a few glimpses of the cliffs and peaks. There were no photographs. The photo here is of the Dardanelles taken on my first day hike.

The first day hike in 2018 began at the St. Mary's Pass Trailhead. I took the trail to the pass, then a dim trail to the summit of Stanislaus Peak (11,233 feet), then went cross country a little way north along the ridge until it was time to turn around. This route was mostly open with some hard-rock terrain.

The Dardanelles, Carson-Iceberg Wilderness

My last hike began at the Corral Valley Trailhead. I hiked west to Poison Flat, then down toward, but not quite to, the Carson River before turning around. Another worthwhile day.

After four separate day hikes I can confirm that this is a nice and interesting area. My favorite part is still the Dardanelles, but I think most hikers would like at least some part of this diverse wilderness.

CALIFORNIA

Emigrant

★ ★ ★

Size: 117,596 acres   **Year Designated:** 1975
Responsible Agency: USFS

The Emigrant Wilderness is located in the Stanislaus National Forest just south of State Highway 108. It shares its eastern boundary with the Hoover Wilderness and its southern boundary with the Yosemite Wilderness. At the time of my visit there was a USFS map dedicated to this wilderness.

My backpack began at the Kennedy Meadows Trailhead off State Highway 108. It was a rather hot day and the trail was steep and sandy, so this was work. My route was south past the Relief Reservoir, then southeast through Saucer Meadow and on to Lunch Meadow where I made my camp. There was a hoard of people on the trail—backpackers, horse pack strings, and a big trail crew coming out. The terrain was classic late-summer Sierra Nevada with dry meadows, lots of bare granite, and some volcanic features. On the second day I went over Brown Bear Pass, past Emigrant Meadow Lake, through Grizzly Basin, through Summit Meadow, and on to Snow Lake where I set up camp. This was all very nice country. I still had time and made a side trip into the Yosemite Wilderness, going through Bond Pass and then to Dorothy Lake before returning to Snow Lake. This was a good day, and I did not see anybody else on the trail. Day three took me southwest to Horse Meadow, then to Maxwell Lake and on to Emigrant Lake. From Emigrant lake (with a few folks camped about) I made a slog over Mosquito Pass and back to Lunch Meadow for my last night's camp. This was a long day. Day four was spent going back to Kennedy Meadows. Once again, this stretch of trail had hordes of people and horses, way too many of both. One reason for the crowds was the beginning of deer hunting season.

At the end of the day, this is a nice classic Sierra Nevada destination that I recommend to almost all hikers unless they are looking for serious solitude.

Snow Lake, Emigrant Wilderness

Monarch

★ ★ ★

Size: 44,216 acres **Year Designated:** 1984
Responsible Agency: USFS

The Monarch Wilderness is located in the Sierra and Sequoia National Forests. The wilderness is in two pieces with State Highway 180 running east-west between the two. The highway provides excellent access. The wilderness shares its eastern boundary with the western boundary of Kings Canyon National Park.

MY VISIT: September 16, 2007 and September 17, 2007

One mistake I made before starting my first day hike was not asking someone questions about how to get to the giant sequoia groves in the wilderness. I looked at my Sequoia National Forest map and it showed an Agnew Grove and a Monarch Grove with a trail coming quite close (a second map showed only the Agnew Grove). I found what I thought was the correct trailhead and started walking north toward the southern boundary of the southern segment of the wilderness. I was concerned from the beginning because this looked like a very obscure, little-visited trailhead with no signs. The trail was difficult, straight up and straight down. After walking what I thought was more than far enough to see the groves, I was in dense forest but saw no giants. The trail started to drop significantly to the west and I didn't want to lose any more elevation so I just turned around. It is possible that I was close to the giants but did not see them because of dense intervening forest. I will probably never know.

The next day was another nice day and I took State Highway 180 east to the Deer Cove Trailhead. I hiked north into the wilderness and through Deer Cove Saddle, on to Wildman Meadow and finally to Frypan Meadow in the Kings Canyon National Park. Most of this route was in timber, but it was open enough to provide views of nearby mountains. The trail appeared to get little use. It was a longish day with 3,000 feet of elevation gain and a fair number of miles, but it seemed easy. I recommend this hike to just about any hiker.

Hain

★ ★ ★

Size: 15,985 acres **Year Designated:** 1976
Responsible Agency: USNPS

The Hain Wilderness is located northeast of the city of Soledad. It can be accessed by State Highway 146. It was designated a national monument in 1908 and then later became Pinnacles National Park. The original name of the wilderness was Pinnacles but was recently changed to honor Schuyler Hain, an early homesteader who gave tours of the area and worked for the area's preservation.

MY VISITS: Day hikes in 1973 and 1974

I made numerous visits for day hikes in 1973 and 1974 during my time working at UC Berkeley. I have no records of exact dates or destinations, but I think I hiked most of the trails. The area is of volcanic origin followed by significant erosion leaving weird, twisted formations and caves. I have no good-quality photos from my visits, but I do remember being fascinated. I recommended the area to friends when I was living in the Bay Area and maintain that recommendation although I have not been back since 1974.

Golden Trout

★ ★ ★

Size: 308,287 acres **Year Designated:** 1976
Responsible Agency: USFS

The Golden Trout Wilderness is located in the Inyo and Sequoia National Forests south of the John Muir and Sequoia-Kings Canyon Wilderness areas and west of the South Sierra Wilderness. The easiest access is from US Highway 395 to the east.

My trip began at the large horse and hiker Horseshoe Meadows Trailhead. My route this day was west over Cottonwood Pass, through Big Whitney Meadow to an unnamed meadow near the trail junction to the Rocky Basin Lakes, where I made my camp for that night. Late that night it began to rain. It rained all night. The next morning, I got up late and did not do much until the rain stopped. At that point I just had time to do a day hike up the trail to the Rocky Basin Lakes. It was a good use of time, as the lakes were a neat destination. I saw absolutely nobody that day. On day three I went south to Little Whitney Meadows. My intention was to make a loop around the Malpais Lava. Despite multiple tries I could not find this trail. Part of the problem was that this area was heavily grazed by cattle. There were little paths everywhere. I tried several, but they were nothing but cow paths. There were no signs. I gave up and decided to backtrack to the Rocky Basin Lakes for my next camp. Again, I saw no other humans. Day four was devoted to touring around the Rocky Basin Lakes and the Boreal Plateau, then going over into the Sequoia-Kings Canyon Wilderness and Funston Lake. Upon returning to my camp I decided I did not like the look of the weather and moved camp to Big Whitney Meadow so that I could get out quickly if the weather turned bad.

This fourth and final night was interesting. I think I gained some insight into why some people think they see evidence of alien activity in the sky. It was a warm night, so I sat outside reading until pretty late. I had my back leaning against a tree and was facing south. Suddenly the sky was illuminated by a great flash from the south. This brilliant light source approached me and then began making a glowing, corkscrew trail. This went on for several seconds, then the light went out. Several more seconds went by and then I heard the fairly common sound of a jet aircraft passing overhead. My best guess is that I witnessed a test launch of some sort of missile from a military aircraft.

Day five began with a serenade. There were a few coyotes around and one individual, not far from my camp, had a long and involved story to tell, and he was determined to tell it all. It was probably the longest coyote song I have ever heard. The rest of the day was spent going back to my truck.

The day hike in 2009 was almost an accident. I had bought a new map and, on the way to the Domeland Wilderness, noted an unnamed trailhead that led north into the Golden Trout to something called Manzanita Point. I had time, so off I went. This was not a long hike, but it went to a wide-open viewpoint allowing me to see many of the peaks of the southern Sierra. It was a neat, worthwhile distraction.

My overall reaction to my days in the Golden Trout Wilderness was one of disappointment. The terrain was just not particularly interesting and there was way too much impact from cattle. If a hiker wants to get a good sense of the Sierra Nevada, there are more attractive destinations.

CALIFORNIA

Ventana

★ ★ ★

Size: 216,500 acres   **Year Designated:** 1969
Responsible Agency: USFS

The Ventana Wilderness is located in the Los Padres National Forest west of US Highway 101 and east of State Highway 1.

MY VISIT: May 17–20, 2005

My four-day backpack began at the large, active Arroyo Seco Trailhead and campground. This was quintessential chaparral country. The trailhead was posted with warning signs about ticks, including deer ticks—the famous vector for Lyme disease. Personally, I hate ticks. To me they are perhaps the forced to turn around before getting to the South Ventana Cone. One scary thought was how difficult it would be to try to hike cross country. Fortunately, the wilderness here has good trails. Later that night the ocean fog rolled in and everything got wet.

Day three saw another day hike, this time west toward the coast. The fog cleared and the views were good. Some of this day was spent hiking along the South Fork of the Big Sur River. I got to the western wilderness boundary at the North Coast Ridge Road near the Cold Springs campsite. The terrain here was more open and there were fewer ticks. Mountain and ocean views were good, making a worthwhile day. The fog returned that night.

Day four was just hiking back out the way I came in. My notes say that I got an early start in the fog because it would be thirteen miles back to my truck. While hiking, the day cleared and I was back to enjoying good views. Because of the late hour back at the trailhead I camped in the Arroyo Seco Campground.

While this area gives a hiker an excellent sense of chaparral country, I must confess that I was not a big fan. This area was certainly pleasant enough, but given the ticks and dense vegetation I don't have a lot of enthusiasm for coming back. Maybe I did not pick the best route, but my recommendation to other hikers is muted. I still give it three stars.

Dense chaparral, Ventana Wilderness

worst item on a list of things that can make a day in the wilderness unpleasant. It was a warm spring after a wet winter and the chaparral brush was growing like crazy. The brush was full of ticks. My route was west on the Marble Peak Trail to a wilderness campsite called Strawberry. The Ventana has many of these little campsites cleared of brush and close to water. The brush was much taller than I was, and ticks kept dropping off the brush and onto me. Constant vigilance was required, and I stopped often to look for and remove ticks from my clothes. Otherwise this was a nice day through moderately scenic terrain.

Day two was a day hike north past the Black Cone and toward the South Ventana Cone. This day the brush was even heavier and the ticks even worse. Too bad because this was otherwise interesting terrain. I finally was

CALIFORNIA

Domeland

★ ★ ★

Size: 130,986 acres   **Year Designated:** 1964
Responsible Agency: USFS and BLM

The Domeland Wilderness is located in the Sequoia National Forest and adjacent BLM lands to the east. The South Sierra Wilderness is to the north and the Kiavah Wilderness is to the south. Access is from roads taking off from US Highway 395 to the east and from roads out of Lake Isabella. At the time of my visits there was a USFS map dedicated to this area.

MY VISITS: April 12, 2007 and April 13, 2007 and April 14, 2007 and October 23, 2009 and October 24, 2009

Before beginning my Domeland hikes, I needed a map and some advice, which I was able to find in Kernvale. I got what I needed and went up a road leading around the east side of the wilderness. I was looking for what my map said was a trailhead for the Rockhouse Meadow. I drove up and down three times and saw no trailhead. Instead I went to a small BLM campground at Long Valley. It was by now pretty late, but there was a trail here that went through the BLM portion of the wilderness and into the USFS portion and to the Kern River. The trail ran along a small stream sliding over bare, smooth granite and moss. Willows and cottonwood trees were starting to show green. While this was not a long hike, it was pretty neat.

The next day I again sought the elusive Rockhouse Trailhead. There were no signs but I thought I could see a trail through some recently burned terrain. I hiked east through BLM land to the USFS boundary which did have a sign, so I was sure that I was at the Rockhouse Trail-Manter Trail junc-

tion. I got to the Kern River, crossed easily, and continued on the trail west into Rockhouse Meadow where there was a small cabin. Here the trail disappeared in an old burn. I continued downstream along the river until it was time to turn around. There were many birds along the river including mountain quail and pygmy nuthatches among large ponderosa pines. The terrain featured a lot of granite, including domes.

The third day I decided to go north along the Kern River. Using the same starting point, I hiked north to the Rockhouse Trail, then to Rockhouse Basin, and continued north to a junction with the PCT. I followed the PCT north until it was time to turn around. The terrain was similar to the previous day, lots of granite and a rather dry forest. The granite was clearly eroded by glaciers leaving strange-looking domes and spires. Upon returning to my truck I looked up and saw a very large black bear running away from me.

The first day hike in 2009 began at a trailhead for Dark Canyon. The trail dropped from typical Sierra forest to sagebrush and mountain mahogany with some oaks and willows. I got to Woodpecker Meadow where there was some water (This was not a backpacking trip because I was not confident that I could find water down here.) I continued down the Woodpecker Trail with great views of the almost countless domes. Very neat granite country. When it was time to turn around, I sat among the domes, ate lunch, then went back to my truck. I spent that night camped at the Dark Canyon Trailhead, a nice spot.

The next day I went a bit farther down the road to a trailhead for Manter Meadow on the west-central wilderness boundary. This trail led to the epicenter of domes north of Manter Meadow. It took me awhile to get there so I didn't have much time to linger, but it was nice terrain. For the first time in this wilderness I saw people, one on foot and one on horseback, both hunters. There was granite in all sorts of shapes and figures. The perfect end for my travels in this area.

Simply stated: I like this wilderness. I recommend it to anybody who likes weird, fascinating rock formations and is tolerant of dry conditions.

Inyo Mountains

★ ★ ★

Size: 245,320 acres   **Year Designated:** 1994
Responsible Agency: USFS and BLM

The Inyo Mountains Wilderness is located in the Inyo National Forest and on BLM lands to the east and south. The easiest access is from roads off US Highway 395, but perhaps also from the Saline Valley Road to the east.

MY VISITS: April 9, 2007 and April 10, 2007 and April 11, 2007

All three of these day hikes were from US Highway 395. (One word of warning is that once one gets off paved roads here signs are scarce. It is hard to know just where one is.) This day started by going up the Mazourka Road off US Highway 395. This road became marginal as it paralleled the western wilderness boundary. My map showed a Tamarack Trail going east from the road. I never saw a sign but believed I had found the trail. It started as an old two-track road but even then was hard to follow. One thing I can guarantee is that this trail had never seen a tamarack tree. At low elevation, the vegetation was pinon and juniper, becoming mostly bristlecone pine (one of my favorites). There were bits of snow in shady spots. I had been warned not to try to backpack here because of lack of water. I was not tempted. Day hikes did just fine. As the map indicated, this trail just disappeared after a few miles. There were a few decent views, but nothing special.

My map showed another trail taking off from my road just a bit beyond the Tamarack Trail. For my second hike I walked up the road and thought I saw this other trail at an old mine. It was a nice morning and I started to climb, first through the pinon and juniper, then through the bristlecone pine, and finally to a high (9,500 feet) "meadow" of bone-dry grass and short shrubs. There were good views of the "real" Sierra Nevada to the west. One must be impressed at just how much different a place can be when it is even only a few miles into the rain shadow of a high mountain range. The trail basically ended here. I climbed 4,000 feet and it seemed like a long day.

Perhaps the best-known hike in these mountains is the Pat Keyes Trail, which climbs up and over the summit ridge and drops down to an abandoned mine. That was my destination for my third hike. It did not start well as I was not willing to take my truck down the road to where the trail supposedly began. Instead, I walked, finally seeing a BLM wilderness boundary sign indicating the beginning of the trail. This wandering around cost ninety minutes of my morning. This was a difficult trail. A climb of 4,500 feet brought me to the summit ridge, but as I descended, I was running out of time. I had to turn around before getting to the mine. After the previous two days with a lot of vertical change, my old knees were complaining on this descent.

I can only conclude after three days here that hiking is difficult with few trails, little water, and steep, austere, perhaps forbidding terrain. I saw no other humans on these three days, and the only evidence of human activity were abandoned mines. Still, hikers looking for obscure areas to explore might find this wilderness interesting.

San Rafael

★ ★ ★

Size: 197,570 acres   **Year Designated:** 1968
Responsible Agency: USFS

Dick Smith

★ ★ ★

Size: 64,700 acres   **Year Designated:** 1984
Responsible Agency: USFS

The San Rafael and Dick Smith Wilderness areas are basically contiguous areas of the Los Padres National Forest northeast of US Highway 101 and southwest of State Highway 166. The two areas are separated only by a fire road not open to the public. I discuss these two areas together because I visited both on the same backpacking trip and because they are very similar in geography, geology, and ecosystems. At the time of my visit I used a privately published map and backcountry guide for this wilderness.

Flowers along the trail to Madulce Peak, Dick Smith Wilderness

MY VISIT: May 27–31, 2005

My initial plan was to begin this trip on the east side and go up the Santa Barbara Canyon. I had read or heard that this was a wonderful trip. When I arrived at the trailhead it looked to be completely deserted, even unused. Well, not completely deserted; the place was full of rattlesnakes. The terrain did not look at all interesting so I decided to go to the west side and begin my trip at the Nira Campground and Trailhead. By now it was quite late and I only managed a short distance before finding camping at the Lost Valley site. The terrain was classic chaparral and the weather was hot.

The second day was again hot and my route took me down the Manzana Trail, then past the White Ledge and on to the South Fork Guard Station where I camped at a site near the station. The terrain this day was more open with lots of exposed rock and vegetation trending to more desert than chaparral, but there was certainly some classic chaparral.

Day three I went mostly southeast along the Sisquoc Wild and Scenic River. The vegetation along the river was lush and dense and the trail crossed the river many times. It was another hot day, so the water crossings were welcome. I got to somewhat higher terrain and camped at a site called Upper Bear. It was cooler here. I saw two other hikers and four people on horseback. What I did not see were California condors. The Sisquoc Trail goes by the northern boundary of the Sisquoc Condor Sanctuary (public entry prohibited). I was hopeful, but no big birds.

Day four was a day hike to the Dick Smith Wilderness. It was just a short hike to the fire road separating the two wilderness areas, then along a ridge trail to the Madulce Peak Trail and on to the summit of Madulce Peak (6,536 feet). This was a nice weather day and there were good views from the summit. The views, however, were obscured by a considerable amount of air pollution. The terrain was open, classic chaparral with other wildflowers. This was the best day of the trip. After I got back to my camp, I packed up and moved down to the Lower Bear camp. I saw absolutely nobody that day.

The next day was spent again along the Sisquoc. This time I counted my crossings. There were thirty! I have this memory of stopping in the trail because a rattlesnake was buzzing and I did not want to proceed until I knew where it was. I camped that night at the White Ledge site. Day five was another hot day going back to the Nira Trailhead.

In all a pretty nice trip. The hike to Madulce Peak was the highlight. The scenery was pleasant, but I just don't get very excited by chaparral terrain. I recommend this area to anyone who does like warm, dry environments. For myself, I don't plan to return.

Sespe

★ ★ ★

Size: 219,000 acres   **Year Designated:** 1992
Responsible Agency: USFS

The Sespe Wilderness is located in the Los Padres National Forest west of Interstate Highway 5 and east of State Highway 33. It is northeast of the city of Ojai. For this trip I used a privately published map of the Sespe from Tom Harrison Maps.

MY VISIT: May 8–10, 2006

This three-day backpack began at the Piedra Blanco Trailhead. I went east on the Sespe River Trail for about nine miles to an unnamed trail campsite beyond the Oak Flat site. The river was running with a fair flow. Each of the several river crossings were wet foot. The river was also quite pretty with good views to the south, first of Piedra Blanco, then of the colorful Topatopa Mountains. The terrain was open with the normal chaparral vegetation. The second day was a day hike with the goal of visiting the Sespe Hot Springs. I did not know what to expect there, but the springs were shown on my map. Multiple water crossings made the trip slow, plus I lost the trail. I decided to turn around before getting to the Sespe Springs. Instead, I went to the Willet Hot Springs on my way back

Topatopa Mountains above the Sespe River, Sespe Wilderness

to camp. These were not worth the detour, just being a couple of tanks filled with hot water. Day three was spent going back to the trailhead, although with a few interesting sightings. The first was a large, totally black rattlesnake in the middle of the trail. It buzzed and coiled and showed no sign of giving up the trail. Both sides of the trail were steep, but discretion dictated that I go around. Not much farther along the trail I met a group of ten Boy Scouts and two adult leaders. I told them about the snake. They responded that they had to abandon their original campsite the previous evening because of the density of rattlesnakes. A bit farther still I met a group of about ten girls (probably scouts) with two adults. Shortly after that I met three equestrians. They were riding mules with donkeys carrying their gear. Two of them were local avocado growers. We talked for a while and upon parting they gave me an avocado. Later when I stopped for lunch, I ate the avocado and it was the best I ever tasted. (Yes, I know, fresh food always tastes great on the trail, but it was still the best.) The trail was clearly crowded this day, with yet another group of boys encountered before getting all the way back to the trailhead. I was glad to get off the trail because by now it was just plain hot.

One small disappointment was again not seeing any California condors. The southeast portion of the wilderness is the Sespe Condor Sanctuary.

Overall, a worthwhile trip. Again, chaparral is not my favorite ecosystem, but I think many hikers would like this area.

San Gorgonio

★ ★ ★

Size: 94,702 acres   **Year Designated:** 1964
Responsible Agency: USFS and BLM

The San Gorgonio Wilderness is located in the San Bernardino National Forest and BLM lands to the east. The area is south and east of State Highway 38 and east of the city of Redlands. At the time of my visit there was a USFS map dedicated to this wilderness. The PCT goes through the BLM portion of the wilderness.

MY VISIT: April 29, 2006

It was early in the year to be hiking in the high country, even in southern California. My trip began by discussing relatively snow-free routes with USFS folks and I took their advice by starting at the Momyer Trailhead. The only problem was crossing Mill Creek just past the trailhead. That went well and I went up the trail to the southern wilderness boundary, then east and south following a 7,200-foot ridge to a junction with the Falls Creek Trail. The Falls Creek Trail climbed some more, up above 8,000 feet and some snow, then traversed southeast slopes to about 9,000 feet with less snow. I didn't quite get to Dollar Lake Saddle before running out of time and turning around. This was another nice day on a nice route with manageable snow. Most of the route was in forest, but there were still good views.

I recommend this hike and this wilderness area.

San Jacinto

★ ★ ★

Size: 32,851 acres   **Year Designated:** 1964
Responsible Agency: USFS

The San Jacinto Wilderness is located in the San Bernardino National Forest south of Interstate Highway 10 and east of State Highways 243 and 74. It is west of the city of Palm Springs. The PCT runs essentially the entire length of the wilderness.

MY VISIT: April 28, 2006

My visit occupied a very full day beginning at the Humber Park Trailhead. My route ran northeast to the PCT at Saddle Junction, then north on the PCT. It was a gorgeous, clear day and there was quite a bit of snow remaining. The views were excellent as I blundered through snow and bare patches until I got to about 8,830 feet elevation by my GPS. Even with other hikers' tracks to follow, I totally lost the trail and had to turn back.

This was a good route on a good day and I recommend this hike and wilderness area to just about any hiker.

Sheep Mountain

★ ★ ★

Size: 43,600 acres   **Year Designated:** 1984
Responsible Agency: USFS

The Sheep Mountain Wilderness is one of five wilderness areas in the mountains surrounding greater Los Angeles. It is located in the Angeles National Forest just south of State Highway 2. There are also access roads from the city of Los Angeles, but this old man from Wyoming will have nothing to do with driving down there. The Cucamonga Wilderness is to the southeast and the San Gabriel Wilderness is to the west.

MY VISIT: September 12, 2007

My Angeles National Forest map showed a trail starting from the Lupine Campground. I tried to get there but the road was mostly blocked by debris from recent rain. I got out of my truck, looked at the debris pile, and decided crossing was not safe and turned around. I would learn later that road blockages, closures, and outright road disappearance were not uncommon after severe rains. I was not to be deterred; my map also showed another branch of the road that skirted the wilderness boundary a bit to the east. I went there and parked in a big turnout. There were no signs, but a dim "trail" took off toward what I thought was Pine Mountain. A little way along the "trail" was a wilderness welcome sign that let me know I was en route to somewhere. The trail led me to the summit of what I later learned was Pine Mountain, elevation 9,660 feet (on the left in the photo). The trail continued along a ridge with good views west along the San Gabriel Mountains and down into Los Angeles, almost invisible in smog. The trail dropped into a saddle where there was a sign pointing south for routes to Mount San Antonio and north to Fish Creek. I took the Fish Creek route because it appeared to lead into the interior of the wilderness. I went down a way, but the route disappeared and I decided to turn around.

In many ways I think my hike was superior to anything I could have done on the "real trail" out of the Lupine Campground because I was able to take a nice ridge route with good views in scenic, mostly open terrain. This wilderness, so close to so many millions of people, still appeared to be pristine and quite lovely. Neither the road nor the trail appeared to get much use. I recommend this area to any hikers finding themselves in greater Los Angeles or who are just curious about the San Gabriel Mountains.

San Gabriel Mountains and Pine Mountain,
Sheep Mountain Wilderness

Death Valley

★ ★ ★

Size: 3,253,028 acres **Year Designated:** 1994
Responsible Agency: USNPS

Most of Death Valley National Park is designated wilderness. However, these three-plus-million acres are fragmented into many smaller pieces separated by roads. The park and wilderness are mostly in California, but some parts are also in Nevada. Access from Nevada is by State Highway 267 from Scotty's Junction and State Highway 374 from Beatty. Access from California is by State Highways 178 on the west and 190 on the east and north. Much of the wilderness and surrounding areas are in the Mojave Desert ecosystem.

MY VISIT: April 6, 2011 and April 7, 2011

I entered the park at Furnace Creek and talked to a ranger about destinations for day hikes. We agreed on two, and on day one I did a day hike up Fall Canyon. There was a marked trail that followed a canyon upstream through the Grapevine Mountains. The area was made up of uplifted and convoluted layers of limestone and basalt. The route appeared to end at an unclimbable dry waterfall, but there was a hard-looking but actually easy work-around. This led to an impressive narrow passage through the limestone. I went about another mile and then turned around and retraced my steps. It was clearly high season in Death Valley as I encountered at least twenty people on this hike.

My second day hike began at the Charcoal Kilns near the Wildrose Campground. There was a trail here that led through open forest to the summit of Wildrose Peak. The wind was howling. As I neared the summit (9,065 feet) I encountered a man who looked at me and said, "You are not dressed for the summit." My response was a dismissive "You Californians are just not accustomed to cold conditions." He gave me a hard (probably offended) stare and replied, "I am from Quebec. You are not dressed for the summit." He was right. A bit farther along I put on my Gore-Tex rain parka. When I got to the summit it was not enough. I could not walk a straight line. The wind howled (I think at least 60 mph) and it was cold. I spent maybe two minutes up there and headed back down.

These were only two hikes in a huge wilderness area, but all I have done so far. I suspect that there are a lot of secret gems scattered around this park, but this was not a place I found especially appealing. This may just be a matter of taste. I would not discourage anyone from exploring the wilderness areas of this park.

Mojave

★ ★ ★

Size: 695,200 acres **Year Designated:** 1994
Responsible Agency: USNPS

Most of the Mojave Reserve is designated wilderness. Like the nearby Death Valley, the Mojave Wilderness consists of several segments divided by roads. The wilderness is bounded on the north by Interstate Highway 15 and on the south by Interstate Highway 40. All of the wilderness is in California with some segments on the Nevada border. There is a visitor information center at the old rail depot in Kelso. The nearest town is Searchlight, Nevada, to the northeast of the preserve.

MY VISITS: October 26, 2009 and March 12, 2018

I did three short hikes into the wilderness in 2009. The first was to the summit of Teutonia Mountain (5,755 feet). There was a trailhead just off

The Kelso Dunes, Mojave Wilderness

Turtle Mountains

★ ★ ★

Size: 177,209 acres   **Year Designated:** 1994
Responsible Agency: BLM

The Turtle Mountains Wilderness is located west of US Highway 95 south of the town of Needles. Access is mainly via the Turtle Mountain Road off US Highway 95 about twenty-five miles south of Needles. The Turtle Mountains Wilderness is immediately south of the Stepladder Mountains Wilderness and east of the Old Woman Mountains Wilderness.

MY VISIT: April 12, 2011 and April 13, 2011

Any visit to the Turtle Mountains Wilderness and other nearby wilderness areas should begin at the BLM district office in Needles. I have been here a few times and always found a knowledgeable person who could tell visitors about hiking opportunities. Getting road information is also important as wilderness access roads are rough.

My first day hike began at the Lisa Dawn Campground and Trailhead on the eastern boundary of the wilderness. This campground was situated in a beautiful spot. It was not easy to get to, but the reward for getting here was considerable. The terrain was tortured volcanic spires and other features rising out of classic Mojave Desert. Lots of desert plants were in bloom. Common in these California desert areas are old, abandoned mines. There was one shaft in the campground. It was covered by what the BLM calls a cupola, a sturdy steel frame with steel bars on the side and a mesh metal top. The purpose is to keep visitors from falling in and to protect wildlife that rely on the mine openings for shelter. My hike was a loop called the Mexican Hat Trail. This was a not-very-long trail that provided an excellent introduction to the volcanic desert environment. I knew I was in a good spot when only a few minutes from the trailhead I interrupted the nap of a desert bighorn ram.

the Cima Road and a trail. The trailhead area was neat with a nice Joshua tree grove and mine shafts (tunnels?) scattered around. A pleasant if not spectacular hike.

The second and longest hike of the day was through Quail Basin. It was standard Mojave terrain with desert scrub and good views of tortured volcanic features to the north.

The last little sortie of the day was into the Kelso Dunes with perfect light for photos. Here I encountered my first sand surfers. They used modified surfboards to slide down the dunes.

The 2018 hike was to the summit of Hackberry Mountain (5,390 feet). The hike began at some corrals near the end of an obscure road west from the Ivanpah Road. The terrain was mostly volcanic with typical Mojave vegetation: yucca, creosote, some cactus, and mesquite. There were some decent views from the summit.

This was not a lot of hiking in a big and diverse area. I don't claim expert status here, but my guess is that any hiker comfortable with desert terrain will enjoy this area. There are few trails, but cross-country hiking opportunities are just about limitless.

After returning to the trailhead I camped at the co-located campground. I saw nobody else on the trail or in the campground and only saw one other truck on the road coming in.

The next day I drove south toward the Coffin Springs Trailhead. On the way I stopped at some more old mine diggings. There was another cupola here and as I approached, I scared out a barn owl that had been roosting there. Instead of taking the Coffin Springs Trail I went up a canyon south of the Mexican Hat area. This canyon was even more spectacular than yesterday's. Lots of flowers and even more twisted spires. I spent the day here until it was time to turn around and drive partway out of the area to a truck campsite not far from the Old Woman Mountains.

I know I took photographs on this trip, but they have disappeared, probably due to my incompetence. This may be my favorite Mojave wilderness and I recommend it to any hiker as an introduction to the California/Nevada desert.

Trilobite

★ ★ ★

Size: 29,626 acres   **Year Designated:** 1994
Responsible Agency: BLM

The Trilobite Wilderness is located south of Interstate Highway 40 and southwest of the Clipper Mountain Wilderness. Access is south from I-40 at the Kelbaker exit. From the Kelbaker Road there is an unpaved pipeline access road to the east that skirts the northern wilderness boundary.

MY VISIT: March 14, 2018

I spent the previous night camped just off the pipeline road. So this morning I left my campsite and dropped into what looked like a "main" wash, crossed this and then went up a secondary wash that looked like it came from some peaks off to the southeast. The early going was through standard volcanic Mojave terrain of mesquite and creosote. I ultimately gained a ridgetop with nice views. To the south there was a deep canyon with some amazing tortured volcanic features with dark lava, pale ash, and blobs of what looked like scoops of pale ice cream. This was a genuinely dramatic canyon. I hiked down partway, then looped back to my entry route, had lunch, and went back to my truck. I recommend this area to any hiker who likes volcanic desert terrain.

Three scoops of volcanic ice cream, Trilobite Wilderness

Mesquite

★ ★ ★

Size: 44,865 acres   **Year Designated:** 1994
Responsible Agency: BLM

North Mesquite Mountains

★ ★ ★

Size: 28,942 acres   **Year Designated:** 1994
Responsible Agency: BLM

I describe these two areas together because they are practically adjacent, are very similar in geology and environment, and I hiked them on consecutive days. The areas are accessible from Interstate Highway 15 by the Kingston Road, which separates the two areas. The Kingston Range Wilderness is to the west and the Mojave Wilderness is to the south.

MY VISIT: March 15, 2018 and March 16, 2018

For these hikes I camped next to the Kingston Road near Winters Pass and just hiked out of my campsite. The first day I went south into the Mesquite Wilderness. My goal was to go up a small summit to the south. The terrain was almost exclusively volcanic with some rather large peaks. It was a typical high Mojave environment with yucca, Joshua tree, barrel cactus, some cholla, and a few grasses. As I approached the summit I saw "caves" in the rock that may have been formed by hot lava draining away from cooler surrounding material. The rock texture was very rough, almost like karst (maybe the rock was really limestone?). It was an interesting area for poking around.

My hike the next day into the North Mesquite Wilderness began at my campsite, then went up a cherry-stem road west from Winters Pass and continued to near the western wilderness boundary. The terrain was, not surpris-

"Caves" in volcanic hills, Mesquite Wilderness

ingly, very similar to that of the previous day, but without any caves. Hiking to the top of a modest volcanic ridge gave good views of the neighborhood. Hikers who like volcanic desert terrain would find these areas attractive.

Chemehuevi Mountains

★ ★ ★

Size: 85,810 acres   **Year Designated:** 1994
Responsible Agency: BLM

The Chemehuevi Wilderness is located on BLM public lands south of the town of Needles, east of US Highway 95, and west of the Colorado River. The northern part of the wilderness is shown on BLM California map Desert District Needles. There are no trails.

MY VISIT: March 17, 2019

My starting point for this day hike was a large parking area and informal camping area just west of US Highway 95 near a rock formation called Snaggletooth. My route was just crossing the highway and heading toward the obvious ridge of the Chemehuevi Mountains. This was standard California Mojave ecosystem with metamorphic rock. Hiking was easy over mostly flat, hard-packed rubble. It was nearly the peak of wildflower blooming and everything was green. The yucca were in bloom along with numerous yellow and purple flowers blanketing large patches of ground. Ocotillo were beginning to bloom. I scared up lots of black-tailed jackrabbits and had one roadrunner stop by for a brief visit as I sat resting on the edge of a wash. Mockingbirds provided background music. I went as far east as the point where the mountains rise sharply. The pale rock was distinctly traversed by basalt dikes twisted by past uplifting and tilting.

This was a very pleasant and worthwhile day in perfect weather conditions. I recommend this area to anybody who likes wandering around in desert terrain, especially if they find themselves in greater Needles.

Two-Star Areas

★ ★

South Warner 70,385 acres, designated 1964, managed by the USFS, located in the Warner Mountains in the Modoc National Forest south of the city of Alturas. The wilderness is east of US Highway 395 and west of the Surprise Valley Road. When I visited there was a USFS map dedicated to this wilderness. My three-day backpack began on September 16, 2004 at the Soup Spring Campground and Trailhead. My route was east on the Slide Creek Trail to a junction with the Summit Trail, where I made my camp in forest at about 7,800 feet. The terrain was forest and meadow. The second day was a day hike north on the Summit Trail to Patterson Lake. This was a nice day through some forest but mostly open, volcanic terrain with brush and grass up to about 9,200 feet. The lake was pretty with basalt cliffs along its west side. I had lunch at the lake, then turned around and went back to my camp. Upon my return I was surprised to see my food bags that had been hanging from a tree were now on the ground and the hanging cord draped in a crazy pattern among the trees. The food in the bags was largely undisturbed. To this day I don't know who or what was at work here, but my chief suspect was squirrels. That night it snowed. In the morning there were a couple of inches of snow on the ground, mostly just a sloppy mess. I went back to the trailhead.

Mount Shasta 36,981 acres, designated 1984, located in the Shasta-Trinity National Forest east of Interstate Highway 5 and northeast of the town of Mount Shasta. At the time of my visit there was a USFS map devoted to the Mount Shasta and Castle Crag Wilderness areas. My day hike on September 29, 2007 began at the Bunny Flat Trailhead. There were already lots of people and vehicles at the trailhead. I went up the trail to Avalanche Gulch, a route for climbers going to the summit. It was a nice, clear day and views of the summit were good. The trail was excellent, sometimes looking like it has been laboriously maintained on its way to some climber shelters at about 9,800 feet, where the trail ended. (Note: a permit was required for going to the summit. That was not my goal.) I tried to follow dim trails farther up the mountain, but I completely lost the route in slopes of rubble. I decided to turn around and went back to the trailhead. The view on the way down was mostly of Interstate Highway 5 and surrounding developed spaces. This view plus the large number of hikers certainly distracted from the wilderness character. This was a pleasant enough day and route, but I have been in much wilder, more attractive volcanic terrain.

Castle Crags 7,300 acres, designated 1984, located in the Shasta-Trinity National Forest just west of Interstate Highway 5 and west of the town of Dunsmuir. At the time of my visit there was a USFS map dedicated to the Mount Shasta and Castle Crags Wilderness areas. I arrived near this wilderness the previous day and camped overnight in the Castle Crags State Park. Then, on the morning of July 20, 2004, still in the state park, I began hiking north on the PCT. After about two miles I got to the southern wilderness boundary and continued north. As the morning progressed, I realized this was going to be a *really hot* day. I kept hiking north through pretty interesting terrain of rugged granite spires. According to my old, marked-up map I got to within two miles of the northern wilderness boundary. My original plan was to go all the way to the northern boundary, but it was just too hot so I turned around. This was a reasonably attractive and interesting area, but I needed to get out of the heat. My recommendation is come and hike here, but don't plan your trip for July.

Yuki 53,339 acres, designated 2006, located in the Mendocino National Forest and BLM land south of the Yolla Bolly-Middle Eel Wilderness and east of the town of Covelo. Because the Yuki was only recently designated as wilderness, its boundaries were not shown on any maps in my possession. I stopped in a ranger station in Covelo to buy an up-to-date map. While I have great respect for the Forest Service, they can be bureaucratic. The only person in the office tried to be helpful, but was a firefighter and was not allowed to handle money and so could not sell me a map. I was allowed to study a map that showed the wilderness boundaries and I set out. My access

on October 22, 2008 was from County Road 162 to Forest Road M1, which forms the eastern boundary of the wilderness. The boundary along Road M1 was signed, so I could tell where I was. To the best of my knowledge, there are no trails in the Yuki. The M1 road followed a ridgetop, so all hikes into the wilderness involved a steep descent. For my hike I picked a likely spot, dropped a way, and then walked parallel to the ridge. It was a magnificent, crystal clear day. The forest was dense with mixed oak and pine, and the oaks were very near their peak of color. There were some open, grassy areas and some volcanic outcrops. (The area also saw cattle grazing.) I encountered a few deer hunters. This was certainly a pleasant hiking day, although I could not call it especially interesting.

Mount Lassic 7,279 acres, designated 2006, located in the Six Rivers National Forest south of the USFS Mad River Ranger Station. The area can be easily accessed from the ranger station. By 2014 I had learned enough about illegal activity in California national forests that I did not go into new territory without checking in with a local USFS office. I stopped in the Mad River Ranger Station before this trip and was advised that the serpentine soils in the higher elevations of this wilderness were not appropriate for the common illegal crop, meaning hiking the high route to the summit of Mount Lassic should be OK. It was late in the day when I learned this, so my friend Maya and I found a nice place to camp in our truck overnight.

The next morning, July 27, 2014, we drove to the wilderness boundary. There were no signs for a trailhead, but we saw a truck parked not far off the road and, upon investigation, there was indeed a trailhead for Mount Lassic. On our drive up, we realized the significance of the rock serpentine. There were literally mountains of the stuff. These mountains looked like volcanoes but they were not. They were heaps of shattered serpentine. It turns out that serpentine is a hydrated metamorphic rock with composition $Mg_3Si_2O_5(OH)_4$. It gets its name because the rock has the appearance of snakeskin. Well, OK, if they say so. There were three named peaks here— Mount Lassic, Black Lassic, and Red Lassic. Only Mount Lassic was in the wilderness. We hiked to the summit of Mount Lassic where there was an old monument to the US Geological Survey and great views of the other Lassic peaks and also out to the ocean, where the coast was covered with fog. This was a rather short hike and, depending on one's tastes, pretty interesting although I only gave it two stars (not likely to return).

Snow Mountain 60,221 acres, designated 1984, located in the Mendocino National Forest southeast of the Yuki Wilderness, east of Lake Pillsbury, and north of Clear Lake. Before attempting a hike here in April, I thought it advisable to talk to the USFS about access to potentially snowy country. I spoke to someone in the Willows Forest Supervisor's Office and was advised that access should be feasible from the south. My goal was to go to one of the two summits of Snow Mountain: either the East Summit at 7,056 feet or the West Summit at 7,038 feet. After a trip on the proverbial long and winding road, Forest Road 10, on April 26, 2007 I arrived at the Summit Springs Trailhead. It was now the crack of noon, but up I went on the Summit Trail. The area featured old volcanic mounds with rather open forest of spruce and Jeffrey pine. I am particularly fond of Jeffrey pine with its enormous branches almost as thick as the trunk, sometimes dipping to the ground. As I climbed there was more and more snow. One hazard of hiking on snow is the ease with which one can lose a trail. I lost the trail. Not only that, I missed a trail junction and ended up on the Milk Ranch Trail, not where I wanted to be. I tried to recover by going cross country to what looked like a local summit. Upon arrival, my GPS said I was at 6,950 feet. Was this close enough to be the 7,038 feet of the West Summit? Maybe. In any event, it was getting late and I needed to go back down, and go I did. I did not see another single soul on this hike, most other hikers knowing it was too early to be here. It was a pleasant area, nothing of outstanding scenic value or interest, but a place many hikers might find worth spending a day.

Owens River Headwaters 14,721 acres, designated 2009, located in the Inyo National Forest just east of the Ansel Adams Wilderness. It can be accessed by State Highway 158, which makes a loop around June Lake from US Highway 395. I visited this area on October 18, 2009, shortly after President Obama signed the bill designating it as wilderness. I was pretty confident I knew where it was and found a map showing the boundaries on the internet. My visit began at a trailhead adjacent to State Highway 158 between Gull Lake and Silver Lake. There had been some significant snow in the area, but another person at the trailhead said hiking was still possible. It was a beautiful morning and the trail was steep, heading south, then east, then southeast up to Yost Lake. Serious snow cover began at about 8,500 feet, but there were other hikers' tracks to follow. I continued south past Yost Lake to Yost Meadow where the other tracks stopped. I still had plenty of time so I kept going south to a pass overlooking Glass Creek Meadows. This was my lunch and turnaround spot. On my way back some very fresh bear tracks crossed the hikers' tracks. This was another day on a nice route in a nice area with easy access and not too strenuous. The terrain was standard Sierra Nevada edge—forest and meadow with views of higher peaks. While I am not tempted to return, I suspect other hikers might just find this a good hike.

Kaiser 22,700 acres, designated 1976, located in the Sierra National Forest just north of Huntington Lake and State Highway 168. On September 18, 2007 I made a good-weather day hike to the summit of Kaiser Peak. I had to blunder around some campgrounds looking for the trailhead. I finally found the Lakeshore Trailhead and started hiking north on the Kaiser Peak Trail. It was a straightforward hike to the 10,043-foot summit. Once out of the timber this was a very nice, scenic hike. The summit views up into Kings Canyon were good, and there were a few small lakes just below the summit. After a summit lunch I went back to the trailhead. Other than two horse riders near the trailhead, I saw nobody all day. A worthwhile day, but nothing exceptional.

Chimney Peak 13,700 acres, designated 1994, located on BLM land just across a road from the eastern boundary of the Domeland Wilder-

Lower Soldier Lake, Sequoia-Kings Canyon Wilderness

ness. The entire wilderness is surrounded by a loop of road. Access is from US Highway 395 to the east and State Highway 178 from the south. According to my Sequoia National Forest map, the Chimney Peak Wilderness was not far from my trailheads for Domeland. Not only that, the PCT runs through Chimney Peak and crosses the loop road at a small BLM campground. I drove to this campground and on April 15, 2007 began a short hike to the north on the PCT. It was a cold, gray, gloomy morning with a little snow, but there were occasional glimpses of sun revealing nearby peaks and some snow-blasted trees. The terrain was dry forest with rugged, rocky outcrops. While this was a pleasant hike, I would recommend hikers look first at Domeland.

Owens Peak 74,060 acres, designated 1994, managed by BLM, separated by a road from the BLM portion of the Domeland Wilderness to the west, from the Chimney Peak Wilderness to the west, and from the Kiavah Wilderness to the southwest. It is accessible from US Highway 395 to the east and State Highway 178 to the southwest. The PCT traverses the wilderness. My day hike on April 17, 2007 began at a signed trailhead for Lamont Peak. I parked and went up the trail to almost the summit. The last bit up the summit block was beyond my rock skills. The views were good and while not long the trail was steep, climbing 1,700 feet. There was open forest almost all the way. This was terrain typical of the transition zone one finds between the southern Sierra Nevada and the more serious desert terrain to the south and west. This hike, like the Chimney Peak above, were what I call "poking around hikes." There were no ambitious destinations, no jaw-dropping scenery, just pleasant hikes in pleasant terrain that gave me a good sense of the neighborhood.

Santa Lucia 21,704 acres, designated 1978, located in the Los Padres National Forest east of US Highway 101 and close to but just east of the city of San Louis Obispo. This was just a day hike on May 3, 2005 in a small but pretty and popular area. Getting to my trailhead was slow as the road made several stream fords. My hike began at the Big Falls Trailhead. Upon my arrival, there were no other vehicles. That did not last long. The trail obviously sees heavy use. In a short while the reason was clear. This was a canyon with a truly beautiful stream with waterfalls and deep swimming holes. The swimmers soon appeared. There was also a contingent of butterfly hunters. I left the pools to the others and wandered up a ridge trail toward the Upper Lopez campsite, but the terrain just became ordinary chaparral with lots of evidence of heavy cattle grazing. I made this a short day and went back to the trailhead. Some hikers may find this a good destination. I have no intention to return.

South Fork San Jacinto 20,217 acres, designated 2009, located, well, south of the San Jacinto Wilderness in the San Bernardino National Forest south of State Highway 74. There is only one trail in this wilderness and I hiked all of it on October 17, 2009. There was a South Fork Trailhead along State Highway 74. The highway was busy and the sound of traffic followed me down the trail for a fair distance. The higher elevations near the highway were standard chaparral. As I dropped toward the creek the canyon deepened and the traffic noise disappeared. When I reached the creek there were nice stands of mixed pine and oak with ferns and cattails near the water. This was a very pleasant spot. The trail continued across the creek and ended near Rouse Ridge where a road divides the wilderness into two pieces. I simply turned around and retraced my steps. I saw no other humans and the area did not appear to get much visitation. This was an enjoyable day in a pleasant place but without any dramatic scenery and little of interest.

Pleasant View Ridge 26,757 acres, designated 2009, located in the Angeles National Forest just north of State Highway 2, the Angeles Crest Highway. It is across State Highway 2 from the San Gabriel Wilderness. I had a hard time getting here. In the time since designation, road travel in this area had been difficult, mostly because of fire and flood closures. When I say flood closures, I am serious. One year a whole section of State Highway 2 had simply vanished due to heavy rain. I was where the road had been, and it was as though no road had ever been there, just a smooth slope down the mountain. There was also a closure of the land including the wilderness because of a study of an endangered toad (frog?) species. By May of 2012 I had a good idea of where the wilderness boundaries were. My first day hike began on May 14, 2012 at the Islip Saddle on State Highway 2. My route went northeast on a trail to a USFS campground called South Fork, through pleasant, rather open forest typical of the San Gabriel Mountains. There were some nice pools in the creek at the campground and several people were enjoying the day. A second day hike on May 15, 2012 was on the Burkhart Trail from the Buckhorn Campground. Some of my route was on the PCT. The trail dropped through forest to creeks and a nice waterfall, then climbed to the Buckhorn Saddle about five miles from the trailhead. From the saddle I climbed cross country to the top of Will Thrall Peak where I had lunch and turned around. I saw nothing here to make me want to come back.

Lava Beds 28,460 acres, designated 1972, managed by the USNPS as part of the Lava Beds National Monument, and located near the town of Tulelake. My day hike on September 30, 2007 was on the Whitney Butte Trail to the relatively recent Callahan Lava Flow. The trail wound through grass and brush and ended at a very rough aa lava flow said to be only about 1,000 years old.

Chanchelulla 8,062 acres, designated 1984, located in the Shasta-Trinity National Forest north of State Highway 36, west of the city of Red Bluff, and east of the town of Wildwood. My day hike on April 19, 2007 began at a trailhead for Chanchelulla Peak in fog, wind, and snow. The trail climbed steeply through big ponderosa pine, cedar, and Douglas fir trees to an open volcanic ridge. Here in the open it was snowing sideways and I couldn't see. There was a Jeffrey pine holding on to the ridge for dear life and its photo captures the conditions of the day and the terrain. I went to the summit of this ridge for lunch before turning around.

Jeffrey pine in snowstorm, Chanchelulla Wilderness

Bucks Lake 23,710 acres, designated 1984, located in the Plumas National Forest west of the town of Quincy. The PCT traverses the area. My day hike on September 14, 2004 began at Silver Lake and went to Gold Lake and by Spanish Peak, and was on some portion of the PCT through terrain of mixed forest and meadow with a fair bit of open granite. There were cattle grazing here.

Dinky Lakes 30,863 acres, designated 1984, located in the Sierra National Forest west of the John Muir Wilderness. My long (sixteen-mile) day hike on September 19, 2007 began at the Cliff Lake Trailhead near the Courtright Reservoir. The terrain was classic gentle Sierra Nevada with lots of exposed granite, meadows, and some rather open forest. My route took me to Cliff Lake, Rock Lake, Dinky Lake Number 2, and finally to a ridge overlooking Dinky Lake Number 1. I never saw another person the entire day. There was nothing wrong with this area; it was pretty and the hiking was easy, but there are simply more interesting and more attractive areas nearby.

Jenny Lakes 10,510 acres, designated 1984, located in the Sequoia National Forest just east of The Generals Highway in Sequoia National Park. The eastern and southern wilderness boundaries are shared with the

Sequoia-Kings Canyon Wilderness. My long day hike on September 15, 2007 began at a trailhead near the Big Meadow Campground. The route was over Poop Out Pass, down to Jenny Lake, and then up to JO Pass into the Sequoia-Kings Canyon Wilderness. Again, this was gentle, quintessential Sierra Nevada lake, forest, meadow, and granite terrain. The surroundings were pleasant and the trail was easy. I had lots of company, as my notes say I passed twenty-two backpackers and three other day hikers.

South Sierra 60,280 acres, designated 1984, located in the Sequoia and Inyo National Forests south of the John Muir Wilderness, north of the Domeland Wilderness, and west of US Highway 395. An overnight backpack began on September 24, 2005 at Sage Flat at the eastern boundary of the wilderness. The parking area was filled with big rigs with horse trailers. I asked some folks unloading horses what was happening and was told that it was the opening of both deer and bear hunting seasons. I decided this was not a threatening situation and hiked up a long hill to Summit Meadows. I set up my camp in a nice spot, then climbed a nearby ridge for views and photos. There were a lot of hunters around on my way up. This looked like good grazing for cattle and I was assured that there were lots of cows here earlier in the year. The land appeared to me to have taken a toll from the grazing. The terrain was typical low-elevation Sierra Nevada with open forest and occasional meadows. There was a lot of granite, but always mixed with trees. A day hike on May 16, 2012 began at the famous Kennedy Meadows at the southern wilderness boundary. I hiked the PCT north along the Kern River, then northwest following Crag Creek. I got to a narrow spot in the canyon and turned around. I must be honest with readers; I really did not like this area.

Silver Peak 31,533 acres, designated 1992, located in the Los Padres National Forest east of State Highway 1 and southwest of Fort Hunter Liggett. My overnight backpack began on May 21, 2005 at the Salmon Creek Trailhead. My route was up to the Ridge Road and what I hoped would be the Lion Den backcountry campground shown on my map. I never found

the campground and needed water, so I backtracked to the Estrella backcountry campground and found a spot among a lot of other hikers. This was a pleasant but not at all interesting day in mixed terrain of forest and chaparral. There were some views out over the ocean.

Matilija 29,600 acres, designated 1992, located in the Los Padres National forest southeast of the San Rafael Wilderness and southwest of the Sespe Wilderness and north of the city of Santa Anna. My day hike on May 7, 2006 began at a trailhead for Matilija Creek. The parking area was full, but I was able to squeeze into a space along the road. There were a lot of people around. The trail went through a private wildlife refuge before entering the wilderness. The trail crossed the creek multiple times. I kept my boots on. It was a nice riparian area. A little way in I came across a group of about twenty Boy Scouts accompanied by about ten adults. These were far from the total number of folks I encountered. Crowds of this magnitude will normally drive me away and they did on this occasion. Back at my truck, the parking area and road were so heavily packed that someone had put up a "Road Closed" sign.

Chumash 37,768 acres, designated 1992, located in the Los Padres National Forest north of the Sespe Wilderness and northwest of the town of Lockwood. My day hike on May 6, 2006 began at the Los Pinos Nordic Ski Center. The parking lot was almost filled with sheriff's department and search and rescue vehicles. I was told that a hiker went missing the previous day and may or may not have been found. I was also told it was OK for me to start my hike. This was a long day because the road to the normal summer trailhead was still closed because of snow. The snow was well consolidated so walking was not too difficult. My route went west to Sawmill Mountain, then south to almost Lilly Meadows where I turned around. Along the way I encountered about a dozen Boy Scouts and one other day hiker, although the area gave no sign of overuse. When I got back to the parking area it was full, this time with a different cast of characters—amateur astronomers setting up for a star party.

Bighorn Mountains 38,502 acres, designated 1994, located in the San Bernardino National Forest and in two separate segments of BLM lands to the east. The area is northeast of the San Gorgonio Wilderness and is south of State Highway 247 and east of State Highway 18. There are no trails. My day hike on April 30, 2006 was pretty simple: I just followed a compass bearing to the east. I got to a ridge with good views to the east of pretty serious desert terrain. To the west were good views of the snow-covered San Bernardino Mountains. The whole route was through Joshua trees and other desert species. I had lunch on this ridge and was pleased to be joined by a flock of pinon jays.

Cahuilla Mountain 5,585 acres, designated 2009, located in the San Bernardino National Forest south of the South Fork San Jacinto Wilderness. This wilderness had only one trail and I hiked all of it on October 16, 2009. At the Cahuilla Trailhead were two bow hunters who had just taken a black-tailed deer. The trail went to the summit of Cahuilla Mountain (5,635 feet). It was another classic chaparral hike.

Santa Rosa 78,576 acres, designated 1984, located in the San Bernardino National Forest and adjacent BLM lands south of Interstate Highway 10 and southwest of the city of Indio. My day hike on April 27, 2006 began at the Sawmill Trailhead at the western edge of the national forest part of the wilderness. This was, I think, the only trail in the wilderness and it was called the Cactus Spring Trail. My route was to about a mile past Cactus Spring where I turned around and retraced my steps. This was classic California Mojave Desert and an easy trail. It was also a good time of year with lots of birds in the brush including my first ever wrentit and second ever Lawrence's goldfinch. Also, a profusion of flowers.

Cucamonga 12,981 acres, designated 1964, located in the Angeles National Forest southeast of the Sheep Mountain Wilderness, separated by the Glendora Ridge Road, west of State Highway 109 and north of the city of Rancho Cucamonga. My day hike on May 1, 2006 began at the Lytle Creek Trailhead at the end of a bad road. It was early in the year and I could see that the higher ridges were buried in snow. The lower country at the end of the road had nice spring conditions. The trail was steep, going through open forest along Lytle Creek. Once past the backcountry campsite called Third Stream Crossing the trail became very dim and then almost disappeared. This would not have been troubling except there were now steep scree slopes that looked like they could send me sliding into a bad place. I kept going, but finally gave up and turned around without gaining the ridgetop. The area appeared to receive little visitation. One other observation this day was just how bad the air pollution was. There were no long-distance views.

San Gabriel 36,118 acres, designated 1968, located in the Angeles National Forest just south of State Highway 2. It is across State Highway 2 from the Pleasant View Ridge Wilderness and a bit west of the Sheep Mountain Wilderness. I had trouble getting here. Segments of State Highway 2 were closed because of flood damage. Part of the highway had simply slid away into a ravine. I finally saw a detour map on a bulletin board at the Big Pines Ranger Station. I went to the portion of State Highway 2 that led to a wilderness trailhead. This also took time to find as there was no sign for the trailhead at the highway. By now it was almost noon, but I began my day hike on September 13, 2007 on the Twin Peaks Trail. It was a good trail to the Twin Peaks Saddle, then an informal trail to the two summits. The terrain was open forest through granite. The views from the summits were not as good as I hoped, but still a worthwhile day. From the summits I retraced my steps and got back to the trailhead in the last of the daylight. I saw no other hikers, but did see deer and a bobcat! The cat and I had a staring contest. If I remember correctly, the cat won. Another example of a wilderness area close to many millions of people with little evidence of visitors.

Funeral Mountains 25,697 acres, designated 1994, located on BLM land just to the southeast of the Death Valley Wilderness near the Nevada state line. Access was from Nevada State Highway 373, then on unpaved roads to and past clay pits as shown on the Death Valley National Park map. My day hike on April 8, 2011 was cold. I was wearing my Gore-Tex shell and gloves. My Death Valley map showed a trail entering the wilderness from the end of a two-track road. Here I started hiking southwest in an obvious, wide canyon. I wandered up to a shallow pass, then headed north into a jumble of volcanic ridges and tortured layers of uplifted basalt in red and tan. There were also lots of volcanic bombs scattered about and sealed-together conglomerates. I sat on a high spot in the wind and had lunch, then turned around and walked back to my truck in light snow.

Ibex 28,804 acres, designated 1994, located on BLM land contiguous with the southeast section of the Death Valley Wilderness. State Highway 127 runs along the southeast wilderness boundary. My day hike here on February 24, 2012 was an introduction to the mother lode of talcum powder. Talc is a hydrated magnesium silicate, formula $Mg_3(Si_2O_5)_2(OH)_2$. It is brilliant white in color and is found in large amounts in greater Death Valley. There are lots of old talc mines in the volcanic hills in this part of California. Because of their whiteness, they can be seen from great distances. My hike started at an old cherry-stem road to the Eclipse Mine, which is a former talc mine. There were still some open tunnels. I went beyond the mine to some ridges close to the Death Valley National Park boundary. The terrain was very broken so there was a lot of side-hill walking to keep elevation. I got to 4,130 feet, more than

Kingston Range from the Pahrump Valley Wilderness

2,000 feet above State Highway 127. I had lunch on a minor summit, then walked back to my truck. There were no trails.

Resting Spring Range 76,280 acres, designated 1994, located on BLM land in California just east of Death Valley National Park and on the Nevada border. Access is by California State Highways 178 and 127. The wilderness is shown on BLM California map Death Valley Junction (no trails). My day hike on February 28, 2012 began at a parking area next to State Highway 178 and went through a canyon between two volcanic ridges, then to the top of a ridge and a minor summit at 4,660 feet. As I approached this summit I stumbled across two bighorn rams that quickly scampered away.

Clipper Mountain 33,905 acres, designated 1994, managed by BLM (no trails), located just south of Interstate Highway 40 south of the Mojave Preserve. Access is from the Essex Road, then an unpaved road to the Goldhammer Mine. My day hike on March 13, 2018 began at the partially restored Goldhammer Mine just south of I-40. I went south through a small wash, then followed an old two-track to another old mine, this one with an unobstructed, open tunnel and a scary-looking open shaft. Except for the old mines and some dried coyote melons, I saw nothing of particular interest.

Kingston Range 199,444 acres, designated 1994
Pahrump Valley 72,528 acres, designated 1994
These two wilderness areas on BLM lands are discussed together because they are very close together and because I visited both on the same day. The land southeast of Death Valley National Park and north of the Mojave National Preserve is mostly public land administered by the BLM. Most of the land is designated wilderness. Access to these areas is from side roads off State Highways 127 and 178 and Interstate Highway 15. The areas are shown on California BLM map Mesquite Lake. My day hike on February 25, 2012 began at the old Western Talc Mine. I hiked south through spare and profoundly dry terrain, cut by numerous washes. I continued to head south farther into the

wilderness. I ultimately ended up on a ridgetop in the Dumont Hills with views to the south of the Dumont Dunes Off Highway Vehicle Recreation Area. My GPS said I had come 5.1 miles, so I turned around and went back to my truck. Once at my truck, I still had a lot of daylight left so I drove back to the Mesquite Valley Road and went to the southern boundary of the Pahrump Valley Wilderness. This western portion of the wilderness is almost dead flat, a featureless desert of yucca, cactus, and creosote (but looked pretty good in this early desert spring). I took a short stroll north into the wilderness until I found a good spot for a photograph with the Pahrump Valley Wilderness in the foreground and the Kingston Range Wilderness in the background. The portion of the Kingston Range in the photo would have made a better hiking destination than the one I went to earlier that day.

South Nopah Range 17,036 acres, designated 1994
Nopah Range 106,571 acres, designated 1994

These two areas on BLM lands are discussed together because they are only separated by the Old Spanish Trail Road and because I visited them on two consecutive days. The terrain in the two areas is identical. The areas are east of the Ibex Wilderness, west of the Pahrump Valley Wilderness, and north of the Kingston Range Wilderness areas as shown on the BLM California map Owlshead Mountains. My first day hike was on February 26, 2012 and it began along the southern boundary of the South Nopah Wilderness. The terrain here, more jumbled limestone and volcanic rock, was not very interesting, so I drove to the northern boundary and began a second hike between two black volcanic peaks. This part of the wilderness was more interesting with good views of the Kingston Range. On February 27 I did a day hike into the Nopah Range Wilderness from the eastern boundary. There is nothing to distinguish these areas from other nearby BLM wilderness areas.

Argus Range 74,890 acres, designated 1994, located on BLM lands west of State Highway 178, across the Panamint Valley from Death Valley National Park. My day hike on April 10, 2011 began at the Minnietta Mine outside the eastern wilderness boundary. I parked by the old mine and walked west up a canyon until the road ended at what I think was the wilderness boundary. From here a distinct trail continued as shown on my Death Valley National Park map. There were a few springs along this trail until it ended at a high spring. I kept going upcanyon until I encountered a wall that pretty much ended my hike. On the way down, I was buzzed by what I thought was a black-chinned hummingbird. I figured "cool." A few yards later I just happened to see a female black-chinned sitting on her tiny nest. She was utterly still, with me only about a meter away.

Old Woman Mountains 162,985 acres, designated 1994, located on BLM lands south of the Old Historic Route 66 Highway southwest of Needles in the Mojave Desert. Most of the wilderness is shown on the BLM map for Amboy, California. My day hike on April 14, 2011 began at the northwest wilderness boundary. I hiked southeast past old mine sites with open shafts, then on to the larger Florence Mine and up on some ridges hoping for expansive views, but there were a lot of obstacles. The terrain was typical Mojave.

Piute Mountains 48,084 acres, designated 1994, located on BLM lands just north of the Old Woman Mountains Wilderness, south of the Mojave National Preserve, and south of the Old Route 66 Highway. The wilderness is shown on the BLM map for Amboy, California. My day hike on April 15, 2011 started at the northwest wilderness boundary. I went up a cherry-stem road to a junction with a sign (!) showing "mine" to the right and "tank" to the left. I went left. The road segment ended at a cattle operation (no visible animals) where there was a spring. I continued on to an old mine with a deep, open shaft. It looked scary to me. I went on through a low pass, up a ridge, then to a high point on that ridge (3,939 feet). I had lunch on this summit and then walked back to my truck.

Agua Tibia 17,986 acres, designated 1975, located in the Cleveland National Forest north of the city of Escondido, east of Interstate Highway 15, and south of State Highway 79. My day hike on May 2, 2006 started at

the Wild Horse Trailhead off State Highway 79. There was a campground here, but it was closed to protect an endangered toad. The trail, however, was open. The terrain was classic California chaparral with lots of plants in flower. There were also oak trees along riparian areas. The area appeared to receive little visitation. I certainly saw nobody.

Pine Creek 13,261 acres, designated 1984, located in the Cleveland National Forest just south of Interstate Highway 8 and east of the city of Alpine. My day hike on May 3, 2006 began at the Horsethief Trailhead at the western wilderness boundary, then went along the Espinosa Trail to the eastern wilderness boundary. The riparian areas along the creek were pleasant. I saw my first Hutton's vireo.

CALIFORNIA

One-Star Areas

★

Ishi 41,840 acres, designated 1984, located in the Lassen National Forest south of Lassen Volcanic National Park. The nearest town is Chester and the easiest access is from State Highway 32. The area is named after the famous last member of a local Native American tribe who lived in this area. I had a lot of trouble finding this wilderness. I was also advised by locals not to go there alone. My day hike on September 27, 2007 began at the Black Rock Campground. I went west out of the campground on the Mill Creek Trail. The terrain was dry timber in a steep-sided basalt valley full of cows. The terrain was neither interesting nor pleasant, and after a few miles I turned around and went back to the trailhead. The only saving feature of this bleak place was the Black Rock itself. It was an old volcanic throat just outside the wilderness. It might be just me, but out of 600 wilderness areas this just might be the one I was most glad to see in my rearview mirror. I do not recommend it.

Granite Chief 25,093 acres, designated 1984, located in the Tahoe National Forest west of State Highway 89 and south of the town of Truckee. The eastern wilderness boundary runs along the top of the Squaw Valley ski area. The PCT runs through the eastern portion of the wilderness. My day hike on September 15, 2004 began at the Parker Pass Trailhead with a lot of other vehicles. I hiked the PCT north, some of it on the eastern wilderness boundary, and I distinctly recall seeing the lift machinery at the top of the ski hill. There were a lot of other people and I just did not like the area.

Sanhedrin 10,571 acres, designated 2006, located in the Mendocino National Forest south of the Yuki Wilderness and northwest of Lake Pillsbury. There were no trails. I attempted two hikes on June 15, 2009. My first attempt began at the top of Big Signal Peak. There was some fog and intermittent rain, but I made an effort to walk west. There was no hint of a trail anywhere and there was nasty, thick, thorny brush. I could tell pretty quickly that I was not going to get very far from here, so I went back and drove down the road a bit to the boundary between the wilderness and private property (posted). I thought this was Vulture Spring. There was a bit of a path here heading northwest into the wilderness. There was moist meadow with springs and a small stream. However, I did not go far until I encountered another private property sign. I gave up and went back to my truck. I had seen nothing remotely interesting. This was not a successful day.

Garcia 14,000 acres, designated 1992
Machesna Mountain 20,000 acres, designated 1984
I discuss these two areas together because they are close together and their terrain is similar, and I hiked them on consecutive days. Both areas are in the Los Padres National Forest east of San Louis Obispo and east of the Santa Lucia Wilderness. My day hike on May 24, 2005 was in the Garcia. I began along Trout Creek. There was a nice riparian area but the trail was dim. I ultimately came to an overgrown backcountry campsite called Buckeye. This area clearly did not get much visitation. Going beyond Buckeye, the trail almost disappeared and there was a lot of poison oak. Because I was

watching my feet, I did not see the big cinnamon bear right in front of me. No problem, he just hustled into the brush. The terrain here was chaparral.

I knew that I wanted to visit the Machesna Mountain Wilderness the next day, so I drove a few miles northeast to the USFS campground called La Panza. The Los Padres has a lot of almost derelict primitive campgrounds and this was one. I was the only human here. However, I was not alone. With the last direct rays of sun hitting my campsite, in fluttered a long-eared owl (not a great horned). She hooted a bit and then left before I could get a photograph. Later, when it was almost dark, she returned, accompanied by five fledglings. I believed this was their very first night out of the nest. They proceeded to put on an amazing show. They practiced hopping along branches of the pine trees. They hopped and fluttered from one branch to another. They were trying all sorts of flight maneuvers, sometimes failing hilariously. This went on until it was truly dark and I just couldn't see, but I thought they left. I will see this performance in my mind for as long as I live. It was probably the most amazing bird behavior I have ever seen.

The next day, May 25, 2005, was a day for a hike in the Machesna Mountain Wilderness. Again, there were no signs, but I drove a short distance to an off-road-vehicle track along the northern wilderness boundary. I started to walk down this track until I came to a locked gate where there actually was a sign for a trail into the wilderness. I know I hiked past Castle Crag because I have a photo so named. I went farther, but the terrain was simply uninteresting and not even pleasant, in part because of obvious heavy cattle use, so I turned around and left.

Magic Mountain 12,282 acres, designated 2009, located in the Angeles National Forest south of the Soledad Canyon Road and north of the communications site on Magic Mountain. On April 11, 2011 I did a day hike from a bit south of the Soledad Canyon Road most of the way up to the communications site. The terrain was pure chaparral *and it was full of ticks*. I must say that this was one of the least interesting wilderness areas I have seen. Multiple signs and sounds of human activity were always present. If there were redeeming features, I did not see them.

Kiavah 80,580 acres, designated 1994, located in the southern Sequoia National Forest and adjacent BLM lands. It is south and a bit east of the Domeland Wilderness, separated by State Highway 178. The PCT runs through the wilderness. My day hike on April 16, 2007 began at the Walker Pass Trailhead off State Highway 178. I went south on the PCT and hiked about one-third of the way to the southern wilderness boundary. The terrain was a transition zone between the southern Sierra Nevada and the true desert to the south with pinon, evergreen oak, sage, and manzanita and ponderosa pine at higher elevations. This area saw heavy use by cattle. I saw no water sources. The air pollution was bad, no use in trying to take photographs of distant mountains. By far the most interesting thing I saw this day was a US Air Force F117A (the original stealth fighter) flying just over my head.

Hauser 5,100 acres, designated 1984, located in the Cleveland National Forest south of Interstate Highway 8 and south of the Pine Creek Wilderness. It is close to the Mexican border. My day hike on May 4, 2006 began with a stop with the USFS to talk to knowledgeable people about the area with questions about safety on my mind. The advice that I got was to hike only the PCT and to avoid Hauser Canyon because of illegal activity. I took this advice and began my day hike at a PCT trailhead in Lake Morena County Park. My route went south a short distance to the wilderness boundary. The trail cut through the southeast corner of the wilderness. I walked this fraction of a mile to the southern wilderness boundary with a view into Hauser Canyon. Nothing on my route was either pleasant or interesting. Other than for PCT through-hikers, I do not recommend this area.

Cirque of the Towers from Popo Agie River, Popo Agie Wilderness.

The Northern Rockies

The Northern Rockies can be described by the biomes temperate coniferous forest with occasional tundra and high-mountain ice at high elevations and dry shrublands at low elevations. Most of the region is dry, much drier than the Pacific Northwest. Some high-elevation areas can capture enough snowfall to allow glacier formation, but the ice is disappearing rapidly with global warming. Temperature variations can be quite large, with cold winters and warm to hot summers. Elevation varies greatly, from near sea level in parts of Nevada to more than 13,000 feet in Wyoming, Colorado, and Utah. Elevation is an important variable for ecosystems found in this region. For my purposes here, I include the states of Idaho, Montana, Wyoming, Colorado, Nevada, and Utah in the Northern Rockies. Some Nevada, and a few Utah areas should probably be included in a desert biome, but other areas fit with coniferous forest and dry shrubland.

A useful reference book for my travels in Colorado was John Fielder and Mark Pearson's *Colorado's Wilderness Areas* published by Westcliffe Publishers.

SAWTOOTH

★ ★ ★ ★ ★

Size: 217,658 acres   **Year Designated:** 1972
Responsible Agency: USFS

The Sawtooth Wilderness is located in the Sawtooth National Forest west of State Highway 75 and south and east of State Highway 21. The famous ski town of Ketchum-Sun Valley is to the south and the small town of Stanley is just to the northeast.

MY VISITS: Multiple backpacking trips from 1979 to 2014

According to my records I have made seven or eight backpacking trips covering at least forty-three days in the Sawtooth Wilderness. This area is an absolute jewel, sharp, rugged peaks, hard rock, dozens of lakes, coniferous forest, and occasional meadows.

My most recent trip in 2014 was to show my friend Maya the beauty of this place on a three-day September backpack around the famous Twin Lakes-Toxaway Lake loop. I had done this hike years earlier and it was marvelous to see it again. The trip began at the Tin Cup Trailhead near Petit Lake. Our route went first to Alice Lake, then to Twin Lakes where we camped our first night. The next day we went over a divide and dropped into Toxaway Lake. Here we deviated from the standard loop and went north to Edna and Imogene Lakes with spectacular views, camping at Edith Lake. On the third day we hiked past Farley Lake and back to the trailhead. I recommend this area and this hike to everybody who likes the outdoors. Some people do this loop hike in one day. Some people *run* the loop in one day. My recommendation is to take at least two days. One thing a hiker will not find here is solitude. The Sawtooth Wilderness has been discovered. The dramatic population growth around Boise has made the area a popular destination.

Toxaway Lake, Sawtooth Wilderness

Ski camp, Sawtooth Wilderness

My first time on the Twin Lakes-Toxaway Lake trails was in early July 1981 on an eight-day trip with a small group of friends from the Midwest (I was then living in Idaho). We went into the Payette River drainage to Virginia, Edna, Ardeth, Spangle and Little Spangle Lakes, Lake Ingeborg, and finally Plummer Lake. From Plummer Lake we day hiked to the summits of Mount Everly (9,867 feet) and Plummer Peak with great views south into the Queens River Valley.

I have done one and perhaps two trips out of the Iron Gate Trailhead to Sawtooth Lake and Mount Regan and the Trailer Lakes, Baron Creek, and the Baron Lakes. I have also backpacked solo from Redfish Lake up to the Cramer Lakes neighborhood. There was at least one solo backpack from the Grandjean Trailhead on the west side of the wilderness, but my notes do not tell me where I went.

In 1984 I did a four-day trip with two friends on a cross-country ski trip. I am a pretty poor skier and am worse when carrying a multi-day pack. We started at Redfish Lake and went to the Stephens Lakes, then across a divide and into the Braxon and Baron Lakes. It was early May and warm, but there was still *a lot* of snow. One memory I have from this trip is the sound of thunder in the afternoons. It was not thunder, but the sound of avalanches. We made our route selections carefully. The photo is a scan of an old print, not the best but a good sense of the time and place.

This is a five-star area. That means go there. I'm serious. This is a great destination.

Absaroka-Beartooth

Size: 943,626 acres   **Year Designated:** 1978
Responsible Agency: USFS

The Absaroka-Beartooth Wilderness is located in the Custer Gallatin National Forest in Montana and Wyoming. Interstate Highway 90 is to the north and US Highway 212 skirts the southern part of the wilderness. Nearby towns are Red Lodge, Cooke City, and Gardiner in Montana. Yellowstone National Park is to the southwest. Today there are two National Geographic Trails Illustrated maps devoted to this wilderness.

MY VISITS: Early July 1984 and September 10–17, 1987 and September 25–27, 2018 and August 8–14, 2019

The first trip was a seven-day backpack (my records do not include the exact dates) with two friends, beginning at the East Rosebud Trailhead. I remember being very impressed with the scenery as soon as we got out of the car. It was early July and there was still a fair bit of snow around. The creeks were running full and the waterfalls were spectacular. Our route ran up the East Rosebud Trail past Rainbow Lake and Lake of the Falls and Dewy Lake. I remember camping at Dewy Lake and then making a day hike to the summit of Mount Dewy (11,436 feet). We continued on up to the base of a divide at Fossil Lake. My memory is very tenuous about the rest of the trip. I think there was quite a bit of snow at Fossil Lake and we did not go much farther but turned around and retraced our steps. Up to this point I had done little in Montana and was really impressed and promised to come back. To this day I still recommend this trip to just about anybody who likes wild places (and I did it again in 2019).

The second trip was very ambitious. There were five of us and we did a vehicle shuttle, starting at a trailhead for the Lady of the Lake Trail near Colter Pass. We went to the Lady of the Lake and north to Lower Aero Lake where the trail ended. We proceeded cross country to Upper Aero Lake and past Rough Lake and then to the Sky Top Lakes. We camped

at the north end of the Sky Top Lakes hoping to climb Granite Peak, the tallest in Montana at 12,799 feet. The next day was to be summit day. There were four of us climbing (and one not). The route from Sky Top to the summit was technical but not difficult. Unfortunately, we had only one rope for four climbers and our progress was slow. We ultimately had to give up because it was getting too late. This portion of the wilderness was high, wide, and open and cross-country travel was not difficult. We continued south to Fossil Lake, then past Mariane Lake to Otter Lake where there was a trail. We took the trail east to Lake Elaine and Green Lake and Kidney Lake, then south on the Beartooth High Lakes Trail past Beauty Lake, Night Lake, and finally Island Lake where we had stashed a vehicle. This was a wonderful trip. The weather was good and the scenery always spectacular.

After a thirty-one-year absence I returned to this wilderness in 2018. I made a visit of the greater Rock Creek area in the eastern part of the wilderness. I first did a quick overnight trip up the Lake Fork of Rock Creek, camping at Keyser Brown Lake. Separately I did a three-day backpack up the West Fork of Rock Creek, camping at the base of Sundance Pass with a day hike over the pass to September Morn Lake. This was a slightly gentler part of the wilderness with meadows and open forest to go along with some dramatic peaks. The photo is from Quinnebaugh Meadow. The Absaroka-Beartooth remains one of my favorite areas.

Bridger   Fitzpatrick   Popo Agie

★ ★ ★ ★ ★   ★ ★ ★ ★ ★   ★ ★ ★ ★ ★

BRIDGER	**Size:** 428,169 acres	**Year Designated:** 1964	**Responsible Agency:** USFS
FITZPATRICK	**Size:** 198,838 acres	**Year Designated:** 1976	**Responsible Agency:** USFS
POPO AGIE	**Size:** 101,991 acres	**Year Designated:** 1984	**Responsible Agency:** USFS

These three wilderness areas are located in the Bridger-Teton and Shoshone National Forests. They are described together here because they are contiguous and make up the bulk of the Wind River Range. The Bridger Wilderness is west of the Continental Divide and the Fitzpatrick and Popo Agie are east of the Divide. On a historical note, Jim Bridger was a famous trapper, explorer, and overall mountain man in Wyoming. Tom Fitzpatrick was a similar early trapper and mountain man known for a severely injured hand. The name Popo Agie is from the local Native Americans and is pronounced Po Po Zhuh.

These areas can be accessed by US Highway 191 on the west, US Highway 287 on the east and north, and State Highway 28 on the south. The nearby towns are Pinedale on the west, Lander on the east, and Dubois on the north. Some of the eastern Wind River Range is on the Wind River Indian Reservation. Access is controlled by the Shoshone and Arapaho tribes. Permits are required to be on reservation land. Please respect the tribes' rights.

These areas are well known and have been thoroughly described. My book shelf includes Finis Mitchell's *Wind River Trails,* Wasatch Publishers, 1975; Joe Kelsey's *Climbing and Hiking in the Wind River Mountains,* Chockstone Press, 1994; and Orrin H. Bonney and Lorraine Bonney's *Field Book Wind River Range,* 1960. This mountain range is world famous among technical climbers as well as ordinary hikers and backpackers. The Bonney and Bonney book is basically a technical climbing guide. Kelsey's book is also mostly oriented to technical climbers but does give useful information for backpackers. Earthwalk Press publishes a two-piece map for the Wind River Range.

MY VISITS: At least 60 backpacking trips covering about 300 days between 1978 and 2017

According to my records I have spent at least 223 days in the Bridger Wilderness, 46 days in the Fitzpatrick, and 25 days in the Popo Agie, not including day hikes. That is a lot of time and a lot of miles. I will attempt to give an overview here of main features and describe a few of my favorite destinations.

The Wind River Range is characterized by large expanses of glacier-carved granite. There are some dramatic sheer walls, many deep lakes, and numerous peaks over 13,000 feet. Lower elevations include huge meadows, often called parks, and forested areas with fir and pine and still more lakes. Because of the high elevations, much of the wilderness is above tree line and the hiker is simply traveling through open granite. This leads to many opportunities for easy off-trail travel. The Continental Divide and its associated Continental Divide Trail (CDT) run through the range.

In the northern part of the range there are some remaining glaciers that are the source of the Green River. A popular access point is the Green River Lakes Trailhead. The hiker is immediately presented with a view of the iconic Squaretop Mountain. The summit of Squaretop can be easily gained from its southern side.

Another popular trailhead for the Bridger Wilderness is at Elkhart Park, located at the end of a paved road from the town of Pinedale. One reason for the popularity is its elevation, just over 9,000 feet. Another reason is its proximity to Island Lake and the climbing Mecca of Titcomb Basin. The photo here shows Island Lake. It was taken on my introductory trip to the Wind River Range in September of 1978. The previous day had been stormy, but on the morning of the photo the lake was mirror smooth. In the right-of-center background is Fremont Peak (13,745 feet). It is a massive peak and not difficult to climb if the weather is good. I summited in August of 1984.

A third major trailhead provides access from the west at Big Sandy Openings. This popular trailhead quickly takes hikers to a network of trails

covering the southern part of the Bridger Wilderness. It is also a favorite entry point for climbers heading to the deservedly famous Cirque of the Towers. One of my favorite routes goes from Big Sandy Openings to Big Sandy Lake, then south to Clear Lake, Deep Lake, Temple Peak, and Temple Lake. The stretch of trail between Clear and Deep Lakes follows an almost continuous flow of water over smooth granite and provides superb views of the Cirque of the Towers.

On the east side of the range a popular trailhead is at the Trail Lake Ranch at the end of a road from US Highway 287 south of the town of DuBois. From here the Glacier Trail goes south into the Fitzpatrick Wilderness and provides climber access to the east side of Gannet Peak, the tallest in Wyoming at 13,804 feet. If a hiker is comfortable with off-trail travel, this trailhead also allows quick access to the Continental Divide via Lake Louise, Ross Lake, Upper Ross Lake, and Mile-Long Lake. Once on the Divide, one can hike south many miles around glaciers and the easily hiked summits of Northwest Peak (13,246 feet), Downs Mountain (13,349 feet), Klondike Peak (13,114 feet), Pedestal Peak (13,340 feet), and Flagstone Peak (13,450 feet). In what may be my lifetime best backpacking trip, two friends and I did pretty much this trip in August of 2003. After Flagstone Peak, we dropped east of the Divide into the Downs Fork drainage, arriving in Downs Fork Meadows. We than hiked the Glacier Trail back to our trailhead.

On a separate trip in 1985 two friends and I took a six-day backpack to the Divide from the Green River Lakes Trailhead (but mostly off-trail). We went to Baker Lake just west of the Divide, then up Yukon Peak. I lobbied to try for the summit of Klondike but was outvoted. In 1993 I did a solo six-day backpack from the Green River Lakes Trailhead on the Roaring Fork Trail past Crescent Lake and on to Faler Lake, then some semi-serious off-trail hiking to (almost) Bear Lake, then up to the Divide and the summit of Northwest Peak. Views to the west were fabulous.

The Popo Agie Wilderness is located east of the Continental Divide and south of the Wind River Indian Reservation. Popular trailheads for access from the east are Dickinson Park and the Worthen Reservoir. Dickinson Park can only be accessed by driving through the Indian reservation. This was not a problem when I went there in 1986, but the tribes may have changed their policies.

My first trip into the Popo Agie from the east was in 1983 when a friend and I departed the Worthen Reservoir Trailhead and headed northwest through Pinto Park and then up the Popo Agie River to the Cirque of the Towers. The view of the Cirque was spectacular. A seven-day trip followed in 1986 beginning at Dickinson Park and going west to Grave Lake, then the South Fork Lakes and Washakie Lake. This was marvelous, gentle country. The peaks were still there, but not so dramatically sharp. There were big lakes, big parks, and good views.

So yes, I really feel attracted to the Wind River Range. As a western Wyoming resident this is my back yard. I still keep going back. I recommend it to anybody who likes mountains. One note of caution, however. The place has been discovered. If you are hiking on a trail you will see other hikers. Because of its size, many visitors hire local outfitters to take them into the wilderness. Hikers are likely to encounter big strings of horses. They are part of the experience. Fishing is a major attraction and many outfitters specialize in fishing trips.

Grizzly bears have been pushed into the northern Wind River Range as Yellowstone populations have increased. I did a four-day backpack in the northern Fitzpatrick Wilderness in 2012, and grizzly scat and tracks were everywhere along with at least one cow killed by a bear. My advice to hikers is to carry pepper spray and be careful not to surprise the beasts.

Island Lake, Bridger Wilderness

Gros Ventre

★ ★ ★ ★ ★

Size: 285,567 acres **Year Designated:** 1984
Responsible Agency: USFS

Between the hectic bustle of Jackson to the west and the busy trails in the Wind River Range to the southeast, the Gros Ventre Wilderness can provide a calm, quiet destination with loads of scenery waiting for hiker explorations. The wilderness is in the Bridger-Teton National Forest, and access is from US Highway 191 to the south and from roads out of Jackson on the west. The tastefully developed Granite Hot Springs at the southern wilderness boundary draws quite a number of folks year-round. Trailheads along the road to the hot springs provide hiker access. In my experience hiker visitation has been light. The area is popular with hunters, and outfitter pack strings are common in season. The area has also been a refuge for grizzly bears.

The terrain features lush, green meadows, waterfalls, lakes, and tall peaks, although the peaks are not as dramatically spiked as those of the Tetons and Wind River Range. The rock is mostly sedimentary (limestone) in contrast with other nearby areas.

MY VISITS: Four backpacking trips and some day hikes between 1993 and 2013

The 1993 backpacks were both in the central part of the wilderness; the first went from the Granite Hot Springs road east to Shoal Creek, past Shoal Falls and on to Shoal Lake, then north into the Crystal Creek valley and the summit of Crystal Peak (10,967 feet). The second trip began at the Goosewing Guard Station along the Gros Ventre River Road. My route was southwest through the beautiful Two-Echo Park, south to the Six Lakes, then east to the Cowboy Camp, then making a loop back to Goosewing. I remember scaring up a large herd of elk on one of these trips.

A 1994 trip took me to Brewster Lake and the summits of Triangle Peak and Darwin Peak. I also remember a woman running up behind me asking if I was carrying a firearm. One of her horses had broken a leg and she wanted to shoot it. I was unable to help as I was unarmed.

The 2013 trip was to show my friend Maya the Gros Ventre. We began at

the Granite Hot Springs and followed Granite Creek partway to Turquois Lake, camping near Granite Creek. The next day we did a day hike to Turquois Lake, then made a loop going to the Cash Creek Divide and back to our campsite. Day three was spent hiking back along Crystal Creek to the hot springs. This was a lovely trip with warm days, sun, and fall colors starting to appear. We pretty much had the wilderness to ourselves.

WYOMING
Washakie
★ ★ ★ ★ ★

Size: 704,529 acres   **Year Designated:** 1964
Responsible Agency: USFS

The Washakie Wilderness is located in the Shoshone National Forest south of US Highway 14/16/20, east of Yellowstone National Park and east of the Teton Wilderness. The city of Cody is to the east.

MY VISITS: August 28–30, 2009 and August 25–27, 2010 and August 23–26, 2012 plus day hikes

I had long wanted to do the first backpack. An Idaho friend and I began at the Double Cabin Trailhead north of the town of Dubois. We went north on the Frontier Creek Trail, then west on the Cougar Creek Trail, and climbed to a high plateau above tree line where we set up camp. The next day we made a long day hike south on the Twilight Creek Trail to Cathedral Peak. This offered wonderful views to the west of the Five Pockets and Raggedtop Mountain. The whole day was spent above tree line.

The 2010 backpack was a solo trip up the Wiggins Fork Trail to Burwell Pass and adjacent high ridges. More days in steep, almost forbidding terrain of highly eroded volcanic features. The photo is from this trip. It gives a clear testament to the condition of the forests in this area. They are dying from insect infestation. The trees here were whitebark pine, an important

Upper Wiggins Creek with dead whitebark pine trees, Washakie Wilderness

Elk near Bear Creek Pass, Washakie Wilderness

food source for grizzly bears. The fire potential from these dead trees is also frightening. The photo also gives one the sense of just how austere this mountain range is.

The 2012 backpack was a solo trip that began at the East Fork (of the Wind River) Trailhead. There were lots of people around with horses, but no other hikers. I went north to near a junction with the Ninemile Trail. The trail here was full of bear tracks. Large bear tracks. My second day I did a day hike to East Fork Pass with a side trip to Coal Chute Pass. Day three I took the Ninemile Trail to upper Bear Creek with a side trip to Bear Creek Pass. There were elk here. I camped in upper Bear Creek. The last day was just going out the way I came in.

A few day hikes are also worth noting. One hike on August 20, 2009 went up Kitty Creek from a trailhead on US Highway 14/16/20. This was a marvelous day with views, an interesting old volcanic cone, and nice meadows. Another hike on August 21 went up from the South Fork (of the Shoshone River) Road to Boulder Ridge, then along the ridge for more great views. The next day, August 22, I went up Deer Creek from the other side of the South Fork Road. I got as far as the Yellowstone Park boundary for at least decent views.

This is a wonderful area. Very wild (although visitors will probably see horse groups) and austere but still scenic with a lot of wildlife, some of which the hiker needs to be careful of.

Jedediah Smith

★ ★ ★ ★ ★

Size: 123,451 acres   **Year Designated:** 1984
Responsible Agency: USFS

Jedediah Smith was an early frontier trapper, hunter, and explorer of the American West. His namesake wilderness is located just west of Grand Teton National Park in the Caribou-Targhee National Forest. It makes up what is known as the west slope of the Tetons. The terrain is quite rugged with mostly sedimentary rock, older than the more dramatic granite of the Tetons. There are several lakes and expansive meadows. The most direct access is from roads off Idaho State Highway 33 near the towns of Victor, Driggs, and Tetonia. The northernmost portion of the wilderness can be accessed from the old Reclamation Road between Ashton, Idaho, and the Rockefeller Parkway.

MY VISITS: Many visits between 1982 and 1993

My record keeping was not the most detailed back in the 1980s and 1990s. Records were pretty much just phrases on my employer's appoint-

Green Lake Basin, Jedediah Smith Wilderness

Teton Canyon Shelf, Jedediah Smith Wilderness

ment calendar and little entries on the edges of slides. However, there are at least 28 calendar entries noting some destination in what is now the Jedediah Smith Wilderness. I remember the terrain, but I don't remember details of the trips like where I started, how long I was out, or who my companions may have been. In these years I was living nearby in Idaho Falls, close enough for day trips. My outdoor-oriented friends were sometimes hard-core cross-country skiers, and the Jedediah Smith had lots of opportunities for skiing, especially in spring. The western slope of the Teton Range gets a lot of snow. Essentially all of these trips originated on the west side of the wilderness.

So, where have I been? In the north I have been to the summit of Hominy Peak (8,263 feet). The north end of the wilderness is relatively gentle and rather heavily timbered. Even in these "old" days, this was known to be grizzly bear country, and I made lots of noise. I have also been up the North Fork of Bitch Creek, perhaps as far east as Conant Pass with Teton Park. I have little memory of these hikes. More interesting were hikes up Badger Creek. Here a trail takes the hiker close to the Teton Park boundary, and a little off-trail exploration leads to two lovely lakes just inside the park. I took multiple friends to see this neat little out-of-the-way destination.

A bit farther south is the North Leigh Trailhead and the Tin Cup Trail to Green Lake, then to the Granite Lake Basin, making a nice loop back to the trailhead. I think I did this trip more than once as both a day hike and as an overnighter. A little cross-country navigation can take one to the summit of Little's Peak on the park boundary for good views into the park.

The most popular trailhead in the wilderness is the one at the end of the Teton Canyon Road. One popular day hike from here is to the summit of Table Mountain (11,106 feet). The early part of this hike gives few views of what is to come, but as one approaches the summit, the Teton peaks are right there staring the hiker in the face. I rate this as one of the best day hikes in the American West. I have hiked it multiple times and skied it once. One Easter weekend (in April) a friend and I decided to ski just below the Table Mountain summit and descend into Cascade Canyon in Teton Park, coming back to a road at Jenny Lake where we had stashed a car. Because it was still winter, the Teton Canyon Road was still snowed in, so the trip required three days and a vehicle shuttle. The weather was warm, and as we started down into Cascade Canyon snow from higher ledges was melting and sliding into the canyon. As we approached the canyon bottom, the sliding snow triggered a large slab avalanche. Had we been just a few minutes earlier we would have been goners.

A second trail from the Teton Canyon Trailhead takes the hiker into the main Teton Canyon. One branch of the trail goes up the Devil's Stairs to the Teton Canyon Shelf, which turns into the Death Canyon Shelf at the park boundary. These "shelves" are well named, a wide bench between two steep cliffs. The other branch of the trail goes more directly to Alaska Basin, another famous destination. Alaska Basin is an idyllic meadow with some trees and small lakes surrounded by dramatic peaks. I have both skied and backpacked into the basin.

South of Teton Canyon is a trailhead at Darby Canyon. The two main attractions here are the Ice Cave and Wind Cave. I have been in the canyon a few times but could never talk myself into entering the caves. The limestone in these canyons harbor multiple other caves, some quite long, but their entrances are kept secret. South of Darby Canyon a trail goes up Fox Creek. I have bad memories of skiing out Fox Creek when three of us had to abandon a multi-day trip because of bad weather. Farther south still, I have done some skiing out of Teton Pass and hiked up Coal Creek and Taylor Mountain. I have also summited Fossil Mountain (10,916 feet) twice (yes, there were fossils) and skied to the summits of Housetop Mountain and Mount Bannon.

Do I like this area? Yes. Do I recommend it? Yes. My only caution would be that this area has truly been discovered. Visitors will see lots of other visitors.

The Maroon Bells,
Maroon Bells-Snowmass Wilderness

Maroon Bells-Snowmass

★ ★ ★ ★ ★

Size: 180,962 acres   **Year Designated:** 1964
Responsible Agency: USFS

There are a lot of nice wilderness areas in Colorado and I had a hard time deciding which got five stars and which got four. This area ended up being my five-star winner. The Maroon Bells-Snowmass Wilderness is located in the Gunnison National Forest southwest of the famous ski town of Aspen. Access is easy via a road taking off from State Highway 82.

MY VISIT: August 25–27, 2005

This three-day backpack began at the West Maroon Trailhead southwest of Aspen. My route was the Four Passes Loop. I did the loop counterclockwise, first going through Minnehaha Gulch, over Buckskin Pass, then to Snowmass Lake, over Trail Rider Pass, up the North Fork of the Crystal River, over Frigid Air Pass and West Maroon Pass, down to Crater Lake, and back to the trailhead. The Bells are indeed maroon, as is some of the surrounding terrain. Both Bells are "Fourteeners," meaning they are over 14,000 feet tall. The terrain is mostly open because it is above tree line.

The Bells are popular with climbers and the wilderness is quite popular overall.

Zion

★ ★ ★ ★ ★

Size: 124,406 acres   **Year Designated:** 2009
Responsible Agency: USNPS

Most of Zion National Park is designated wilderness. The park is in southwest Utah east of Interstate Highway 15 and north of State Highway 9. The nearest city is St. George with smaller towns just outside the park. The northern part of the park, called the Kolob, can be entered directly from I-15. Nine small BLM wilderness areas are contiguous with the park. There is a National Geographic Trails Illustrated map dedicated to the park.

MY VISITS: October 26–28, 2011 and October 29–30, 2012 and a few day hikes

The first backpack was in the Kolob section of the park. It began at the Lee Pass Trailhead and followed the La Verkin Creek Trail. It was a cold, windy morning with fresh snow at the Kolob Canyons Visitor Center, but down in the canyons it was sunny and quite pleasant. I needed to obtain an overnight camping permit at the visitor center. I was in a gorgeous neighborhood. Zion is noted for its deep, sometimes narrow sandstone canyons. One reason for visiting the park late in the year is the low sun angle that makes the walls glow. In my not-so-narrow canyon the walls were glowing a brilliant red. On my way I made a small side trip to the well-known Kolob Arch. Back on the main trail I stopped at my assigned campsite, number 14. It was a cold night and I was early in the tent.

Day two of the trip was a day hike to the end of the La Verkin Creek canyon. It was an almost cold day, but with brilliant sunshine. Because of the sun angle, my route was mostly in shade, but the walls were once again on fire. Adding color was the last of the fall leaves on oak, maple, and cottonwood. Instead of following the park's Willis Creek Trail, I bushwhacked up La Verkin Creek into the BLM La Verkin Creek Wilderness until the canyon almost disappeared. Day three of the trip was spent hiking back to the trailhead.

Later, I did a day hike on the Taylor Creek Trail near the beginning of the Kolob Canyons Road. This was a lovely route on a brilliant, cool but sunny day. The trail ran between two large sandstone monoliths, ending at a nice spot called the Double Arch Alcove, although I only saw one arch. The Park Service trail ended but the canyon continued and I gave it a go. The canyon was steep and full of rubble. There was a nice waterfall on one side and some frozen waterfalls farther up. The canyon narrowed considerably beyond the waterfalls and I turned around.

On another day, I drove along State Highway 9 and a side road to a trailhead for the Chinle Trail. The trail began near an upscale residential area and the sounds of civilization lingered for a while. However, once inside the wilderness boundary it became a very neat route, providing "backside" views of some of the park's famous features including the West Temple and the Towers of the Virgin. After passing the first two official campsites, I decided to leave the trail where it began to descend and instead bushwhacked up a ridge for better views. It was another brilliant clear day and the views were spectacular.

The 2012 backpack began at the West Rim Trailhead near Lava Point. I had a permit for campsite number 8, the only site on this mesa that had water. The hike was on the West Rim Trail, which followed the Horse Pasture Plateau. My campsite was only four miles in and the spring was just barely flowing, but I set up my camp and began a day hike to my real destination: views of the famous towers and of the Virgin River. It was another beautiful, crystal clear day. I continued on the West Rim Trail and, as hoped, there were marvelous views of the towers. The towers had different color sandstone at different depths. The terrain on top was covered with trees, shrubs, and grass. I stayed on the West Rim Trail past campsites 7, 6, 5, 4, and 3, where I was able to see down into the main Virgin River Canyon. It was getting late and I had to turn around. Back at my campsite there were quite a few deer. They seemed to be annoyed by my presence because I was camped at their watering hole. They soon got over it and ignored me. The next day I returned to the trailhead.

Hikers, put this area on your bucket list.

IDAHO

Selway-Bitterroot

★ ★ ★ ★

Size: 1,340,450 acres   **Year Designated:** 1964
Responsible Agency: USFS

The Selway-Bitterroot Wilderness is located in the Nez Perce, Clearwater, and Bitterroot National Forests in the states of Idaho and Montana. Access from the east is by roads from US Highway 93, from the north from US Highway 12 and from the south by Montana State Highway 473 and Idaho State Highway 14. Depending on the destination, access may be time consuming, as this wilderness is a bit out of the way. The Frank Church-River of No Return Wilderness is to the south. At the time of my second visit, the USFS had two maps dedicated to this wilderness.

At the time of my first visit to the western part of this wilderness, a fire had been burning near my planned starting point. On my way to the trailhead I passed a fire camp. The fire crew members were cheering. It was snowing.

My starting point was the Big Fog Trailhead not far from where the Selway River (a coveted river permit) exits the wilderness. Again, this being 1992, I was not keeping detailed notes. I know where I went from my photo labels, but not my exact route. The terrain was not especially high, but quite rugged and all hard rock with forest at lower elevation. Lakes were common. The area was called the Selway Crags.

I know I took the trail past Big Fog Mountain. From there I think I stayed on a trail to the east and north, probably leaving the trail and travelling cross country to the Three Links Meadows and then up to the North Three Links Lakes. This is very open country, either too high or too rocky for forests. From the lakes I climbed a ridge, followed the ridge over Fenn Mountain (8,021 feet), and then dropped down to Florence and Lloyd Lakes. Somewhere in here I dropped into the South Three Links Lakes, probably finishing the trip by way of a trail past the Cove Lakes, then back to the trailhead.

I have a distinct memory from this trip of sitting in my camp a bit after dark and a large owl leaving a nearby tree and gliding right over my head, landing in a different tree. I turned around to face where I thought the owl had gone. After a few seconds, the scene was repeated, the owl swooping just over my head. A second time I turned around and a third time the owl swooped over my head. At that time the owl probably got bored because I did not see it again. It was too dark for me to identify the owl, but I am guessing great horned as it was fairly large. Neat.

This trip was certainly in a wild place. I don't think I saw a single other person. It was a scenic destination and I recommend it to anybody who likes wild, rocky, lake-filled country.

The second backpack was from the Montana side. I began at the Sam Billings Campground just off State Highway 473. My trail went up along Boulder Creek. I started looking for a campsite, but most suitable places had been overused by folks with horses. Two other hikers recommended I go closer to a pass into Idaho. This was good advice and I found a scenic spot. Since I was already close to Idaho, I decided to make a day trip to some unnamed lakes in Idaho. Unfortunately, getting to those lakes required off-trail travel and I ended up in dense timber and very rough terrain. I gave up, turned around, and hiked past my camp to pleasant Boulder Lake and up to Lake Crystal (no trail). Here I turned around and went back to my camp. Day three was spent going back to the trailhead.

Florence Lake in the Selway Crags,
Selway-Bitterroot Wilderness

Frank Church- River of No Return

★ ★ ★ ★

Size: 2,358,133 acres   **Year Designated:** 1980
Responsible Agency: USFS

The Frank Church-River of No Return Wilderness is located in central Idaho in the Nez Perce, Salmon, Payette, Challis, Boise, and Bitterroot National Forests. It is the largest wilderness outside of Alaska. Perhaps the biggest attractions are the Middle Fork and Main Fork of the Salmon River. Both are part of the national Wild and Scenic River System. Both are very popular with boaters and floaters. Even though motorized transport is prohibited in most wilderness areas, jet boats are permitted on the Main Fork of the Salmon and a few airstrips are still allowed. The area is also quite popular with hunters and fishers. Horse-supported trips are common. Gold has been sought and occasionally found in and around the wilderness. Even today the area is remote. Access is typically from US Highway 93 in the east and State Highways 75 and 21 to the south. Many trailheads will require a long time on unpaved roads. This area is often densely timbered and in recent decades has seen large, severe fires. Most of my twenty-first-century trips have been through large stretches of black sticks. For my recent visits, the USFS had two maps dedicated to this wilderness.

Frank Church was a senator from Idaho and was the US Senate sponsor of the 1964 Wilderness Act. Somewhere I have heard that the term River of No Return is the way the local Native Americans referred to the Salmon River.

MY VISITS: Five backpacking trips and some day hikes between 1982 and 2014

My first three trips began at the Crags Trailhead in the eastern part of the wilderness and went through the Bighorn Crags in dramatic hard-rock terrain dotted with lakes.

A 1993 trip was with several friends on their annual steelhead fishing trip on the Main Fork of the Salmon River. We began at the Corn Creek Trailhead and hiked downstream, setting up the fishing camp. I do not fish, but this was a perfect opportunity to see a different part of the wilderness. The terrain here was much less dramatic than the Bighorn Crags, mostly forest and the river was pretty big. While the others fished, I hiked, mostly just along the river.

My friend Maya and I did a day hike on September 23, 2013 starting at the Langer Lake Trailhead and hiking up past Langer Lake and then to Roughneck Lake and Peak and Island Lake. We went to a pass overlooking the Finger Lakes and hoped to do a loop hike back to Langer Lake. The map showed this as a feasible route. However, the entire area had a severe fire in 2012 and another fire before that, so the trail was very indistinct in places, there was a lot of deadfall, and the trail signs had disappeared. My old girlfriend Prudence suggested that we turn around, so we did.

Later that fall Maya and I returned to "The Frank." From State Highway 21 we took a good but unpaved road to the Blue Bunch Trailhead. While it was dry at the trailhead, there had been some recent snow. We took the Blue Bunch Mountain Trail to its snowy summit. The snow had time to become firm sitting in the sun, so the hiking was pretty easy. It was also pleasant with good views in most directions. Some of the surroundings had seen recent fires although Blue Bunch Mountain itself had been spared. This portion of the wilderness was unlike the Bighorn Crags or Salmon River canyons. It was thinly timbered and quite open with large meadows at lower elevation. The terrain was much gentler than the Crags.

The next day Maya and I drove north to the Dagger Falls Trailhead. This is a very famous spot for river runners to begin a trip down the Middle Fork of the Salmon River. We hiked upstream on a nice fall day with just a few late remnants of color. This was my first and most likely only view of the famous Middle Fork.

Another part of this wilderness of which I have heard tales of various heights is the Loon Creek area. From State Highway 75 we took an unpaved road to the old ghost town of Bonanza, which is now a historical site.

The main feature was an old dredge that had once forced its way up the Yankee Fork of the Salmon River sifting gravel for gold. I considered it worth a visit. Continuing on up the road we arrived at a USFS station (unoccupied) and a guest ranch. We did not immediately see where a trail started up Loon Creek, so we went to the guest ranch and got our directions. We set out and one of the first things we saw were signs that said, "Danger, Explosives Bunker," and back in the trees was a large metal box on a concrete pad. I had *no* idea who was storing explosives or what their purpose would have been.

Not very far up the trail we entered burned forest, spotty at first, then essentially 100 percent burned. Someone had tried to mark the trail with lines of stones or burned sticks. After a pretty serious climb, we finally got to Horseshoe Lake and found a campsite away from dead trees. The next day we did a day hike up the trail to Knapp Pass, then along a ridge north for views of Horseshoe Lake and four higher lakes. We also had good views of the Knapp Lakes and surrounding peaks and ridges, especially Mount Loening. We had lunch on a small summit above Fish Lake, and then made a roundabout path back to our Horseshoe Lake camp. We had a thunderstorm during the night. The next day we went back to our truck. We never saw another soul on this trip.

This wilderness contains a huge variety of terrain. Its size makes it difficult for a hiker to see all the sights. My conclusion is that it is certainly worth four stars, but my recommendation is that hikers might find the Bighorn Crags their best first choice.

IDAHO

Cecil D. Andrus-White Clouds

★ ★ ★ ★

Size: 90,769 acres   **Year Designated:** 2015
Responsible Agency: USFS

This wilderness is located in the Sawtooth National Forest. Access can be from the west and State Highway 75 or from the northeast from US Highway 93 and a road that runs along the East Fork of the Salmon River. There is a map that includes the White Cloud Wilderness published by Adventure Maps.

I cannot resist telling a tale about decisions on wilderness designation in Idaho. There was a major round of new designations in the early 1980s, especially 1984. This round was quite contentious in Idaho. Conservationists wanted more wilderness designation and resource businesses wanted less. In a classic decision-making process, protagonists on each side decided to lock themselves in a room with maps and not leave until they had an agreement. On the pro wilderness side was Idaho governor Cecil D. Andrus. His opponent was US senator Jim McClure. They came out with a proposal for just over one million acres of new national forest wilderness. When the compromise was made public, the environmental organizations were furious. Their attitude was there was just too much left out. They wanted the deal defeated. I attended a meeting in Idaho Falls where the pro wilderness groups urged defeat of the plan. I supported the plan. One of the opponents stuck his face a few inches from

Big Boulder Basin, Cecil D Andrus-White Clouds Wilderness

my face and called me a traitor to the wilderness cause. Without support from environmental groups the compromise was defeated. There were zero new acres designated. Fast forward to 2015. Finally, three new areas were designated. One of them was the Cecil D. Andrus-White Clouds Wilderness, one was the Hemmingway-Boulders Wilderness, and the third was the Jim McClure-Jerry Peak Wilderness. Their total acreage was 275,665 acres. In 1984 supporters could have had a million acres. (Some BLM wilderness areas were designated in 2009.)

MY VISITS: A two- or three-day backpack before 1983 and September 3–9, 1983

I was not keeping detailed notes in the 1980s, and I have no record of my first visit, only a memory of beginning at a trailhead near Livingston Mill (an old gold mining site) and hiking up among some lovely pale peaks and blue lakes among sparse timber. I was favorably impressed. In 1983 I did record dates for a three-day backpack with a coworker, again starting at Livingston Mill. Our destinations were recorded on photographs. Our route ran south along an ATV-legal trail until a hiking trail past the Boulder Chain Lakes, then off-trail into a canyon with Shallow, Noisy, and Scree Lakes. Next, we scrambled up to a trail that led us into the Boulder Chain Lakes and back to the ATV-legal trail, making a balloon-shaped route. We were both impressed. This was very nice country and I recommend it to just about any hiker.

Craters of the Moon

★ ★ ★ ★

Size: 43,243 acres   **Year Designated:** 1970
Responsible Agency: USNPS

Much of the Craters of the Moon National Monument is designated wilderness. It is located west of the city of Idaho Falls and south of the small town of Arco. Access is easy because US Highways 20/26/93 pass through the monument.

MY VISITS: Many times, especially in the 1980s

This area was in my back yard when I lived in Idaho Falls. I went there often, especially on day hikes. I often took out-of-town visitors there. The terrain is completely volcanic and is one of the best examples of volcanic features I have seen (along with Lassen Volcanic). There are cinder cones, splatter cones, lava tube caves, and huge expanses of lava flows to the south. Most of the volcanic activity was non-explosive, just huge flows of lava from rifts. The volcanic activity was fairly recent. My memory is that some activity was just a few thousand years ago.

The wilderness portion of the monument is in its southern section. I spent a fair bit of time there just poking around and enjoying the quiet. My impression was that the wilderness got few visitors.

I did decide one weekend that I wanted to spend one night sleeping in a volcano. My choice was Crescent Butte, not very far south of the end of the road. It was indeed a quiet night.

I recommend this wilderness to just about any hiker. One word of caution, however. Bring a GPS. As you can see in the photo, beyond Crescent Butte the lava flows are pretty featureless. One can easily get lost.

Crescent Butte,
Craters of the Moon Wilderness

MONTANA
Anaconda-Pintler

★ ★ ★ ★

Size: 158,615 acres   **Year Designated:** 1964
Responsible Agency: USFS

The Anaconda-Pintler Wilderness spans the Continental Divide in the Bearverhead-Deerlodge and Bitterroot National Forests. The area is southwest of the town of Anaconda and can be accessed by Forest Service roads from State Highways 38 (north) and 43 (south).

MY VISIT : September 16–19, 1992

Once again, the notes on my trip are very cryptic. I have some labeled slides and entries on a calendar, but nothing more. My best recollection of my route is that I started this backpacking trip at the north side of the wilderness, probably on the Hi Line Trail. My timing was good; the weather was perfect and the western larch, also called tamarack, a deciduous conifer, was in full fall color. The terrain was a nearly perfect mix of forest, lakes, and tall, jagged peaks. I have photos from Carpp Lake (also spelled Carp), Johnson Lake, and Mount Warren. I clearly remember being very impressed. While the terrain was rugged, the hiking was easy, and I recommend this area to anybody who likes to hike.

MONTANA
Cabinet Mountains

★ ★ ★ ★

Size: 94,272 acres   **Year Designated:** 1964
Responsible Agency: USFS

The Cabinet Mountains Wilderness is located in the Kaniksu and Kootenai National Forests south and west of US Highway 2. At the time of my visit there was a USFS map dedicated to this wilderness.

MY VISIT: August 31–September 2, 2006

My three-day backpack began at the Cedar Creek Trailhead where my vehicle was the only one at the trailhead parking. There was rain that day and I decided to make camp at Cedar Lake, a very nice spot. The next day was brilliantly clear and perfect for a day hike along a north-south ridge past Dome Mountain and Sugarloaf Mountain to just above Sky Lake. The summit of Snowshoe Peak and its Blackwell Glacier were almost always lurking in the background. The terrain here was dominated by bare, hard rock at

Cedar Lake, Cabinet Mountains Wilderness

high elevations and coniferous forest below. During my hike I was visited by a few just-fledged sharp-shinned hawks and I was later able to identify a peregrine falcon. This was a perfect hike in a wonderful little area. My route the third day was just going back to the trailhead.

Cloud Peak

★ ★ ★ ★

Size: 195,000 acres   **Year Designated:** 1984
Responsible Agency: USFS

The Cloud Peak Wilderness is located in the Bighorn National Forest west of the town of Buffalo. At the time of my visit there was a National Geographic Trails Illustrated map devoted to this area.

MY VISIT: September 5–7, 2007

This three-day backpack began at the West Tensleep Trailhead. My route was up a trail along West Tensleep Creek past Lake Helen, Lake Marion, and Mistymoon Lake. I continued north past Mistymoon and then left the trail where Paint Rock Creek intersects the trail. The off-trail hike up Paint Rock Creek was easy in almost completely open granite terrain and I made camp at a small lake at 10,725 feet. The second day was dedicated to going up to the summit of Cloud Peak (13,167 feet). My memory is a bit fuzzy about this day, but I think the route was pretty easy. Views were excellent. To me, this wilderness area is a lot like those making up the Wind River Range to the southwest—open granite, big lakes, scattered trees, and meadows. The Cloud Peak area, however, is much smaller and more compact. I recommend Cloud Peak to any hiker.

Lake Helen, Cloud Peak Wilderness

Teton

★ ★ ★ ★

Size: 585,468 acres   **Year Designated:** 1964
Responsible Agency: USFS

The Teton Wilderness is located in the Bridger-Teton and Shoshone National Forests west of the Washakie Wilderness and south of Yellowstone National Park. Access is from US Highways 26/287 to the south and US Highway 89/191/287 to the west. At the time of my visits there was a USFS map dedicated to this wilderness.

MY VISITS: August 20–25, 2007 plus a few day hikes

This area is big, wild, and remote. It is part of a large complex of protected land including the North Absaroka, Washakie, and Teton Wilderness areas and the backcountry of southeast Yellowstone National Park. Parts of this complex are the farthest from a road in the lower forty-eight states. The Continental Divide and its namesake trail run through this wilderness. There is a good trail system and, like other large western wilderness areas, many visitors use the service of horsepacking guides. Hunting and fishing are popular.

My "big trip" was a six-day backpack with two friends from Idaho. The trip began at a trailhead at Brooks Lake. (Even if one is not a hiker, Brooks

Headwaters of the Yellowstone River, Teton Wilderness

Lake is worth a visit for its scenic value.) Our route was north through Bear Cub Pass then into the Cub Creek drainage to the Angle Lakes Trail to the Angle Lakes. Most of this day was in relatively gentle, forested terrain sprinkled with small lakes. Our second day continued in timbered, rather gentle country with some large meadows, crossing the South Fork of the Buffalo River, then crossing Lake Creek and taking the Lake Creek Trail to a nice campsite overlooking the creek. Day three had a little rain early as we hiked north to Ferry Lake where we broke out of the trees. We made a camp at Ferry Lake with lots of daylight left, so I and one of the others decided to make a side trip east to Marston Pass. This side trip of 5.5 miles each way was the highlight of the trip for me. We were in gentle terrain above 11,000 feet through huge meadows beginning to get their fall colors. At the pass we had fabulous views into the Washakie Wilderness with its weird spires and volcanic cliffs. Wind and mists were boiling up from the Washakie, ultimately leaving us in thin fog. As we looked at the sky it was pretty certain that we would be punished for our intrusion. We were. The trip back to camp featured thunder and lightning, wind, rain, and hail. Even in August, storms at 11,000 feet can be intimidating.

On day four we left Ferry Lake and went on to Crater Lake. On the way we made a short side trip to the Continental Divide looking into the Yellowstone River Valley. We continued past Crater Lake down into the timber to Newlin Meadows where there was an unoccupied Forest Service cabin and a black bear mother with a cub and where we made a camp. On day five we worked our way back toward the trailhead, crossing the South Fork of the Buffalo River and camping above Cub Creek. Day six was a repeat of the first part of day one, going through Bear Cub Pass to Brooks Lake.

The day hikes were not particularly noteworthy. One hike in 2005 began at the Sheffield Creek Trailhead and went up to Huckleberry Mountain in the far northwest part of the wilderness. This was wild, timbered terrain that appeared to get very little traffic. Another day hike in 2010 went from a trailhead in Grand Teton National Park up Pacific Creek. This was through nearly flat meadows with scattered trees and views of the Tetons. Pacific Creek is famous as prime grizzly bear habitat although I did not see any bears.

Collegiate Peaks

★ ★ ★ ★

Size: 167,994 acres   **Year Designated:** 1980
Responsible Agency: USFS

The Collegiate Peaks Wilderness is located in the Gunnison, White River, ,and San Isabel National Forests southeast of the resort town of Aspen. Access is from State Highway 82 in the north and from Forest Road 306 in the south. The area is on the National Geographic Trails Illustrated map Buena Vista/Collegiate Peaks.

MY VISIT: August 22–24, 2005

This three-day backpack began at the Denny Creek Trailhead at the southern boundary of the wilderness. My route took me up Denny Creek, through Browns Pass and up to Lake Rebecca where I camped the first night. The second day I made a short side trip to the ridge above Rebecca Lake for a view into Missouri Basin. I then packed up and moved my camp to the head of Magdalene Gulch with a stop at the Magdalene Mine. There was a lot of fascinating old mining equipment scattered about slowly becoming rust. My memory tells me that there was still an open mine shaft. The morning of the third day I went back up the ridge behind the gulch and to an unnamed summit at 13,964 feet. I then returned to my camp, packed up, and went back to the trailhead. This was a very nice, easy little trip through mostly open terrain above tree line. I found the old mine interesting, and recommend the area to just about any hiker.

Collegiate Peaks Wilderness

Hunter-Fryingpan

★ ★ ★ ★

Size: 82,729 acres   **Year Designated:** 1978
Responsible Agency: USFS

Fryingpan Lakes, Hunter-Fryingpan Wilderness

The Hunter-Fryingpan Wilderness is located in the White River National Forest east of the resort town of Aspen and north of the Collegiate Peaks Wilderness. Access is by State Highway 82 on the south and to the north by Forest Service roads out of Aspen.

MY VISITS: August 28, 2005 and September 25–26, 2014

My day hike in 2005 began at a trailhead along State Highway 82, going up the Roaring Fork River, past Independence Lake and Lost Man Lake, and on up to South Fork Pass. This was a very scenic hike; easy going, almost always above tree line with some meadows and nice, big lakes.

The backpack in 2014 was with my friend Maya. We began at the Fryingpan Lakes Trailhead at the north wilderness boundary. Our route was south along the Fryingpan River through a mix of forest and meadow with steep ridges over 13,000 feet on both sides. Our timing was almost perfect with fall colors near their peak. The lakes were small and surrounded by thick willows glowing gold in the sun. In fact, the entire valley was glowing gold. I recommend this area.

Holy Cross

★ ★ ★ ★

Size: 121,883 acres   **Year Designated:** 1980
Responsible Agency: USFS

The Holy Cross Wilderness is located in the San Isabel and White River National Forests northeast of the Hunter-Fryingpan Wilderness and southwest of the resort town of Vail. The easiest access is from US Highway 24 to the east of the wilderness. The area is home to the Mount of the Holy Cross (14,003 feet). The name is derived from large, cruciform fissures in the mountain that collect snow and keep the resulting white cross for much of the year. There is a National Geographic Trails Illustrated map (Holy Cross/Ruedi Reservoir) for the area.

MY VISIT: June 22–23, 2007

This overnight backpack began at the Missouri Lakes Trailhead at the eastern edge of the wilderness. My route was through forest to the Missouri Lakes, near tree line at about 11,500 feet. The scenery here was fabulous. There was still a lot of snow, and it was quite sloppy as it was a warm and very sunny day. I went over Missouri Pass (11,986 feet) where there was a lot of snow and some postholing, which I hate, but I kept going. I dropped into Cross Creek with some meadow and trees, then took a side trail (hard to see in snow) to Harvey Lake where I made my camp. Given the snow conditions I was surprised to see a couple of large groups of hikers along my route. The next day was spent going back to the trailhead on another sunny, even warmer day. The snow made it a bit of a slog, but manageable. Like the day before, every direction I looked from every location, there was fabulous scenery. Back at the trailhead, lots of other folks were packing up to start into the wilderness. This is clearly a popular area and a well-known trailhead. I certainly recommend it.

Eagles Nest

★ ★ ★ ★

Size: 133,688 acres   **Year Designated:** 1976
Responsible Agency: USFS

The Eagles Nest Wilderness is located in the White River and Arapaho National Forests west of the town of Silverthorne and northeast of the Holy Cross Wilderness. Access is from State Highway 9 on the east and from roads off Interstate Highway 70 to the south and southwest. The resort town of Vail is just to the west.

MY VISITS: October 16, 2004 and October 17, 2004 and July 14, 2008 and October 3, 2014

The two October 2004 hikes covered the same ground so I will discuss only the hike of the 17th. This day hike began at the Eaglesmere Trailhead at the northern wilderness boundary. There was snow on the ground, but there were lots of folks around because it was elk hunting season. My memory is that it was cold. The hike was a loop, first on the Gore Range Trail to the Eaglesmere Lakes, then a side trip south to Cat Lake and Upper Cataract Lake, then back to the Gore Range Trail, past Surprise Lake, and then on the Surprise Trail back to Lower Cataract Lake. The evening after this hike weather moved in and I decided to bail out given the time of year and the possibility of major snow.

The 2008 hike was my favorite for this area. The hike began at the Blue Lake Trailhead and followed Elliot Ridge to the summit of Meridian Peak (12,426 feet), then down to the Soda Lakes area, turning around and going back to the trailhead. This was all in good weather and open terrain with 360-degree views. There was still some snow but it was never a problem. Along the way I scared up a herd of thirty-five to forty elk.

The 2014 hike was supposed to be an overnight backpack to Gore Lake with my friend Maya. I was not too optimistic as we could see fresh snow down to pretty low elevations. We began at the Gore Creek Trailhead just outside Vail. It did not take long for the trail to be snow covered. We passed two backpackers coming out who told us that they lost the Gore Lake Trail in the snow. We continued on anyway to the Gore Lake junction and the graves of two early settlers, but we agreed that we needed to turn around. It was a nice-weather day and there were still some autumn colors, so our day was not wasted.

While I have not spent a lot of time in this area, everywhere I went has had wonderful scenery and I recommend it as a destination.

Elliot Ridge, Eagles Nest Wilderness

Weminuche

★ ★ ★ ★

Size: 492,418 acres   **Year Designated:** 1975
Responsible Agency: USFS

The Weminuche Wilderness is located in the San Juan and Rio Grande National Forests northeast of the city of Durango. Access is by US Highway 55 to the west and US Highway 160 to the south. Access is also possible via the Durango & Silverton Narrow Gauge Railroad.

MY VISITS: September 16–18, 1985 and September 19–20, 1985 and September 14–17, 2017

The first backpack began at the Vallecito Trailhead. My route was north along Vallecito Creek, then west up Johnson Creek and through Columbine Pass into Chicago Basin. There were lots of other folks along the way. This was a very popular route and trailhead, in part because Chicago Basin is a Mecca for technical climbers. The lower part of the route was in forest, but upper Johnson Creek was above tree line. The only problem with this hike was the weather—very rainy. I did have good luck though, as there was some sun at Columbine Pass, which had superb views of the aptly named Needle Mountains. Another interesting feature near Columbine Pass was the old mining remnants scattered about.

The following overnight backpack began at the Thirtymile Trailhead near the Rio Grande Reservoir. My route was southwest through Weminuche Pass, then west toward the Rio Grande Pyramid where I camped. Unfortunately, there was a pretty big dump of snow that night and I decided to bail out in case of more snow. Before departing there was a brief period of sun with great views of the Rio Grande Pyramid.

After an absence of thirty-two years I returned in 2017 to do a four-day loop backpack that started at the Williams Creek Trailhead. Again, the weather was problematic with heavy thunderstorms much of the first day. I camped just below tree line near the headwaters of Williams Creek. The next day was cold and windy with hints of snow. I quickly got above tree line and hiked to the Continental Divide Trail (CDT), then east to Trout Lake where I camped. There were lots of elk, at least sixty, along this route as well as a few other backpackers using the CDT. Day three was again on the CDT. It was still cold and windy but with hints of sun. There were neat views of the Williams Lakes, Squaw Mountain, and Cimarrona Peak. I found a nice campsite on a shelf with small lakes above the CDT. Day four was mostly rolling downhill on the Cimarrona Creek Trail back to the access road half a mile from my truck.

The Weminuche is big, high, and very scenic. It is popular and visitors will see other hikers and people with horses. Unless one puts solitude first on their list of wilderness characteristics, I heartily recommend this area.

Storm over ridge, upper Cimarrona Creek Trail, Weminuche Wilderness

West Elk

★ ★ ★ ★

Size: 167,092 acres   **Year Designated:** 1964
Responsible Agency: USFS

The West Elk Wilderness is located in the Gunnison National Forest northwest of the town of Gunnison. Access is via roads leading from State Highway 92 on the west and from county roads out of Gunnison to the east.

MY VISITS: September 21, 1985 and June 27–29, 2007

My day hike in 1985 was a long time ago, and I remember some things and do not remember other things. I remember that it was still raining after a couple of other rainy hikes. I remember the access road was in poor condition. I vividly remember looking at The Castles as they were enveloped by fog, then briefly illuminated by sun along with gold from the aspen trees. The Castles are highly eroded volcanic tuff forming the wall of the valley of Castle Creek. I *probably* began this hike at a trailhead for Castle Creek along the east side of the wilderness. I do remember being very impressed with the scenery (I have a few surviving, poor-quality scans of photos).

I have notes and photos from the three-day backpack in 2007. The trip began at the Cliff Creek Trailhead off the West Elk Loop Scenic Road. I first went southwest, then through Beckwith Pass, then continued on the Cliff Creek Trail to a junction with the South Fork of Cliff Creek. There were good views in all directions. I made my camp near this junction. The day was quite warm and there was water everywhere from snowmelt. This produced very large numbers of mosquitoes. The second day was a day hike to the summit of Storm Ridge. I took the Castle Creek Trail to Castle Pass, then hiked cross country to the ridgetop at about 11,800 feet. It was mosquito free, with great views in all directions including north into the Raggeds Wilderness where I had been on my previous hike. I hung out on the bug-free ridge as long as I could before going back down to my camp. Day three was spent going back to the trailhead. On my way out I counted twenty-three people, six on horseback, coming into the area. My guess was early Fourth of July visitors.

Looking toward The Castles from Storm Ridge, West Elk Wilderness

The West Elk is scenically dense with a good trail system and easy access. I highly recommend it.

Rocky Mountain National Park

★ ★ ★ ★

Size: 249,339 acres   **Year Designated:** 2009
Responsible Agency: USNPS

Most of Rocky Mountain National Park is designated wilderness. Access is primarily from US Highway 34 on the north and west and State Highway 7 on the east. At the time of my visit there was a National Geographic Trails Illustrated map devoted to the park. The Park Service requires permits for any overnight backcountry camping, and camping is only allowed at specific sites. There are limits on the number of people at any site. Bear-proof food storage containers are also required.

MY VISIT: September 19–21, 2014

My friend Maya and I did this three-day backpack beginning at the East Inlet Trailhead adjacent to Grand Lake east of US Highway 34. We wound our way up 2,500 feet to our assigned Upper East campsite, which we had to ourselves. This day's hiking was pretty much all in timber, but with a few views. There were late afternoon thunderstorms, common in Colorado. Our big day was day two when we made a day hike to the end of the trail at Fifth Lake. Most of this day was in open meadow or at tree line, so the country was quite open and there were great views. Our timing could not have been any better; the fall colors were at their peak and this was a very nice weather day. I had hoped we could find an off-trail route up to the Continental Divide from around Spirit Lake, but the route simply became too steep so we went back to the trail. Fifth Lake itself was spectacular (see the photo).

This wilderness area is another with high scenic density. Like some other Colorado areas, this wilderness is very popular. Visitors are almost guaranteed to see other visitors. Still, the area is easy to get to and has a great trail system. I recommend this area to all but the most intent on solitude.

Black Ridge Canyons

★ ★ ★ ★

Size: 75,439 acres   **Year Designated:** 2000
Responsible Agency: BLM

The Black Ridge Canyons Wilderness is located in western Colorado and eastern Utah south of Interstate Highway 70, southwest of the town of Fruita, and just west of the Colorado National Monument. The easiest access is probably from the Rim Rock Road through the Colorado National Monument. The wilderness is within the McInnis Canyons National Conservation Area. At the time of my visit there were BLM brochures with maps of the wilderness and its immediate surroundings.

MY VISITS: May 28, 2012 and May 29, 2012

My day hikes began at the Upper Bench Road off the Rim Rock Road through the Colorado National Monument. I did not drive to the trailhead at the end of the road because I was not convinced that my truck could survive the road. (In hindsight it could have). The first day was to explore Mee Canyon. The BLM handout for the area said that there was a cairned route to the canyon bottom, but I lost the route and completely failed to find any way down.

The second day was much more successful. I walked to the end of the road to the Rattlesnake Canyon Arches Trail and began a truly spectacular 2.5-mile stroll to some of the nicest sandstone arches I have ever seen. The whole neighborhood is nice, typical of much of the southern Utah sandstone country with its bare rock, dry washes, pinons, and junipers. The arches, however, were special. If a hiker likes sandstone, they need to come here.

dramatic views of the multi-colored limestone spires and cliffs in the monument and later similar features in the wilderness area. The rock formations here are very similar to those seen in the better-known Bryce Canyon National Park. The trail lost elevation as it wound its way south to a junction with the High Mountain Trail at the western edge of the wilderness. Here I simply turned around and went back to the trailhead. The hike took me through typical southern Utah terrain of high-elevation forest to juniper scrub at lower elevations. I did not see any other hikers on this day.

I recommend this hike to anybody who likes colorful rock and pleasant forest in a very quiet setting.

Ashdown Gorge

★ ★ ★ ★

Size: 7,085 acres   **Year Designated:** 1984
Responsible Agency: USFS

The Ashdown Gorge Wilderness is located in the Dixie National Forest southeast of Cedar City. It shares a boundary with the Cedar Breaks National Monument to the east and south.

MY VISIT: June 20, 2006

This day hike began at a trailhead in Cedar Breaks National Monument for the Rattlesnake Trail. The starting elevation was about 10,000 feet in a lovely pine forest. The trail skirted the northern monument boundary with

Dark Canyon

★ ★ ★ ★

Size: 46,353 acres   **Year Designated:** 1984   **Responsible Agency:** USFS

Dark Canyon, Dark Canyon Wilderness

The Dark Canyon Wilderness is located in the Manti-La Sal National Forest north of Natural Bridges National Monument and west of the town of Blanding. Access is by unpaved roads to the south and west of the wilderness. The area was within the original boundary of the controversial Bears Ears National Monument. I don't know if it remains in the much smaller proposed boundary.

MY VISIT: June 1–2, 1987

Earlier in 1987 I had done a backpacking trip in Grand Gulch in southern Utah. During that trip I spoke with a BLM employee who had spent a lot of time in southern Utah. I asked him what his favorite canyon hike was and he said, "Dark Canyon." I made it my next destination. I remember the hike and the terrain because I have photos. What I do not have are any notes with such information as where I began or my exact route. I do know that I was in both Woodenshoe and Dark Canyons. My starting point was probably from Woodenshoe Road, then down Woodenshoe Canyon to its intersection with Dark Canyon and a short way up Dark Canyon. It was a marvelous trip with water flowing over huge expanses of sandstone, plunge pools, and cliffs rising over 1,000 feet above the canyon bottoms. It was a good time of year because water was relatively easy to find. I remember camping near a large flowing spring surrounded by blooming cacti. I also remember seeing no other people.

While my memory fades, I still consider this one of my best ever desert trips. I encourage others to visit.

Dark and Woodenshoe Canyons, Dark Canyon Wilderness

Side canyon in Dark Canyon, Dark Canyon Wilderness

High Uinta

★ ★ ★ ★

Size: 453,890 acres   **Year Designated:** 1984
Responsible Agency: USFS

The high Uinta Wilderness is located in the Wasatch-Cache and Ashley National Forests. Access to the western part of the wilderness is from State Highway 150. Northern trailheads are accessed by roads in Wyoming from Evanston, Robertson, and Lonetree. There is a USFS map dedicated to this wilderness.

MY VISITS: July 1998 and July 6–7, 2013 and August 22–24, 2013

This wilderness is pretty much in my back yard. Living in Wyoming, my trips have mostly used north-side trailheads. I describe here my overnight trips and one day hike. In addition, I have made several one-day visits, mostly on cross-country skis, in the winter.

A friend and I began the first backpacking trip at the East Fork of the Blacks Fork Trailhead. I do not have any detailed records from that trip, but we went first to the area of the Red Castles for a couple of days, then through Anderson Pass and to the summit of Kings Peak (13,528 feet, tallest in Utah). I simply don't remember our route back to the trailhead. I do remember both of us being impressed with the scenery in general and the area around the Red Castles in particular. The Uinta Mountains have nice areas of forest with lodgepole pine down low, Colorado spruce and Douglas fir at higher elevations. There are lots of big, green meadows, some large lakes, and large areas of rock and meadow above 11,000 feet. As of this writing, it is painful to see these forests devastated by disease, with many slopes having 50 percent dead timber.

The overnight backpack in 2013 began at the Henrys Fork Trailhead. This trailhead had often been a cross-country ski destination. On this occasion my route was south along the Henrys Fork, past Dollar Lake to a campsite just below Gunsight Pass. My timing was not good as it was still Fourth of July time and there were a lot of other hikers around. What was

good at the time was the near maximum wildflower density. The next day I made a short trip to Gunsight Pass, came back to my camp, packed up, and took a slightly different route back to my truck, going past Henrys Lake, Grass Lake, and Bear Lake. Most of the return trip was in rain. My original intent was to camp a second night, but decided instead to go all the way out, getting to my truck after dark. The photo was taken near my campsite.

Later that summer I made a three-day backpack from Spirit Lake near the northeast corner of the wilderness. I had done a day hike from here years earlier but wanted to get a more thorough look. My route was through McCoy Park, then cross country toward Round Lake. The second day was a day hike past Round Lake to Island Lake and back to my campsite. Day three was spent going back to the trailhead. Once again, this was in a mix of forest and meadow with lakes scattered about.

The only day hike I will describe was from the very popular east-side High Line Trailhead along Utah Highway 150. There were *a lot* of vehicles at the trailhead. This was on July 17, 2017, and the route was first along the High Line Trail, then a side trail to Wilder, Wyman, and Packard Lakes. This route was not very interesting until the end. The Packard Lake outlet flowed over a very steep canyon wall into the East Fork of the Duchesne River with good views of the river valley. A truly worthwhile reward for a day's hiking.

In summary, this is a very nice area. The only negative comment I can make is that it gets a *lot* of visitors because of easy access from the Wasatch Front cities of Salt Lake and its neighbors. There are lots of hunters, fishers, and hikers.

Flower-filled meadow below Gunsight Pass
High Uinta Wilderness

Mount Timpanogos

★ ★ ★ ★

Size: 10,750 acres   **Year Designated:** 1984
Responsible Agency: USFS

The Mount Timpanogos Wilderness is located in the Uinta National Forest east of Interstate Highway 15 and east of the town of Alpine. The easiest access is via State Highway 92. There was a National Geographic Trails Illustrated map dedicated to the Lone Pine, Mount Timpanogos, and Mount Nebo Wilderness areas.

MY VISITS: August 2, 2005 and October 15, 2014

My notes for the day hike in 2005 are sketchy, but they do tell me that I started at the trailhead for the Mount Timpanogos Trail (Aspen Grove) at the eastern wilderness boundary with the intention of going to the summit. My plan was thwarted by deep lingering snow and high water from melting runoff. I was, however, really impressed with the beauty of the place and my notes said "Must come back." It took me nine years, but I did come back with my friend Maya in 2014. This time our day hike began at the trailhead for the Timpooneke Trail at the northern wilderness boundary with the goal of getting to Emerald Lake just below the summit. The trail went up the Giant Staircase, a big climb with a lot of switchbacks. The route was through relatively open forest at low elevation, then to mostly meadow and sedimentary rock at high elevation. There was still some fall color. We were able to get just beyond two small lakes in Timpanogos Basin but not to Emerald Lake because we were running out of daylight. That did not matter as we were again impressed with this very scenic area. This might just be my favorite of the several small wilderness areas in greater Salt Lake City.

*Roberts Horn from the Timpooneke Trail,
Mount Timpanogos Wilderness*

Jarbidge

★ ★ ★ ★

Size: 113,167 acres   **Year Designated:** 1964
Responsible Agency: USFS

The Jarbidge Wilderness is not easy to get to. It is located in the northeast corner of Nevada in the Humboldt-Toiyabe National Forest, west of US Highway 93 and east of the Charlston-Deeth county road off Interstate Highway 80. At the time of my visit there was a USFS map dedicated to this wilderness.

MY VISIT: July 3–6, 2003

My visit began at the "real" end of a county road along the Jarbidge River. Most readers will not remember the controversy over the missing segment of road that ended at a wilderness trailhead. Sometime before 2003, the last few miles of road were washed away by floodwaters. Much of the road simply disappeared. The locals wanted the road replaced but the USFS said no

Jarbidge Spine from Saint Marys River Peak

because the construction would harm fish habitat. The locals were incensed. They famously organized "shovel brigades" to do the construction. The brigades were nowhere adequate to replace miles of missing road, but they became an anti-government rallying point. The county never recognized that the road was missing. They simply posted a sign that said "Road Damage Ahead" at the beginning of the washout. Nonetheless, I hiked up along the river to the old trailhead and began my four-day backpack.

The timing was very good for this trip. There was still some snow around, the small lakes still had water, and the whole area was green. My route was up the Jarbidge River, then to Emerald and Jarbidge Lakes with side trips to the summits of Prospect Peak and Marys River Peak. The Marys Peak summit provided excellent views of the lush green open space, including God's Pocket, a name I found appropriate. The terrain was mostly open with hard rock and wide expanses of grassy slopes and a little forest scattered about.

Given its remoteness, I was a bit surprised to see lots of other hikers, although it was around July Fourth and an attractive time of year. I found the area very appealing and recommend it to other hikers.

Ruby Mountains

★ ★ ★ ★

Size: 95,620 acres **Year Designated:** 1989
Responsible Agency: USFS

The Ruby Mountains Wilderness is located in the Humboldt-Toiyabe National Forest southeast of the city of Elko. Access is easy to the northern part of the wilderness by State Highway 227 and then a road from Lamoille to Lamoille Canyon. At the time of my visit there was a USFS map dedicated to the Ruby Mountains and the nearby East Humboldt Wilderness areas.

MY VISIT: June 30–July 2, 2003

My three-day backpack began at the Lamoille Canyon Trailhead. It was early in the hiking season and there was some snow, but the hiking was easy and there were few other hikers. My route was the Ruby Crest Trail. This trail is true to its name. Once on the crest, the trail stayed high, mostly above tree line, so the terrain was very open with lots of lakes. I made a camp at Favre Lake, and on day two did a day hike south past Wines Peak until it was time to go back to my camp. Day three was spent going back to the trailhead.

This is a very nice area and I had ideal conditions. I recommend it.

Liberty Lake near the Ruby Crest Trail, Ruby Mountains Wilderness

Muddy Mountains

★ ★ ★ ★

Size: 48,097 acres   **Year Designated:** 2002
Responsible Agency: BLM and USNPS

The Muddy Mountains Wilderness is located just east of Las Vegas. Most of the wilderness is managed by the BLM, but the southeast corner is part of the Lake Mead National Recreation Area and is managed by the Park Service. The easiest access to the southeast corner is via State Highway 169 from Interstate Highway 15, and then from the North Shore Highway.

MY VISIT: October 28, 2014

This visit was only in the National Park Service part of the wilderness. From the North Shore Road, the unpaved but serviceable Calville Wash North Road led to a trailhead for the Bowl of Fire. The trailhead was not obvious, but a few parking places and wilderness boundary signs were good in-

dicators. It is only a short hike to as spectacular a collection of fiery red rock as I have ever seen. The only drawback to the area is the very large number of helicopters flying overhead taking sightseers from Las Vegas to the Grand Canyon. The Bowl of Fire itself is small and can be seen in its entirety in a little over an hour. Any hiker who likes red rock must see this place.

Gospel Hump

★ ★ ★

Size: 206,053 acres   **Year Designated:** 1978
Responsible Agency: USFS

The Gospel Hump Wilderness is located in the Nez Perce National Forest east of US Highway 95 and northeast of the community of Riggins. The southern wilderness boundary is the Salmon River, and the Frank Church-River of No Return Wilderness is south of the river. Within the wilderness is a summit called Gospel Hill and another summit called Buffalo Hump, hence the name. The summits are quite rounded, looking just like humps.

MY VISIT: July 8–10, 2005 and July 11, 2005

My three-day backpack began at the end of a cherry-stem road at the Square Mountain Trailhead. My route was east from this trailhead through a mix of forest and meadow along a gentle ridge, finding a campsite not far from the Buffalo Hump. It was a beautiful weather day with good views but a lot of mosquitoes. The next day was rainy and I did a day hike to the eastern wilderness boundary where a big chunk of land was left out of the wilderness because of active mining claims. I wandered around the edges of this mining area and it did look like there was some human activity but nothing of any size. I went to the foot of the Buffalo Hump, then looked for Mirror Lake but failed to find it. I got back to my camp just in time for the rain to stop. Day three was rain most of the day and I just went back to my truck.

The day hike on the eleventh was from a nearby trailhead for Hanover Mountain. This was a perfectly clear day and I went to the summit of Hanover (7,966 feet) for good views all around and of Indigo Lake just below.

This area was always pleasant if not spectacular. It was mostly gentle terrain with forest, meadow, lakes, and some bare, worn, hard-rock summits. In my four days I never saw another person. Hikers seeking a quiet place to see gentle country would like this area.

IDAHO

Hells Canyon

★ ★ ★

Size: 219,006 acres   **Year Designated:** 1975
Responsible Agency: USFS and BLM

The Hells Canyon Wilderness is located in the Nez Perce and Payette National Forests and BLM public lands in both Oregon and Idaho. The Snake River Canyon (Hells Canyon) splits the wilderness. The area is west of US Highway 95 and west of the community of Riggins. The map I used for this area was the USGS 7.5-minute He Devil quadrangle.

MY VISIT: July 7–9, 2003

My visit was to the Seven Devils portion of the wilderness on the Idaho side of the river on national forest land. A quick look at the map and one sees how this place got its name. The official USGS map names peaks He Devil, She Devil, The Ogre, The Goblin, Mount Belial, the Tower of Babel, the Devils Throne, the Twin Imps, the Devils Tooth, and the Devils Farm (that makes ten devils). Not to be intimidated, I began a three-day backpack into this area starting at the Windy Saddle Trailhead. Day one was rainy and I dropped down to Basin Lake and set up a camp. Day two had good weath-

er and I did a day hike south to Shelf, Gem, Rock Island, Appendix, and Sheep Lakes, then turned around, went back to my camp, and hiked north toward a fire lookout on Dry Diggins Ridge, then back to camp. Day three was spent going back to the trailhead. This was a very scenic and interesting trip. The terrain was pretty steep and not heavily forested so mostly bare, eroded volcanic rock with many lakes sprinkled about. I recommend hiking this part of the wilderness to just about anybody.

IDAHO

Hemingway-Boulders

★ ★ ★

Size: 67,998 acres   **Year Designated:** 2015
Responsible Agency: USFS

The Hemingway-Boulders Wilderness is located in the Salmon-Challis National Forest north of State Highway 75 and north of the town of Ketchum. The area is within the Sawtooth National Recreation Area and is home to the Boulder Mountains. Access is easy from a road leaving State Highway 75 at the national recreation area visitor center. At the time of my visit there was a USFS map of the trails of the Sawtooth National Recreation Area.

View south from West Pass, Hemingway-Boulders Wilderness

Ernest Hemingway had a long association with greater Sun Valley, Idaho. He owned a home in Ketchum, where he died in 1961. The home is now owned by The Nature Conservancy.

MY VISIT: September 15–16, 2016

My overnight backpack began at the Sawtooth National Recreation Area Visitor Center where I obtained a map that included this newly designated wilderness area. I mentioned my planned route to a USFS employee who warned me that my route would be an arduous climb. She was right. The trip began at the North Fork of the Big Wood River Trailhead just beyond the visitor center. It was a beautiful fall day with just a hint of snow at high elevation. Soon after starting I encountered a hunter who was, through binoculars, monitoring some comrades who were bow-hunting elk. I watched for a bit with my own binoculars but did not linger. After a short distance on rather level ground the real climb began. At age seventy-two I was really slow and sometimes wondered if I would get to my destina-

tion. Being slow was not a problem here as the scenery from the trail was always good. The trail quickly left the forest and the views were excellent. Finally, I got to West Pass where the views were even more expansive and where I looked for a campsite. Fortunately, the recent snow had provided enough moisture for a small stream to be flowing just below the pass and I found an excellent site. I was too tired to venture any farther. The next day I packed up and retraced my steps to the trailhead, descending a lot more quickly than I had climbed.

I had driven past this area many times but had always passed by, heading for the Sawtooth or White Cloud Mountains. I am really glad I stopped here this time and got to see this nice area. I am even more pleased that this area has finally been given formal wilderness status along with the White Clouds and the Jim McClure-Jerry Peak areas.

Jim McClure-Jerry Peak

★ ★ ★

Size: 116,946 acres   **Year Designated:** 2015
Responsible Agency: USFS and BLM

This wilderness area is located in the Salmon-Challis National Forest and adjacent BLM public lands northeast of the Hemingway-Boulders Wilderness and east of the Cecil D. Andrus-White Clouds Wilderness. Access is via the East Fork of the Salmon River Road on the west and the Trail Creek Road on the south. Jim McClure was a long-serving US senator from Idaho who was probably better known as a supporter of extractive industries than of conservation.

Bowery Peak, Jim McClure-Jerry Peak Wilderness

My overnight backpack began at the Hunter Creek Trailhead in the southwest part of the wilderness. There were a lot of vehicles at the trailhead with license plates from all over the West. It was bow-hunting season for elk. My route crossed Hunter Creek Summit and followed East Pass Creek to a junction with Bowery Creek where I set up my camp. This day was mostly in timber with some meadows along the creek and occasional views of higher volcanic features. There was one nice waterfall on East Fork Creek. There was some overnight rain and even a little fresh snow. The next morning was sunny and the views of Bowery Peak with lingering fall color and snow were marvelous. I made a side trip west to the headwaters of Bowery Creek before packing up my camp. My original intention was to spend another night in the wilderness, but afternoon rain changed my mind and I walked back to my truck, the last part in the dark.

This wilderness does not have the scenic density of the Sawtooth, White Clouds, or Boulder Mountains, but is still quite pleasant and worth a visit.

IDAHO

Big Jacks Creek

★ ★ ★

Size: 52,826 acres   **Year Designated:** 2009
Responsible Agency: BLM

The Big Jacks Creek Wilderness is located in BLM public lands west of State Highway 51 and southwest of the community of Bruneau.

MY VISIT: June 5, 2014 and June 6, 2014

Southwest Idaho is a very remote. The terrain is volcanic plains cut through occasionally by creeks or rivers. The area is quite dry. The flat parts are used for grazing. The rivers are used by some floaters when there is suf-

ficient water. Hiking is not common and trails are rare. There are not many roads, and some of the roads that are here are bad. In 2009 a wilderness bill was passed protecting six pieces of this rough country. The protected areas are mostly along creek and river courses. The main rivers are the Bruneau and the Owyhee with their various forks and tributaries. Big Jacks Creek is probably the easiest wilderness to access, being just west of State Highway 51 and then west on the Wickahoney Road.

I did a day hike here starting at the marked Parker Trailhead. The trail went a short distance through cow-grazed sagebrush then steeply down through multiple volcanic layers to the creek. The creek provided a startlingly bright green band of vegetation, especially willow and cottonwood. The area around the creek was quite pleasant, although hiking very far would have been difficult because of cliffs and dense vegetation. The next day I did another day hike farther south, from the Zeno Trailhead. Here there was not even the pretense of a trail. I worked my way down to the creek, but again was stopped by cliffs and dense vegetation. I returned to the canyon rim and hiked a ways upstream but was stopped by cliffs.

There are five other BLM wilderness areas scattered around this far corner of Idaho. I have been to four of them and none are as nice or as interesting as Big Jacks Creek (I rate them two stars). The sixth and largest is the Owyhee River Wilderness, but my attempt to access it failed.

Great Bear

★ ★ ★

Size: 286,636 acres   **Year Designated:** 1978
Responsible Agency: USFS

The Great Bear Wilderness is located in the Flathead National Forest south and west of Glacier National Park and north and west of the Bob Marshall Wilderness. The easiest access is from US Highway 2 along the northern boundary. The Middle Fork of the Flathead River flows through the area. At the time of my visit there was a USFS map dedicated to the Great Bear, Bob Marshall, and Scapegoat Wilderness areas.

MY VISIT: August 2–4, 2010

My three-day backpack began at the Devil Creek Trailhead. My route went south to Elk Lake where I set up camp. The terrain here was heavily forested with thick understory at low elevation. There were several other people camped at the lake. Day two was a day hike of the open ridges above Elk Lake. My goal was the summit of Forster Mountain, but weather moved in and the mountain was shrouded in mist, so I went back down and headed for Tranquil Basin. At least I could see here, and the basin was indeed an idyllic spot with two lakes surrounded by forest. I turned around and went back to my camp at Elk Lake where I was now the only camper. Day three was just going back to my trailhead.

Readers will tire of seeing my response to many areas; this place was pleasant but not especially interesting. While I would not discourage anyone from visiting, I cannot claim this as a must-see area based on my limited experience.

Bob Marshall

★ ★ ★

Size: 1,009,356 acres   **Year Designated:** 1964
Responsible Agency: USFS

The Bob Marshall Wilderness is located in the Flathead and Lewis and Clark National Forests astride the Continental Divide. It is south and east of the Great Bear Wilderness and northwest of the Scapegoat Wilderness. The headwaters of the Flathead and Sun Rivers are in the wilderness. Access roads are west of US Highway 89, west of the town of Choteau. The Continental Divide Trail crosses the wilderness. Bob Marshall was a forester and an early advocate of wilderness preservation. He was the founder of the Wilderness Society and held a PhD degree in plant physiology (!) The wilderness area is sometimes referred to as just "The Bob."

MY VISIT: August 7–12, 1988

On this backpacking trip I was a tagalong member of what was for me a largish group. I have no detailed notes from this trip, but I do have a USFS map of the Great Bear, Bob Marshall, and Scapegoat Wilderness areas marked with our route. Our trip began at the Mortimer Gulch Trailhead. We went west along the Gibson Reservoir, then south along the Sun River through the aptly named Pretty Prairie. The terrain here was gentle, open with lots of meadows and some timber. Next, we went up the West Fork of the Sun River to Indian Creek and just below White River Pass. I remember a side trip to the summit of Red Butte (8,590 feet). We returned to the Sun River and continued north along the eastern side of the famous Chinese Wall to Moose Creek. I remember camping at Moose Creek with a huge plume of smoke from a forest fire off to the east as we retired for the night. Our last day was down Moose Creek making a loop back to the trailhead.

The terrain on this trip was very open with large meadows, open limestone along the Chinese Wall, and some not-very-dense forest. It was always pleasant if not densely scenic. I know that this is considered one of the nation's premier wilderness areas, but I still "only" give it three stars.

Scapegoat

★ ★ ★

Size: 239,936 acres   **Year Designated:** 1972
Responsible Agency: USFS

The Scapegoat Wilderness is located in the Lolo, Lewis and Clark, and Helena National Forests. The area is south and east of the Bob Marshall Wilderness. Easy access is from State Highway 200 to the south. The closest community is Lincoln. The Continental Divide Trail traverses the wilderness.

MY VISIT: August 25–29, 2011

This five-day backpack was with two friends from Idaho. We began at the Indian Meadows Trailhead and, with the drive from Idaho, had time only to go as far as Heart Lake where we camped for the night. The second day we backpacked to what my map shows as Middle Fork Creek and my notes say is North Fork Creek. We camped here among a fair amount of grizzly bear sign. There also was lots of sign along the trail. We saw no bears. These first two days were mostly in timber with occasional meadows.

Day three was a long day hike on a ridge trail up to a summit called "Crow" on my map (8,611 feet). Here we finally broke out of the trees and got some nice views in all directions including Scapegoat Mountain and Olson Peak. On our way up the ridge we came across substantial diggings. Our best guess was that a grizzly bear had been devouring a group of ground squirrels. It looked like a backhoe had been at work. We decided to descend by a different trail, but had a difficult time negotiating a large burned area. There were just enough old blaze marks to keep us on course.

Day four we intended to go northeast past Crow Creek to the Continental Divide Trail, then take the CDT south to Heart Lake. At this we failed. We simply could not find the trails, mostly due to old fires. We backtracked to the previous campsite, then on to Webb Lake, and camped near a USFS guard station. Upon rising the next morning, we watched a moose feeding as it waded in the lake. We packed up and went back to the trailhead.

Like the Great Bear, this wilderness earns the dreaded pleasant but not especially interesting rating. I would neither encourage nor discourage hikers for coming here.

Mission Mountains

★ ★ ★

Size: 73,877 acres   **Year Designated:** 1975
Responsible Agency: USFS

The long, skinny Mission Mountains Wilderness is located in the Flathead National Forest west of State Highway 83 and east of the Flathead Indian Reservation. The easiest access is west from State Highway 83. The nearest town is Polson, northwest of the wilderness.

MY VISIT: July 28 and July 29, 2007

The first day hike began at a trailhead for Piper Lake. The trail went up Piper Creek to Piper Lake then through a pass to Cedar Lake. The day was quite warm and there was considerable smoke in the air. The terrain was timber at lower elevation, then open rock and meadow at higher elevation. The pass was quite scenic, reminding me somewhat of the Selway-Bitterroot area. I encountered some people on horseback who said they had seen grizzly bears earlier that day. I saw no bears, but knowing of their presence helped me decide to keep doing day hikes here.

The second day hike was from a trailhead in the southern part of the wilderness taking me to very pretty Glacier Lake, then up to Lagoon and Lance Lakes and ultimately up to Turquoise Lake where the trail ended. It was another very warm day with lots of smoke. The views, however, were still good. In the near background was Glacier Peak and there did appear to be a possible glacier there. I saw several other hikers this day, but no bears.

Glacier Peak, Mission Mountains Wilderness

Lee Metcalf

★ ★ ★

Size: 254,288 acres   **Year Designated:** 1983
Responsible Agency: USFS

The Lee Metcalf Wilderness is located in the Beaverhead-Deerlodge and Gallatin National Forests west of US Highway 191 and southwest of the city of Bozeman. It is just north of the ski resort of Big Sky. Lee Metcalf represented Montana in the US House of Representatives and the US Senate for twenty-five years and was a strong advocate for wilderness.

MY VISIT: October 2–4, 1987

This three-day backpack into the Spanish Peaks with two friends was a long time ago and my memory is dim. I still have the USGS 15-minute map Spanish Peaks with markings of our route. I also have a few photos. I remember being concerned that this trip would be at high elevation in Montana in October, so I packed for cold conditions. All three days were beautiful and quite warm.

The trip began at a trailhead at the USFS Spanish Creek Ranger Station. We went up along the South Fork of Spanish Creek, then up Falls Creek in timber until breaking out into open rock and meadow. There were lots of little lakes in little cirques and good views of the peaks of the Madison Range with summits around 10,000 feet. I think we camped in this area. Our second day we went back to the upper South Fork of Spanish Creek to Summit Lake and Thompson Lake where we may have camped. Most of this day was above tree line. Our third day was down, then up to Beacon Point, across Indian Ridge, reentering the timber at Arrow Lake, and exiting via Little Hell Roaring Creek. We had made a perfect loop.

I certainly liked this area, as did my two companions. My memory is that we saw no other hikers. I recommend this area and this hike to just about anybody.

Winegar Hole

★ ★ ★

Size: 10,715 acres   **Year Designated:** 1984
Responsible Agency: USFS

The Winegar Hole Wilderness is located in the Caribou-Targhee National Forest just south of Yellowstone National Park. The western wilderness boundary is the Idaho-Wyoming state line. Access is via the old, unpaved Reclamation Road that runs between US Highway 89/191/287 in Wyoming and Ashton, Idaho.

MY VISITS: Sometime in 1985 and July 6, 2017 and August 31, 2017

This is a very obscure wilderness area. I learned of its designation in 1984 when I was living in eastern Idaho. I had never heard of the area and went out of curiosity in 1985. I have no recollection of that trip other than thinking it was not very interesting. As I got more interested in wilderness areas, I decided that I needed to go back.

The timing of the first 2017 visit was not good. The road was still muddy and the mosquitoes were very dense. I did make a bushwhack hike beginning at the Reclamation Road. The terrain was nearly flat for the whole area with lots of lakes and ponds and wetlands, but also lots of mainly lodgepole pine and willows. The lakes and ponds are probably leftovers from when the area was covered by glaciers. What was good this time of year was the wildflowers, nearly at their peak. There were also nesting sandhill cranes and some other birds. Given the mosquito density I decided to come back later in the year.

The late August trip was much better with dry roads and few mosquitoes. I was able to start a hike at a real trailhead and travel on a real trail. The trail only went a short way until it entered Yellowstone National Park. It was used mostly by people on horseback visiting some of the waterfalls of southwest Yellowstone. I used the trail to get to Fish Lake and Junco Lake. Junco Lake provided a fine example of ecosystem succession from shallow lake and its aquatic birds to near-shore grassy wetland to edge-of-wetland shrubs to lodgepole pine forest.

While the area is not especially scenic, it does have some interesting features. My guess is that most hikers would prefer to use the area as an access point to a little-visited part of Yellowstone.

WYOMING

North Absaroka

★ ★ ★

Size: 350,488 acres   **Year Designated:** 1964
Responsible Agency: USFS

The North Absaroka Wilderness is located in the Shoshone National Forest south of US Highway 212, north of US Highway 14/16/20, and northwest of the city of Cody. The western wilderness boundary is the eastern boundary of Yellowstone National Park.

MY VISITS: October 3, October 4, and October 5, 2006 and August 19, 2009 and September 14, 2018 and September 15, 2018

I have done six different day hikes from six different trailheads in this wilderness. The terrain was pretty similar throughout the wilderness, mostly volcanic with dense forest low and some open meadows and then open ridges up high. Wildlife was plentiful, including grizzly bears. Hunting is popular, especially for elk, and horses were common.

The three hikes in 2006 followed a spell of rain and all the trails were quite muddy and the creeks were high, making crossing difficult. The first hike was from the North Crandall Trailhead and went up North Crandall Creek. There were a few good views of cliffs and still some fall color remaining. The second hike began at the Dead Indian Trailhead near the eastern part of the wilderness. The Trout Mountain Trail followed Dead Indian Creek south and then west and was mostly in forest until more open country around Dead Indian Meadows where I turned around. The third hike

began at a trailhead for Sam Berry Meadow off US Highway 14/16/20 at the southern wilderness boundary. The trail went mostly through burned forest to the meadow where I turned around. This was not a very interesting or attractive hike.

The hike in 2009 began near a lodge off US Highway 14/16/20 where a dim trail led north up Mormon Creek, eventually disappearing near the Sleeping Giant, a long ridgetop. There were excellent views from a cirque above the Giant, especially south into the Washakie Wilderness. This was a worthwhile hike. The first 2018 hike began at the Pilot Creek Trailhead off US Highway 212. The attraction here was the jumbled volcanic remains known as Pilot and Index. Other than this there was not much of interest and the trail just seemed to disappear near the Yellowstone boundary. The following day's hike began in the Yellowstone gateway community of Cooke City on the Republic Pass Trail, which climbed to the pass at the Yellowstone boundary. Most of the route was through forest with open terrain near the pass. Much of this day I followed grizzly bear tracks in the trail. While pleasant, I can think of better destinations.

COLORADO

Mount Zirkel

★ ★ ★

Size: 160,568 acres   **Year Designated:** 1964
Responsible Agency: USFS

The Mount Zirkel Wilderness is located in the Routt National Forest just south of the Wyoming state line and north of US Highway 40. Access is best from Forest Roads 129 and 400 along the west side of the wilderness. The Continental Divide Trail runs the length of the wilderness. There are two National Geographic Trails Illustrated maps that cover this wilderness.

MY VISIT: August 12–15, 2004

This four-day backpack began at the Slavonia Trailhead on the west side of the wilderness. My route took me east up Gold Creek past Gold Lake then north on the Red Dirt Trail to nearly Red Dirt Pass for my first night's camp. The country here was very open, mostly above tree line in dry, grassy, fairly gentle terrain. The second day began with a day hike to the summit of Mount Zirkel (12,180 feet). I went back to camp, packed up and went back to Gold Lake, but then headed south on the Wyoming Trail to the Continental Divide Trail and made camp above North Lake. Another day in mostly open, brown, almost baked-looking country. The third day was a day hike south on the CDT past Lost Ranger Peak and Pristine Lake to the summit of Mount Ethel (11, 924 feet). There I turned around and went back to my camp. Day four was spent going back to Gold Lake and then the trailhead.

I have no memory about weather conditions in 2004 but was surprised at how dry the land looked. The creeks still were flowing and the lakes looked healthy. The land, however, was very brown. As in so much of the American West, a disturbing fraction of the trees were dead.

This is indeed a nice area, especially for someone who likes wide-open country. While I saw nothing outstanding, I would recommend this area to just about anybody.

COLORADO

Rawah

★ ★ ★

Size: 73,899 acres   **Year Designated:** 1964
Responsible Agency: USFS

The Rawah Wilderness is located in the Roosevelt National Forest west of State Highway 14, northwest of Rocky Mountain National Park, and east of the town of Walden. The National Geographic Trails Illustrated map 112 (Colorado) covers the wilderness.

MY VISIT: August 12–13, 2007

This overnight backpack began at the West Branch Trailhead on the eastern side of the wilderness. There were a lot of people at this trailhead and lots of other people on the trail. It was hot. Later, clouds and a misty rain cooled things off. My route was up the West Branch (of the Laramie River) Trail to the Camp Lake Trail to Camp Lake, which had lots of other campers so I continued on to Upper Camp Lake for the night. The terrain here was very open, just at tree line. The second day finished a loop going west past Upper and Lower Sandbar Lakes, then south on the scenic Rawah Trail past Rawah Lake Number 3, over Grassy Pass, to the junction with the West Branch Trail, and then to the trailhead. There were still lots of folks around.

This was certainly a pleasant trip in a pleasant neighborhood, even given the number of other hikers. While I would not beat the drum about this area, I can still recommend a visit.

COLORADO

Neota

★ ★ ★

Size: 9924 acres   **Year Designated:** 1980
Responsible Agency: USFS

The Neota Wilderness is located in the Roosevelt National Forest just off State Highway 14. The Rawah Wilderness is to the northwest and the Comanche Peak Wilderness is to the east. The National Geographic Trails Illustrated map 112 (Colorado) covers the wilderness.

MY VISIT: August 15, 2007

This day hike began at a turnout off State Highway 14 that served as a trailhead for Zimmerman Lake. The trail ended at the lake at the wilderness boundary and I hiked off-trail for a short while through timber and then broke out into open country with easy access to a high, open ridge. I got to the top, then wandered south to a high spot (11,727 feet), had lunch, turned around, and went back to my truck. After the crowds in the Rawah, this day was a treat as there was never another soul in sight. I can recommend this hike to anyone looking for an obscure, quiet but still scenic, and trailless destination.

Forest, meadow, and ridges, Neota Wilderness

Never Summer

★ ★ ★

Size: 20,692 acres   **Year Designated:** 1980
Responsible Agency: USFS

The Never Summer Wilderness is located in the Routt and Arapaho National Forests just outside the northwestern boundary of Rocky Mountain National Park. The Continental Divide and its namesake trail go through the area. The mountains are part of the Never Summer Range. Peaks on or close to the divide include Mounts Nimbus, Stratus, Cumulus, and Cirrus. Most of the wilderness is on the National Geographic Trails Illustrated map for Rocky Mountain National Park.

MY VISIT: August 14, 2007

This long day hike began where a sign on a Forest Service road along the South Fork of the Michigan River said that the road was now a four-wheel-drive road. I looked at this road and parked my four-wheel-drive pickup truck. As I hiked up the road, I was very glad I had parked where I did because I considered the road undrivable. It was just 1.5 miles to the end of the road at the wilderness boundary. I continued on the trail in forest and intermittent rain to Baker Pass at the park boundary. Views from the pass were good even with heavy cloud cover. There was not much lightning, so I decided to climb higher on the completely open divide. I stopped for photos and lunch at the site of an old mine.

On the way down, I encountered a couple of backpackers on their way up. They said that they drove the last 1.5 miles of road and had no trouble. When I got to their vehicle, I saw that it was a Nissan Frontier four-wheel-drive pickup just like mine. I paid close attention to the road on the way down and I still say that there was no way I would try to drive up that stretch of road.

This was a good day even though the weather was not the best. The Never Summer is a nice area and I recommend it. I do not include any photos because they were too dark.

Mount Massive

★ ★ ★

Size: 30,540 acres   **Year Designated:** 1980
Responsible Agency: USFS

The Mount Massive Wilderness is located in the San Isabel National Forest west of US Highway 24 and southwest of the city of Leadville. The Continental Divide forms the western wilderness boundary and the Continental Divide Trail goes through the eastern part of the wilderness. The National Geographic Trails Illustrated map 127 (Colorado) covers the area.

MY VISIT: July 17, 2008

The goal this day was the summit of Mount Massive. I knew it would be a long day. I got a 6:00 am start on the trail. There is a Mount Massive and Mount Elbert Trailhead and from there I went north on the Continental Divide Trail to the Mount Massive Trail. I was slow and plodding. There were other hikers. I distinctly remember one man with a child of about five years, way too young to be attempting this hike, but dad was insisting that this would work (I think it did). It took me five hours to get the 14,421-foot summit. The weather was not the best, and I worried a little about thunderstorms. Summit views were good, 360-degree vistas of mountains. I did not dally at the summit because of weather and retraced my steps back to my truck. It took another five hours to get down, so a long day. There was a little rain and thunder on the way down.

This was certainly a pleasant day, but I must admit that I did not see anything of special interest. For anyone who is a peak bagger, go here. Personally, I have no interest in coming back, but that should not deter anyone else from visiting this area.

COLORADO
Flat Tops
★ ★ ★

Size: 235,214 acres   **Year Designated:** 1975
Responsible Agency: USFS

The Flat Tops Wilderness is located in the Routt and White River National Forests north of Interstate Highway 70, east of the town of Meeker, and north of the town of Glenwood Springs. At the time of my visit there was a small USFS map dedicated to this wilderness, although I consider the White River National Forest map more useful if somewhat clumsy.

MY VISIT: August 5–8, 2004

My four-day backpack began at the Wall Lake Trailhead and I proceeded to hike up to Wall Lake in the rain and camp for the night. The terrain here was mostly volcanic and Wall Lake sits at the base of a volcanic cliff. The second day I went mostly east to Deer Lake through scenic, open terrain with good views. There was a little rain. Day three I went from Deer Lake to West Lake. This segment required traversing the famous Devils Causeway. The causeway is a very narrow hogback with steep drops on both sides. There were numerous other hikers around, each trying to test their level of fear at crossing. For me, the test was could I do it walking upright? The answer was no, I had to get down on my hands and knees. While I was watching, the most confident traverse of all was made by a beagle. I blamed my big pack for my hesitation. This was a nice hiking day in very open terrain above tree line through some rock and some high meadow. On my last day I hiked to the Skinny Fish Trailhead. I had to hike the road back to my truck, but that was OK with me because I was able to make a nice loop. And yes, there were a few high spots with *very* flat tops.

This is a nice area. I liked the scenery and the open terrain. I recommend the area to just about anybody.

Thunderstorm approaching Trapper Peak, Flat Tops Wilderness

COLORADO
Indian Peaks
★ ★ ★

Size: 77,711 acres   **Year Designated:** 1978
Responsible Agency: USFS

The Indian Peaks Wilderness is located in the Arapaho and Roosevelt National Forests south of Rocky Mountain National Park and west of the city of Boulder. Access is via State Highways 7 and 72 on the east and roads from US Highway 34 on the west. National Geographic Trails Illustrated maps 102 and 103 (Colorado) cover this wilderness.

MY VISITS: July 18, 2008 and July 20, 2008 and July 7, 2009

What a shock. After looking at my map I picked an east-side trailhead for what I hoped would be an overnight trip. I got to this trailhead and it was a total mob scene with huge numbers of cars, people, and dogs. There was literally no place to park. In addition, unknown to me, overnight trips required permits. I would have no part of this. I found another trailhead, still crowded but at least I could find a parking place. This was at the Mitchell Lake Trailhead, and my destination for this day hike was Blue Lake and an off-trail scramble to a higher lake. There were other hikers, but tolerable. The valley was very scenic, the lake pleasant, and the scramble to the upper lake was fun.

Two days later and in an effort to avoid crowds I went to the west side of the wilderness and began a day hike from the Devils Thumb Trailhead. This is an access point for the Continental Divide Trail (here also called the High Lonesome Trail). I went east to the actual Divide, then south on the Divide. Here the number of other hikers became large. I continued south past Bob and Betty Lakes and to an overlook of King Lake where I turned around. The terrain was mostly wide open and easy, gentle hiking. The scenery was good but nothing special.

The third hike in 2009 was a better experience. I began again on the west side of the wilderness at the Roaring Fork Trailhead. It was a day of perfect weather. The trail climbed steeply through timber before breaking out on open ridges with excellent views. The trail went to a very pretty Stone Lake and then ended at what my map called Upper Lake. I saw exactly one other hiker this day.

Overall, this is a nice enough area with good scenery and an extensive trail system. Is it really wild? Certainly not on the east side, based on my experience. I know better hiking destinations elsewhere in Colorado.

Vasquez Peak

Size: 12,300 acres   **Year Designated:** 1993
Responsible Agency: USFS

The oddly shaped Vasquez Peak Wilderness is located in the Arapaho National Forest west of US Highway 40 near Berthoud Pass. The area is shown on National Geographic Trails Illustrated map 103 (Colorado).

MY VISIT: July 19, 2008

This day hike began at the Henderson Mine Trailhead. The trail climbed steeply to a junction with the Continental Divide Trail at the wilderness boundary. The trail followed the Divide to a junction with an obscure trail that I took northwest across the wilderness to the summit of Mount Nystrom (12,652 feet). This was a day of good weather through mostly open terrain with some nice if not spectacular views. I recommend this hike and area to most hikers.

Byers Peak

★ ★ ★

Size: 8095 acres   **Year Designated:** 1993
Responsible Agency: USFS

The Byers Peak Wilderness is located in the Arapaho National Forest south of US Highway 40 and west of the Winter Park ski resort. It is west of the Vasquez Peak Wilderness. The area is shown on the National Geographic Trails Illustrated map 103 (Colorado).

MY VISIT: September 18, 2006

My day began with getting very confused with county roads and Forest Service roads whose names did not match the names on my map. I finally found my Lake Evelyn Trailhead at an elevation of 9,800 feet where there was significant snow on the ground. But I was prepared and made the short hike to Lake Evelyn in good time. The map showed the trail continuing past the lake, but I couldn't find it in the snow, so I bushwhacked up the hillside and indeed found the trail again. The trail followed a wide-open scenic ridge to an elevation of 11,829 feet. I continued north to a prominent point at 11,605 feet and had lunch in the sun. I then basically retraced my steps back to the trailhead, passing three other hikers along the way.

Even considering the snow, this was a nice hike on a nice day, an easy route with good views. I recommend it.

James Peak

★ ★ ★

Size: 17,084 acres   **Year Designated:** 2002
Responsible Agency: USFS

The James Peak Wilderness is located in the Roosevelt National Forest south of the Indian Peaks Wilderness and west of State Highway 119. Access is via the Rollins Pass Road. At the time of my visit no maps showed the boundaries of this wilderness.

MY VISIT: July 8, 2009

My day hike began at the East Portal of the famous Moffat Tunnel (a long railway tunnel). My route went southwest to Heart Lake then up to Rogers Pass and the Continental Divide Trail, then south to the base of James Peak where I stopped and turned around. This was a perfect weather day and the hiking was mostly in open terrain. Heart Lake was lovely. There were plenty of other hikers, but I did not have a sense of being crowded. One of my favorite wildflowers is the rarely seen alpine forget-me-not. I saw some here near James Peak. This was a worthwhile day and an area I can recommend.

*Alpine forget-me-nots,
James Peak Wilderness*

Mount Evans

★ ★ ★

Size: 74,401 acres   **Year Designated:** 1980
Responsible Agency: USFS

The Mount Evans Wilderness is located in the Arapaho National Forest north of US Highway 285, south of State Highway 103, and southwest of the town of Idaho Springs. The area is shown on the National Geographic Trails Illustrated map 104 (Colorado).

MY VISIT: June 20–21, 2007

This overnight backpack began at the Abyss Trailhead near the southwest corner of the wilderness. My route was pretty easy, just going northeast up the Abyss Trail to Abyss Lake where I camped. The lake is pretty, surrounded by lots of meadow with views of lots of rock above, including Mount Evans itself at 14,265 feet. The lake elevation is 12,650 feet.

Within about two seconds of setting my pack down, I was approached by a marmot who had obviously seen lots of other backpackers. As soon as I could I attached a cord to my food bags and jammed the other end of cord into a crack in a nearby boulder. The varmint appeared to have seen this practice before as well, staring up at the bags and looking for the other end of the cord. There was a definite look of frustration.

This was a nice hike in a nice area although without any especially interesting features. I recommend it.

Food bags? What food bags?
Marmot, Mount Evans Wilderness

Lost Creek

★ ★ ★

Size: 120,700 acres   **Year Designated:** 1980
Responsible Agency: USFS

The Lost Creek Wilderness is located in the Pike National Forest south of US Highway 285, north of US Highway 24, and east of the town of Fairplay.

MY VISIT: September 19–20, 2006

My original intent was to do an overnight loop trip from the east side of the wilderness, but that side had recently suffered a severe fire. Instead I turned around and went over to the west side. I found a trailhead for Ute Creek and started walking northeast toward Bison Peak. The area was quite dry and I camped near the last flowing water in Ute Creek. The terrain was gentle and open with lots of old, worn granite. The next day I made an off-trail day hike to the summit of Bison Peak (12,431 feet). This was a fascinating stroll through highly eroded Pikes Peak granite spires with a few pine trees scattered around. The weather was about perfect and the light was good for photos. After taking lots of photos I turned around, went back to my camp, packed up, and went back to the trailhead. Unfortunately, my developed photos (prints) were of poor quality.

This is a worthwhile destination. I recommend it to just about any hiker.

Mount Sneffels

★ ★ ★

Size: 16,505 acres   **Year Designated:** 1980
Responsible Agency: USFS

The Mount Sneffels Wilderness is located in the Uncompahgre National Forest west of US Highway 550 and north of the resort town of Telluride. The National Geographic Trails Illustrated map 141 (Colorado) covers the area.

MY VISIT: July 17, 2006

I was taken aback when arriving at the Blue Lakes Trailhead as there were multiple school buses and lots of other vehicles parked nearby. My route (and just about everyone else's route) went up the Blue Lakes Trail past the three Blue Lakes and to Blue Lakes Pass at the eastern edge of the wilderness. The early part of the day had beautiful weather and the route was scenic. I didn't see many other hikers until the area around the pass. These folks were looking to climb Mount Sneffels, one of Colorado's fourteeners, which sits north of the pass on the wilderness boundary. I took a quick look at the mountain but did not see an easy route for a nontechnical climber. I had lunch on the pass and started back down. Not attempting the summit turned out to be a good choice as rain and thunder began soon after leaving the pass. My notes remind me that on my way down I slipped on some mud and made a major mess of myself. This is a pretty area and I recommend it.

Navajo Lake, Lizard Head Wilderness

Lizard Head

★ ★ ★

Size: 41,496 acres   **Year Designated:** 1980
Responsible Agency: USFS

The Lizard Head Wilderness is located in the San Juan and Uncompahgre National Forests north and west of State Highway 145 and southwest of the resort town of Telluride. The National Geographic Trails Illustrated map 141 (Colorado) covers this area.

MY VISIT: July 16, 2006

This long day hike began at the Navajo Lake Trailhead at the southern wilderness boundary. The route went north and then east to Navajo Lake (pictured), continuing east past the lake, then turning north to the Rock of Ages Mine in a pass near the northern wilderness boundary. The wilderness is home to two fourteeners, El Diente Peak and Mount Wilson. Lizard Head itself is only 13,113 feet. The day had glorious weather and a very scenic route of forest, meadow, lake, and tall mountains. The thunder and rain held off until I was back at the trailhead. It was a long day with a lot of elevation gain, but quite worthwhile. I recommend this area.

Raggeds

★ ★ ★

Size: 65,019 acres   **Year Designated:** 1980
Responsible Agency: USFS

The Raggeds Wilderness is located in the Gunnison and White River National Forests northwest of State Highway 135 and northwest of the town of Crested Butte. The National Geographic Trails Illustrated maps 133 and 128 (Colorado) cover the area. The Ruby Range mountains form the area's backbone.

MY VISIT: June 25—26, 2007

This overnight backpack began at the Horse Ranch Park Trailhead. My route went north through forest, meadow, and small lakes with views of the Ruby Range, then on to the Oh Be Joyful Trail. Here the scenery got even better as the trail neared my destination of Oh Be Joyful Pass. It was still pretty early in the season, and there was some snow and a lot of meltwater. I made a camp in upper Swan Basin and then hiked to the top of the pass. Views were very good and there were no boot tracks going down through the snow into Democrat Basin. To this day I wonder if the very tall man just visible below was John Kerry.

The next morning there was a small band of seven elk near my camp. One appeared to be almost albino with only a few patches of tan. I packed up and had a leisurely hike through nice scenery back to the trailhead. This is a nice area and I recommend it.

Marcelina and the Chair, Raggeds Wilderness

La Garita

★ ★ ★

Size: 226,455 acres   **Year Designated:** 1993
Responsible Agency: USFS and USNPS

The La Garita Wilderness is located in the Gunnison and Rio Grande National Forests north of State Highway 149 and north of the town of Creede. The Continental Divide and its namesake trail run through and along the southern boundary of the wilderness. The San Juan Mountains run along the southern boundary, and the La Garita Mountains run through the eastern portion of the wilderness. The area is covered by National Geographic Trails Illustrated map 139 (Colorado).

MY VISIT: July 21–22, 2006

This overnight backpack began at the Mineral Creek Trailhead on the north side of the wilderness. My route was south along Mineral Creek, then up the West Fork of the creek. The early hiking was in timber, then broke out in high, open, almost tundra terrain. On the way I met an outfitter on horseback and we talked about the local wildlife. He predicted that I would see bighorn sheep. I found a nice campsite well below the Continental Divide because thunderstorms were almost guaranteed later in the day. There was still time, however, to wander up to the Divide for views to the south, including Snow Mesa. I went back to camp at the first sound of thunder. I dived into the tent just as it began to hail.

There was enough of a break in the weather to allow me to fix dinner, but then it was back into the tent for a heavy-duty storm with enough hail to turn the ground completely white. Later, after things calmed down, I got out of the tent and just above me, as predicted, were a few bighorn sheep.

The next day I went back to the Divide and the CDT, hiking east to the head of the East Fork of Mineral Creek and then back to the trailhead.

Another nice area that I can recommend to just about anybody.

The Precipice, Uncompahgre Wilderness

Uncompahgre

★ ★ ★

Size: 102,668 acres   **Year Designated:** 1980
Responsible Agency: USFS

The Uncompahgre Wilderness is located in the Uncompahgre National Forest west of State Highway 149 and northwest of the town of Lake City. The area is covered by National Geographic Trails Illustrated map 141 (Colorado).

MY VISIT: July 18–19, 2006

This overnight backpack began at a trailhead for the Middle Fork of the Cimarron River. The trail went south through timber along the river. The forest was open enough so that dramatic cliffs above the river were always in view. Precipice Peak was particularly impressive. Once above timberline the view was dominated by Matterhorn Peak and Wetterhorn (14,015 feet) Peak. I ascended to a pass between Matterhorn and Uncompahgre Peaks. Thunderstorms were gathering and I decided to make camp south of Uncompahgre Peak. Just about dark I heard and then saw a flock of domestic sheep. There was a little rain after dark.

The next day's goal was the summit of Uncompahgre Peak. It looked like it should be safe and easy. This time of year, any summit attempt must begin early and I did get an early start. Approaching the base of the peak I encountered a group of young people from Outward Bound who were putting on climbing helmets. I was worried that the route may be hazardous, but they assured me it was not. I did reach the 14,309-foot summit in good shape. Views, especially north down the Cimarron River, were splendid. Just as I began to descend, the clouds were building and it really was time to go back down to my camp. I packed up, went back to the Matterhorn-Uncompahgre Pass, and descended the way I came up. By the time I got back to my truck it had been a twelve-hour day with a lot of vertical. I was truly tired.

I doubt that many hikers would be disappointed in this area.

COLORADO

Sangre de Cristo

★ ★ ★

Size: 226,455 acres   **Year Designated:** 1993
Responsible Agency: USFS and USNPS

The Sangre de Cristo Wilderness is the home of the Sangre de Cristo Range in the San Isabel and Rio Grande National Forests. It is north and east of State Highway 150 and can also be accessed from roads off State Highway 17 to the west and State Highway 69 to the east. The closest town to the east is Westcliffe. The area is home to five peaks over 14,000 feet. There is a National Geographic Trails Illustrated map that covers this wilderness plus Great Sand Dunes National Park.

MY VISITS: July 10–11, 2009 and June 3–4, 2012 and June 5, 2012 and June 8, 2012

The first overnight backpack began at the trailhead for the North Fork of Crestone Creek. The trail led to Venable Pass. The day was hot and buggy, and after climbing over 3,000 feet I made camp in a scenic spot just below the pass. I saw only one other hiker and the trail seemed little used. The next day I went to the top of the pass with views of Venable Lake, then along the main ridgeline to Comanche Pass. Wonderful views from this pass. There were lots of other hikers and backpackers here. From this pass I descended the Comanche Trail along the Lake Fork of North Crestone Creek and back to the trailhead.

The second backpack began on the east side of the wilderness at a trailhead for the Lakes of the Clouds. It was obvious from the beginning that this area received heavy use. Lots of trash and lots of people camped right on the shore of a lake posted for no camping within 300 feet. Still, I put up my camp well away from the lake, and just in time as the almost-certain rain began at 3:00 p.m. There was enough hail associated with the rain to turn the ground white. Speaking of white ground, there was still a little snow here at lake level of 11,500 feet. When the weather calmed down, I did a stroll up the trail until I had a view of all three lakes. Above the lakes there was considerably more snow. It turned out that I had a companion near my campsite—a snowshoe hare. Day two all I did was retrace my steps to the trailhead.

The June 5, 2012 day hike began near the end of the Mosca Pass Road. I had encountered a trail crew the previous day and they told me about an unofficial trail to Carbonate Mountain. I found this "trail" and followed it for a steep climb to a false summit where there were good views of the Great Sand Dunes National Park. I was going to turn around here, but after a bit of wandering about the summit I saw a cairned route continuing up a ridge to a derelict log shelter with a higher peak, presumably Carbonate, still beyond. By now it looked like thunderstorms were forming, and the route to the true summit was very exposed in case of lightning. I decided it was safer to turn around so I just went back to my truck. As it turned out, there were no thunderstorms that day.

The June 8, 2012 day hike was also from the east side of the wilderness beginning at the Horn Lake Trailhead. The trail followed Horn Creek through timber and climbed to timberline above 11,000 feet where I chose the left fork going to the larger Horn Lake. This was a nice weather day and a nice destination. Here I had a lunch companion, a large marmot that just looked like it wanted somebody to hang out with for a little while.

I have spent some time in this area and I like it. I "only" give it three stars mostly because it does not have quite the "wow" factor as some other areas do, but I still recommend it to just about anybody.

COLORADO
Great Sand Dunes
★ ★ ★

Size: 75,225 acres   **Year Designated:** 1976
Responsible Agency: USNPS

Much of the Great Sand Dunes National Park is designated wilderness. The easiest access is via State Highway 150, which ends in the park. The National Geographic Trails Illustrated map for the park and the Sangre de Cristo Wilderness map covers this area. The Sangre de Cristo Mountains form the physical eastern boundary of the Great Sand Dunes Wilderness.

MY VISIT: June 6–7, 2012

This overnight backpack began at the "Point of No Return" at the beginning of a four-wheel-drive road ending at the Sand Ramp Trailhead. I scouted the four-wheel road for a bit and decided not to risk taking my truck, so I parked and walked. From what I saw coming and going this was a good choice. The four-wheel route required a deeper water crossing than I was willing to do and deeper sand than I wanted to do. So I carried my pack up the "road" to the Sand Ramp Trailhead and followed the trail northwest into the wilderness. The going was much more difficult than I anticipated. The terrain was about 99 percent sand and the day was hot. To be honest, I was not having fun. After about eight or nine miles I arrived at a permitted campsite at Cold Creek, short of my nominal destination of Sand Creek. I decide to camp at Cold Creek. This was a pleasant site with a wren's nest in the aspen trees. There were no other humans anywhere close. There were some good views along my route over toward Carbonate Mountain and, of course, of the dunes.

My backcountry permit allowed me to stay a second night, but I decided to go out my second day. It was another difficult slog in soft sand. When I got back to my truck I made the decision that I had now filled my lifetime quota of miles carrying a pack in soft sand.

While I will never claim to have had a wonderful time in this area, I will still give it a three-star rating because of its uniqueness. I do not discourage anyone else from visiting this area.

Spanish Peaks

★ ★ ★

Size: 17,885 acres   **Year Designated:** 2000
Responsible Agency: USFS

The Spanish Peaks Wilderness is located in the San Isabel National Forest west of Interstate Highway 25 and east of State Highway 12.

MY VISIT: July 9, 2009

These mountains have dorsal fins. It is their claim to fame in addition to acting as easily recognizable guideposts to early travelers. My day hike began late at a trailhead near Wahatoya Camp. The route went south through pleasant forest. Near timberline I took the trail to the West Spanish Peak. Once above timberline views of the dikes were good. The peaks are of granitic rock, and in the distant past there were magma intrusions that, after erosion, formed dikes that look as though the mountains have dorsal fins. Due to a late start I did not get to the summit, but the views I did get seemed sufficient. From my limited time here, I rate the area as interesting because of the dikes as well as a pleasant place for a hike.

South San Juan

★ ★ ★

Size: 158,790 acres   **Year Designated:** 1980
Responsible Agency: USFS

The South San Juan Wilderness is located in the Rio Grande and San Juan National Forests east of the city of Durango, east of US Highways 84 and 160, and northwest of State Highway 17. The area is home to the San Juan Mountains. The Continental Divide and its namesake trail traverse the wilderness. The area is covered by the National Geographic Trails Illustrated map 142 (Colorado).

MY VISIT: August 18–21, 2001

This five-day backpack did not start well. It began at a trailhead for the Adams Fork Conejos River just above the Platoro Reservoir, and I went up the Adams fork not very far when I found myself behind a huge herd of sheep (a couple of thousand). The stench was overwhelming. There was no way I was going to continue up this trail. My intention was to go north on the Continental Divide Trail, but that was the direction the sheep were going, so I made a quick decision to go south on the CDT. I got as far as the headwaters for the North Fork of the Conejos River and camped for that night. The next day I went back to the CDT and continued south to Blue Lake and made a second camp, encountering a second large (multi-thousand) band of sheep. The terrain around Blue Lake was quite lovely. Day three was the highlight of the trip. I did a long day hike in perfect weather from Blue Lake northeast on the Glacier Lake Trail to Glacier Lake with its large snowbank, past Twin Lakes, then up to the summit of Conejos Peak (13,172 feet) and back to Glacier Lake by a different trail. This was a very scenic day, almost all of it above tree line. The terrain was wide open, with nice meadows, lakes, and hard rock. Day four was a day hike to Fish Lake. My route out was circuitous: the CDT to the Middle Fork of the Conejos, then the Three Forks Trail back to the Platoro Reservoir.

In many ways this was a nice trip, but the sheep detracted. I talked to other hikers who said there was no time to avoid large numbers of livestock; one got either cows or sheep depending on the time of year. The area was also clearly popular, with quite a few other hikers and some people on horseback.

COLORADO
Black Canyon of the Gunnison

★ ★ ★

Size: 15,999 acres   **Year Designated:** 1976
Responsible Agency: USNPS

The Black Canyon of the Gunnison Wilderness is located east of US Highway 50 and north of the city of Montrose. The easiest access is via State Highway 347. Much of Black Canyon of the Gunnison National Park is designated wilderness.

MY VISIT: May 15, 2011

This day hike began on the canyon rim and I followed the Warner Route down to the Gunnison River. The canyon here was 2,770 feet deep. The route was quite steep but safe. The river was running fast. The "Black" in the name came from the fact that the canyon is narrow and gets very little sunlight.

My impression was that this is more of a river runner's area than a hiker's. I think my trail was the only trail in the wilderness portion of the park. This was a nice hike and I recommend it.

UTAH
Mount Naomi

★ ★ ★

Size: 44,350 acres   **Year Designated:** 1984
Responsible Agency: USFS

The Mount Naomi Wilderness is located in the Wasatch-Cache National Forest just south of the Idaho state line, east of US Highway 91, and northeast of the city of Logan in the northern part of the Wasatch Range.

MY VISITS: June 6, 2002 and October 9, 2014

Both of these day hikes began at the High Creek Trailhead in the northwest portion of the wilderness. Both hikes went up the Naomi

Peak National Recreation Trail. The first hike was just too early in the season, with lots of snow and high-water levels in High Creek. Twelve years later and a different season provided a very nice hike. The weather was perfect and fall colors were still dominant. The trail climbed significantly to a pass at the eastern edge of the wilderness where I stopped. The summit of Naomi Peak was easily visible, but it was time to turn around. My memory is that I did not see any other hikers. I would describe the terrain as gentle Wasatch: not many cliffs, nothing dramatic, but quite lovely. As a general statement for all Wasatch areas, fall is a great time to visit.

This is a nice area. Come and do a hike here.

Mount Olympus

★ ★ ★

Size: 15,292 acres   **Year Designated:** 1984
Responsible Agency: USFS

The Mount Olympus Wilderness is located in the Wasatch-Cache National Forest just east of greater Salt Lake City. The Big Cottonwood Canyon Road to the Brighton ski resort runs along the southern wilderness boundary and State Highway 213 is just to the west. The spine of the Wasatch Range runs through the wilderness.

MY VISIT: June 29, 2005

This day hike began at a trailhead along the Big Cottonwood Canyon Road. I went north to the Wasatch Crest, then continued along the crest until it was time to turn around. The Wasatch here are very rugged with summits over 11,000 feet looming over the densely populated Salt Lake Valley. There are good if sometimes steep trails and hiking is popular. On my hike there was still a lot of snow around and the views were excellent, especially

to the south into the Twin Peaks Wilderness. Lower elevations had pleasant evergreen forests with lots of aspen, small oak, and other deciduous trees that turn brilliant colors in the fall.

The three wilderness areas adjacent to Salt Lake City—Mount Olympus, Twin Peaks and Lone Peak—are very similar and all three are good hiking destinations. I recommend all three.

Twin Peaks

★ ★ ★

Size: 11,436 acres   **Year Designated:** 1984
Responsible Agency: USFS

Just south of the Mount Olympus Wilderness and across the Big Cottonwood Canyon Road is the Twin Peaks Wilderness. The southern wilderness boundary is the Little Cottonwood Canyon Road leading to the Alta ski resort. State Highway 210 is just to the west.

MY VISIT: June 28, 2005

This day hike went from a Big Cottonwood Canyon trailhead south on a trail to Lakes Florence, Blanche, and Lilian. While I don't have detailed notes from this hike, I remember going mostly through timber to lakes that were basically still in snow. The terrain was very similar to that of Mount Olympus.

Lone Peak

★ ★ ★

Size: 30,736 acres   **Year Designated:** 1978
Responsible Agency: USFS

The Lone Peak Wilderness is just south of the Twin Peaks Wilderness. Little Cottonwood Canyon Road is the northern boundary and American Fork Canyon Road (State Highway 92) is the southern boundary. There is a National Geographic Trails Illustrated map, Utah 701, for this area.

MY VISITS: June 30, 2005 and October 16, 2014

The first day hike began at a trailhead along Little Cottonwood Canyon Road and I went south to Red Pine Lake. The route was mostly through forest and here I clearly remember the lake completely surrounded by snow. I also remember liking the area, saying that I needed to come back.

Come back I did nine years later. This day hike began at the Silver Lake Trailhead off the American Fork Canyon Road. There is a good trail climbing a rather short way to a very pretty Silver Lake surrounded by gleaming pale rock. It was a gorgeous weather day and there was still a lot of fall color. There were also a *lot* of other hikers, including many children, in part, I suppose, because it is an easy hike.

There was also romance in the air. Close to the trail were three moose: two young bulls and one cow (a second cow was a little distance away). The larger bull was fending off advances on the cow by the smaller bull. There were mock charges and lots of grunting, the most moose vocalization I had ever heard. I got close enough to take the photo seen here (look closely, the big dark thing is a bull moose), then decided it was best not to hang around too long.

Once again, I recommend all three of these areas—Lone Peak, Mount Olympus, and Twin Peaks—to just about any hiker.

Bull moose in aspen, Lone Peak Wilderness

Deseret Peak

★ ★ ★

Size: 25,500 acres   **Year Designated:** 1984
Responsible Agency: USFS

The Deseret Peak Wilderness is located in the Wasatch-Cache National Forest south of Interstate Highway 80 and west of the town of Tooele, not far west of Salt Lake City. The Stansbury Mountains make up most of the wilderness.

MY VISIT: June 29, 2003

My day hike began at a trailhead at the end of South Willow Road. The trail climbed south and a bit west to the summit of Deseret Peak. The trail began in timber, then climbed steeply up to and above tree line. The terrain here was pretty dry but there was still a little snow around. The views from the summit (11,031 feet) were good but not great.

What was striking on this hike and the drive to the trailhead was the enormous number of Mormon crickets. Mormon crickets are katydids, not crickets, and they thrive in the sagebrush country of the American West. They can get to be three inches long and are plump. They can also swarm in very large numbers, becoming numerous enough that when squashed by cars on roads the road surface becomes slippery. There was a big infestation the day of my hike. I started rather late and I returned from the summit as it was getting dark. The "crickets" were crawling all over boulders along the trail and in the poor light the boulders appeared to be moving. Going lower still, I brushed against a spruce tree and scared up a cloud of miller moths, making things even a little spookier. Miller moths are the adult form of army cutworms, also famous for appearing in very large numbers.

Given the insects and the terrain, I found this a pretty interesting trip. I can recommend the area.

*Mount Nebo from North Peak,
Mount Nebo Wilderness*

Mount Nebo

★ ★ ★

Size: 27,057 acres   **Year Designated:** 1984
Responsible Agency: USFS

The Mount Nebo Wilderness is located in the Uinta National Forest east of Interstate Highway 15, north of State Highway 132, and northeast of the town of Nephi. It is in the southern portion of the Wasatch Range. The National Geographic Trails Illustrated map 701 (Utah) covers this wilderness.

MY VISITS: June 19, 2006 and October 14, 2014

The first day hike began at a trailhead for the Nebo Bench Trail which went up Andrews Ridge. My goal was to get as close to the Mount Nebo summit as I could. I failed, in part because of a poor choice of trailheads. The elevation of my trailhead was 6,400 feet. The Mount Nebo summit, at 11,928 feet, would be a big climb even in good conditions. Conditions were not good. There was still a fair bit of snow around and I lost the trail when it made a switchback. I eventually found the trail again, but the higher I got the more snow covered the trail. The snow was steep in some of the chutes and I considered it unsafe. I gave up and turned around after climbing about 3, 400 feet. This was a nice area and my intention was to come back. I saw nobody on this hike.

Eight years later and in a different season I did come back. This day hike began at an obscure, little-used trailhead north of Mount Nebo. It was a ridge trail with good views all the time, always dim, and occasionally pretty steep. The terrain was classic Wasatch limestone, mostly above tree line. The area around the trailhead had obviously been heavily grazed by cattle. There was still a little fall color left but was well past its prime. I managed to get to and over North Peak (11,174 feet) and into Wolf Pass. To me, the summit of Mount Nebo did not look feasible from this vantage point, so I just turned around. The photo shows Mount Nebo's summit. This was another day of solitude, no other hikers and the trail seemed to get little use. It was a nice day on a nice route in a nice area. I recommend it.

Pine Valley Mountain

★ ★ ★

Size: 50,216 acres   **Year Designated:** 1984
Responsible Agency: USFS

The Pine Valley Mountain Wilderness is located in the Dixie National Forest west of Interstate Highway 15 and east of State Highway 18. The town of Central is to the west, the town of Leeds is to the southeast, and the much larger city of St. George is nearby to the south. The Pine Valley Mountains make up much of the area.

MY VISITS: June 21, 2006 and October 14, 2012

My notes are very sparse for my first day hike. I do know that I began at the Oak Grove Trailhead on the east side of the wilderness. My destination was the Summit Trail via the Oak Grove Trail. After an hour or so I concluded that I was not on the Oak Grove Trail, but probably on the Cottonwood-Harmon Trail. I turned around and went back to the trailhead. Indeed, there was a much less obvious trail that went up to the Summit Trail. This trail was steep and the day was getting pretty hot as I went through a long series of limestone cliffs. I eventually did get to the Summit Trail, but neither my notes nor memory tell me what I did after getting to Deer Flat. Given the wasted couple of hours earlier, I probably did not do much more. Another case of come back later.

Later turned out to be six years later and in fall after conditions turned cooler. This hike began on the west side of the wilderness at the Whipple Trailhead. There were several folks at the trailhead taking photos of a young woman in wedding attire.

This was a lovely, brilliantly clear, cool day with even a little snow visible at high elevation. My route was to Whipple Valley and somewhat beyond. The terrain was mostly forest with occasional views. It was a pleasant day in a pleasant area and I can recommend it, but with the warning that summer can be really hot here.

Box-Death Hollow

★ ★ ★

Size: 25,750 acres   **Year Designated:** 1984
Responsible Agency: USFS

The Box-Death Hollow Wilderness is located in the Dixie National Forest north of State Highway 12 and north of the town of Escalante. The best access is via the Hells Backbone Road, built by the Civilian Conservation Corps in the 1930s. It is a very scenic drive and I would recommend it even to nonhikers. The views from the Hells Backbone Bridge are worth the road trip. There is a guidebook, *Hiking the Escalante* by Rudi Lambrecht, that covers this area. I have used USFS handouts for wilderness trails and how to access them.

MY VISITS: May 1, 1986 and April 11–12, 2014

During the 1980s I was living in southeastern Idaho and springtime was time to go hiking in southern Utah. We could get there in a reasonable day's driving. The greater Escalante was often a destination as were Harris Wash and Coyote Wash on BLM lands. One of the most infamous hikes was Death Hollow. This hike required a lot of time in water, swimming and diving into plunge pools, negotiating thorns and other obstacles. I have never done that part of what is now the wilderness.

The day hike in 1986 was with a small group of Idaho friends and was along Pine Creek, a tributary to the Escalante River. I have no detailed notes and do not remember where we began. I do remember (from a few remaining photos) hiking through gray, tan, and occasionally yellow or red eroded sandstone amid pine trees and some aspen.

The 2014 trip began at a new visitor center getting advice on destinations in the wilderness. A BLM employee recommended Lower Box Canyon and gave us a handout. We exchanged tales of Death Hollow, and she told me that it is much worse than in the 1980s because the canyon had filled with poison ivy. My friend Maya and I began our backpack at a trailhead along the Hells Backbone Road for Lower Box Canyon. It was a nice weather day, not too hot. This neighborhood can get very hot in the summer. The

trail followed the creek, crossing often. The USFS handout said that the Upper Box Trail crosses the creek fifty-four times. On this day I counted about twenty-two crossings. This was a very pretty canyon with some of the most brilliant sandstone I have seen. The terrain was not desert, but very green with big ponderosa pine, some Douglas fir, juniper, cottonwood, and willow with blooming manzanita. We made camp where the canyon started to narrow, taking care to avoid the numerous prickly pear cacti. The next day we retraced our steps back to the trailhead. The morning light really set the sandstone colors on fire, as shown in the photo.

UTAH
Red Mountain
★ ★ ★

Size: 18,729 acres   **Year Designated:** 2009
Responsible Agency: BLM

The Red Mountain Wilderness is located just northwest of the city of St. George and just west of State Highway 18. A map of this area and its one trail can be found on a map of the Red Cliffs Desert Reserve.

MY VISIT: November 4, 2011

My day hike began at a trailhead just off State Highway 18 (but hard to see from the highway). The early part of the hike was not very interesting, just the usual pinon and juniper on rather flat sandstone. All of a sudden there was a side trail with dramatic views down into Snow Canyon, most of it in a state park. Back on the main trail, I continued south to some wide-open gray slickrock with bands of red and yellow and more dramatic views of Snow Canyon. I kept going south until my watch dictated it was time to turn around. I had no idea what to expect on this hike, but it certainly turned out well. This is an area I recommend to anyone.

UTAH

Canaan Mountains

★ ★ ★

Size: 44,531 acres   **Year Designated:** 2009
Responsible Agency: BLM

The Canaan Mountains Wilderness is located south of Zion National Park and south of State Highway 9.

MY VISIT: October 31, 2011

This day hike began at more-or-less of a trailhead for the Eagle Crags, a rather impressive rock formation. The trail was easy to the crags. I found the crags neat but then noticed that the trail sort of kept going upcanyon, marked by cairns. I followed. At first there were boot tracks and the trail held steady elevation. But there were nasty gullies to cross and I began to wonder where this trail was going. There were no obvious ways out of the canyon because of cliffs. The trail became ever dimmer and I finally decided to just turn around.

The terrain here was standard southern Utah sandstone with pinon, juniper, sagebrush, rabbitbrush, and bitterbrush vegetation. The two noteworthy attractions are the crags and superb views of the major features of southeastern Zion National Park. These two features are enough to allow me to recommend this area, but also adivse not going beyond the crags.

NEVADA

Calico Mountains

★ ★ ★

Size: 64,984 acres   **Year Designated:** 2000
Responsible Agency: BLM

The Calico Mountains Wilderness is located in the Black Rock Desert-High Rock Canyon-Emigrant Trails National Conservation Area just west of the Soldier Meadows Road, north of the small town of Gerlach just off the end of State Highway 447. The name comes from the orange, yellow, and sometimes red lichen-covered volcanic material found throughout the area. There were no trails.

MY VISIT: May 22, 2017

I just parked along the Soldier Meadows Road and started hiking west through completely open terrain. After a few miles and a 2,400-foot climb I got to a minor summit with good views and stopped for lunch, then turned around and went back to the road.

The photo shows the lower (nonwilderness) portion of the river playa. This gypsum playa is probably the defining feature in this neighborhood. It is huge and makes up almost all of the nearby Black Rock Desert Wilderness.

This was a nice weather day with a nice hiking route in a nice area. I recommend it to just about any hiker who likes desert terrain.

NEVADA

Goshute Canyon

★ ★ ★

Size: 42,544 acres   **Year Designated:** 2006
Responsible Agency: BLM

The Goshute Canyon Wilderness is located on BLM public land west of US Highway 93 and north of the town of Ely. The wilderness is shown on BLM maps Currie Nevada and Kern Mountains Nevada. The Cherry Creek Mountains run through the wilderness.

MY VISIT: May 2, 2014 and May 3, 2014

The first day hike began at the mouth of Goshute Creek. My route was directly up along the creek. There was no trail, but the route was obvious if slow. It was a nice day, early in the season, and snowmelt at higher elevations made the creek run deep and fast. There was a lot of brush along the creek and the terrain was steep with cliff bands to negotiate. My original intent was to get to open country at the headwaters of the creek, but that was not going to happen given the difficulty of the terrain and the visible snow remaining in the open area ahead. I turned around and went back to my truck and camped that night in a nice camping/parking area by the mouth of the creek.

Both my map and a sign near Goshute Creek mentioned a cave just a bit to the north. So the next day I looked for and found a trailhead for the Goshute Cave. There was indeed a cave and, with only my camping headlamp, I went in. I was not really prepared for cave exploration, but there were certainly passages leading to I knew not where and I poked around some before turning around. One thing that always worries me in caves is being able to find my way back out. From what I could see, the Cherry Creek Mountains are all limestone, a good source for caves.

I enjoyed my two days in and around this wilderness. Like much of Nevada, the area was grazed by cattle. Otherwise there was not much sign of human activity. I recommend the area for hikers looking for a quiet, scenic destination.

Entrance to Goshute Cave, Goshute Canyon Wilderness

High Schells

★ ★ ★

Size: 121,497 acres   **Year Designated:** 2006
Responsible Agency: USFS

The High Schells Wilderness is located in the Humboldt-Toiyabe National Forest east of US Highway 93 and west of State Highway 893. It is east of the town of McGill and northeast of Ely. The mountain backbone is the Schell Creek Range.

MY VISIT: July 29, 2011 and July 30, 2011 and August 4, 2011

The first day hike began at the Berry Creek Campground/Trailhead east of McGill. There is not much of a campground and getting to it required a serious-looking ford of the creek. I decided to just park before the ford. The first day I forded Berry Creek on foot. My nominal goal was the summit of South Schell Peak. The route began as an old two-track through a pleasant valley with views of limestone bluffs and ridges. It was another Cheshire Cat route: the farther one went, the dimmer the trail. Finally, near timberline, the trail disappeared completely. However, I could now see the summit ridge and did not need a trail. Progress was good until near the summit where the rock was very steep and loose. I decided to turn around here, which was a pretty good choice as clouds had built up and the thunder began. I managed to have lunch before the rain. Overall, this was a pleasant day and I really liked the limestone.

The second day hike began at the same trailhead as the previous day but went along the Berry Creek-Worthington Trail to the southeast along Berry Creek. This was a scenic route with more nice limestone bluffs. At the high point of the trail was what I thought was an outfitter's camp. The trail to Worthington Canyon disappeared here so I just continued along a ridge to about 10,850 feet for excellent views. Another worthwhile day.

Day hike number three began on the east side of the wilderness near the Clive Creek Trailhead. I was near and not at the trailhead because I decided I did not want to take my truck through the three fords on the way to the trail-

Ridges above Berry Creek, High Schells Wilderness

head. I put on my Crocs and walked the last two miles of road. I began hiking what I thought was the Kolchek Trail, and after way too long realized that I was not on the trail I wanted, so I turned around and finally found the desired trail. This trail climbed steeply through pinon, juniper, and mountain mahogany to a forest of bristlecone pine and other high-elevation conifers. This route went through a very pleasant Kolchek Basin, then south below a ridge. By now I was at 9,654 feet and running out of water and time, so I turned around and went back to my truck (at 6,900 feet).

I really liked this area and recommend it to just about any hiker. Nice forest, great limestone, and from what I saw, very few visitors.

*Bristlecone pine on The Table,
Mount Mariah Wilderness*

Mount Mariah

★ ★ ★

Size: 88,671 acres   **Year Designated:** 1989
Responsible Agency: USFS and BLM

The Mount Mariah Wilderness is located mostly in the Humboldt-Toiyabe National Forest just west of the Utah-Nevada border. It is north of US Highway 6/50, east of the High Schells Wilderness, and north of Great Basin National Park. There was a USFS map dedicated to this wilderness.

MY VISIT: July 8–9, 2006

This two-day backpack began at the Hampton Creek Trailhead on the eastern edge of the wilderness. The route went west along Hampton Creek through some nice riparian areas in forest, then north to climb steeply through timber with good views of nearby cliffs before reaching timberline and "The Table" at about 10,800 feet. This was a beautiful spot. It was still early summer and there were lots of flowers. The Table looked like a high,

relatively dry meadow with an open forest of bristlecone pine. In my short time on The Table I saw deer, elk, and bighorn sheep. I expected to find snow here as a water source and I did, camping next to a big, old snowbank. Day two was pretty much just packing up and going back to my truck. I really liked this area and recommend it to any and all hikers.

Arc Dome

★ ★ ★

Size: 129,555 acres   **Year Designated:** 1989
Responsible Agency: USFS

The Arc Dome Wilderness is located in the Humboldt-Toiyabe National Forest south of US Highway 50 and west of State Highway 376. The nearest towns are Austin to the north and Tonopah to the south.

MY VISIT: June 11–13, 2004

I do not have any detailed notes from this trip but do know the dates and that I began at the Stewart Creek Trailhead and hiked south on the Toiyabe Crest National Recreation Trail. I remember having trouble losing the trail for a while and spending the first night along the Reese River. I also know that I went to the summit of the Arc Dome (11,775 feet) on the second day but have no recollection of where I spent the second night. The third day was spent going back to the trailhead. I definitely remember liking this area with typical Nevada dry, mostly open pinon and juniper forest and other conifers at higher elevations and along water. There was some snow remaining as old drifts along the high ridges. I remember the terrain as rather gentle with few dramatic features. The area seemed to get a fair bit of visitation.

Alta Toquima

★ ★ ★

Size: 35,581 acres   **Year Designated:** 1989
Responsible Agency: USFS

The Alta Toquima Wilderness is located in the Humboldt-Toiyabe National Forest just across the Big Smokey Valley from the Arc Dome Wilderness. State Highway 376 is to the west and State Highway 82 is to the east (according to my Toiyabe National Forest map). The mountains of the Toquima Range run through the wilderness.

MY VISIT: June 18, 2004

This ambitious day hike began at the Pine Creek Trailhead and went southwest past the south summit of Mount Jefferson, then north to the middle summit of Mount Jefferson (11,685 feet). It was a day of perfect weather. There was forest down low and wide-open, mostly flat, sparse pasture land up high with a little remaining snow. Early in the hike I unwittingly got too close to a goshawk nest. If there is one raptor that will not tolerate human presence near a nest it is the goshawk. I was repeatedly dive-bombed until I was well out of the way. Up on the high pasture was a small group of bighorn sheep. This was a really nice day and I would recommend the area to just about anybody.

Table Mountain

★ ★ ★

Size: 92,627 acres   **Year Designated:** 1989
Responsible Agency: USFS

The Table Mountain Wilderness is located in the Humboldt-Toiyabe National Forest east of the Alta Toquima Wilderness and east of State Highway 82. The nearest (but not near) town is Tonopah.

MY VISIT: June 15–17, 2004

This three-day backpack began at the Barley Creek Trailhead. I hiked north up Barley Creek with a horse-supported trail crew on their way to a trail-rebuild project. It was nice to have company and they were an interesting group. Low elevation was mostly aspen forest and higher elevation was wide-open, see-forever pasture. We all stopped that afternoon and camped below the high, open country to avoid lightning from thunderstorms.

The second day had better weather and I hiked north across The Table to the Danville Summit (10,888 feet), then turned around and hiked south to Lees Camp, an old cow camp, where I camped for the night. Day three was spent hiking south back to the trailhead.

Was The Table flat? Yes, very flat.

Very flat table, Table Mountain Wilderness

Grant Range

★ ★ ★

Size: 52,451 acres   **Year Designated:** 1989
Responsible Agency: USFS

The Grant Range Wilderness is located in the Humboldt-Toiyabe National Forest east of the Railroad Valley, southeast of US Highway 6, and west of State Highway 318.

MY VISIT: September 17, 2005

This day hike began at the end of a road partway up Schofield Canyon on the east side of the wilderness. This is classic central Nevada featuring rugged limestone mountains with sparse timber. There were no trails. My hike was straight up the canyon, then a scramble up a ridge for views. From the ridge I could see that Troy Peak, the highest in the wilderness, was not far off to the north. I hustled back to my truck and took a different road to the mouth of a different canyon and hiked toward the peak. Unfortunately, I was starting too late and the terrain was too rough, so I did not get to the summit. I did, however, get some more good views. This was another nice day in rugged, little-visited terrain. This area would be good for any hiker looking for a quiet, scenic destination.

Far South Egans

★ ★ ★

Size: 36,384 acres   **Year Designated:** 2004
Responsible Agency: BLM

The Far South Egans Wilderness is located on BLM public lands just south of the South Egan Range Wilderness, east of State Highway 318, and west of US Highway 93. The unpaved Shingle Pass Road separates the two wilderness areas. The BLM Nevada maps Garrison and Wilson Creek Range cover this area.

MY VISIT: June 2, 2016

As I crossed Shingle Pass the previous day, I noticed a prominent limestone peak to the south in what must have been the Far South Egans Wilderness. It was. On this day, my hike began at some corrals just off the Shingle Pass Road. There were no trails in this area, but it was easy to hike cross country to a major canyon north of the prominent peak seen the previous day. My route was upstream in the canyon with dramatic limestone cliffs on both sides. The lower elevations were normal pinon and juniper, but with ponderosa pine, bristlecone pine and Douglas fir higher up. To my modest surprise the canyon had been logged, based on the density of old tree stumps. There was some elk sign. At no point was there water in the canyon, although there was water near the corrals. This was a neat day, one of my better days in the Nevada BLM wilderness areas. I saw essentially no sign of human activity. This would be a good destination for hikers looking for a quiet, out-of-the-way destination.

Mount Grafton

★ ★ ★

Size: 78,754 acres   **Year Designated:** 2006
Responsible Agency: BLM

The Mount Grafton Wilderness Area is on BLM public lands just west of US Highway 93 and south of the town of Ely. It is just east of the South Egan Range Wilderness, the two separated by the Cave Valley. The BLM Nevada map Garrison covers the wilderness.

MY VISIT: June 1, 2016

This day hike began at the end of an unpaved road that runs along North Creek off US Highway 93 south of Ely. An old two-track continued for a bit over a mile, then disappeared. There were no trails in this area. For a while I bushwhacked up North Creek, but the route became very difficult because of deadfall from a past fire. I decided to be adventurous and make an attempt on the summit of Mount Grafton. This route was steep and ultimately became a boulder scramble. Unfortunately, this beautiful day was my first really serious hike of the season and I was not in the best of condition. After a climb of about 3,600 feet I was running out of gas. It was at least another 500 feet to the summit and I just had to stop. I had a long lunch in a snow-covered bristlecone pine grove, then turned around and went back down. By the time I was back at my truck my knees were making loud complaints and I was glad to stop. Still, a very nice day in a nice area. I recommend it to most hikers.

South Pahroc Range

★ ★ ★

Size: 25,671 acres   **Year Designated:** 2004
Responsible Agency: BLM

The South Pahroc Range Wilderness is located on BLM public lands south and east of US Highway 93. The nearest town is Caliente. It is home to the South Pahroc Range mountains.

MY VISIT: May 9, 2017

This day hike began along an old two-track on the east side of the wilderness. The dominant feature here was the huge expanses of piled-up jumbles of connected boulders. Some of these jumbles were scattered along the flat valley bottom and some lined the sides of ridges at higher elevation. There were also obviously volcanic features, so I guessed that the boulder jumbles could be eroded volcanic tuff like those in the Big Rocks Wilderness. In any case, I hiked due west with the goal of getting to the summit ridge. This day I was successful. The pass I was in was gentle and quite green with lots of flowers including phlox and Mormon tea. The ridge to the north was more jumbled boulders. After turning around and heading back down, I scared up a bighorn ewe and her very small lamb. They scrambled up through the boulders with the lamb having a little trouble keeping up with mom. Both scampered out of sight. This was a worthwhile day in a neat place.

Clover Mountains

★ ★ ★

Size: 85,668 acres   **Year Designated:** 2004
Responsible Agency: BLM

The Clover Mountains Wilderness is located on BLM public lands east of State Highway 317 and south of the town of Caliente. There is a BLM map dedicated to this wilderness.

MY VISIT: March 11, 2013 and March 12, 2013

The first day hike began along an unpaved road behind a BLM sign announcing the Clover Mountains Wilderness. I did not have a map but decided to go for a hike anyway, feeling confident that I was indeed in the wilderness. The terrain was mostly volcanic with jumbles of eroded tuff and harder materials. The canyon sides were steep with a few dry waterfalls. Eventually the terrain flattened out and an obscure road appeared. No longer confident that I was in the wilderness, I turned around and went back to my truck, drove into Caliente, and bought a map from the BLM. It turned out that my route was mostly in Pennsylvania Canyon along the western wilderness boundary. I will still call this a day spent hiking in a wilderness.

The next day, armed with a map and advice from a BLM employee, I headed back down State Highway 317 and its unpaved extension looking for Cottonwood Canyon. I had trouble finding the canyon, but ultimately caught a glimpse of a BLM sign and drove under the Union Pacific Railroad and into the mouth of the wash of Cottonwood Creek. I did not want to try to drive far up the wash because I feared getting stuck in the soft sand, so I parked by the BLM sign and started hiking northeast into the canyon. My goal was the Fountain of Youth Spring shown on my map. The canyon was pretty and I got to a corral shown on the map. There was a small band of wild horses (pictured) including a mare with a foal. I came to a second corral but no spring. The creek was now flowing pretty well and I guessed that the Fountain of Youth was the source, so I continued upstream well past where the map said the spring should be, but no luck. Finally, I ran out of time and had to turn around without finding the spring, thus being doomed to old age.

Tunnel Spring

★ ★ ★

Size: 5,341 acres   **Year Designated:** 2004
Responsible Agency: BLM

The Tunnel Spring Wilderness is located on BLM public lands adjacent to the Utah state line and just north of the Beaver Dam State Park. It is southeast of US Highway 93, and access is via the Beaver Dam Road. The closest town is Caliente, and the wilderness area is shown on the BLM Nevada map Caliente. There are no trails in the wilderness.

MY VISIT: May 8, 2017

This day hike began at the previous night's campsite off an unpaved road that skirted the western side of the wilderness. There was an old, rutted two-

Wild horses, Cottonwood Canyon, Clover Mountains Wilderness

Stone goblins,
Tunnel Spring Wilderness

lins" in the photo are one example. I followed the creek upstream looking for and finding the Tunnel Spring, basically just two large seeps. If there was any connection to a tunnel, I failed to see it. I really enjoyed this hike. Even without a trail it was easy walking and the route was certainly scenic. I recommend it to just about anybody.

Meadow Valley Range

★ ★ ★

Size: 123,508 acres   **Year Designated:** 2004
Responsible Agency: BLM

The Meadow Valley Range Wilderness is located on BLM public lands east of US Highway 93, southwest of the Clover Mountains Wilderness, west of the Mormon Mountains Wilderness, and east of the Delamar Mountains Wilderness. The BLM Nevada maps Clover Mountains and Overton cover the wilderness. There is also a BLM handout with a map of the wilderness. There are no trails. The easiest access is from the Kane Springs Road on the west.

track that went to the wilderness boundary, but I elected to walk that last mile. There was a BLM sign for the wilderness and an old corral at the end of the road. The terrain at the trailhead was nearly flat with pinon, juniper, and sage and no features of interest. I dropped into a canyon behind the sign and soon came to an old roadbed that went down through sedimentary rock to a pretty valley with a flowing creek. It was a nice time of year to be here with lots of green, birds, and flowers. The most interesting feature to me was the formations of nearly pure white, very soft rock. The "gob-

View north from the summit of Sunflower Peak,
Meadow Valley Range Wilderness

This day hike began at the end of a two-track road taking off from the Kane Springs Road. I had camped here the previous night. My goal was the summit of Sunflower Peak. This was wide-open desert terrain with few if any trees. I believed the terrain to be volcanic with nice ridges and mounds of solidified but easily eroded tuff and pumice. Hiking was pretty easy. The views from the summit (5,022 feet) were good. While on the summit I had a visit from an F-15 fighter from one of the nearby air bases. This was definitely a neat day in a neat place. I recommend it.

NEVADA
Mormon Mountains

★ ★ ★

Size: 157,716 acres   **Year Designated:** 2004
Responsible Agency: BLM

The Mormon Mountains Wilderness is located on BLM public lands north of Interstate Highway 15 and northeast of State Highway 168. It is just east of the Meadow Valley Range Wilderness and south of the Clover Mountains Wilderness. There was a BLM handout of the wilderness including a map and the wilderness is covered by BLM Nevada maps Clover Mountains and Overton. The nearest town is Overton. There are no trails.

MY VISIT: March 13, 201

All my maps showed a road going south past the Meadow Valley Range Wilderness and then along the west side of the Mormon Mountains Wilderness. There was indeed such a road, but before getting to the Mormon Mountains there was a tall, locked gate across the road with a big "No Trespassing" sign from the Union Pacific Railroad. My options were limited, so I turned around and took a BLM road to the east that then went south along the eastern wilderness boundary. I took a 3.5-mile-long cherry-stem road to the southwest that ended at some stock tanks where I began my hike. The terrain here was steep and rugged, maybe volcanic, maybe standard sedimentary (limestone). My route was up a pretty big wash, then some smaller washes to some nice ridges. I continued climbing until I got close to a prominent summit that I could not climb. It was getting late, in part because of my late start, so it was time for the standard have lunch, turn around, and go back to the truck.

NEVADA
La Madre Mountain

★ ★ ★

Size: 47,267 acres   **Year Designated:** 2002
Responsible Agency: BLM and USFS

The La Madre Mountain Wilderness is located on BLM public lands on the east and the Humboldt-Toiyabe National Forest on the west. The BLM portion is just a few miles west of the city of Las Vegas and receives heavy use. The west side can be accessed from northbound USFS roads off State Highway 160. The west side sees less heavy use. The east side can be accessed by roads off State Highway 159. At the time of my visit there was a Green Trails map of the Red Rock Canyon National Conservation Area that covered much of the wilderness.

MY VISIT: April 5, 2011

Unfortunately, I was visiting a new wilderness area and did not have my camera, so *no photos*.

My first stop on this trip to the eastern side of the Rainbow Mountain/La Madre Mountain Wilderness areas was at the BLM visitor center where I purchased an up-to-date map. This was a big help. Even from this vantage point, it was clear that the east-facing bluffs were spectacular with reds, yellows, and tans coloring high cliffs. My choice for a hike was the 6.3-mile White Rock Loop beginning at the White Rock Spring Trailhead. There was lots of colorful rock, almost always with good views. Near the end of the hike, sitting on a sandstone ledge about waist high was a rattlesnake that found me sufficiently dangerous to activate his rattle. It was obvious that this area got a lot of use. I was here on a Tuesday with nice weather and there were *a lot* of people about.

Both La Madre Mountain and Rainbow Mountain make for very scenic destinations when approached from the east. The only caution is that any visitor must be prepared for lots of company.

NEVADA

Mount Charleston

★ ★ ★

Size: 56,819 acres   **Year Designated:** 1989
Responsible Agency: USFS

The Mount Charleston Wilderness is located in the Humboldt-Toiyabe National Forest and a small chunk of BLM public lands. It is northwest of the city of Las Vegas and northwest of the La Madre Mountain Wilderness. Access is by State Highways 156 and 157 from Las Vegas. The area sees heavy visitor use. The wilderness area is now part of the Spring Mountain National Recreation Area.

MY VISIT: June 22, 2006

This day hike began with confusion. My intention was to hike the South Loop Trail beginning at the Cathedral Rock picnic area, but the area was gated and locked (I was too early). I tried another nearby trailhead but the trail did not go where I wanted, so I started on the North Loop Trail at the Trail

*The Cockscomb,
Mount Charleston Wilderness*

Canyon Trailhead. This was, in fact, a good choice. The North Loop Trail was very scenic, climbing through pine and fir forest at low elevation to ridges covered with bristlecone pines and great views at higher elevations. Views of the Cockscomb (pictured) were most impressive. I did not get to the summit of Charleston Peak, but it was still a worthwhile day. I recommend this area to just about anyone who does not mind hiking in a heavily used area.

NEVADA

Bridge Canyon

★ ★ ★

Size: 7,761 acres   **Year Designated:** 2002
Responsible Agency: USNPS

The Bridge Canyon Wilderness is located in the Lake Mead National Recreation Area northwest of the town of Laughlin. Access is by State Highway 163 and an unpaved road around the east and north sides of the wilderness.

MY VISIT: October 31, 2014

My friend Maya and I began a day hike up Grapevine Canyon at a trail-

Goldfinches at a spring, Bridge Canyon Wilderness

Fortification Range

★ ★ ★

Size: 30,658 acres   **Year Designated:** 2004
Responsible Agency: BLM

The Fortification Range Wilderness in located in BLM public lands east of US Highway 93 and west of the Atlanta Road. Access may be from either side. At the time of our visit there was a BLM handout for this wilderness area.

MY VISIT: June 24, 2013

My friend Maya and I did two hikes here on the same day, starting from the Atlanta Road. Our first hike was in the northern part of the range that featured eroded, nearly pure white, soft rock (perhaps volcanic tuff). To me, one isolated monolith looked like two hands folded together in greeting or supplication (pictured). We continued past this formation to the summit of Patterson Peak (8,028 feet). Upon returning to our vehicle we drove south to Cottonwood Canyon and a short trail that led to a very nice cirque. The walls along the sides of the canyon did look like walls of a fortress. The terrain here was a mix of forest, soft, eroded rock, and some hard rock. We were both impressed with this obscure but scenic area. If you like poking around in nice, quiet surroundings, this area is for you.

Folded hands, Fortification Range Wilderness

head next to the unpaved road along the eastern wilderness boundary. The first feature we encountered at the mouth of the canyon was a pretty extensive collection of petroglyphs. This was the only destination for most visitors. We continued on up the canyon, encountering dense masses of grapevines, the source of the canyon name. There were weirdly eroded granite formations plus a segment that was quite narrow. Beyond the narrow part was a small spring forming a pool with tadpoles and a flock of goldfinches. An almost magical spot. I recommend this area.

Jimbilnan

★ ★ ★

Size: 18,879 acres   **Year Designated:** 2002
Responsible Agency: USNPS

The Jimbilnan Wilderness is located just east of the Pinto Valley Wilderness in the Lake Mead National Recreation Area. There are no trails.

MY VISIT: October 28, 2014

This day hike was pretty simple. I got up at my previous night's campsite and walked across the Boathouse Cove Road for a hike in the Jimbilnan Wilderness. My route was to the northeast, sometimes in a wash, sometimes side-hilling around obstacles in the wash. The terrain was truly desert, no trees. The rock seemed to be pretty much only volcanic, rather loose and steep. The goal again was to get to some ridge summit for a good view. I did ascend to a ridge and this time got a "wow" moment with excellent views of the Cathedral Peaks and a bit of Lake Mead. Best, there were four young desert bighorn rams just below me, not appearing to be too frightened. I doubted that I would find a better spot this day, so I decided to have lunch here and turn around and go back to my camp.

Guys just hanging out,
Jimbilnan Wilderness

Two-Star Areas

★ ★

IDAHO

Bruneau-Jarbidge Rivers 89,996 acres, designated 2009, located on BLM public lands east of State Highway 51 and south of the community of Bruneau. This area is visited mostly by river floaters. There were no trails. My day hike on June 6, 2014 began at a spot along the Grasmere-Rowland Road at the headwaters of Marys Creek. According to my downloaded BLM map, this was at the very edge of a thin band of wilderness around Marys Creek leading to a confluence with Sheep Creek, which is a tributary to the Jarbidge River. There was a BLM sign here and I just walked along Marys Creek. This route had been heavily impacted by cattle. Hiking was difficult and, to be honest, not very pleasant. It was definitely sagebrush country. My guess is that hikers are rare.

Pole Creek 12,533 acres, designated 2009, located on BLM public lands south of the Owyhee Uplands Backcountry Byway (also called Mud Flat Road) and west of Hurry Back Creek. There are no nearby towns. There were no trails. My day hike on June 7, 2014 began at a turnout along the Owyhee Uplands Backcountry Byway where there was a BLM sign describing the wilderness, including a map. The terrain was almost completely open with just a few juniper trees. My route was cross country south for about two miles to the top of the Avery Table. There were a couple of stock ponds and the area was heavily impacted by cattle. The table was indeed flat and covered with red grass.

North Fork of the Owyhee 43,413 acres, designated 2009, located on BLM public lands north of the Owyhee Uplands Backcountry Byway (Mud Flat Road) just west of where Current Creek crosses the road. Pole Creek Wilderness is just to the east. The North Fork of the Owyhee River does flow through the center of the wilderness. There are no nearby towns.

There were no trails. My day hike on June 7, 2014 began just a bit west of the Pole Creek Wilderness and on the other side of the Owyhee Uplands Backcountry Byway at a BLM sign for the North Fork of the Owyhee Wilderness. My route was parallel to the shallow Current Creek Canyon through mostly juniper forest and some open grassy areas with volcanic outcrops along the canyon.

Little Jacks Creek 50,929 acres, designated 2009, located on BLM public lands south of the Owyhee Uplands Backcountry Byway northwest of Big Jacks Creek Wilderness and west of State Highway 51. The closest community is Bruneau. There were no trails. This day hike on June 8, 2014 began just east of the BLM Poison Creek Picnic Area adjacent to the Owyhee Uplands Backcountry Byway, which follows the wilderness boundary along its northwest edge. I climbed up a rather steep sagebrush slope to the top of a ridge that provided a long view of an almost bare tableland cut by two obvious drainages. One of these was Little Jacks Creek. This was spare country whose most obvious occupants were cattle. I hiked the ridge northwest to a minor summit overlooking the Poison Creek drainage.

MONTANA

Rattlesnake 32,976 acres, designated 1980, located in the Lolo National Forest north of Interstate Highway 90 and northeast of the city of Missoula and south of the Flathead Indian Reservation. My day hike was on June 6, 2006, the Sunday of Labor Day Weekend and I was concerned about crowds. I picked the Gold Creek Trailhead in the northeast corner of the wilderness hoping it would be away from any crowds. It was. There was exactly one other vehicle at the trailhead parking area. My route was west to Fly Lake, mostly through timber. The lake, while pretty, was not in a particularly scenic spot. Just as I sat down for lunch, I was joined by a Montana game warden. We chatted a bit, including our surprise at the lack of other visitors. I did not see anything interesting here.

Gates of the Mountains 28,562 acres, designated 1964, managed by the Helena National Forest, located east of Interstate Highway 15 and northeast of the city of Helena. As I understand the tale, the name was given by Lewis and Clark for the limestone cliffs along the Missouri River. At the time of my visit there was a USFS map dedicated to this wilderness. I stopped in at a USFS ranger station to pick up a map and discuss hiking options. I was informed that hiking in the wilderness was difficult because a severe fire had gone through the area in 2007. One trail that was still in good shape was Refrigerator Canyon. So my hike on July 29, 2008 began at the Refrigerator Canyon Trailhead. The first part of the route had nice views of spiked pinnacles and ridges of limestone and was quite scenic. Farther along, the trail was through dense forest with only glimpses of limestone, then plunged into intensely burned forest. At this point I turned around. I did not find this area especially interesting but would not discourage others from visiting.

Welcome Creek 28,135 acres, designated 1978, located in the Lolo National Forest south of Interstate Highway 90 and southeast of the city of Missoula. Access is easiest from Forest Road 102 that runs along the eastern wilderness boundary. At the time of my visit there was a USFS map dedicated to the wilderness. My day hike on September 4, 2006 began at the Welcome Creek Trailhead off Forest Road 102. The route was simple, just follow Welcome Creek through timber northwest past the Cinnabar Cabin, then past the Carron Cabin, then turn around where Carron Creek flowed into Welcome Creek. The route was essentially all in forest with occasional openings but nothing of great interest.

WYOMING

Huston Park 30,726 acres, designated 1984, located in the Medicine Bow-Routt National Forest north of the Colorado state line, south of Wyoming State Highway 70, and southwest of the town of Encampment. At the time of my visit there was a USFS handout with map for this wilderness and the nearby Encampment River Wilderness. The Continental Divide and its namesake trail run through the wilderness. This day hike on July 29, 2004 began at the Green Mountain Trailhead. My route went south to the Continental Divide Trail (CDT), then northwest on the CDT to its junction with the Roaring Fork Trail where I turned around and retraced my steps back to the trailhead. The route was mostly through rather nondescript forest with occasional meadows.

Encampment River 10,400 acres, designated 1984, located in the Medicine Bow-Routt National Forest east of the Huston Park Wilderness, south of State Highway 70, and south of the town of Encampment. At the time of my visit there was a USFS handout with map for this wilderness and the Huston Park Wilderness. This day hike began on July 30, 2004 at the Hog Park Trailhead near the southern wilderness boundary. My route was north through timber along the Encampment River until I was at about the midpoint of the wilderness, where I turned around and retraced my steps back to the trailhead. I do not recall any interesting features.

Platt River 22,749 acres, designated 1984, located in the Medicine Bow-Routt National Forest south of State Highway 130, southwest of the city of Laramie, and southeast of the town of Saratoga. At the time of my visit there was a USFS handout with map for this wilderness. A tiny part of the wilderness is in Colorado. The North Platt River runs through the western part of the wilderness. This one-day loop hike on July 31, 2004 began and ended at the Platt Ridge Trailhead. The route was north and west up Platt Ridge, then east and south to Douglas Creek, following the creek back to the trailhead. I did not see anything of special interest or scenic value.

Savage Run 15,260 acres, designated 1978, located in the Medicine Bow-Routt National Forest south of State Highway 130 and north of the Platt River Wilderness. The closest towns are Laramie to the east and Saratoga to the northwest. At the time of my visit there was a USFS handout with map for the wilderness. My day hike on August 1, 2004 began at the Cottonwood Creek Trailhead. My route was north to the wilderness boundary at Cottonwood Creek, continuing north to Savage Run Creek and partway up the Savage Run Trail before turning around and retracing my steps. Almost all of this hike was in lodgepole pine forest with little of interest to me.

COLORADO

Cache La Poudre 9,238 acres, designated 1980, located in the Roosevelt National Forest south of State Highway 14 and north of Rocky Mountain National Park. The closest city is Fort Collins to the east. This day hike on September 14, 2006 began at a trailhead in the USFS campground Mountain Park. There was only one trail in the wilderness and it was a four-mile loop that went up Mount McConnel at the northern edge of the wilderness. My notes from this hike are sparse but say that it was a pretty hike without anything particularly interesting. There was a lot of smoke that day and I took no photos.

Comanche Peak 66,791 acres, designated 1980, located in the Roosevelt National Forest just east and south of State Highway 14. The southern wilderness boundary is contiguous with Rocky Mountain National Park. The National Geographic Trails Illustrated map 112 (Colorado) covers the area. The Cache La Poudre River flows through the area. I have few recollections of my two day hikes and there are no surviving photos, just some notes on a calendar and a route marking on a map. The first hike, on September 15, 2006, began at the Browns Lake Trailhead, went south on Browns Trail to Browns Lake and then on to Comanche Lake. My calendar notes say that Browns Lake was very nice and that it snowed on the way back. They also say that it snowed more overnight and that I made the second hike along Beaver Creek (probably from the Fish Creek Trailhead) in the snow.

Sarvis Creek 47,140 acres, designated 1993, located in the Routt National Forest south of US Highway 40 and east of State Highway 131. The closest major town is Steamboat Springs to the north.

My notes are once again very cryptic for this area. My day hike on September 17, 2006 began at the western wilderness boundary and went east up Sarvis Creek. It was a cold, gray, and windy day. There had been snow and there was snow on the ground for at least part of the trip and the trail was muddy. My notes again say that the hike was pretty but that there was nothing particularly interesting. I have no recollection of the hike or what the terrain was like. I have no surviving photos and most likely took none.

Ptarmigan Peak 13,175 acres, designated 1993, located in the White River National Forest just north of Interstate Highway 70 and east of State Highway 9. It is a bit northeast of the town of Silverthorne. It is shown on the National Geographic Trails Illustrated map 108 (Colorado). This day hike on July 15, 2008 began at a trailhead for the Ptarmigan Trail on the eastern side of Silverthorne. The route was north then northeast to the western wilderness boundary and then northeast to the summit of Ptarmigan Peak (12,948 feet). It was a big climb but easy on a good and well-used trail. There was some fresh snow. The hike began in timber and ended in totally open, gentle ridges. Views from the summit were good. The drawback to this area is that one is never actually away from civilization. The sight and sound of the traffic on I-70 and of other human activity never disappeared. One neat thing I did see on this hike was down in the trees where an American three-toed woodpecker was teaching a youngster how to work a tree to find insects, occasionally leaning over and stuffing a bug in the little guy's mouth.

Powderhorn 60,100 acres, designated 1993, located in the Gunnison National Forest north of State Highway 149 and just northwest of the La Garita Wilderness. The closest town is Lake City to the southwest. The wilderness is shown on the National Geographic Trails Illustrated map 139 (Colorado).

This hike on July 20, 2006 was frustrating. I intended to do an overnight trip, but my first and second choice trailheads were so crowded I could not find a place to park (it was a weekday). Somewhat discouraged, I found a spot at the Powder Park Trailhead. This resulted in a late start and thunderstorms were forming. I decided to make this a day trip, not knowing if I would find water along the trail. The trail ran northwest through a little timber but mostly open meadow to a junction with the East Fork Trail, which I took north through a very large, flat Powderhorn Park and on to Robbers Roost where I turned around. This was not particularly interesting terrain.

Buffalo Peaks 43,410 acres, designated 1993, located in the Pike National Forest east of US Highway 24 and north of the town of Buena Vista. The southern part of the wilderness is shown on National Geographic Trails Illustrated map 129 (Colorado). My day hike on July 16, 2008 began at the Fourmile Trailhead at the southern wilderness boundary. The last couple of miles of road to the trailhead were dicey, but I got there. I hiked the Tumble Creek Trail north to a shallow pass near tree line, then left the trail for a route east to the summit of West Buffalo. There were at least ten other hikers on this ridge. I got to the 13,326-foot summit for good views into the Collegiate Peaks Wilderness. This high area was mostly open meadow with willows and gentle peaks. I stopped here and turned around.

Fossil Ridge 33,060 acres, designated 1993, located in the Gunnison National Forest north of US Highway 50 and northeast of the town of Gunnison. Access is via the Gold Creek Road. This day hike on June 24, 2007 began at the Lamphier Lake Trailhead at the Gold Creek Campground. I took the trail to a pleasant lake then climbed to the top of a nearby ridge for some views. Were there any fossils? Yes, billions and billions, all the same creature and all metamorphosed into almost unrecognizable shapes.

Greenhorn Mountain 22,040 acres, designated 1993, located in the San Isabel National Forest north of State Highway 69, south of State Highway 165, and northwest of the town of Walsenburg. I had trouble finding a trailhead for this area and was forced to ask directions. I was successful and began this day hike on May 14, 2007 at the Bartlet Trailhead on the eastern side of the wilderness and took the Bartlet Trail up toward the summit of Greenhorn Mountain. It was still only May and there was a lot of snow in high elevations. This trail was a good choice of routes because it had a lot of southern exposure. The hike was pleasant, starting in oak, then changing to aspen then pine. Unfortunately, there were a lot of ticks. There was significant snow above 11,000 feet and I started postholing at 11,300 feet. After a few yards of this I left the trail and found a snow-free ridge at 11,500 feet. I was not far from the summit, but from my ridge to the summit was all rotten snow so I stopped, had lunch, and turned around. The view from my ridge spot was mostly to the east, and I could see a long way across flat terrain. I was truly at the edge of the mountains.

Hermosa Creek 37,236 acres, designated 2014, located in the San Juan National Forest east of State Highway 145 and west of US Highway 550. The closest city is Durango to the south. Hermosa Creek forms the eastern wilderness boundary. Hermosa is Spanish for beautiful. This visit on June 29, 2015 was just one year after designation so no maps showed the wilderness boundaries. I did mark up some of my old maps with boundaries I saw on the wilderness.net website. My access was via the Roaring Fork Road off State Highway 145. It had rained significantly the day I arrived and the road was quite muddy. The road climbed to a ridge and led to what looked like an access point for the Colorado Trail, which ran along the western wilderness boundary. I camped there that night. The next morning, I explored a bit and there was indeed a dim trail leading to the Colorado Trail. This was the beginning of my day hike. The forest had several openings along this ridge with good views to the north and east over the heavily forested wilderness. I went south a bit and found a USFS trail sign for Salt Creek heading down and to the east. I took this trail, which quickly entered a thick spruce forest along Salt Creek. The trail was quite dim and appeared to not see much use. I continued down a few miles and decided to turn around before reaching Hermosa Creek because it did not look like I would see anything much different from where I was.

Dominguez Canyon 66,280 acres, designated 2009, located on BLM public lands southwest of US Highway 50, southeast of State Highway 141, south of the city of Grand Junction, and west of the city of Delta. At the time of my visit there was a BLM handout with map for the wilderness (called a wilderness study area at that time). This day hike on May 14, 2011 began at the Bridgeport Trailhead at the end of the Bridgeport Road off US Highway 50. My hike was straightforward, up Big Dominguez Creek for about six miles. The upper canyon had lots of cottonwood, pinon, and juniper in a sandstone canyon. There were a few petroglyphs and lots of evidence of cattle grazing. I saw a few other hikers and one bighorn ewe. At about six miles upcanyon I turned around and retraced my steps. There are many destinations in Colorado that are more pleasant and interesting.

Gunnison Gorge 17,700 acres, designated 1999, located on BLM public lands just west (downstream) of the Black Canyon of the Gunnison National Park and wilderness. It is east of US Highway 50, south of State Highway 92, and east of the town of Olathe. Access from the west is via the Peach Valley Road. The wilderness is part of the Gunnison Gorge National Conservation Area. At the time of my visit there was a BLM handout with map for this area. This day hike on September 24, 2017 began at the Bobcat Trailhead at the "end" of the Bobcat Road at the western boundary of the wilderness. End is in quotation marks because it is as far as one can go in a pickup truck, but the road continued along the western boundary for ATVs and dirt bikes. The Bobcat Trail began at the canyon rim and descended steeply toward the river. The terrain was pinon and juniper and hard rock. Close to the river I lost the trail and do not indeed know if the trail really went to the river, but I did not see a safe way down so I stopped, had lunch, and turned around. There were decent views of the river.

UTAH

Wellsville Mountain 23,850 acres, designated 1984, located in the Wasatch-Cache National Forest east of State Highway 69, west of State Highway 23 and southwest of the city of Logan. This day hike on June 5, 2002 began at the Deep Canyon Trailhead near the northeast corner of the wilderness. The trail climbed steeply to the backbone ridge of the Wellsville Mountains. The trail then followed the ridge south over Mendon Peak and Scout Peak to Pleasant View Point and on to Stewart Pass where I turned around. I have very little memory of this hike and few notes. I do remember finding a tiny lake along the trail and having good views from Pleasant View Point of two cities—Logan and Ogden.

Cedar Mountain 99,428 acres, designated 2006, located on BLM lands south of Interstate Highway 80 and east of the town of Wendover. Access is from I-80 on a road south from the Aragonite exit. The wilderness is home to the Cedar Mountains. The tale I heard about this wilderness designation was that the State of Utah wanted to block access to a site proposed for aboveground storage of radioactive waste from nuclear power plants. I have no opinion about the veracity of this tale.

There are no cedar trees in the Cedar Mountain Wilderness. As was often the case, early visitors and settlers saw juniper trees and called them cedars. Juniper trees were in abundance here. To the best of my knowledge, there were no trails in this area. My day hike on May 12, 2017 was from an old gravel pit alongside a road just outside the western wilderness boundary. I had camped in this spot the previous night. I hiked to the summit ridge through a mix of grass, shrubs, and juniper with pines (probably limber pine) at the highest points. There were views of the Stansbury Mountains to the east. It was a nice time of year to be here; everything was still green and there were lots of wildflowers. I suspect this area becomes pretty brown and burned-out looking later in the year. The terrain was not dramatic, just gentle slopes broken by limestone fins and outcrops. Nothing special here, but still a pleasant place to spend a day.

Cougar Canyon 10,409 acres, designated 2009, located on BLM public lands just east of Nevada's Beaver Dam State Park. The wilderness is contiguous with the Tunnel Spring Wilderness in Nevada. The easier access is probably via the Beaver Dam Road from the west. This day hike on June 4, 2016 began at the Waterfall Trailhead in the Beaver Dam State Park in Nevada. At the end of the park trail I bushwhacked east into the Sheep Creek Canyon of the wilderness. The going was hard. There was dense brush both in the canyon bottom and on the adjacent hillsides. I was constantly flailing around, stumbling, and getting tangled in thickets. The terrain was sandstone with some color, but nothing very interesting. It was starting to get pretty hot and I decided I had struggled enough so I turned around. I had a nice visit with an ash-throated flycatcher at my turnaround point. On the way back, I stumbled on a brilliantly marked snake. I had no idea what it was but looked it up when I got home and it was a milk snake. Upon returning to my trailhead the temperature in the shade was exactly 100 degrees F. That is my limit and I decided to end my trip and go home.

La Verkin Creek 445 acres, designated 2009, located on BLM public lands just outside the Zion National Park Wilderness in the northwestern part of the park. I did a very little hike in this very little wilderness on October 27, 2011. The easiest access, and the route I used, was from the park's La Verkin Creek Trail. Near the northern park boundary, the Park Service trail leaves La Verkin Creek and goes up Willis Creek. If a hiker leaves the trail

Bear Basin, Bridger Wilderness, Wyoming

and goes up La Verkin Creek he is soon in the La Verkin Creek Wilderness. The BLM wilderness is not nearly as scenic or interesting as the park. I only made this side trip because the map said the BLM area was there.

Cottonwood Forest 2,643 acres, designated 2009, located in the Dixie National Forest just west of Interstate Highway 15, south of the Pine Valley Mountain Wilderness, and north of the Cottonwood Canyon Wilderness administered by the BLM. Easiest access is probably via the Forest Service road from Leeds that goes to the Oak Grove Campground. The wilderness and its surroundings are shown on the BLM visitor's map for the St. George Field Office. There were no trails in this wilderness. My day hike on April 5, 2010, just after wilderness designation, began along the Forest Service road that goes north of the wilderness. Between my map and GPS, I was confident that I had reached the new wilderness boundary. I bushwhacked roughly south and a bit east. The terrain was relatively open—some evergreen trees and a lot of red sandstone. Progress was slow but not difficult. I eventually came to a sandstone dome with views and photo opportunities. The day was overcast and the lighting was not the best, but it was an attractive area. One drawback is the proximity to the I-15 corridor and other human activities.

Cottonwood Canyon 11,712 acres, designated 2009, located on BLM public lands just west and north of Interstate Highway 15 and northeast of the city of St. George. It is wholly within the Red Cliffs National Conservation Area and contiguous with the Cottonwood Forest Wilderness along part of its northern boundary. My first day hike on October 29, 2009 began at the BLM Red Rocks Recreation Area. There was a campground here and I grabbed a spot and then began my day hike from the campground. The route went through some very pretty red sandstone in a little canyon that sometimes became quite narrow. There was one tricky bit where I needed to traverse a pool using carved hand- and footholds and a rope. Unfortunately, after another short stretch I was blocked by a dry waterfall surrounded by smooth rock. I had no idea how to get around so I had to give up and go back to the campground.

The second hike on November 3, 2011 began at the southern edge of the wilderness on the Red Reef Trail. This trail meandered through washes with few interesting features. The terrain was not nearly as nice as that I saw in the northeast part of the wilderness or as nice as the terrain in the Cottonwood Forest Wilderness.

NEVADA

Government Peak 6,313 acres, designated 2006, located on BLM lands just west of the Utah-Nevada border, east of State Highway 893, and just north of the Mount Mariah Wilderness. The northern portion of the wilderness is shown on the Kern Mountains Nevada BLM map. The wilderness is in two parts separated by an old two-track road. It took me a while to find this place. I will call it obscure even by Nevada standards. Fortunately, there was a BLM sign along a northern boundary road announcing the wilderness area. Just looking at a map, I did not hold out much hope for this area, but once on the ground I was pleasantly surprised. There were no trails, but the most obvious hiking route was just up to and then along the north-south spine of this northern end of the Snake Range. The route was slow, dodging obstacles along the mostly broken karst summit ridge. There was sparse pinon and juniper forest, but quite open with good views of more impressive limestone to the south. I distinctly remember one shallow pass with a very large pile of wild horse droppings where some band was marking its territory. Ultimately, I arrived on the summit of Government Peak (about 8,000 feet) where I had lunch and then turned around and went back to my truck. I did this day hike on June 12, 2017.

Becky Peak 18,119 acres, designated 2006, located on BLM lands just west of US Highway 93 and north of the town of Ely. Most of the wilderness is shown on BLM map Kern Mountains Nevada. The mountain is part of the Schell Creek Range. For no particular reason I decided to access this wilderness from the east where unpaved BLM Road 4023 runs along the range. There were no trails in this area, but multiple obscure two-track roads get fairly close to the eastern wilderness boundary. I stopped along one at a

BLM sign for the wilderness and, on June 13, 2017, began hiking up what may or may not have been an old cherry-stem road. My route was west toward a large bowl along the mountain crest. There was a lot of pinon and juniper at low elevation, giving way to Douglas fir higher up. Limestone outcrops were common. Everything was green since there was still a little high snow providing water. On this day I was not feeling well and my progress was slow with frequent stops. The east-facing summit bowl was now clearly in view and I climbed to tree line but stopped there as I was tired and definitely not feeling my best. This was a nice weather day in a nice neighborhood that appeared to see few visitors. There was nothing special here, but certainly a pleasant place.

Currant Mountain 47,311 acres, designated 1989
Red Mountain 20,490 acres, designated 2006
Bald Mountain 22,366 acres, designated 2006
Shellback 36,143 acres, designated 2006
White Pine Range 40,013 acres, designated 2006

Southwest of the town of Ely and west and north of US Highway 6 and south of US Highway 50 ("The Loneliest Road") is a cluster of five wilderness areas in the Humboldt-Toiyabe National Forest. One of these areas I visited in 2005 and the others on four consecutive days in 2011. I have rated all five areas two stars. At the time of my visit the USFS map for these areas showed boundaries only for the Currant Mountain Wilderness. There was a USFS travel map that showed all five boundaries. From my visits I concluded that these see very little human visitation, although, as in most of Nevada, all are grazed by domestic livestock. Trails were almost nonexistent. I describe all five areas together because they are close together and share many features.

My Currant Mountain day hike on September 16, 2005 began on the west side of the wilderness at the end of an obscure two-track. I camped here the previous night and was treated to a magnificent sunset that produced an intense red color on the limestone cliffs. Indeed, these areas are pretty much defined by their limestone rock formations studded with pinon and juniper

trees. The two-track continued a bit into the wilderness, then disappeared as I hiked east into Broom Canyon. Douglas fir trees appeared as I gained elevation. The upper canyon was dry, but the stream bed made for easy hiking. The canyon became quite narrow, then abruptly ended in a jumble of unclimbable cliffs. This was a nice day in a nice place for a quiet, easy day hike, but I am not likely to return.

The Red Mountain Wilderness day hike on July 31, 2011 began just east of the Currant Mountain Wilderness and went east to the summit of Red Mountain (9,332 feet). Yes, the rock was red. The terrain was mostly open through bare, broken rock with pinon and juniper giving way to other conifers at higher elevation. There were no trails, but cross-country hiking was easy. The most notable features of this day were the views of the nearby limestone cliffs of the Currant Mountain Wilderness. Also notable was the density of the remains of cattle grazing.

My Bald Mountain Wilderness day hike on August 1, 2011 began along Forest Road 10 just north of what my map showed as the Ellison Guard Station, although I never saw the station. This was another area of exposed rock with pinon and juniper, then open ridges higher up. I ascended one

Currant Mountain from the Bald Mountain Wilderness

of these ridges and was able to get to the summit of Bald Mountain (8,853 feet). The summit was still green with deer and elk sign scattered about. Views of the neighborhood were good if not spectacular.

My Shellback Wilderness day hike on August 2, 2011 began along Forest Road 400 just south of US Highway 50. There was a sign for "Aspen Springs" and I parked there and walked up an obscure two-track to the springs at the wilderness boundary. There were no trails, but the terrain was very open with long, bare ridges. I climbed to one ridgetop at about 9,000 feet and found a lunch spot with good views. There were mule deer nearby in some mountain mahogany. While eating my lunch a band of fourteen elk wandered into view. To my amazement they were accompanied by two wild horses (at least I think they were wild). Also nearby was a bow hunter looking for elk.

My White Pine Range Wilderness day hike on August 3, 2011 began at Indian Garden Spring, a starting point recommended to me by a USFS employee in Ely. There were no trails in this area, so I bushwhacked up a bit and found an old two-track and followed it to a surprise. There was a fenced-off exclosure featuring what I will call a plastic-lined bathtub and two low, covered structures that looked like little Quonset huts. I suddenly realized that this was a "guzzler," a facility for providing water for wildlife but not cattle. I continued on up past a wilderness boundary sign to the top of a ridge with pinon, juniper, and mountain mahogany, then along the ridge to a high (9,400 feet), open area with views of a west-facing escarpment of limestone cliffs. This was a neat spot and I stopped and had lunch. Clouds were building and thunder was beginning, so I decided to turn around.

High Rock Lake 59,094 acres, designated 2000, located on BLM lands in the Black Rock Desert-High Rock Canyon-Emigrant Trails National Conservation Area just north of the Calico Mountains Wilderness and west of the Soldier Meadows Road out of Gerlach. My day hike on May 23, 2017 began on the west side of the Soldier Meadows Road. I just parked along the road and hiked west. Here the terrain was gentler than in the Calico Mountains and greener. Again, there were no trails, but the country was almost completely open and free of major obstacles, so a route straight west

worked. The terrain was still volcanic, but with only a few low, basalt cliff bands and ribs. There were lots of flowers. I made a few miles to a minor summit with some views, had lunch, turned around, and hiked back to the road. This area was certainly pleasant, but less dramatic and, to me, less interesting than the Calico Mountains.

Pahute Peak 56,890 acres, designated 2000, located on BLM lands in the Black Rock Desert-High Rock Canyon-Emigrant Trails National Conservation Area east of the High Rock Lake Wilderness and east of the Soldier Meadows Road. My day hike on May 24, 2017 began at a spur road off the Soldier Meadows Road at the northwest corner of the wilderness. Right at the wilderness boundary was an old mine complete with an open tunnel. The wilderness itself was one enormous jumble of volcanic debris and there were no trails. I began a day hike up a promising-looking wash, but it soon ended with cliffs all around. I decided to try and string together relatively gentle slopes to work my way higher. Ultimately this too failed and I was stuck on a minor summit with no way forward. I stopped and had lunch with a pronghorn buck for company. There were some good views, dominated by a big mountain to the east called, according to my map, Big Mountain. I returned to my truck about the same way as I came in.

Little High Rock Canyon 48,355 acres, designated 2000, located on BLM lands in the Black Rock Desert-High Rock Canyon-Emigrant Trails National Conservation Area west of the High Rock Lake Wilderness, south of the High Rock Canyon Wilderness, and north of the town of Gerlach. My day hike on May 25, 2017 was accessed by County Road 34, which runs west of the conservation area boundary. The BLM map showed another road going to the wilderness boundary, but when I visited, this second road could only be taken partway to the wilderness. A culvert had been washed out and, a bit scary, someone had removed sections of a cattle guard so that a vehicle would fall through the cross members. Past the cattle guard the road skirted the wilderness boundary, and once past a small reservoir a hiker could enter the wilderness and hike downstream through Little High

Rock Canyon. The canyon was very green with moderately tall basalt cliffs covered with lichen. The creek was flowing most of the way downstream with thick brush on both sides. There were boot tracks in mud telling me that some other hiker had been here. I went downstream until it looked like the terrain would continue with no new features, so I turned around and went back upstream. On my way back, I saw a cave at the base of a cliff, almost certainly an old lava tube, with a steel mesh grating preventing human entry. There was a BLM sign saying that the cave was a prehistoric site and was not to be disturbed.

High Rock Canyon 46,464 acres, designated 2000, managed by BLM
East Fork High Rock Canyon 52,617 acres, designated 2000, managed by BLM

These two wilderness areas are adjacent to each other in the Black Rock Desert-High Rock Canyon-Emigrant Trails National Conservation Area east of County Road 34 and north of the town of Gerlach. They are separated by the Applegate National Historic Trail. My access to these two areas was via BLM Road 37032, which formed the northwest boundary of the High Rock Canyon Wilderness. The Applegate Trail is seasonally open to motor vehicles, but I do not recommend anyone attempting the trail in even an ordinary four-wheel-drive pickup. Some sort of ATV would almost certainly be best.

I hiked both areas on October 16, 2018. The first hike began at the BLM road along the northeast wilderness boundary of the High Rock Canyon Wilderness. I hiked a short way east from the road through an almost flat sagebrush plateau broken by some volcanic outcrops. This was spare country even by northwest Nevada standards, mostly sage with some other small shrubs, grass, and a hint of mountain mahogany. I encountered a lone, rather shy wild horse.

After returning to my truck I drove east and then south to the Applegate Trail. I parked near the northern gate because I did not want to take my truck down the trail. Instead, I hiked down the trail in the dry stream bed between the two wilderness areas. Crumbling basalt cliffs lined both sides of the canyon. After a couple of miles, I climbed east out of the canyon to a very flat sagebrush plateau and then to an overlook of the East Fork of the High Rock Canyon. Looking back to the west, I had the sense of standing on the edge of a sagebrush ocean. Both these areas appeared to be quite wild.

Black Rock Desert 314,835 acres, designated 2000, located on BLM lands southwest of State Highway 140. Access on the east side is by County Roads 214 and 216 off State Highway 140. The area consists of the ancient playa of the Quinn River. My day hike on October 13, 2017 began along BLM Road 2014, a continuation of County Road 216 in the northeast part of the wilderness. The terrain was almost exactly flat, slowly dropping to the south. Here in the north there were hummocks of grass and shrubs sticking above the gypsum. In the south there was just a bare expanse of old river playa. I spent a couple of hours wandering through the hummocks. This area is huge: 314,835 acres (but no trails). The nonwilderness portion of the area is home to the (in)famous Burning Man celebration. In my perhaps unjust judgment, the area is mostly featureless. It is, however, unique. As a hiking destination, I only give the area two stars. Having said that, it still may be worth a peek if one is in the neighborhood.

Gypsum plain, Black Rock Desert Wilderness

South Jackson Mountains 54,535 acres, designated 2000, managed by the BLM

North Jackson Mountains 23,438 acres, designated 2000, managed by the BLM

Both of these areas are located east of the Black Rock Wilderness and just east of BLM Road 2049, accessed from State Highway 140 and County Roads 214 and 216. I visited South Jackson first on October 14, 2017. It was on a beautiful, chilly fall day. I began at BLM Road 2049 and hiked east into the Jackson Mountains, following a flowing stream. The streamside was quite brushy, but also provided some fall color. The terrain was mostly very dark lava, perhaps the origin of the Black Rock name. There were some dramatic cliffs. There were no trails in this area and the going was slow because of descending basalt ribs. My memory is that I got as far as the beginning of the creek water flow, then turned around because daylight was scarce in mid-October. I did not get anywhere close to the crest of the mountains. On October 15 I visited the North Jackson, starting again from BLM Road 2049. I followed Deer Creek upstream. Hiking was again slow in very rough volcanic terrain and I ran out of time before getting to the summit ridge. This day's hike was pretty similar to the South Jackson except that the terrain was less dramatic.

Pine Forest Range 24,015 acres, designated 2014, located on BLM public lands west of State Highway 140, southeast of the Sheldon National Wildlife Refuge, and northwest of the town of Winnemucca. There was a sign along State Highway 140 for an unpaved road to Blue Lake. This road is not for the faint of heart or for vehicles without good ground clearance. The road was worrisomely narrow and I kept hoping I would not meet another vehicle. After a seemingly endless time on a gnarly road, I gave up hope of getting to the Onion Valley Reservoir where there was supposedly a trail to Blue Lake. Instead, I found an old hunters' camp at the wilderness boundary, parked, and, on October 14, 2018 hiked up a ridge through sage and aspen on a clear, cold fall morning. Near the top of the ridge the pine forest appeared. I remain uncertain if they were limber or whitebark pine, but they were a neat addition to the other dryland species. The terrain was quite rugged with exposed spires and sharp ridges. After a while, the Onion Valley Reservoir appeared and I think I was able to just see Blue Lake nestled among some trees. There was still some fall color left in the aspens, making this a very neat spot. However, I have no urge to come back.

Santa Rosa-Paradise Peak 32,072 acres, designated 1989, located in the Humboldt-Toiyabe National Forest just east of US Highway 95, west of State Highway 290, and north of the city of Winnemucca. There was a USFS map available dedicated to this area. I had planned this trip to be an overnight backpack and I was carrying my heavier pack. The hike began on June 30, 2008 at the Singas Creek Trailhead. My route was south along a trail toward the Abel Creek Trailhead. At low elevation the trail went through dense aspen forest with brush and lots of flowers. At times the flowering plant aromas were almost overwhelming. There was lots of flowing water as there was still snow at higher elevations. The trail was easy to lose. I was able to find the trail from Abel Creek, but lost it when climbing up to the west. The terrain opened up and I made a beeline for the ridge and, indeed, got back on the trail to Abel Summit. I had my lunch on this summit and was joined briefly by a coyote. After the coyote came two hikers to my considerable amazement. The area appeared to see little visitation by humans, but there was lots of evidence of cattle grazing. The day was now more than half gone and I did not see any inviting campsites, so I decided to make this a day hike and went back to the trailhead. My notes tell me that this day hike was more than fifteen miles and about twelve hours.

Mount Rose 31,197 acres, designated 1989, located in the Humboldt-Toiyabe National Forest just north of Lake Tahoe and the ski resort of Incline Village. The easiest access is by State Highway 431 on the east side of the wilderness. My visit really began on July 1, 2008 when I tried to find a campsite near the wilderness to allow an early start the next day. I bought a North Lake Tahoe Basin map at a USFS station in Carson City and thought I would hike Whites Creek but drove up and down State Highway 431 without seeing any signs or indication of trailheads. I was sufficiently frustrated to stop and ask directions at a convenience store. To my surprise the store manager knew how to get there and I would never have found it without directions. Upon arriving at the trailhead there was a sign announcing a trail closure for fuel removal (dead tree removal). There was, however a Thomas Creek Trailhead. At this trailhead there was *both* a trail and a road. I walked the trail to a real trailhead at the end of a road. By now it was so late that I had to turn around and camp near my truck. At least I knew where to go for tomorrow's hike.

My hike then began at the "real" Thomas Creek Trailhead. My map said there was no trail beyond the wilderness boundary, but there was. The trail climbed west, then contoured around the Thomas Creek headwaters, then climbed steeply up a ridge dividing the eastern and western parts of the wilderness. There were good views of Mount Rose from the ridge. I went south a little way, found a scenic spot, had lunch, and turned around. My memory is that the trail ended here, but this memory cannot be trusted. This was a pleasant enough area although nothing special.

East Humboldt 37,797 acres, designated 1989, located in the Humboldt-Toiyabe National Forest south of Interstate Highway 80, west of State Highway 232, north of State Highway 229, and southwest of the town of Wells. There was a USFS map devoted to the East Humboldt and Ruby Mountains Wilderness areas. The first day hike here was on July 22, 2004 and began at the Angel Lake Trailhead. My route was north on a trail to Greys Lake. The terrain was mostly open with lots of exposed rock, steep mountainsides, some grass and brush, and some isolated timber. Greys Lake was certainly a pretty destination. For hikers really wanting a wilderness experience, this may not be your route as I-80 and traffic was visible for most of the hike. Nonetheless, a nice hike on a nice day. The second day hike, this time on July 5, 2008, also began at the Angel Lake Trailhead, but this time my route was south on a trail to Winchell Lake. Again, lots of bare rock, a few trees, and a pretty spot around the lake. While a pleasant enough destination, I did not find this area particularly interesting.

Wovoka 49,018 acres, designated 2014, located in the Humboldt-Toiyabe National Forest east of State Highway 338. The nearest town is Bridgeport, California. There were no trails in the area. Because of its recent designation, there was little information about this area, especially any map that showed wilderness boundaries. I drove up and down State Highway 338 a few times without seeing any signs of entry points. I then drove to Bridgeport in California and asked at the USFS ranger station there what they knew. They did not know much but printed off a map for me from the wilderness.net website. This showed some small roads from State Highway 338 leading to the western wilderness boundary. I went back into Nevada and took one of those roads close to what I was confident was the wilderness boundary and camped in my truck for that night.

The next morning, June 11, 2015, I made my day hike to the east up what I am pretty certain was Long Doctor Canyon. This was again classic pinon, juniper, and sage country with some aspen in the lower parts. I followed an old two-track until it disappeared, then bushwhacked toward a distant ridge, climbed that ridge to tree line, then walked up completely open, grassy slopes toward Bald Mountain, the highest point in the wilderness. By the time I got to a small summit west of the main peak it was getting late and I needed to turn around. My GPS said I was at about 9,200 feet compared to 9,407 feet for the Bald Mountain summit. As I was leaving, the sun was shining on the west slope of Bald Mountain through a gap in some clouds. As the clouds moved, the light through the gap moved the illuminated pattern on the mountain slope, making it look like light was flowing like a stream. It was a neat sight.

Boundary Peak 10,521 acres, designated 1989, located in the Inyo National Forest on the Nevada-California border east of US Highway 6 and west of Nevada State Highway 264. The nearest town is Bishop, California. This wilderness area gets a lot of hikers because Boundary Peak is one of the fifty-state "High Points" as the summit on the state line is the highest point in the state of Nevada. At the time of my visit on July 3, 2008 there was a handout for the Boundary Peak area with map available at the USFS ranger station in Bishop, California. There were no trails in the wilderness and in particular no trails to the summit. My hike began (as does almost everybody's) at the end of the road in Trail Canyon. The problem was *not* that there was no trail but that there were *too many* trails leaving the end of the road. Which very visible, well-used path to take? I was clueless and chose a route that was less than the best. I will admit that this was early in the hiking season and I was not in my peak of physical condition, but my chosen route was very difficult, going steeply up through sand and gravel. When I finally got to the summit ridge with the summit in pretty clear view, I was just too tired to continue. The spirit was willing but the flesh was weak, so I turned around. My down route was much easier because I could now see the "correct" route that avoided some of the loose conditions I had on my way up. I did not enjoy this day or this area.

Quinn Canyon 26,310 acres, designated 1989, located in the Humboldt-Toiyabe National Forest just west of the Grant Range Wilderness and east of State Highway 375. My day hike on September 18, 2005 began at the Cherry Creek Trailhead on the eastern wilderness boundary. The trail followed Little Cherry Creek to the northwest, ultimately exiting the wilderness on the western side. For my visit the trail was in poor condition and hard to find. There were a few overgrazed, brushy riparian areas with little of scenic value. I do not recommend this area.

Mount Irish 28,274 acres, designated 2004, located on BLM public lands north of State Highway 375, west of State Highway 318, and west of the town of Caliente. There were no trails. From my map, the most promising access to this wilderness was a cherry-stem road from State Highway 375. I went up this road on May 9, 2017. The terrain along the road was not appealing. The road ended at an old, derelict cabin alongside a mine with an open tunnel. There was an old, partially filled watering trough with a great horned owl face down, dead in the water. I wandered around a bit and decided there was no place worth hiking from here, so I went back to the highway and found a place to camp near the northern part of the wilderness.

My May 10 hike began near a BLM sign announcing the wilderness and a smaller sign pointing to some petroglyphs. I went south to the close-by petroglyphs and continued walking south into the wilderness. The mostly volcanic terrain was totally uninteresting and I did not go very far.

Highland Ridge 68,622 acres, designated 2006, located on BLM lands just west of the Utah state line and just south of Great Basin National Park. State Highway 894 is just to the west. The closest town is Ely to the northwest. At the time of my visit there was a BLM handout with map for the wilderness area. I did day hikes here on June 25 and 26, 2013. The first day hike began from a cherry-stem road through Murphy Canyon in the southwest portion of the wilderness. My route was southeast through Johns Wash. This was a nice neighborhood. There was still-green vegetation and tall, gray limestone cliffs. There were lots of flowers among the aspen and pine forest. It was a day of perfect weather in pleasant terrain. The second day hike began in the northeast corner of the wilderness at a National Park Service trailhead for the Lexington Arch. Instead of hiking into the park, my route was southwest into the wilderness. The early part of the hike was on an old two-track that soon disappeared. I bushwhacked up a nearby 8,800-foot-high summit for views of the arch and the surrounding terrain. Again, a pleasant place, but nothing of special interest.

Parsnip Peak 43,512 acres, designated 2004, located on BLM lands just west of the White Rock Range Wilderness, west of the Mount Wilson Back Country Byway, and east of US Highway 93. The closest town is Pioche. The Nevada BLM Wilson Creek Range map covers the wilderness. The wilderness mountains are part of the Wilson Creek Range. There were no trails in this wilderness. My day hike on May 5, 2014 began in the northern portion of the wilderness along the edge of the Mount Wilson Back Country Byway, a scenic if slow drive. I knew I was at the wilderness boundary because there was a BLM sign at the mouth of a wash announcing the Parsnip Peak Wilderness. My route was simple; I just walked up the wash. This went alright for a while, but the wash grew full of brush, especially mountain mahogany, and I was constantly leaving the wash for the pinon and juniper hillside only to return to the wash because of deadfall. Finally, I was able to see a clearer path up a hillside to more open terrain. I ended up on a small summit with a huge stone cairn. There were some good views, but now I was stuck. Every direction was down steep slopes through heavy brush with no obvious next destination. So I decided to turn around. This was a nice enough day in a nice enough area, but I did not see anything especially interesting or attractive.

Weepah Spring 51,305 acres, designated 2004, located on BLM lands west of State Highway 318. The nearest towns are Pioche and Caliente. The BLM Nevada map Timpahute Range covers most of the wilderness area but does not show the boundaries because the BLM map is dated 2004, the same year as designation. There were no trails in this area. I had trouble finding this area. I drove up and down State Highway 318 a few times until I saw a likely side road to the wilderness. At the end of this short road was a wilderness study area sign, so I was confident I was in the right place. There was a lot of old iron pipe and plastic hose here from someone's attempt to get water for cattle. On May 4, 2004 my hike began up the wash at the end of the road. At first there was nothing interesting, but then there was a lot of holey rock, probably old, eroded welded tuff. There were some eroded rock columns farther up the wash. I went to the top of a ridge to get some views.

From here I could see a green spot that I bet harbored the spring. I headed for that spot. It was indeed a spring coming out of an indentation in the tuff. There were birds and dense vegetation, especially stinging nettle. This was the perfect spot for lunch and a turnaround back to my truck. This area appeared to get very little visitation, and I saw nothing of particular interest.

Worthington Mountains 30,594, designated 2004, located on BLM lands north of State Highway 375 and west of State Highway 318. The closest town is Caliente. The easiest access and the access I used was the Mail Summit Road (unpaved), which runs northwest around the east side of the wilderness. There were no trails in this area. My day hike on May 11, 2017 began beside an old two-track running south from the Mail Summit Road. The terrain here was quite dry and there was a mix of volcanic and sedimentary rock. Given the absence of trails I just looked over the dry, flat cow pasture and chose a likely entry point to the range. My nominal goal was to get to the top of the main ridge. I basically went straight west a mile or two across the pasture to a wash running through a jumble of highly eroded sedimentary rock. Hiking was slow because of rather dense pinon, juniper, and mountain mahogany and a lot of loose rock under my feet. This place was basically a maze of intersecting little washes, picturesque in its own way. I did not get to the summit ridge because the terrain got too steep and the rock too crumbly. My enthusiasm for this area was limited. Farther south the mountains appeared less crumbly with tall cliffs of sedimentary rock. The 8,768-foot Meeker Peak anchors the southern end of the range. From my vantage I could not see a sensible way up that peak.

Big Rocks 12,930 acres, designated 2004, located on BLM public lands just north of US Highway 93 and east of State Highway 318. The nearest town is Caliente. There was a BLM handout with a map and driving directions available at the Caliente BLM field office. My day hike on March 16, 2013 began at a brand-new trailhead for the brand-new Boulder Springs Trail on the northeast side of the wilderness along the Boulder Wash Road. The route was simple—hike south on the trail until it ended, then a bit

A spot of color, blooming cactus, South Egan Range Wilderness

farther south to the little summit that is the highest point in the wilderness at 7,016 feet. Went there, did that. The trail was mostly in trees (pinon and juniper) and desert shrubs and grasses. The terrain was relatively level and there were indeed big rocks, leftovers of highly eroded volcanic welded tuff. There was a lot of elk sign and, this being Nevada, lots of cattle sign. A few tiny patches of snow remained in the shady spots. There was little sign of human visitation, but it was early in the season. This was a pleasant hike, but I do not plan to return.

Delamar Mountains 111,006 acres, designated 2004, located on BLM public lands just east of US Highway 93 and north of Las Vegas. At the time of my visit there was a BLM handout with map for this area. There were no trails. This day hike on March 14, 2013 really began at the BLM field office in Caliente. I got handouts, maps, directions, and advice from an employee familiar with the wilderness areas in the local district. It was probably the only time in all my hiking days that I was advised not to visit a wilderness area because it was not worth visiting. The area? The Delamar Mountains. Not to be deterred, I drove down to the end of a cherry-stem road into the

southeast part of the wilderness and began my day hike. I will admit, the terrain in front of me was uninspiring. But hike I did. The terrain was true desert, the features volcanic. I went up a wash to a spring that a rancher had tried to develop for watering cattle, then to a minor summit with a curious view. Spread around me to the northeast was a huge expanse of what I believed was volcanic tuff eroded into vertical fat fingers a few feet in diameter and perhaps ten to twelve feet tall. The sheer number of these fingers was impressive. Other than this one feature the person in the BLM office was right; there was not much interesting here.

South Egan Range 67,214 acres, designated 2006, located on BLM lands west of US Highway 93 and east of State Highway 318. The town of Ely is to the north and the town of Pioche is to the south. The BLM Nevada map Garrison covers most of the wilderness. My day hike on June 3, 2016 began along an unpaved but decent road that ran along the eastern wilderness boundary north of Shingle Pass. There were no trails in this wilderness and my starting point was unremarkable; I would probably not be able to recognize it again. This was dry country. There was easy walking to some cliffs of red rock, then a scramble through the cliffs and spires to an extensive bench with pinon, juniper, sage, and grasses, mostly cheatgrass. It was still early enough for flowers, especially buckwheat, daisies, and cacti. I did find by accident a tiny spring providing a few square feet of extra green. I was very glad for my GPS on this hike because the terrain had few features and did not offer many opportunities to hike in a straight line. I certainly went away with the impression that this area sees very few visitors.

Rainbow Mountain 25,113 acres, designated 2002, located in the Humboldt-Toiyabe National Forest (west) and on BLM lands (east). The BLM portion is just a few miles west of the city of Las Vegas and receives heavy use. The west side can be accessed from State Highway 160 to the south and is less heavily visited. At the time of my visit there was a Green Trails map of the Red Rock Canyon National Conservation Area that included parts of the Rainbow Mountain and La Madre Mountain Wilderness areas.

The author can sometimes (maybe often) be a true space cadet. *I left my camera at home. There are no photos from this wilderness area or the La Madre Mountain Wilderness.*

My day hike on April 4, 2011 began along an unpaved USFS road running north from State Highway 160. My map was out of date and referred to a Pine Creek Wilderness Study Area just to the east. This is now the Rainbow Mountain Wilderness. There were no trails here on the west side, so the hike was a literal bushwhack east through brushy shale and limestone hills. There was some pinon and juniper. I hiked east until I got close to the sandstone bluffs. There was clearly some interesting rock there, but I was running out of time and had to turn back.

Black Canyon 17,220 acres, designated 2002, located in the Lake Mead National Recreation Area (administered by the USNPS) south of US Highway 93 and east of US Highway 95. The Colorado River is the eastern wilderness boundary. The nearest town is Boulder City. The wilderness area and approved backcountry roads are shown on a USNPS map for the Hoover Dam area. There were no trails. I had trouble finding access to this area. I was forced to ask directions. Twice. I was lucky because had I found the route I was looking for I might well have got stuck in deep sand according to the first person I asked. She gave me directions for a different route and I still had trouble finding it until a postman finally got me on the right path. My day hike on October 29, 2014 began off Backcountry Route 58. I first went east to an overlook of the Colorado River, then south parallel to the canyon rim. This area was not wild. US Highway 93 was visible much of the route, Boulder City was also visible, and the air was filled with the noise of helicopters taking flightseeing tourists to the Grand Canyon. The terrain here was stark and spare, mostly jumbled, black volcanic rubble. It was true desert with very little vegetation. I strongly suspect this area sees few hikers. I promise that I will not return.

Eldorado 31,950 acres, designated 2002, located in the Lake Mead National Recreation Area (administered by the USNPS) just south of the Black Canyon Wilderness and east of US Highway 95. The Colorado River is the eastern wilderness boundary. The area and its approved backcountry access roads are shown on the USNPS map for the Hoover Dam area. There were no trails. My day hike on October 30, 2014 began near the end of approved Backcountry Route 51. I just hiked cross country to the southeast through volcanic peaks and ridges to a rim dropping off toward the Colorado River (not visible). Again, this was true desert terrain with little vegetation. Like Black Canyon, I doubt that this area sees many hikers.

Bristlecone 14,095 acres, designated 2006, located on BLM public lands west of US Highway 93, west of the town of McGill, and north of the town of Ely. The wilderness is shown on BLM Nevada maps Ely and Kern Mountains. The mountains are part of the Egan Range. There were no trails. I spent the previous night camped near the end of an obscure two-track close to what my map called "The Cove," which was at the northern wilderness boundary. There were no trails in this area, but on the morning of June 13, 2015, I started hiking south on the two-track until it disappeared, then hiked cross country toward a high ridge. The terrain was mostly open with some scattered pinon and juniper. The ridge was steep and walking the ridgeline would have been almost impossible because of jumbled rock and thick stands of mountain mahogany. There were good views of McGill, the Steptoe Valley, and the High Schells beyond. I made a loop here, dropping down to a pleasant meadow for lunch and taking a different route back to my truck. I only saw one bristlecone pine tree on this trip. Presumably there are more elsewhere in the wilderness. There were even a few Douglas firs in the higher elevation. June was still an early month here and everything was nice and green. Still, nothing very interesting.

Spirit Mountain 33,518 acres, designated 2002, administered by the BLM and the National Park Service in the Lake Mead National Recreation Area north and east of the Bridge Canyon Wilderness. Access is by USNPS Backcountry Road 20, which runs from State Highway 163 in the south to US Highway 95 in the west. There were no trails. My day hike on October 31, 2014 began at the end of a little spur road (20A) called the Pipe Spring Road off the USNPS Road 20. The obvious thing to do here was park and walk down Pipe Spring Wash, so that was what I did. I hiked down a couple of miles through jumbled sandstone and volcanic terrain in a true desert environment of brush and cactus. The farther down the wash I went the less interesting the terrain, so I found a small summit, took a photo, and turned around. The scenery at the head of the wash was the nicest in the immediate area, especially Spirit Mountain itself. The mountain looks like a severely tortured mass of sedimentary rock. A hike up there might have been more interesting. The area appeared to receive very little visitation.

Ireteba Peaks 32,745 acres, designated 2002, administered by the BLM and the National Park Service in the Lake Mead National Recreation Area east of US Highway 95. Access is from the paved road to Nelsons Landing on USNPS Backcountry Roads 42 and 43. There were no trails. I had some trouble getting here. USNPS Road 43 was in bad condition so I went to Nelsons Landing, then up the Eagle Wash Road to get on a better stretch of Road 43. This road followed a powerline just north of the wilderness. My goal was to get to the crest for my hike, but the closer I got to the crest the more jumbled and rougher the terrain, so I went back down partway, parked at a transmission tower, and hiked south into the wilderness and parallel to the crest. This was once again true Mojave Desert, just brush, a little grass, and cactus (lots of cholla). I was east of the crest of the Eldorado Mountains, which are just big volcanic mounds and jumbles. Hiking was pleasant but slow as there were lots of washes to cross. This was stark, spare country, but I do not particularly recommend it to hikers. I did my hike on November 2, 2015.

Pinto Valley 39,173 acres, designated 2002, administered by the National Park Service within the Nevada portion of the Lake Mead National Recreation Area just south of State Highway 169 and west of USNPS Road 97, the Boathouse Cove Road, and north of the Virgin Basin of Lake Mead. There were no trails. There were a few campsites available along the Boathouse Cove Road, which ran between the Pinto Valley and Jimbilnan Wilderness Areas. On October 27, 2014 I picked what looked like a good candidate site and began a day hike southwest into the Pinto Valley Wilderness. The terrain seemed to be a mix of volcanic and sandstone features (pictured), and I tried to get to the crest of the very volcanic-looking Black Mountains. I came up just a bit short. This was a pleasant enough day in terrain that appeared to get very little foot traffic. I do not plan to come back.

Nellis Wash 16,423 acres, designated 2002, located in the Lake Mead National Recreation Area (administered by the USNPS) east of US Highway 95 and southeast of the town of Searchlight. Access is by the paved Cottonwood Cove Road from Searchlight to USNPS Backcountry Road 30 which runs along the northeast wilderness boundary. There were no trails. This day hike on November 3, 2015 began at the side of USNPS Road 30 along the southeast wilderness boundary. My route was up a large wash through rather flat Mojave Desert terrain. As I gained elevation Lake Mojave came into view. A modest ridgetop provided a good lunch spot and views of the summit of Spirit Mountain to the south.

White Rock Range 24,249 acres, designated 2004, located on BLM public lands just west of the Utah state line. The Mount Wilson Back Country Byway is to the west. The nearest town is Pioche. The BLM Nevada map Wilson Creek Range covers this wilderness. The area is home to the White Rock Mountains. I had a difficult time finding this area. There were a lot of obscure, unsigned roads going who knew where. I stopped to camp just off a road that at least had a lot of white rocks surrounding it. The next morning, I did more wandering around and then found a road that led to what I believed to be White Rock Peak. I parked as close to this peak as I could and, on May 4, 2014, I started hiking. The terrain was very open so hiking was easy. The day was cold and windy and I was bundled up in a hat, gloves, and my Gore-Tex raincoat. I kept to the ridgetops until White Rock Peak was in sight and went to the summit (9,146 feet). The area around the summit was home to not much more than grass and some low shrubs. It was also

home to mule deer and wild horses. I only saw one curious but ultimately shy mare. The more sheltered areas had some large pine trees and old snow where I had lunch before returning to my starting point. I had the impression that the area gets very little visitation. It was not especially interesting.

Wee Thump Joshua Tree 6,050 acres, designated 2004, located on BLM public lands just north of State Highway 164 and west of the town of Searchlight. I visited this area on March 17, 2018 with a brief day hike through the Joshua trees starting from a BLM sign off State Highway 164. I doubt that many hikers would consider this a prime destination, but it does give a good introduction to this iconic desert plant. The terrain is rather flat, but the trees are the main attraction. The name comes from the local Native American term for the "Old Ones," because these Joshua trees are perhaps a few hundred years old.

View from the summit of Mount Bangs, Paiute Wilderness, Arizona

The Desert Southwest

Much of the interior American West is desert. The southwestern states of Arizona, New Mexico, and West Texas have wilderness areas that provide excellent examples of different desert types. We have already included true desert areas in southern California, southern Utah, and parts of Nevada because I have been trying to keep wilderness areas together by state. In this desert section I include wilderness areas that are surrounded by desert although not really desert themselves. Both New Mexico and Arizona have high-elevation areas made up of coniferous forest and even bits of tundra. I have included the dry Guadalupe Mountains Wilderness here and not with the other very wet Texas areas.

The American Southwest has four types of desert. The Great Basin Desert probably covers the most area. It is mostly found in Nevada and Utah. It is the northernmost desert type and is distinguished by cold winters and lots of sagebrush. The Mojave is found in southern Nevada and southeastern California. It is less cold than the Great Basin and is also home to several species of brush and some cacti. The Sonoran Desert is found in southwestern Arizona and southeastern California. It is home to several iconic cacti, including the saguaro. Finally, the Chihuahua Desert is found in southwestern Texas and parts of southeastern New Mexico.

I found two books very helpful for finding wilderness areas in Arizona and New Mexico. First, Tom Dollar and Jerry Sieve's book *Arizona's Wilderness Areas,* Westcliffe Publishers, 1998, gives driving direction, specific route recommendations, and descriptions of many of the state's wilderness areas. Second, Mike Hill's *Guide to the Hiking Areas of New Mexico,* University of New Mexico Press, 1995, gives driving directions, background information, and descriptions of both wilderness and nonwilderness areas in New Mexico.

Superstition

★ ★ ★ ★

Size: 160,200 acres   **Year Designated:** 1964   **Responsible Agency:** USFS

The Superstition Wilderness is located in the Tonto National Forest just east of greater Phoenix. Access is easy from trailheads along State Highway 88 on the western and northern boundaries and from US Highway 60 along the southern boundary. At the time of my visit there was a USFS map dedicated to the wilderness.

MY VISIT: February 28–March 2, 2005

This three-day backpack began at the Peralta Trailhead at the southern wilderness boundary. It was a wet winter in greater Phoenix. The desert was green. Finding water for campsites was easy; the springs were working and there was often water flowing in stream beds. My route was a counterclockwise loop, first going northeast past the Miner's Needle and camping by the Whiskey Spring. Day two was a hike to the northwest past La Barge Spring, Oak Spring, Music Canyon, Marsh Valley, Needle Canyon and to a campsite near the base of Black Top Mesa. The third day closed the loop by going south through Boulder Canyon, over Fremont Saddle, and dropping back to the trailhead. This was a marvelous route and a perfect introduction to the Sonoran Desert. The weather was perfect with lots of sun but not hot. All the desert plants were present: beavertail, saguaro, cholla, and ocotillo. The birds seemed to be enjoying the conditions, including a Costa's hummingbird that I watched flycatching during one lunch stop. There was a lot of eroded volcanic rock with some dramatic spires and needles. It was a great trip and I recommend it to anybody who likes to hike. Once away from the Peralta Trailhead there were few other hikers, but there were lots within a few miles of the trailhead.

Volcanic terrain in the Sonoran Desert, Superstition Wilderness

Chiricahua National Monument

★ ★ ★ ★

Size: 10,290 acres　　　**Year Designated:** 1976　　　**Responsible Agency:** USNPS

The Chiricahua National Monument Wilderness is located in the Chiricahua National Monument east of State Highway 181 in the southeast corner of the state. The nearest town is Douglas.

MY VISIT: February 27, 2005

Millions of years ago the land that is now the national monument was buried by debris in the eruption of a nearby volcano. Subsequently this mostly rhyolite material was eroded, forming a forest of towers and spires in many fanciful shapes. My day hike started at the monument visitor center, went east on the Rhyolite Trail, and then made a loop around the Heart of Rocks on the same-named trail and the Echo Trail and back on the Rhyolite Trail. The rock formations were numerous and fabulous. This was a very worthwhile trip. I recommend this area to just about anybody. Note, though, that overnight camping is not allowed in the wilderness.

Spires in old volcanic debris, Chiricahua National Monument Wilderness

Aravaipa Canyon

★ ★ ★ ★

Size: 19,410 acres | **Year Designated:** 1984 | **Responsible Agency:** BLM

The Aravaipa Canyon Wilderness is located on BLM public lands southeast of the town of Winkelman and north of the city of Tucson. The area can be accessed on the west side by a good road off State Highway 77. Access to the east side is possible by a more difficult road. At the time of my visit there was a BLM map dedicated to this wilderness. A permit was required to hike in this area. The number of visitors was limited to fifty per day, thirty from the west and twenty from the east. I obtained my permit in person at the BLM office in Safford.

MY VISIT: March 3, 2006

My day hike began at the west entrance to the wilderness. My route was simple as could be—walking upstream along or in Aravaipa Creek. In the creek was a fair fraction of the time. This was a very pretty canyon. It was spring, birds were active, and the vegetation was lush green. The canyon did not have the dramatic walls of some other southwest canyons like the Grand Canyon or Zion, but was always pleasant and relaxing, the perfect place to spend a fine spring day. There were certainly other hikers, both day hikers and backpackers, but it never seemed crowded. I recommend this hike to just about anybody who does not mind getting his feet wet.

Araviapa Canyon

Kofa Refuge

★ ★ ★ ★

Size: 516,000 acres   **Year Designated:** 1990   **Responsible Agency:** USFWS

The Kofa Refuge Wilderness occupies most of the Kofa National Wildlife Refuge. Easy access is from the west off US Highway 95 south of the crossroads town of Quartzite.

MY VISITS: April 6, 2010 and May 9, 2014 and May 10, 2014 and May 11, 2014

The name Kofa is really an acronym for King of Arizona, given by early miners. There are still semi-active mines within the refuge, one named King.

The first two of these day hikes were to the modestly famous Palm Canyon. This canyon is very deep and narrow with crevices and ledges along the rock walls. Some of the crevices and ledges provided an environment supporting a remnant of California fan palm trees left over from an earlier and wetter time. It was a neat place. The canyon was also home to a nesting colony of white-throated swifts. The birds were active during the 2010 visit. Later in the hiking day in 2010 I went up Kofa Queen Canyon north of Palm Canyon. Typical of the refuge, there were large, dramatic eroded volcanic cliffs and towers.

The May 10, 2014 day hike also began at the Palm Canyon Trailhead, but instead of going into the canyon I hiked south along the base of the volcanic cliffs through classic Sonoran Desert, exploring side canyons along the way. The impressive volcanic spires and cliffs were still present. The final day hike began near the old King Mine and went around Kofa Butte.

I like this area and recommend it to anyone interested in desert terrain.

Sonoran Desert,
Kofa Refuge Wilderness

Pecos

★ ★ ★ ★

Size: 223,667 acres   **Year Designated:** 1964
Responsible Agency: USFS

The Pecos Wilderness is located in the Santa Fe National Forest northeast of the city of Santa Fe. There are many options for access to this area. Popular roads to trailheads include State Highways 63 from the south, 475 from the west, 76 from the north, and 65 and 105 from the east. At the time of my visit there was a USFS map dedicated to this wilderness.

MY VISITS: 1970s overnight backpack, October 28, 2013 and September 19–20, 2017

I have no written records of my first visit sometime in the late 1970s. I do remember it as an overnight backpack with two friends from Los Alamos. I think we began at the Santa Fe ski resort and I remember standing on the summit of Santa Fe Baldy (12,622 feet). I also remember being favorably impressed with the area.

The day hike in 2013 began at the Jacks Creek Trailhead. It was a beautiful fall day with some color still clinging to the aspens. There had been some recent snow and it was deer hunting season with some hunters on horseback coming and going near the trailhead. My route was north past Round Mountain and continuing north to Pecos Baldy Lake where I stopped for lunch. For lunch companions I had a very friendly flock of gray jays. The terrain was classic high-elevation New Mexico with lots of aspen and conifers mixed in with open meadows. The snow was patchy at low elevation and nearly continuous at higher elevation. All of this provided a perfect scenic backdrop at the lake.

The 2017 trip was an overnight backpack beginning at the Trampas Campground Trailhead. As I was getting my pack organized a couple of large trucks arrived, one pulling a horse trailer. The other truck had a cargo of live fingerling fish. Two New Mexico game wardens had the horses and they loaded one horse with fish-carrying paniers. Their task for the day was to go to the Trampas Lakes and Hidden Lake and release the fish. My task for the day was to go to the Trampas Lakes and find a camping spot. The lakes were in a very pretty setting among pine trees near tree line. This was not a difficult hike and could have been done as a day hike. A side effect of this easy access was that the area clearly got a lot of use. There were many obvious campsites with fire rings. The next day I made a side trip to Hidden Lake, then returned to my campsite, packed up, and went back to the trailhead. It was definitely a worthwhile way to spend two late-summer days.

I like the Pecos and recommend it. Access is easy, the trail system is excellent, and the scenery is almost always good. Solitude may be hard to find, but on balance a nice destination.

*Pecos Baldy Lake,
Pecos Wilderness*

Bisti/De-Na-Zin

★ ★ ★ ★

Size: 38,381 acres   **Year Designated:** 1984
Responsible Agency: BLM

The Bisti/De-Na-Zin Wilderness is located on BLM public lands south of the city of Farmington in northwest New Mexico. Access is easy via good unpaved roads off State Highway 371 to the west and State Highway 57 to the east.

MY VISITS: May 30, 2012 and September 23, 2017

The routes of these two hikes were essentially the same. I repeated the trip in 2017 because my camera failed on the 2012 trip and I really wanted photos. Besides, this is a neat area and well worth a second visit. The trips began at a signed trailhead and parking area in standard southwest juniper scrub terrain with a trail descending through sandstone into a wash. The wash contained a fascinating collection of erosion features. There were hillsides of powdery, dry mud often revealing buried rock of odd shapes. Some looked like mushrooms sticking out of ancient soil. A lot of the rock was petrified wood, including large sections of intact tree trunks as shown in the photo. Some of the petrified wood had subtle color components. There were also more common balanced rock formations and other eroded sandstone.

This is a wilderness area where the details of the land are the attractions, not vast scenic expanses. I highly recommend this area for anyone who likes poking around in unusual landscapes.

Petrified tree trunks, Bisti/De-Na-Zin Wilderness

Mount Bangs, Piute Wilderness

Paiute

★ ★ ★

Size: 87,900 acres   **Year Designated:** 1984
Responsible Agency: BLM

The Piute Wilderness is located on BLM public lands south of Interstate Highway 15. The nearest town is Mesquite, Nevada. The Virgin River makes up most of the northern wilderness boundary. This part of Arizona is called the Arizona Strip. It is nearly inaccessible from other parts of Arizona, and access is mostly via unpaved roads from Nevada or Utah. Navigation here can be difficult. The quality of the unpaved roads varies from well maintained to barely passable. There was a BLM map of the Arizona Strip including this wilderness available from the BLM in St. George, Utah.

Yes, the first day hike was in January. My goal was to do a hike from the Cougar Springs Trailhead, but the road was poor in addition to being snow covered. I turned around before getting to the trailhead and was grateful to get out at all. My next choice was to go up what my map called Hatchet Valley, just behind a BLM wilderness sign at the southern wilderness boundary. The terrain was standard Utah/Nevada pinon, juniper, and cactus with little of interest. A look around convinced me that there could be some interesting hikes and I decided to come back later.

That later was in October. This time, again with confusion, I was able to get to the Cougar Springs Trailhead. The route was basically north, taking a side trail to the summit of Mount Bangs (pictured). It was a beautiful fall day with good color from some scrub oak. The 8,012-foot summit provided an excellent view of the Virgin Mountains. After leaving the summit, I continued north on the Virgin Ridge Trail to an overlook to the north. Mesquite, Nevada and I-15 were just visible in the distance. Here I turned around and went back to the trailhead.

This was a very nice day in what I concluded was probably the nicest part of the wilderness. I recommend it to any hiker with a vehicle that can tolerate not-so-great roads. The area gave little evidence of visitation. I never saw another soul on the trail or on the road on either visit.

ARIZONA

Kanab Creek

★ ★ ★

Size: 68,250 acres   **Year Designated:** 1984
Responsible Agency: USFS

The Kanab Creek Wilderness is located mostly in the Kaibab National Forest with a small portion in the western part on BLM land. US Highway Alt 89 is to the northeast. The nearest town is Fredonia to the north. Part of the southern wilderness boundary is the northern boundary of Grand Canyon National Park.

Looking at a map of the Kanab Creek Wilderness one obvious feature is a tentacle sticking out of the northern part of the body heading to the east. This tentacle is Snake Gulch, a not-very-deep, red sandstone canyon with a trail and trailhead. My day hike was up this apparently famous canyon. Its fame is a large collection of high-quality Native American rock art, certainly among the best I have seen although I am not an expert. On the day of my visit the only other people there were a pair of professional photographers carrying serious camera gear. We chatted a bit and I just wandered upcanyon a few miles, turned around, and went back to the trailhead. While the scenery is nothing special this would be a good destination for anyone wishing to see old, native artwork.

Reclining flute player (Kokopelli), Kanab Creek Wilderness

Paria Canyon-Vermillion Cliffs

★ ★ ★

Size: 110,816 acres   **Year Designated:** 1984
Responsible Agency: BLM

The Paria Canyon-Vermillion Cliffs Wilderness is located on BLM public lands south of US Highway 89 in the Vermillion Cliffs National Monument just west of the town of Page. The northern part of the wilderness is in Utah and the southern part in Arizona.

MY VISIT: October 31, 2012 and November 1, 2012

I had heard a few tales about the Paria. Some of them pretty scary. The canyon is popular and is often done as a multi-day trip. I was neither physically or mentally prepared for more than a day hike. The hike began at the White House Trailhead next to the Paria River. For a while the river flowed through open terrain before entering its water-worn canyon. The river was pretty gentle at this time of year, but it was downright cold. Once in the canyon, hiking was in boots and socks with water as high as knee deep. Good footwear with traction was essential. The narrow parts of the canyon were impressive. I was quite amused by some of the erosion patterns in the pale rock that looked to me like multi-family Hobbit housing. I met seven backpackers coming upstream who told me I should make a real effort to get to the confluence of the river and Buckskin Gulch as it was very scenic. Unfortunately, I did not have enough time to get there and back in daylight.

After returning to the White House Trailhead I drove to the nearby Buckskin Trailhead to camp for a cold night. I left my super-saturated boots on the top of my truck. The next morning, they were frozen solid—simply not useable. Fortunately, I had low-cut shoes for backup. This second day hike was down Buckskin Gulch. Again, the beginning of the hike was in fairly open terrain, then dropped down into a narrow stretch. Eventually the canyon opened into a pleasant amphitheater occupied by several other hikers. My intention was to continue downstream, but after a short distance I met three backpackers coming upstream who warned me not to go much farther because the canyon got very narrow with deep, muddy, cold pools. I went just a bit farther, saw one of the deep pools and immediately turned around. On the way back, I made a side trip up to the Wire Canyon narrows to another trailhead.

Taken together these were two interesting and scenic days. The area is obviously popular—on the second day I encountered seventeen other hikers and this was the off-season. I certainly recommend the area to any water-tolerant hikers. Earlier in the fall might be a better choice of visiting times.

Multi-family Hobbit housing, Paria River, Paria Canyon-Vermillion Cliffs Wilderness

Saddle Mountain

★ ★ ★

Size: 40,600 acres | **Year Designated:** 1984 | **Agency:** USFS

The Saddle Mountain Wilderness is located in the Kaibab National Forest south of US Highway Alt 89 and just east of State Highway 67. The nearest town is Fredonia to the north. Most of the southern wilderness boundary is the northern boundary of Grand Canyon National Park.

MY VISIT: April 25, 2006

I did not have any carefully thought out plan for this wilderness, but looked for a trailhead I could drive to without hurting my truck. I was lucky. My trailhead was for the Nankoweap Trail. It started in pretty mundane terrain of pinon, juniper, and ponderosa pine with some red sandstone cliffs within view. After only a few miles I came to a saddle and there right in front of me was a gorgeous view of the Grand Canyon. I was standing on the North Rim. I sat down to take it all in. As I sat, I saw one of the area's problems—air pollution. While spectacular the view was definitely not clear. After a few minutes a second problem became evident—helicopter noise. Yes, a lot of helicopter passes were quite audible. After sitting awhile, I hiked along the park boundary for a way but lost the panoramic views, so I turned around and went back the way I came. This was certainly a worthwhile day.

Grand Canyon from
Saddle Mountain Wilderness

Mount Nutt

★ ★ ★

Size: 27,660 acres   **Year Designated:** 1990
Responsible Agency: BLM

The Mount Nutt Wilderness is located on BLM public lands west of Interstate Highway 40, north of the Oatman Road, and southwest of the city of Kingman. The Black Mountains run through the wilderness.

MY VISIT: March 7, 2014

This day hike began at a trailhead for Cave Spring just across a street at the western edge of a housing development adjacent to southwestern Kingman. Before my friend Maya and I even started walking, five cars pulled into the parking area and disgorged fifteen other hikers. All of us hiked the short distance to Cave Spring, a running spring coming out of a cave large enough to walk in to the water source. All the other hikers stopped at the spring, but Maya and I continued south and west to a ridge with good views of the Black Mountains to the west. This was volcanic terrain and the range was well named—much of the rock was black. Before going very far we needed to turn around because of time, but this stark, somewhat forbidding area looked like it could be worth spending more time. On our way back, we saw what was probably a family group of wild burros. We watched and listened with interest for a while. I have often seen wild horses; this is one of the few times I have seen burros.

This was a nice hike in some interesting country. I recommend it.

Taylor Cabin, Sycamore Canyon Wilderness

Sycamore Canyon

★ ★ ★

Size: 55,937 acres   **Year Designated:** 1972
Responsible Agency: USFS

The Sycamore Canyon Wilderness is located in the Kaibab and Coconino National Forests south of Interstate Highway 40 and west of State Highway 89A. The nearest towns are Sedona to the east and Cottonwood to the south.

MY VISIT: April 11–13, 2005

This three-day backpack began about two miles before the Dogie Trailhead. The road to the trailhead was closed because of mud. I was already getting a late start and it was almost dark when I got to a part of Sycamore Creek with water for my camp. Day two was a day hike from my campsite to the Taylor Cabin. This was a very nice hike through classic Arizona red sandstone along Sycamore Creek, which was running intermittently. The cabin was quite interesting and located in a truly beautiful spot. Day three was spent going back to my truck. This was certainly a pleasant, easy trip and I recommend this wilderness to just about anybody. The area clearly saw some use but, on my visit, it was certainly never crowded.

Red Rock-Secret Mountain

★ ★ ★

Size: 47,194 acres | **Year Designated:** 1984 | **Responsible Agency:** USFS

The Red Rock-Secret Mountain Wilderness is located in the Coconino National Forest just east of the Sycamore Canyon Wilderness. The area is south of Interstate Highway 40 and west of State Highway 89A. The closest town is Sedona to the east.

MY VISIT: April 14, 2005

This rather long day hike began at the Loy Canyon Trailhead at the southern wilderness boundary. It was another day in lovely red sandstone. My route was north up the Loy Canyon Trail to the northern wilderness boundary, then east and south on the Secret Mountain Trail to the Secret Cabin. Here I turned around and retraced my steps back to the trailhead. Like its immediate western neighbor, this area should provide a good hiking opportunity for just about anybody. As an aside, I never did learn what the secret was, so a secret it remains.

Sandstone bluffs from the Loy Canyon Trail, Red Rock-Secret Mountain Wilderness

Wet Beaver

★ ★ ★

Size: 6,700 acres   **Year Designated:** 1984
Responsible Agency: USFS

The Wet Beaver Wilderness is located in the Coconino National Forest a few miles east of Interstate Highway 17. The nearest town is Camp Verde to the southwest. Access is easy via a paved road to the Beaver Creek Campground near the western wilderness boundary. The wilderness runs mostly west to east along Wet Beaver Creek and a few tributary creeks.

MY VISIT: April 20, 2005

My day hike on April 20 began at a trailhead for the Bell Trail near the campground. My route ran west to east upstream along the creek through red sandstone in classic juniper and cactus with lots of deciduous trees and shrubs near the water. A very pretty canyon. At the wilderness boundary I saw my first hooded oriole with its brilliant orange and black. The creek had a substantial water flow and there were lots of pools inviting immersion. Partway into the wilderness my map showed the trail crossing the creek and continuing east and leaving the canyon. I did cross the creek, but was unable to find the continuation of the trail, so I turned around and went back the way I came. This was a nearly perfect day in a very nice area. The trail is easy to get to and easy to hike. The canyon almost begs the hiker to go slowly, enjoying the water, the trees, and the birds. This is another area I recommend to just about anyone.

West Clear Creek

★ ★ ★

Size: 15,238 acres   **Year Designated:** 1984
Responsible Agency: USFS

The West Clear Creek Wilderness is located in the Coconino National Forest east of Interstate Highway 17 and north of State Highway 260. It is a few miles south of the Wet Beaver Wilderness. The wilderness boundary runs just north and south of the main branch of West Clear Creek. When looked at on a map the wilderness looks something like a centipede—long and skinny with little legs sticking out along tributary streams.

MY VISIT: March 14, 2006

My intention was to hike this area the day after I hiked the Wet Beaver Wilderness in 2005. I did drive up to the trailhead, but immediately encountered two problems. First, someone had camped near the trailhead, built a fire, and then left with the fire still burning. My first action was to go to the creek, get water, and put out the fire. As I was doing this, I saw two teenagers taking stuff out of the back of a pickup truck parked nearby. I thought nothing of this until a bit later when the owners of the pickup came back and found their things in the truck stolen. They asked me if I had seen anybody and I said I had and described the two kids. The men wandered down the road and soon returned with the teenagers and asked if they were the ones I had seen. I said yes. There ensued an argument. One complicating aspect of the argument was the butcher knife in the hand of the older teenager, although he was not directly threatening anyone. The argument was not going anywhere, and the men acknowledged that the kids stole only their beer and cooler and they were not willing to make too big a deal over beer. The men then left. That left only myself and the teenagers in the trailhead area. I did not like this arrangement and departed, vowing to come back to the area at some later date.

That date was on March 14, 2006. This time there were no complications. I began my hike at the Bull Pen Ranch Trailhead, the same trailhead where I had parked before. This was another hike in a riparian area along a nice creek. My route was just upstream a few miles until the trail left the creek and then left the wilderness to the north. Here I just turned around and retraced my steps. The trail crossed the creek multiple times each way, so my feet were pretty wet. There was some red rock and snow on some higher cliff tops, but nothing dramatic. The deciduous trees along the creek were just beginning to leaf out. Another easy, pleasant day hike in a pleasant place that I recommend to other hikers.

Fossil Springs

★ ★ ★

Size: 11,550 acres   **Year Designated:** 1884
Responsible Agency: USFS

The Fossil Springs Wilderness is located in the Coconino National Forest south of State Highway 260 and southeast of the town of Camp Verde. It is south of the West Clear Creek Wilderness.

MY VISIT: April 23, 2005

I don't remember many details about this hike, but my notes tell me that I hiked both the Flume Trail and the Mail Trail in a long day. I remember walking next to a flume for a couple of miles before entering the wilderness. Fossil Creek had substantial flow, deep and with lots of moss. There were many clear pools, especially around the springs. It was also obvious that this very pretty spot had been discovered. There were a lot of folks around including families with young children. The springs were neat, a considerable volume of water bubbling up around big tree roots. I failed in my attempts to photograph the upwelling water.

Kachina Peaks

★ ★ ★

Size: 18,960 acres   **Year Designated:** 1984
Responsible Agency: USFS

The Kachina Peaks Wilderness is located in the Coconino National Forest north of the city of Flagstaff and between US Highway 89 to the east and US Highway 180 to the west. The wilderness is home to the San Francisco Peaks.

Maya on the top of Arizona, Kachina Peaks Wilderness

This was relatively high country for Arizona and there was still a lot of snow in the San Francisco Peaks on my first visit. I chose a trailhead for the Weatherford Trail because the trail climbed up south-facing slopes much of the way. My route was simple—hike north for as far as I could get. Even though south facing, there was still a fair bit of snow on the trail. I was able to get to Doyle Saddle for some really good views on this day of glorious weather. I met one other party of hikers coming down, and their judgment was that this was the most scenic trail in the wilderness.

This was volcanic country. There were lots of cones rising from the surrounding flat terrain. It was also heavily forested, unlike many other Arizona areas.

The 2013 visit was to introduce my friend Maya to northern Arizona. The hike was the very popular trail to Humphreys Peak. It was a Saturday and a day of brilliant sunshine after a cold night. Flagstaff, only a few miles away, is home to Northern Arizona University. There was an ant parade of people, obviously students, up and down the trail. Some, still wrapped in sleeping bags, said they had spent the night on the summit for star gazing. Humphreys is the highest point in Arizona at 12,643 feet. It is one of the few "High Points" I have done. The crowds notwithstanding, this was a very worthwhile day. Once again, I recommend this area to any hiker.

Saguaro and poppies in the Rawhide Mountains Wilderness

ARIZONA

Rawhide Mountains

★ ★ ★

Size: 38,470 acres   **Year Designated:** 1990
Responsible Agency: BLM

The Rawhide Mountains wilderness is located on BLM public lands north of US Highway 60, southwest of US Highway 93, and southeast of Lake Havasu City. It is south and west of Alamo State Park. There are no trails.

MY VISIT: March 9, 2017

I had some trouble finding this area, wandering about on some doubtful roads and then, almost ready to give up, I saw a BLM sign telling me that the Rawhide Mountains Wilderness was behind that sign. I quickly began a day hike. This was much volcanic terrain with old lava flows and outcrops of volcanic material. It was also a spring following a rather wet winter. That meant flowers and a perfect time to be visiting these Sonoran Desert areas. The color here was from California poppies in great numbers. I hiked south away from the road in very open, easy-walking terrain. There were no obvious destinations so I just wandered around until it was time to leave. This was a worthwhile day with perfect weather, nice views, and a variety of desert vegetation.

Harcuvar Mountains

★ ★ ★

Size: 25,050 acres   **Year Designated:** 1990
Responsible Agency: BLM

The Harcuvar Wilderness is located on BLM public lands north of US Highway 60, east of the Alamo Road, and southeast of the Rawhide Mountains Wilderness. The nearest town is Parker to the west. There are no trails. Access is probably best via unpaved roads going east from the Alamo Road.

MY VISIT: March 8, 2017

This hike was made on the day previous to the nearby Rawhide Mountains hike. The terrain was quite similar, volcanic with standard Sonoran Desert vegetation. It was a nice day and, like the previous day, things were green after a wet winter. Things were also orange as the California poppies were in great profusion. The hike began at the northern wilderness boundary and my route was south to a minor volcanic summit. After a summit lunch I more or less retraced my steps. Again, a nice example of desert terrain. My sense was that visitors were rare in this area.

Petrified Forest

★ ★ ★

Size: 50,260 acres   **Year Designated:** 1970
Responsible Agency: USNPS

Most of Petrified Forest National Park is designated wilderness. It is located just north of Interstate Highway 40 and northeast of the town of Holbrook. At the time of my visit there was a USGS map for the park, including the wilderness.

MY VISIT: February 25–26, 2006

This overnight backpack began at the Chinde Point lookout and picnic area. A permit was required for overnight travel. It was winter and pretty chilly, but this was not a trip I wanted to do when it was hot. I was able to carry all the water I needed for this short, cool-weather trip. There were no trails in this area and I did not even have a specific destination in mind other than to get a sense of the terrain and see some petrified trees. I began by dropping down into Lithodendron Wash, crossed the wash, and headed northwest up a tributary wash into what looked like potentially interesting terrain. I was in no hurry—this was another case of "poking around in" country. I hiked maybe four or five miles until the terrain turned flat and uninteresting. I turned around and found a nice, sheltered campsite in a side wash.

The next morning was spent exploring the nearby higher terrain looking for petrified wood. I found some. Actually, a lot. A real forest although the trees had fallen. I remember that many of the trees were black, unlike most other petrified wood I had seen. This was a really cool place. After poking around most of the morning I went back to my campsite, packed up, and walked back to my truck. My recollection is that I was glad I had my GPS as landmarks were scarce. I must have taken some photographs, but none remain. I certainly recommend the area to curious hikers.

Eagletail Mountains

★ ★ ★

Size: 100,600 acres   **Year Designated:** 1990
Responsible Agency: BLM

The Eagletail Mountains Wilderness is located on BLM public lands south of Interstate Highway 10, west of the city of Phoenix, and east of the Kofa National Wildlife Refuge.

MY VISIT: April 8, 2010

This day hike was in terrain very much reminiscent of the Kofa Refuge Wilderness just to the west. I began at a "guzzler" wildlife water tank near Courthouse Rock. I knew there was supposed to be a trail called the Ben Avery Trail here but had trouble finding it. After some cross-country hiking I did find the trail and followed it. The terrain was classic Sonoran Desert with lots of cacti, some blooming, and nice volcanic spires and ridges. The trail eventually descended into a wash and the terrain became less interesting so I just turned around. This was another worthwhile hike and I recommend it.

*Volcanic spires and Sonoran Desert,
Eagletail Mountains Wilderness*

Table Top

★ ★ ★

Size: 34,400 acres   **Year Designated:** 1990
Responsible Agency: BLM

The Tabletop Wilderness is located on BLM public lands just south of Interstate Highway 8 and southeast of the town of Gila Bend. Access is easiest from an unpaved road that runs south from I-8.

MY VISIT: March 13, 2015

This day hike began at a formal BLM campground and trailhead at the western wilderness boundary. The campground was quite lovely. Yes, there was really a trail that went to the top of the table. I got the impression that this area was rather popular, plus it was within easy traveling distance from greater Phoenix. The trail to the summit was easy and the terrain was much like other nearby Sonoran Desert areas. After lunch on the summit (4,373 feet) and on our descent we passed one other party of hikers and later received a visit from a low-flying US Air Force A-10. It was a pleasant hike in a pleasant area.

Pusch Ridge

★ ★ ★

Size: 53,933 acres   **Year Designated:** 1978
Responsible Agency: USFS

The Pusch Ridge Wilderness is located in the Coronado National Forest adjacent to the northeast suburbs of Tucson. This proximity guarantees heavy use of the area.

MY VISIT: February 19–21, 2005

This three-day backpack began at a trailhead in the Catalina State Park adjacent to the western wilderness boundary. It was President's Day Weekend after a wet winter. When I told the state park people that I intended to go backpacking they told me I *must sign a waiver* acknowledging that I might not be able to leave the park when I wished because the park entrance road was subject to flooding. Indeed, floodwater had recently dumped so much sand and debris on the road that it had been closed. I agreed and signed. By now it was too late to start a backpack, so I spent the night in the park. It rained that night and the road was "washed in" and impassable. That was no problem for me because that morning I started hiking.

My trail was the Romero Trail, recommended to me by a USFS employee at the Sabino Visitor Center near the southern wilderness boundary. The first couple of miles had dry weather, but rain began shortly thereafter and it rained most of the rest of the day. The going was slow because of crossings of a normally small stream that was no longer small. I made my camp at about 4,800 feet on one of the last relatively flat spots before Romero Pass. Most of this day was hiking in rather heavy timber. That night was exciting. After crawling into my tent, two thunderstorms drifted through. Heavy thunderstorms with lots of lightning and yet more heavy rain. I could hear water running past my tent and I occasionally stuck my head out to be sure I was not about to be washed away.

The second day began gray but not raining. I decided to do a day hike and went over Romero Pass, then around the head of the West Fork of Sabino Canyon, past Cathedral Rock, finally stopping at Window Rock at 7,468 feet. At this point the day was beginning to clear, although my memory is that views were limited. I went back to my camp.

Day three was spent going back to the trailhead. It was a nice, dry day and I passed day hikers coming in. They told me that the state park people were working on opening the road. As I got closer to the state park, I could hear the sound of a wheel loader working. I still had time to get a park shower, then the road was open and I was able to get out. In truth, I think I was really pretty lucky with this trip.

I am somewhat ambivalent about this area. It certainly sees a lot of traffic and I do not remember any especially nice scenery, but I would not discourage others from hiking here.

ARIZONA

Galiuro

★ ★ ★

Size: 76,317 acres   **Year Designated:** 1964
Responsible Agency: USFS

The Galiuro Wilderness is located in the Coronado National Forest northeast of the city of Tucson and southwest of the town of Safford. Access to the west side of the wilderness is from State Highway 266.

MY VISIT: March 3–6, 2006

This three-day backpack began at the Deer Creek Trailhead on the west side of the wilderness. Water was scarce in this area and I had spoken to USFS people in Safford who recommended Powers Garden as a destination with reliable water. So my route was west from the trailhead to Powers

View from the summit of Grassy Peak, Galiuro Wilderness

Garden. On my way west, I was mildly surprised to see a pack string coming east. Upon arriving at the garden, I realized the packer's mission. The area was filled with tents and people. It turned out that I had accidentally wandered into a class in leave-no-trace practices put on by the National Outdoor Leadership School (NOLS) for land managers from various state, federal, and private agencies. Given that the only water source was here I would need to join their camp. They invited me to participate, and that evening's subject was how to build a leave-no-trace campfire.

There was another class the next morning in which I also participated, then the NOLS group departed. I used the rest of the day to do a day hike up Grassy Ridge then south to the summit of Grassy Peak (6,690 feet). This was a perfect weather day in rugged, remote terrain. It was not really desert, although there were lots of thorny plants, and not really forest, although there were some coniferous trees. Yes, there were grasses on Grassy Peak. Day three all I did was pack up and go back to the trailhead.

I quite liked this area. It was not too difficult to get to, had a pretty good trail system and good scenery, and, notwithstanding my experience, seemed to get little human visitation. I certainly recommend it.

Dos Cabezas Mountains

★ ★ ★

Size: 11,998 acres   **Year Designated:** 1990
Responsible Agency: BLM

The Dos Cabezas Mountains Wilderness is located on BLM public lands south of Interstate Highway 10, north of State Highway 186, and southeast of the town of Willcox.

MY VISIT: March 10, 2015

A friend and I began this day hike at a BLM picnic area at the northeast wilderness boundary. The terrain was jumbled sedimentary rock with lots of curious little formations. It was dry, but without many of the usual Sonoran cacti. There was a small stream flowing out of the higher country and we decided to follow it to its source and, if possible, get to a ridgetop for some views. There were some very inviting pools along the stream. Dos Cabezas means "two heads" in Spanish. I did not give this name much thought as we were hiking, but the view from the ridgetop made it very plain, as is obvious in the photo. According to my map, though, the heads were actually outside the wilderness area.

The Two Heads, Dos Cabezas Mountains Wilderness

Peloncillo Mountains

★ ★ ★

Size: 19,440 acres   **Year Designated:** 1990
Responsible Agency: BLM

The Peloncillo Mountains Wilderness is located on BLM public lands north of Interstate Highway 10. The eastern wilderness boundary is the Arizona-New Mexico state line. There are no trails in the area.

MY VISIT: March 9, 2015

This day hike with a friend began by driving up and down an obscure two-track road along the western wilderness boundary looking for Ward Canyon where we wanted to do our hike. We ultimately saw some wilderness area wands and decided we must be in Ward Canyon. Our route was east up the canyon a few miles to a pass looking into Doubtful Canyon. The terrain in Doubtful Canyon did not look especially interesting, so we decided to stop on the pass and have lunch. After lunch and almost as soon as we had put our packs on our backs, we heard noise—a lot of noise. As we looked down Ward Canyon, we saw a very low-flying USAF C-130 that roared over our heads, went over the pass, and banked sharply to the north. We both just said, "Wow." A few minutes later as we headed back to my truck, another C-130, this one from a different air force, performed the same maneuver. This process continued for several minutes. I am not certain how many aircraft there were, but I guess at least four, some flying the route more than once. While the terrain in this wilderness was not particularly interesting, the lunchtime visitors sure were.

C-130 visits hikers, Peloncillo Mountains Wilderness

Mount Wrightson

★ ★ ★

Size: 25,260 acres **Year Designated:** 1984
Responsible Agency: USFS

The Mount Wrightson Wilderness is located in the Coronado National Forest east of Interstate Highway 19, southwest of the city of Tucson, and northeast of the town of Green Valley. Access is easy via a paved road from I-19, and the area's proximity to Tucson guarantees heavy visitation. The area is famous for its birding.

MY VISIT: February 24, 2005

Mount Wrightson is one of the best examples of "sky islands," mountains that rise significantly above the surrounding desert terrain and that support ecosystems not expected in southern Arizona. Some species found on these islands are indeed isolated because they cannot find their way to other members of their species. They could be at risk of deleterious genetic isolation.

This day hike began near the Bog Springs Campground. My route was a figure-eight path using the Super Trail and the Mount Baldy Trail. My goal was the Mount Wrightson summit at 9,435 feet. I was warned that there would be snow before the summit. I encountered snow at the Mount Baldy saddle, but kept going up. Before the summit I spoke with a few hikers coming down who said they had to give up because the route was quite icy. I kept going up anyway but also had to give up because of ice. Nonetheless, this was a very nice day in nice, forested terrain. It was certainly a cold day for southern Arizona. I recommend this area to anyone who does not mind hiking in very popular, potentially crowded places.

Pajarita

★ ★ ★

Size: 7420 acres **Year Designated:** 1984
Responsible Agency: USFS

The Pajarita Wilderness is located in the Coronado National Forest west of Interstate Highway 19 and west of the city of Nogales. Access is via unpaved roads beyond the end of State Highway 289. The southern wilderness boundary is the Mexican border.

MY VISIT: February 25, 2005

My first stop on this day was at the Nogales USFS ranger station. I knew the wilderness was possibly sensitive given its location on the Mexican border, so I wanted official input on conditions there. I was advised that if I did go, I should exercise caution, mostly not to engage people I did not know in conversation and certainly not to pick up any objects that were not mine. Apparently, the area was an entry point for illegal weapons and drugs. On a more positive note I was told that tourists and hikers had not experienced any problems.

I drove to the Sycamore Canyon Trailhead and the only other vehicle in sight was a USFS pickup truck. I parked and began hiking south. I had read that the canyon was well known and quite beautiful. The terrain was mostly forested, including sycamore trees, with sandstone canyon walls and some other desert vegetation. I did not go very many miles, maybe just two, until I ran into a real obstacle—a deep, cold pool with steep sandstone on both sides. I explored ways around the obstacle but saw nothing that made any sense. I poked into the pool with a stick. It was deep. As I am generally a chicken when it comes to water I decided to turn around. Not long after turning around I heard voices coming down the trail. There were four people and they were armed—with butterfly nets. They looked like my community college students. Shortly after that encounter I met a youngish couple who looked like they had just stepped out of an Eddie Bauer catalog. By the time I got back to the trailhead I passed two other casual hikers. My conclusion was that this was indeed not a dangerous destination for hikers. Unfortunately, I probably missed the most scenic part of the canyon because I was afraid of a pool of water. This area might be better visited a little later in the year, and hikers should be prepared for being in water.

ARIZONA

Chiricahua

★ ★ ★

Size: 87,700 acres   **Year Designated:** 1964
Responsible Agency: USFS

The Chiricahua Wilderness is located in the Coronado National Forest west of State Highway 80 and just west of the New Mexico state line. The town of Douglas is to the southwest and the town of Willcox is to the northwest. Portions of the wilderness, especially near the South Fork of Cave Creek, are famous as a destination for birders.

MY VISIT: March 10, 2006 and March 11, 2006

Before beginning this trip, I visited the USFS ranger station in Douglas. I asked about backpacking, but was told that I should plan to carry all the water I might need. I decided to do day hikes. The first hike began at the Morse Canyon Trailhead. It was a cold, gray, and windy day and I was wearing a warm hat, gloves, and rain gear. The mountains were periodically socked in producing a coating of hoar frost on the trees. Most of the day's route was through a recent burn. Low elevations had oak forest with ponderosa pine higher up. I eventually got to the summit of Monte Vista Peak (9,357 feet) and its fire lookout tower. Unfortunately, there was heavy cloud cover so no views. I continued on the Crest Trail, then the Mormon Ridge Trail, down into Mormon Canyon, and closed a loop by walking down a road to my truck. This was a long day.

The second day hike was from the east side of the wilderness beginning at the famous birding spot that is the Cave Creek Canyon Recreation Area. There was not a lot of bird activity on this cold, gray, and windy day. My route was up the South Fork of Cave Creek through deciduous forest down low and coniferous forest up high. There were colorful cliffs and spires of eroded rock. This was definitely a lovely canyon. Somewhere after mile six the trail pretty much disappeared, so I sat down, had lunch, and then went back to the trailhead.

Even though the weather was not the best on this trip, this was a very nice area and I recommend it.

Organ Pipe Cactus

★ ★ ★

Size: 312,600 acres   **Year Designated:** 1978
Responsible Agency: USNPS

The Organ Pipe Cactus wilderness is located on the Mexican border within the Organ Pipe Cactus National Monument, south of the town of Ajo. State Highway 85 runs through the monument, splitting the wilderness into two parts.

MY VISITS: March 13, 2006 and March 13, 2014 and March 14, 2014

The 2006 hike began at the monument's visitor center for a chat with a park ranger about hiking destinations. Her recommendation was the Alamo Canyon Trail in the Ajo Range in the eastern part of the wilderness. This was a good suggestion. The trail went past an old ranch and then up a cairned route to a very scenic canyon with colorful volcanic cliffs. The Sonoran Desert plants were getting nice and green, including the organ pipe cactus.

In 2014 I wanted to show my friend Maya this lovely bit of desert. We arrived pretty late on the 13th and only had time to do a day hike to the old gold/silver Victoria mine. The next day we did a day hike on the Bull Pasture Trail to the summit of Mount Ajo (4,808 feet). This was a beautiful day through blooming cacti, lush greenery, and tortured volcanic formations topped off by good views from the summit. It was a long, strenuous day but well worth the effort. I heartily recommend this area to all hikers.

Latir Peak

★ ★ ★

Size: 20,506 acres   **Year Designated:** 1980
Responsible Agency: USFS

The Latir Peak Wilderness is located in the Carson National Forest east of State Highway 522 and north of the resort town of Taos. The Sangre de Cristo Mountains run through the wilderness. At the time of my visit there was a USFS map dedicated to the Latir Peak, Wheeler Peak, and Columbine-Hondo Wilderness Study Area (now designated).

MY VISIT: June 9–10, 2003

This overnight backpack began at the Cabresto Campground and my route was the shape of a balloon, going up Lake Fork Creek to Heart Lake for my camp and returning over Latir Mesa, past Venado Peak, and then along Bull Creek back to Lake Fork Creek and the campground. My notes from this trip are sparse, but I did see both elk and bighorn sheep and enjoyed the wide-open meadows above tree line. This area looked nothing like the desert southwest. It is not far from Colorado and the terrain looked very much like southern Colorado. I quite liked this area and recommend it as an easy yet worthwhile destination.

Columbine-Hondo

★ ★ ★

Size: 45,000 acres   **Year Designated:** 2014
Responsible Agency: USFS

The Columbine-Hondo Wilderness is located in the Carson National Forest west of State Highway 522 and north of the resort town of Taos. It is south of the Latir Peak Wilderness and north of the Wheeler Peak Wilderness and the Taos Ski Valley resort. The quest of wilderness status for this area was decades long, finally ending with success in 2014.

MY VISIT: July 1, 2015

I did this long day hike with a friend. We began at the Columbine Campground and hiked south through dense timber along Columbine Creek. There were seven creek crossings. The first two had bridges, but the rest required wet feet because the creek was high with snowmelt. After a climb of 3,200 feet we reached a trail running along a ridge above the road to the Taos ski resort. Thunderstorms began before we got to the ridge and there was a fair bit of lightning. Off to the east was a bare summit that would have provided better views, but I really thought discretion was the better part here and we turned around.

Wheeler Peak

★ ★ ★

Size: 20,000 acres   **Year Designated:** 1964
Responsible Agency: USFS

The Wheeler Peak Wilderness is located in the Carson National Forest east of State Highway 522, north of the resort town of Taos, and just south of the Columbine-Hondo Wilderness.

MY VISIT: June 11, 2003

Again, my notes from this trip are sparse. I distinctly remember that it was supposed to be an overnight backpack so that I would have time to go up Wheeler Peak, the tallest in New Mexico. To say that my plan was premature was an understatement. I began at a trailhead along the eastern wilderness boundary and went several miles in pretty good conditions, but as the trail started to climb significantly the snow got deeper on north-facing slopes. Eventually I completely lost the trail and began postholing. I had made it into the wilderness area, but was never going to get to Wheeler Peak. I had to turn around.

This hike was pleasant enough, but it was just too early in the year for my chosen route. I have little memory and no photographs from this day.

Gila

★ ★ ★

Size: 559,040 acres   **Year Designated:** 1964
Responsible Agency: USFS

The Gila Wilderness is located in the Gila National Forest east of US Highway 180. State Highway 15 provides access from the south. The closest city is Silver City to the south. The Mogollon Mountains run through the wilderness.

MY VISITS: May 19–20, 1998 and June 1, 2012 and October 22–25, 2013

The 1998 backpack was supposed to go along the Mogollon Crest, but there was too much snow at the 10,000-foot trailhead. So I dropped 1,000 feet and began at the Redstone Trailhead. The trail went east then south through coniferous forest to Whitewater Creek and Redstone Park near where I made a nice camp. Whitewater Creek earned its name as it was running high and fast with the snowmelt. The second day was just going back to the trailhead.

I intended to come back someday and do the Mogollon Crest Trail. This day came in 2012. Bad timing. When I arrived the entire northern part of the wilderness was on fire. I clearly needed a different destination, so I drove to Silver City and visited the USFS headquarters. Without commenting an employee led me into a meeting room where maps showed the extent of the fire. It was huge, eventually becoming the largest wildfire in the history of New Mexico. However, there were still a few trails open in the southeast part of the wilderness so I drove to a trailhead at the Rocky Canyon Campground in the southeast corner of the wilderness. Here I began a day hike to Brannon Park. It was hot, dry, and smoky. The terrain was pretty gentle with alligator juniper, oak, and tall ponderosas. I had hoped to go beyond Brannon to Apache Creek, but I lost that trail so I turned around and went back toward the trailhead. Now I will admit that my mind was wandering somewhat on the return segment, but in an area with some brush I almost rear-ended a bear! How can one rear-end a bear? He was ambling

Honey bear, Gila Wilderness

Aldo Leopold

★ ★ ★

Size: 203,524 acres   **Year Designated:** 1980
Responsible Agency: USFS

The Aldo Leopold Wilderness is located in the Gila National Forest east of the Gila Wilderness, separated by USFS Road 150. State Highway 159 is to the north and State Highway 152 is to the south. The closest city is Silver City. The Black Range runs north-south through the wilderness. Aldo Leopold was an early twentieth-century writer, environmentalist, and advocate for wilderness protection.

MY VISIT: May 21–24, 1998 and May 25, 1998

The four-day backpack in 1998 began at the southwestern wilderness boundary near McKnight Mountain. My route ran almost exactly north along the crest of the Black Range. This was a fitting name for these mountains as they were heavily timbered with large ponderosa pines and Douglas fir higher up. I have little memory of this trip and there are no surviving photos. I don't think I took many photos. The northern portion of the hike was on the Continental Divide Trail. The area did not appear to get much human visitation. In my four days I saw only one other party that was hiking the range north to south. I do remember that once I was north of Reed's Meadow the area had significant impact from recent fire. I also remember it being a good time and place for birds and I encountered lots of wild turkeys. I also encountered a pale blond bobcat. My route took me over at least a couple of 10,000-plus-foot summits, but my memory is that views were limited because of dense forest.

The day hike on May 25 was along the far southern wilderness boundary. The hike began at Emory Pass on State Highway 152. The route was north for about five miles to the summit of Hillsboro Peak (10,011 feet). Like the backpacking trip the terrain was oak and ponderosa pine at lower elevation and Douglas fir at higher elevation. The summit view was better than any on the backpacking trip. This area might make a good destination for hikers looking for seclusion in a forest environment.

along in the trail in front of me and I did not see him until I was quite close. He offered almost no reaction to me but did stroll slowly from the trail occasionally looking back over his shoulder. He was a large bear and the only honey bear I have ever seen. Cool.

The 2013 backpack was with two friends. We checked in with the USFS folks at the Gila Visitor Center and were warned that a lot of trails were closed and impassable due to post-fire floods. We decided to stay in the southwest part of the wilderness, beginning at the Woody's Corral Trailhead. We went up Little Creek, camping near its headwaters. The terrain was through mostly oak and ponderosa. There was a lot of evidence of various past fires. It was quite dry but the creeks were mostly flowing. The second day we did a side trip to the summit of Granite Peak (8,723 feet). The views were good but somewhat limited by trees. From here we went into the upper part of Turkey Creek, finding a campsite near Miller Spring. On day three we went past an old cabin by a stock pond (the area sees cattle grazing). We continued through pleasant Little Turkey Park and back to Little Creek. We could have easily gone back to the trailhead but decided to spend one more night out. Besides, Bill Gates was also camped there and the four of sat up late talking about lots of things. (This Mr. Gates was in the real estate business in New Mexico.) We went back to the trailhead in the morning.

Apache Kid

★ ★ ★

Size: 44,650 acres   **Year Designated:** 1980
Responsible Agency: USFS

The Apache Kid Wilderness is located in the Cibola National Forest west of Interstate Highway 25, east of State Highway 52, and southwest of the town of Socorro.

MY VISITS: May 27, 1998 and May 26, 2013

I liked this hike so much I did it twice. Both times the route was the same, beginning at the Springtime Campground and ending at the summit of San Mateo Peak (10,145 feet). The first hike was solo, the second to introduce my friend Maya to this neighborhood. This was volcanic terrain with twisted and uplifted swirls of solidified material. Typical of this part of New Mexico there was ponderosa pine at low elevation with spruce and Douglas fir near the summits. The area did not seem to get much human visitation. I certainly recommend this hike to anyone in the area.

White Mountain

★ ★ ★

Size: 46,850 acres   **Year Designated:** 1964
Responsible Agency: USFS

The White Mountain Wilderness is located in the Lincoln National Forest west of State Highway 37, north of State Highway 532, and northwest of the town of Ruidoso. At the time of my visit there was a USFS map dedicated to this area.

MY VISIT: June 17, 2003

The Rio Blanco Mountains of New Mexico are somewhat analogous to the sky islands of Arizona. Going up to elevations over 11,000 feet the terrain leaves the mostly desert lower elevation climbing to areas of oak, pinon, juniper, and mountain mahogany, then to coniferous forests and open grassy summits. My guess is that the name White Mountain comes from the pale grassy cover found on the highest summits. This day hike began at a trailhead adjacent to the South Fork Campground along the South Fork of the Rio Bonito. The trail went southwest up the South Fork toward White Horse Hill. Before reaching Whitehorse Hill, I took a trail over an unnamed summit of 10,518 feet and then descended through the Bluefront Canyon back to the South Fork, making a twelve-mile loop. This was a very nice day hiking through forest and then the open, grassy slopes of the gentle peaks. There were lots of birds and I saw a cinnamon bear with a cub, a whole herd of elk, and one wild turkey hen with ten chicks. Yes, the afternoon brought thunderstorms with rain and hail, but this was expected in New Mexico in the late spring. I found this a very worthwhile area and readily recommend it to other hikers.

Guadalupe Mountains

★ ★ ★

Size: 47,061 acres | **Year Designated:** 1978 | **Responsible Agency:** USNPS

The Guadalupe Mountains Wilderness is located in western Texas just south of the New Mexico state line. The closest city is Carlsbad, New Mexico. Access is via New Mexico State Highway 137 to the north and US Highway 62/180 to the east.

MY VISIT: May 20, 2007

I came into this park from the north into Dog Canyon. I hurried to get here from Carlsbad, New Mexico, because it was a late Friday afternoon and I was afraid I might not get a campsite in the park. I did not need to worry. I was the only visitor. Indeed, I was greeted first by a dog with a frisbee firmly clamped in her teeth. She was soon joined by the resident ranger and we talked about the park and possible hikes. Water was very scarce so I decided to do a long day hike the next day.

My hike began at the Dog Canyon Campground. My route was first west and then south on the Bush Mountain Trail, returning north on the Tejas Trail to make a fifteen-mile loop. The terrain was varied, but always dry with mostly shrub and grass vegetation with occasional coniferous trees and even some Texas madrone (pictured) and lots of cacti typical of the Chihuahuan Desert. There were some nice views from ridges along the Bush Mountain Trail with some exposed cliffs of sedimentary rock. Not too surprising, the area looked a lot like New Mexico and nothing at all like the wilderness areas of east Texas, which is why I include this area in this section. I certainly enjoyed my day here and recommend it to other hikers.

Texas madrone (left) and other Chihuahuan desert plants, Guadalupe Mountains Wilderness

Two-Star Areas

ARIZONA

Mount Trumbull 7,880 acres, designated 1984, located on BLM public lands just northwest of Grand Canyon National Park, south of Arizona State Highway 389, and south of the somewhat infamous Mormon polygamist community of Colorado City. The area can also be accessed by unpaved roads from Nevada to the west. The Mount Logan Wilderness is just to the southwest. The BLM map for the Arizona Strip shows the wilderness and its access routes.

My access route to this area was from Mesquite, Nevada, to the west. On November 1, 2011 and after about sixty-five miles on a very dusty road I found a trailhead for the summit of Mount Trumbull. Near the trailhead the terrain was volcanic with the standard pinon and juniper vegetation becoming a rather dense ponderosa pine forest near the summit at 8,080 feet. There were few views because of the dense tree cover, although the Grand Canyon was just within view.

Grand Wash Cliffs 37,300 acres, designated 1984, managed by BLM within the Grand Canyon-Parashant National Monument. It is south of the Piute Wilderness and is accessed by the same network of unpaved Arizona Strip roads. I did a day hike here on January 6, 2013. I simply went up the Grand Wash itself, then climbed a ridge for better views. It was standard Great Basin Desert-type terrain, but drier and fewer trees than in the Piute. Some Joshua trees were present. There was some nice color in the rock. To my vague amazement there were fences here. What I remember most about this day was the brilliant red color on the cliffs from a very red sunset. The area appeared to get little visitation; I saw exactly one other vehicle on the roads. To me the area was less scenic than the nearby Piute.

Mount Logan 14,650 acres, designated 1984, managed by BLM within the Grand Canyon-Parashant National Monument, located east and a bit

south of the Grand Wash Cliffs Wilderness. Some of the eastern wilderness boundary is shared with Grand Canyon National Park. My visit on November 2, 2011 was another day of realizing what it is like trying to find a specific destination in the web of roads and "roads" in the Arizona Strip. The map said there was a primitive road that went to the wilderness boundary, but I could not find it. By chance I saw another truck whose occupants told me that the road was there and there was a sign, but anyone coming from the west (that's me) would never see the sign. They were correct and I got to the wilderness boundary. I parked in a pullout and started hiking down a dim trail along a canyon rim. This was a nice route following a rim above Hell's Hole and a flat peninsula sticking out into Grand Canyon National Park. This was a day in a very out-of-the-way edge of the Grand Canyon. There are almost certainly better viewpoints for the North Rim of the Grand Canyon.

Kendrick Mountain 6,510 acres, designated 1984, located in the Coconino and Kaibab National Forests west of US Highway 180 and northwest of the city of Flagstaff. My day hike on April 23, 2006 began at the Kendrick Mountain Trailhead and went north on the Kendrick Mountain Trail to, you guessed it, the summit of Kendrick Mountain (10,418 feet). The terrain was mostly forested with oak and pine at low elevation and fir and spruce at high elevation. There was an old fire lookout on the summit. I don't remember much from this hike, but there were lots of other folks about and the views were less than spectacular.

Strawberry Crater 10,743 acres, designated 1984, located in the Coconino National Forest east of US Highway 89, just northeast of the Sunset Crater Volcano National Monument, and northeast of the city of Flagstaff. The wilderness is in two segments. The northern part is a lava flow around the crater and the southern part is gentle, open terrain sloping to the southeast. My day hike on April 24, 2005 began at the side of USFS Road 545 along the southeast wilderness boundary. My route was literally a compass bearing to the north through, no surprise, volcanic but not particularly interesting terrain. It was a cold, blustery, gray day. I eventually got to the northern segment of the wilderness and traversed a short segment of the lava flow from the crater. I returned to my truck using my GPS and was glad I had it. There are better destinations for seeing volcanic remnants.

Granite Mountain 9,800 acres, designated 1984, located in the Prescott National Forest just northwest of the city of Prescott. The easiest access is via USFS Road 10 and then USFS Road 374. My day hike on April 18, 2005 began near Granite Basin Lake. My route was up the Granite Mountain Trail through the normal pinon, oak, and juniper at low elevations and ponderosa pine at higher elevations. There was lots of exposed granite in the form of boulders that provided practice for technical climbers. I met one climber who told me he was preparing for a trip to the Wind River Range. The area appeared to get a lot of human visitation. I found the area neither interesting nor attractive.

Apache Creek 5,628 acres, designated 1984, located in the Prescott National Forest, west of State Highway 80 northwest of the city of Prescott. It is home to the Santa Maria Mountains. There were no trails. For my visit on October 28, 2009 I did not have a great map and needed to ask for directions. It was hunting season and there were a fair number of folks on the back roads. It was also cold. I awoke at my campsite to frozen water bottles. With my directions in mind I drove down a USFS road that supposedly went close to the southern wilderness boundary. This road was in bad condition, so I parked and hiked to the road's end near Pinetop Mountain. I took out my compass and started hiking north. I got to the top of a ridge with views to the west. This was classic oak, pinon, juniper, agave, prickly pear, and ponderosa terrain with enough rock formations and views to make it somewhat attractive. I wandered around along the ridge for a bit before turning around. Snow squalls alternated with sunny spells in the later part of the day. There was nothing spectacular in the scenery or anything especially interesting.

Harquahala Mountains 22,880 acres, designated 1990, managed by the BLM, located south of US Highway 60 and west of the town of Wickenburg. Access is easiest via unpaved roads going south from US 60. Old descriptions of this area discuss a trail to the summit of Harquahala Mountain starting at a US Highway 60 rest area. That rest area has been demolished and the old two-track road going to the trailhead appeared to me to be impassable. Instead I went back toward the eastern part of the wilderness and found an old two-track that terminated at a locked gate at the signed wilderness boundary. This day hike on March 17, 2016 started at that gate. The two-track continued perhaps two miles into a rather wide canyon and ended at a mine. My guess, based on the green rocks surrounding the mine tunnel, was that the miners were looking for copper. There were hand-lettered signs around the tunnel announcing that the mine was still active into the 1980s. The tunnel might have been enticing for some, but not for me. I continued up the canyon to an obvious pass where I stopped for lunch, looking south into more terrain like that I had just traversed. Here again, another hike in pleasant if not interesting Sonoran Desert country.

Castle Creek 25,517 acres, designated 1984, located in the Prescott National Forest, west of Interstate Highway 17 and southeast of the city of Prescott. My day hike on April 19, 2005 began near the Turkey Gulch Campground and went down the Algonquin Trail to Horsethief Creek. The terrain was mostly forest and there was a lot of deadfall on the trail. The best feature of this place was the great number and variety of birds. The area appeared to get very little visitation. There was supposed to be a mine and cabins down here but I could not find them, so I just sat down, had lunch, and turned around.

Woodchute 5,923 acres, designated 1984, located in the Prescott National Forest north of State Highway 89A and northeast of the city of Prescott. My day hike on April 16, 2005 began at a trailhead for the Woodchute Trail near the Potato Patch Campground. There was only one trail here and it ran five miles east-west through the wilderness. The trail basically crossed a mesa top forested with oak and pine. I saw nothing of particular interest.

Munds Mountain 18,109 acres, designated 1984, located in the Coconino National Forest between Interstate Highway 17 and State Highway 179 and southeast of the town of Sedona. My day hike on April 15, 2005 began at the Jacks Creek Trailhead and went north six miles through Jacks Canyon from the southern wilderness boundary to the northern wilderness boundary. I got a pretty early start and the air was filled with the sound of Gamble's quail calling from nearby fences. I also saw a Scott's oriole and a western wood peewee. I did not find the canyon itself very interesting, especially when compared to other nearby wilderness areas.

On my return trip I fell into conversation with two budding young scientists—graduate students studying biology and medicine. We were absorbed in our talk and nearly did not see a black rattlesnake stretched across the trail. As the snake slowly left the trail, it waved its rattles in an almost soundless motion, its tail moving at the speed of windshield wipers set on intermittent.

Gibraltar Mountain 18,790 acres, designated, 1990, located on BLM public lands east of the town of Parker and east of State Highway 9. My day hike on October 17, 2013 began near an informal camping area off the Shea Road. My route was north up a large wash until gaining enough elevation to turn back south along a volcanic ridge to the summit of what I think was Gibraltar Mountain. This was 100 percent volcanic terrain. The ridge and peak were very dark rock and there were some views of similar terrain all around. There was a lot of cacti—cholla, barrel, and ocotillo with the cholla sticking to all it touched, especially boots. I saw nothing of particular interest.

Hellsgate 37,440 acres, designated 1984, located in the Tonto National Forest south of State Highway 260, east of State Highway 87, and east and a bit south of the city of Payson. This day hike on February 17, 2005 began after a lot of rain. Unpaved roads were mud and creeks were very high. I began at the Hellsgate Trail, dropping through forest for about four miles until arriving at the wilderness boundary. Once in the wilderness area, the trail had views of what is probably an intermittent creek but one that was now running full. My goal was to get to the Hellsgate itself, presumably where Tonto Creek goes through a narrow stretch. The only way to get to this point required crossing Tonto Creek, and I can assure all readers that no sensible hiker would have attempted that crossing on that day. So I just turned around and went back up the hill to the trailhead. In better conditions, this might be an interesting hike, but not on the day I was there.

White Canyon 5,800 acres, designated 1990, managed by BLM, located west of State Highway 177 and southeast of the city of Apache Junction in greater Phoenix. Access is easiest via an unpaved road off State Highway 177. My day hike on March 2, 2006 began at the upper end of the canyon where a lot of vehicles were parked. I simply hiked down the canyon until it was time to turn around. There were other hikers. I did not find anything particularly pleasant or interesting here.

Mazatzal 252,200 acres, designated 1964, located in the Tonto National Forest west of State Highway 87 and west of the city of Payson. At the time of my visit there was a USFS map dedicated to this wilderness. My first day hike was on April 20, 2006 on the Barnhardt Trail. There were colorful cliffs in the canyon and some water in the creek. There had been recent fires here, but the vegetation was returning. After a few miles the trail left the canyon and the terrain was more open and the fire damage more evident. I saw about six other hikers and the area seemed to be pretty popular.

The second hike on April 21, 2006 began at the City Creek Trailhead and went up City Creek until the trail left the creek and continued climbing southwest to a feature called Knob Mountain. The elevation gain from the trailhead was about 2,000 feet. It was a nice route, though not as nice as the previous days. In my opinion there are more attractive and interesting destinations in this neighborhood.

Salome 18,530 acres, designated 1984, located in the Tonto National Forest just west of State Highway 288 and southeast of the town of Payson. My day hike on April 25, 2005 began at the Reynolds Creek Campground just off State Highway 288. I took the Hells Hole Trail to its namesake destination, Hells Hole on Workman Creek. The terrain was what was now familiar—cacti and pinon and juniper with more deciduous trees and other vegetation in riparian areas. There was some red rock. There was nothing hellish about Hells Hole, just a low spot along the creek. What surprised me here was encountering (1) the responsible wilderness ranger, (2) a crew of "owl surveyors," and (3) a trail crew. All this in an area that did not look like it got much human visitation.

Sierra Ancha 20,850 acres, designated 1964, located in the Tonto National Forest east of State Highway 288 and southeast of the town of Payson. My day hike on April 26, 2005 began at a trailhead for the Parker Trail and the Rim Trail. The vegetation was by now completely familiar—desert scrub down low with a transition to pinon and juniper with ponderosa pine at the higher elevations. There were also sandstone cliffs although nothing dramatic. Parker Canyon itself was nice, but along the Rim Trail recent fire had done serious damage resulting in a lot of deadfall. The Rim Trail became ever fainter as I went farther along until I eventually just turned around. The day was partly enlivened by my first sight of a Grace's warbler.

Salt River Canyon 32,800 acres, designated 1984, located in the Tonto National Forest east of State Highway 288, northwest of US Highway 60, and north of the town of Globe. There were no trails. My day hike on February 28, 2006 began at the end of USFS Road 303, or more exactly, a mile or two before the end of the road because the road condition was worsening quickly and I decided to walk before the road ended. My Tonto National Forest map labeled the road's end as a put-in point for boaters. My strong impression was that this area was visited mostly by river floaters. I hiked downstream along the southern riverbank. The northern bank here was the Fort Apache Indian Reservation. The riverbank was quite crumbly so sometimes I walked a bit away from the river through Sonoran Desert thorns. I do not try to claim that this was a pleasant hike.

Mount Baldy 6,819 acres, designated 1970, located in the Apache-Sitgreaves National Forest west of State Highway 273 and southwest of the town of Springerville. The wilderness shares its western boundary with the Fort Apache Indian Reservation. It is part of the White Mountains. Its namesake peak, Bald Mountain (11,403 feet), is on the reservation. This small wilderness sits at relatively high elevation, mostly between 9,000 and 11,000 feet. This elevation range produces heavily forested country with pine, fir, and spruce species. There were occasional open meadows. My day hike on April 19, 2006 began at the West Fork Trailhead and followed the Little Colorado River upstream to the west. I spoke with some USFS folks before this hike and was told there would not be any remaining snow. Not true. There was intermittent snow after about 2.5 miles, then continuous snow after that. Fortunately, the snow supported my weight although the going was slow. I went between five and six miles to about 11,000 feet and turned around. There were a lot of elk. I saw absolutely no other hikers.

Escudilla 5,200 acres, designated 1984, located in the Apache-Sitgreaves National Forest east of US Highway 191, southeast of the town of Springerville, and east of the Mount Baldy, Wilderness. This wilderness is not far east of Mount Baldy and the two areas are quite similar. Both are high and heavily forested with pine, fir, and spruce. The Escudilla has only one trail and I hiked all of it on March 1, 2006 beginning at the Escudilla Trailhead at 9,400 feet. The USFS folks advised me there was no snow on the ground. However, after taking about three steps on the trail it began to snow. There was falling snow and wind for the rest of the day. I got to a fire lookout at about 10,800 feet by which time I was wearing every piece of clothing I had, including a warm hat and gloves. This was the end of the trail and I turned around.

Four Peaks 60,740 acres, designated 1984, located in the Tonto National Forest northeast of greater Phoenix and north of the Superstition Wilderness. State Highway 87 is to the west and State Highway 188 is to the east. My day hike on February 27, 2006 began at the Four Peaks Trailhead in the northeast part of the wilderness. I hiked south on the Four Peaks Trail along the crest of the Mazatzal Mountains. The trail skirted around the four highest peaks in the range, including Browns Peak at 7,657 feet. There had been fire through this part of the wilderness in the not-too-distant past. The terrain was very rugged, very dry, and typical of the Sonoran Desert areas of Arizona. There were views to the south across Tonto Basin and into the Superstition Mountains. The air quality was quite poor and distant mountains were almost lost in the haze. This was a long day in a pleasant enough place, but there was little of interest and hikers can find much nicer routes in the Superstitions.

Bear Wallow 11,080 acres, designated 1984, located in the Apache-Sitgreaves National Forest west of US Highway 191, north of the town of Clifton, and just east of the Fort Apache Indian Reservation. I began my day hike on April 18, 2006 at a trailhead for the Bear Wallow Trail in the southeast corner of the wilderness. The trail then proceeded west and north along Bear Wallow Creek to the western wilderness boundary. The area was heavily timbered and was said to have stands of virgin ponderosa pine along with fir and aspen. But the trail went mostly through a riparian area along the creek with various deciduous trees and shrubs. There was no doubt that the area was truly wild with little sign of human activity. Otherwise, there was little of scenic interest.

Santa Teresa 26,780 acres, designated 1984, located in the Coronado National Forest southwest of US Highway 70 and west of the town of Safford. I had trouble finding an access point for this wilderness, finally choosing a road that would get me close to the southern wilderness boundary. The road was in poor condition and on March 7, 2006 I walked the last couple of road miles to a trailhead for Cottonwood Canyon. I followed the canyon north and then northeast to a pass at 7,265 feet where the trail basically disappeared. I have little memory and few notes from this hike other than I did not find it particularly interesting or scenic.

Rincon Mountain 38,590 acres, designated 1984, located in the Coronado National Forest north of Interstate Highway 10 and east of the city of Tucson. Looking at a map, the Rincon Mountain Wilderness is shaped like jaws clamped around the eastern portion of Saguaro National Park and its wilderness area.

I had trouble finding a place to camp here in greater Tucson. I ended up happily in Colossal Cave County Park close to Saguaro National Park. The park was easily within walking distance of the Rincon Mountain Wilderness, but getting there would require crossing private property. I asked a park employee if that would be alright and was told to ask the next day when I could get a definitive answer. I waited and the answer was that I was good to go. So this day hike on February 22, 2005 began as a bushwhack through some very thorny terrain to the southwestern part of the wilderness. There was not much of a trail, but I was able to pick my way around Shaw Canyon to Quemada Canyon and then up the canyon to just about its northeastern end. The environment was classic Sonoran Desert. I did not find anything particularly interesting here but had a successful time birding, seeing my first verdin, curved-billed thrasher, and canyon towhee. Earlier I had seen my first cactus wren in my campsite.

Saguaro 70,905 acres, designated 1970. Most of the Saguaro National Park is designated wilderness. There are two pieces to the wilderness, one just east of the city of Tucson and one just to the west. A February 23, 2005 hike began at a trailhead for the Tanque Verde Ridge Trail, and I followed the trail until I reached the Juniper Basin campsite where I turned around. I remember not finding it a very interesting hike although I did see my first black-tailed gnatcatcher and my first black-chinned sparrow.

A March 12, 2006 day hike began at a trailhead for the King Canyon Trail. I took this trail to the summit of Wasson Peak (4,687 feet), then made a loop via the Hugh Norris Trail and the Sendero Esperanza Trail back to the trailhead. The proximity to a large city was always obvious, plus there was nothing of particular scenic value and little of interest.

New Water Mountains 24,600 acres, designated 1990, located on BLM public lands south of Interstate Highway 10, east of US Highway 95, and southeast of the crossroads community of Quartzite. The Kofa Refuge Wilderness is just to the south. There were no trails. My day hike began at the end of a two-track off a pipeline access road that took off from US Highway 95. My route was simply north up a wash through open Sonoran Desert terrain. It was not a long hike. The terrain was spare, almost grim when compared with the more scenic and interesting Kofa Refuge Wilderness to the south. My recommendation to hikers is go to the Kofa, not here.

Hummingbird Springs 31,200 acres, designated 1990, located on BLM public lands north of Interstate Highway 10 and west of the city of Phoenix. There were no trails. My Arizona Atlas and Gazetteer made it look like this area should be easy to find. It wasn't. I had to ask directions *twice*. I finally found a gravel road going between the Hummingbird Springs and the Big Horn Mountains Wilderness, then parked at the end of a cherry-stem road where the Arizona Game and Fish folks had a "guzzler" providing water for wildlife. From here my route on March 15, 2014 was north up a wash. Once again, standard Sonoran Desert ecosystem, but without much scenic value or anything of particular interest.

Imperial Refuge 15,056 acres, designated 1990, located within the Imperial National Wildlife Refuge (managed by the USFWS) along the east bank of the Colorado River, west of US Highway 95, and north of the city of Yuma. This not-very-long day hike on April 7, 2010 began at a two-track off the Red Cloud Mine Road. I hiked down the two-track to Clear Lake where I thought the wilderness boundary was. I then hiked along game trails upstream along the riverbank. I was eventually stopped by a very steep-walled side canyon. This place did not seem even remotely wild. I did see my first and only brown-crested flycatcher and also some rough-winged swallows tending a nest.

Miller Peak 20,190 acres, designated 1984, located in the Coronado National Forest west of State Highway 92 and south of the town of Sierra Vista. Part of the northern wilderness boundary is the southern boundary of the Fort Huachuca Military Reservation. The southern wilderness boundary is about two miles from the Mexican border. The Huachuca Mountains run through the wilderness. My day hike on February 26, 2005 began at the USFS ranger station in Sierra Vista. Here I was told that the wilderness was on a much-used route for illegal immigrants. I was told that I might be offended by the large amount of trash left behind by those passing through. The USFS was frustrated because no amount of cleanup effort could keep up with the amount of trash deposited.

My hike began at a trailhead in Miller Canyon. I had camped near the trailhead the previous night and had a couple of visits from the Border Patrol. My route was up the Miller Canyon Trail to the Crest Trail and then to the summit of Carr Peak (9,230 feet) where a group of Boy Scouts was on some sort of outing. I had good views of Miller Peak to the south and could see that there was a fair bit of snow on its north side, too much to consider making the side trip to this slightly higher summit. And yes, there was a *lot* of trash along my route. Food and beverage containers of all sorts and, to my surprise, a huge amount of discarded clothing. While not an unpleasant place, I have no desire to come back.

Cabeza Prieta 803,418 acres, designated 1990, located on BLM public lands north of the Mexican border, south of the town of Ajo, and west of State Highway 85. This area used to be a bombing range and is adjacent to still-active military installations. A permit is required for all human entry. At the time of my visit a permit could *only* be obtained over the internet. The process was neither short nor simple and I needed help from a librarian in Ajo. My access was west from State Highway 85 on the Charlie Bell Road. While on the road, I was stopped by law-enforcement agents from the US Fish and Wildlife Service who wanted to see my permit. The road ended at a locked gate at Charlie Bell Pass where I parked and did a day hike on

March 15, 2019. I went down the gated road until coming to a flowing well in a small, green clearing below the pass. There was a wildlife "guzzler" there and basalt boulders bore lots of petroglyphs. The terrain was pure Sonoran Desert, very green with lots of saguaro, ocotillo, and cholla. Charlie Bell Pass provides a way through the Growler Mountains to a large, flat desert plain.

On March 16, I did a longer day hike north from Charlie Bell Pass, cross country to a higher pass to the west. I went through the pass, almost to the plain, and then turned around. Here there were lots of palo verde and other shrubs. I saw what I think were bighorn sheep tracks and also some deer tracks. The refuge is home to reintroduced pronghorn, but I did not see any. Before beginning my hike this day, a group of volunteers came to the pass to begin search operations for people reported missing in the desert. I spoke with them and they said that many immigrants cross the border into the refuge and that they were probably just looking for the bodies of those who perished on their journey. My advice to hikers is that the Organ Pipe Cactus Wilderness might be a better destination, but I do not discourage people wanting to visit the Cabeza Prieta Wildlife Refuge.

NEW MEXICO

Chama River Canyon 50,300 acres, designated 1978, located in the Santa Fe National Forest north of State Highway 96 and east of State Highway 112. I have almost no memory of this hike and my notes are sparse. I do know that on June 14, 2003 I went up Ojitos Canyon and I think that there was no trail. The terrain was sagebrush and sparse grass with cliffs of tan and red and pinon and juniper on the higher tops. My notes say that I did a "long day hike in a nice desert setting."

Cruces Basin 18,902 acres, designated 1980, located in the Carson National Forest west of US Highway 285, south of State Highway 17, and east of the town of Chama. At the time of my visit there was a USFS map dedicated to this area. I have no recollection of this hike that I made on June 15, 2003. My notes tell me that for an area with no trails I saw a lot of other folks. My hike began at the end of a cherry-stem road at the southern wilderness boundary. I hiked up Beaver Creek with a side trip up Diablo Creek. There were faint footpaths along the creeks and some people fishing. From three surviving photos I see that the area was mostly open, rolling terrain with meadows and stands of aspen and conifers, and with a thunderstorm under way.

Cebolla 61,600 acres, designated 1987, located on BLM public lands in the El Malpais National Conservation Area south of the city of Grants and east of State Highway 117. El Malpais is Spanish for "The Bad Lands." This day hike on June 18, 2003 began just off State Highway 117 near the Ventura Arch, which is very close to the highway. Somehow, and I don't remember exactly how, I got onto the Narrows Rim Trail, which follows the western rim of the wilderness for a few miles. The terrain was standard sandstone, pinon, and juniper with views to the west of the very volcanic land of the El Malpais National Monument. It was a nice weather day; the views were good and there was nobody else around.

West Malpais 39,400 acres, designated 1987, located on BLM public lands in the El Malpais National Conservation Area south of the city of Grants and north of State Highway 117. Access is from unpaved County Road 42. I had spent the previous evening driving up and down County Road 42 looking for a good place to do a day hike. Most of this road was OK, but there were big signs telling people not to drive on the road if it were wet. Having seen some of the ruts I took this advice seriously. My choice of routes for a day hike on September 22, 2017 was the Continental Divide Trail south. My not-so-great map had the CDT running outside the wilderness, but the BLM signs on the ground showed it running through the wilderness. I chose to believe the BLM. The terrain was, of course, volcanic with some pinon and juniper and grass. Cattle used the area. This portion of the trail was pretty flat with some higher mountains in the distance. Sometimes the trail got pretty dim and I saw no other hikers. The area was pleasant enough, but there are more scenic and interesting destinations in New Mexico.

Manzano Mountain 36,970 acres, designated 1978, located in the Cibola National Forest west of State Highway 55 and south of the city of Albuquerque. Manzano in Spanish means apple. There were apple trees (not native) in these mountains in the old days. My day hike on May 1, 1998 began at the Red Canyon Campground. The route was simple, about a seven-mile loop up the Red Canyon Trail to the Crest Trail and then down the Red Canyon Trail back to the campground. The terrain was the standard pinon and juniper with larger conifers along the crest. The high point of the trip was the summit of Gallo Peak at 10,003 feet. I have no real recollection of this trip and there are no surviving photos.

San Pedro Parks 41,132 acres, designated 1964, located in the Santa Fe National Forest south of State Highway 96 and northwest of the city of Los Alamos. At the time of my visit there was a USFS map dedicated to the area. This overnight backpack began on June 12, 2003 at a trailhead for the Vacas Trail at the southern wilderness boundary. I followed this trail north through open meadows (parks) with stands of spruce and aspen. I camped near San Pedro Park and made a side trip to a summit of the San Pedro Peaks. There were other people about and the area was grazed by cattle (*vaca* is Spanish for cow) as well as elk.

Sandia Mountain 37,256 acres, designated 1978, located in the Cibola National Forest immediately east of the city of Albuquerque. Interstate Highway 40 is to the south and State Highway 14 is to the east. At the time of my visit there was a USFS map dedicated to this wilderness. I actively disliked this area. Perhaps I was in an uncharitable mood, but I was put off by the urban bustle along the eastern trailheads. Especially obnoxious were parking lots with signs every ten feet telling one that "YOU MUST PAY" to park. There were a lot of people around. I did, however, pay and park at the Cienega Trailhead on June 19, 2003 and hiked the Cienega Trail to its intersection with the Crest Trail and maybe a bit of the Crest Trail. I do not intend to come back.

Dome 5,183 acres, designated 1980
Bandelier 23,267 acres, designated 1976

The western boundary of the Bandelier Wilderness is the eastern boundary of the Dome Wilderness. The Dome Wilderness is in the Santa Fe National Forest. The Bandelier Wilderness is within the Bandelier National Monument and is managed by the National Park Service. Both areas are south of State Highway 4 and south of the city of Los Alamos. The two areas are described together because I visited both on the same hike. My access point for this hike on May 17, 2007 was the Dome Lookout Road (USFS Road 289), a road not in the best condition when I visited. I began the hike from the eastern side of the road, hiking northeast into the Dome Wilderness, crossing Sanchez Canyon, and entering the Bandelier Wilderness at Turkey Springs. I continued northeast until my trail descended into Capulin Canyon where I turned around. It was a classic pinon and juniper ecosystem with some volcanic cliffs and outcroppings. There were also lots of soft, powdery volcanic remnants. Fire had been through here in the not very distant past. I must confess that I did not see anything very interesting on this hike, although my choice of routes may not have been the best as it did not include any archaeological sites.

Ojito 11,823 acres, designated 2009, located on BLM public lands southwest of the Dome and Bandelier Wilderness areas and southwest of US Highway 550. The closest city is Albuquerque to the southeast. There were two short trails in this wilderness and I hiked both of them on September 21, 2017 from an unpaved BLM road that ran along the southern and western wilderness boundaries. The first trail was the Hoodoo Trail, which meandered through eroded sandstone with some mildly interesting formations. The second trail was the Seismosaurous Trail, which went to the site of a dinosaur fossil find. The dinosaur was named the Seismosaurous because of its enormous size, causing the ground shake whenever it took a step. The entire beast was removed to a museum in Albuquerque, leaving nothing behind for hikers to admire. There was also some petrified wood in the area.

Blue Range 29,180 acres, designated 1980, located in the Gila National Forest just west of US Highway 180. The western wilderness boundary is the Arizona state line. The neighboring region in eastern Arizona in the Apache National Forest is the Blue Range Primitive Area, which still does not have formal wilderness status. The areas are controversial because Mexican gray wolves have been introduced in Arizona and local ranchers hate wolves. A hike on May 1, 1998 was basically a bird walk from the Pueblo Park Campground trailhead on the northern wilderness boundary. The trail ran south through mostly coniferous forest. I have no recollections of this hike other than the area seemed to receive little human use. A second hike on May 31, 2012 also began at the Pueblo Park Campground and went south on the WS Mountain Trail. The trail followed a major drainage through ponderosa pine and juniper and some deciduous shrubs through old basalt formations. There were bear tracks on the trail. At a junction with the Tige Canyon Trail I turned around. This was the year of the huge fire in the Gila Wilderness and the entire day was smoky. I did see two other hikers on my way back to the trailhead. All three of us agreed that it was amazing to find other hikers here.

Withington 18,889 acres, designated 1980, located in the Cibola National Forest between State Highway 107 on the east and State highway 52 on the west and southwest of the town of Magdalena. The San Mateo Mountains run through the area. The Apache Kid Wilderness is a bit to the south. This day hike on May 18, 2007 began at the higher-elevation end of the Potato Trail and went literally downhill from there. The San Mateo Mountains are volcanic, but much more rounded than those in the Apache Kid Wilderness. At high elevation, just over 10,000 feet, there were a lot of open, grassy areas, turning into ponderosa pine, fir, and aspen as the trail dropped. I turned around when I got into the common pinon and juniper of low elevation. On my way down, I unknowingly got too close to a goshawk nest and paid the price of repeated dive-bombing runs. There was elk sign everywhere along the trail, but I never actually saw any elk. I got a bit concerned returning uphill because of thunder, lightning, hail, and a little rain, but all was OK.

Capitan Mountains 35,822 acres, designated 1980, located in the Lincoln National Forest north of US Highway 380, south of State Highway 246, and northeast of the town of Ruidoso. The White Mountain Wilderness is to the southwest. At the time of my visit there was a USFS map devoted to this wilderness. This long (fourteen miles and 3,800 feet elevation gain and loss) day hike on May 22, 2007 began at the northern wilderness boundary at a trailhead for the Capitan Peak Trail. It was a cloudless, perfect weather day. The destination was the summit of Capitan Peak at 10,083 feet. Unfortunately, the hike was through heavily burned terrain with few remaining trees, although there was some regrowth of oak, aspen, and wildflowers. There was also a lot of new growth of invasive weeds. My most interesting sight on this hike was a ground-level nest of a Townsend's solitaire (a thrush) complete with recent hatchlings. Otherwise I saw nothing of particular interest or scenic value.

Bosque del Apache 30,427 acres, designated 1975. The Bosque del Apache Wilderness sits astride the Rio Grande River on both sides of State Highway 1 and Interstate Highway 25 and just south of the town of San Antonio. All the wilderness is within the Bosque del Apache National Wildlife Refuge (managed by the USFWS). In the "old" days there were three wilderness areas here separated by roads (the Chupadera, Indian Well, and Little San Pascual). Now there is only one area, the Bosque del Apache. I have been to this refuge on several occasions, but only one dedicated to a wilderness hike. My other visits were strictly for birding along refuge roads. This day hike on May 17, 2007 was in what was then called the Chupadera. This was a volcanic area with typical desert flora. I hiked the Chupadera Trail, which began by walking through a culvert under I-25! The route climbed through reddish volcanic outcrops and blooming cacti to an open summit where I turned around.

As hiking destinations go, this area is nothing special. As a birding destination it is an absolute must-visit. This is a hiking guide, so this wilderness is buried with the two stars. That does *not* mean don't come here. Come here and look for birds. Hikers will frighten birds and they won't see much.

Cars don't scare birds as much, so viewing is best done from a vehicle. In this sense I highly recommend visiting the refuge.

One recommendation I got from New Mexico birders was, after visiting the refuge, to go to the (food-serving) Owl Bar in nearby San Antonio. I rarely go to bars when traveling, but I had this from a reliable source so I went. It had been a hot day. Servers patrolled the patrons with pitchers of iced tea. After I was seated near the bar a man came in with an aluminum bowl and asked the bartender to please fill the bowl with water for his dog. The bartender did. I figured I was in a pretty good place.

Carlsbad Caverns 3,125 acres, designated 1978. Most of the *surface* of Carlsbad Caverns National Park is designated wilderness. It is located just west of US Highway 62/180 near the town of Whites City and just north of the Texas state line. At the time of my visit there was a National Geographic Trails Illustrated map dedicated to the park both above and belowground. My day hike on May 21, 2007 began at a trailhead for the Rattlesnake Canyon Trail along the park's Scenic Loop Drive. The trail descended into the canyon and ended at the southern park boundary after about 2.25 miles. This was a classic Chihuahuan Desert with huge prickly pear (or perhaps beavertail) cacti in bloom and also some blooming claret cups. Otherwise, not much of scenic interest. Before the hike I stopped by the visitor center and did indeed see some cave swallows, found only in southeast New Mexico and southwest Texas.

One-Star Areas

★

ARIZONA

Juniper Mesa 7,554 acres, designated 1984, located in the Prescott National Forest south of Interstate Highway 40, just north of the Apache Creek Wilderness and northwest of the city of Prescott. This day hike on April 17, 2005 began at a trailhead off USFS Road 125 in the southwest part of the wilderness. I climbed to the top of the mesa and hiked east almost to the end of the trail at the eastern wilderness boundary. I have no recollection of the area other than finding it neither attractive nor interesting. There were a lot of flycatchers about, especially ash-throated and dusky.

Cedar Bench
Pine Mountain

16,005 acres, designated 1984. The Pine Mountain and Cedar Bench Wilderness areas are located in the Prescott National Forest (and partly in the Tonto National Forrest for Pine Mountain) south of State Highway 260 and west of the town of Payson. The two areas are close to one another and are northwest of the Mazatzal Wilderness, southwest of the West Clear Creek Wilderness, and west of the Fossil Springs Wilderness. Because of their similarity, proximity to each other, and having hiked them on consecutive days, they are combined here. The Pine Mountain hike on April 21, 2005 began at the end of USFS Road 68 on the northwest side of the wilderness. The route was a "balloon" loop that included the Pine Mountain summit (6,814 feet). The trail was littered with deadfall and easy to lose. I found the area neither pleasant nor interesting.

The Cedar Bench hike the following day began at the Chasm Creek Trailhead. The trail crossed the wilderness from the northeast to southwest boundary. I saw nothing interesting or inviting.

Prairie along Sage Creek, Badlands Wilderness, South Dakota

The Great Plains

Much of the central United States is made up of temperate grasslands. Like temperate grasslands in other parts of the world, those in the central United States have been taken over by humans for agriculture. There is very little of this biome left intact. The biome is characterized by minimal topographic variation, enough precipitation to allow many crops to be produced, and, even though winters can be harsh, the growing season allows many crops to thrive. Soils tend to be very thick, supporting many native grasses and some isolated segments of forest.

Tracts of grasslands that are still intact and in their more-or-less natural state are found around the edges of the grasslands and in isolated pockets that have escaped development. Of those surviving intact spaces, very little has the protection of wilderness designation. The states of Iowa and Kansas have no designated federal wilderness. As the natural grasslands were disappearing under human activity, there were efforts at local levels, often private efforts, to preserve a single acre still hosting native species.

Today, the USFS does oversee some sizeable acres in national grasslands, although none have wilderness status. There are several small grassland wilderness areas managed by the US Fish and Wildlife Service, typically around waters supporting bird migrations. The grassland wilderness areas I have visited and described here are on the periphery of the biome in the Dakotas, Nebraska, and Oklahoma. Other areas I have not visited are Chase Lake (4,155 acres) and Lostwood (5,547 acres) in North Dakota, Fort Niobrara (4,635 acres) in Nebraska, and Agassiz (4,000 acres) and Tamarac (2,180 acres) in western Minnesota. These five unvisited areas are managed by the US Fish and Wildlife Service.

Badlands

★ ★ ★ ★

Size: 64,144 acres **Year Designated:** 1976
Responsible Agency: USNPS

The Badlands Wilderness is located in southwest South Dakota south of Interstate Highway 90, east of State Highway 79, and southwest of the famous town of Wall. The park has two units, north and south. Most of the North Unit is designated wilderness. The wilderness area has two units, Sage Creek and Conata.

MY VISIT: October 10–11, 2011 and October 12, 2011

My visit was to the Sage Creek unit. I began with an overnight backpack starting at the Conata Picnic Area. My destination, after consulting a park ranger, was Deer Haven. There was no trail, but other visitors had produced a somewhat dim path through the grasslands. I was told there was no reliable water in Deer Haven, so I carried enough for two days of cool weather. The hiking through the prairie was easy, but once in Deer Haven it became difficult because of steep-sided gullies in great, chaotic abundance. The haven had trees while the prairie had none. It was a day of perfect weather

Bighorn sheep, Badlands Wilderness

and I found a perfect campsite for the night. The next morning also had perfect weather and I took time to wander around the weirdly magnificent, erosion-carved pinnacles of soft rock. On my way out of the haven I decided to take a small detour into a "canyon" through some of the "badland" erosion formations. For a detour, this proved lucky. There was a group of bighorn sheep here. I counted eleven, including ewes, lambs, and young rams. Some wore tracking collars. They showed no reaction to my presence.

The third day I did a day hike out of the Sage Creek Primitive Campground. There was no trail, but I followed the South Fork of Sage Creek for about four miles before turning around. Now this was true prairie. The creek had steep banks and lots of oxbows, but the low autumn flow made crossings easy. There were trees only along the creek, with vast expanses of prairie in all directions. There were a *lot* of bison plus prairie dog towns and mule deer. I ended up spending the night in the campground and the bison were constant companions for all the campers.

I found this a really neat area. The badland terrain near Deer Haven was spectacular and the prairies truly representative of the temperate grassland biome. I recommend this area to just about any hiker.

Eroded badlands near Deer Haven, Badlands Wilderness

Theodore Roosevelt

★ ★ ★

Size: 29,920 acres   **Year Designated:** 1978
Responsible Agency: USNPS

Approximately half of Theodore Roosevelt National Park is designated wilderness. Like the park, the wilderness is in two sections, north and south. Both sections are north of Interstate Highway 94 and west of US Highway 85. The town of Bellfield is east of the south unit and the town of Watford City is northeast of the north unit.

MY VISIT: October 13, 2011 and October 14, 2011

The first of these day hikes began at a trailhead for the Petrified Forest Loop Trail in the southern unit of the wilderness. The loop went east to the Maah Daah Hey Trail, then north back to the Petrified Forest Trail for a total of eleven easy, mostly level hiking miles. It was a chilly, windy day and I saw no other hikers. The terrain was somewhat broken with rock outcrops, but mostly grass with some trees. There were some petrified tree stumps. There were times on this hike when I had to make detours around bison, plus there were pronghorn and even elk within view.

The second day hike was in the northern section beginning at a trailhead for the North Auchenbach Trail, which went east almost to the banks of the Little Missouri River (see the photo), ending at the park scenic drive road, which was closed to vehicles. Given that the road was closed I chose to hike the road back to my trailhead to make a loop. There were mandatory detours to avoid bison on or next to the road. This was another windy, chilly day, but I did see one other hiker. I recommend this area to just about any hiker.

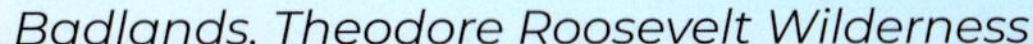

Badlands, Theodore Roosevelt Wilderness

Rock fins from the summit of Harney Peak, Black Elk Wilderness

Black Elk

★ ★ ★

Size: 13,426 acres   **Year Designated:** 1980
Responsible Agency: USFS

The Black Elk Wilderness is located in the Black Hills National Forest south of State Highway 244, north of State Highway 87, and southwest of Rapid City.

MY VISIT: November 2, 2005

This day hike began at a trailhead for the summit of Harney Peak, the highest point in South Dakota at 7,242 feet. Given its status as a "High Point," there were other hikers even on a chilly November day. The trail was mostly through timber and, as my notes say, ponderosa pine. The destination was an old, stone fire lookout, admirably built and wonderfully maintained. Summit views were excellent. What I did not expect were the rock fins and other rock formations surrounding the summit. This was a day of perfect weather and a nice route to a scenic destination. I recommend this hike, especially for visitors not familiar with South Dakota. It may not be typical of the great prairies, but it is worth a visit.

Two-Star Areas

NEBRASKA

Soldier Creek 7,794 acres, designated 1986, located in the Nebraska National Forest north of US Highway 20 and west of the town of Crawford. Fort Robinson State Park is just east of the wilderness. At the time of my visit there was a USFS map devoted to this wilderness. My day hike on November 3, 2005 began at the Soldier Creek Trailhead on a cold, windy day. My route, probably the most popular in the area, was a 10.6-mile loop covering most of the wilderness area on its east-west axis. The early part of the hike was through a pleasant riparian area along Soldier Creek. After a couple of miles, the trail left the creek and crossed rolling prairie sand hills with a few scattered trees. It was obvious that the terrain had been greatly altered by a large fire in 1989 that eliminated most of the trees. I must admit that this open terrain on a *very* windy day was less than pleasant. It did remind me, however, of what the early settlers experienced in this then-wild country where wind dominated everything. I was glad when I got back to my truck. From a hiking perspective, I do not particularly recommend this area unless the hiker wants to see what the early settlers faced.

OKLAHOMA

Wichita Mountains 8,570 acres, designated 1970, located in the Wichita Mountains National Wildlife Refuge north of US Highway 62, east of US Highway 183, and northwest of the city of Lawton. The wilderness portion of the refuge has two units: North Mountain in the north and Charon's Garden in the south. The North Mountain unit is closed to the public to protect wildlife including bison and longhorn cattle. Charon's Garden is open to the public and has trails. My day hike on February 24, 2007 began at a trailhead for the Charon's Garden and Elk Mountain Trails. Both trails were short. The Wichita Mountains are low remnants of an old hard-rock range eroded down to rounded shapes set among oak and prairie. While neither especially interesting nor greatly scenic, it was a pleasant place.

Little Missouri River, Theodore Roosevelt
Wilderness, North Dakota

Cypress trees and knees, Congaree National Park Wilderness, South Carolina

The Eastern Forests

The biome of temperate broadleaf and mixed forests dominates the eastern United States, including most of the Great Lakes region. Some of the Southeast, including Florida and the southeast coast, may be better characterized as temperate coniferous forest, but here I combine these two as just eastern forests.

Like the grasslands of the Great Plains, the eastern forests have been greatly impacted by human activity. Once the forests were cleared, large-scale agriculture could prosper. Like the Great Plains, winters could be cold, but the growing seasons were long enough and mild enough and the soils typically fertile enough to provide humans with good places to live and produce food.

In the nineteenth and early twentieth centuries, the original forests were almost totally removed for timber. Only a very few tracts of virgin timber remain. However, second-growth forest now covers a significant portion of the eastern United States. Some of these forests have been partly protected by incorporation into the US national forest system. Some of the least-human-impacted areas have been given wilderness designation.

Most eastern wilderness areas are small simply because large tracts of naturally intact land are relatively scarce. Some of the larger wilderness areas are in lands deemed unattractive by humans such as the swamps in the Okefenokee Wilderness in Georgia and the Marjory Stoneman Douglas Wilderness in the Florida Everglades.

Some portions of the Atlantic Coast also have obtained wilderness status, protecting some of the last undeveloped coast in the country. Most of the coastal areas are managed by the US Fish and Wildlife Service as part of the National Wildlife Refuge system.

Hiking in the eastern wilderness is not quite like hiking in the big western areas. The hiker may find reminders of past human activity. Trails or access routes are sometimes on old roads or even railroad beds that served long-ago logging activity. One also encounters old stone walls or developed springs or old foundations of buildings or even intact buildings. I have more than once stumbled upon an old cemetery. Many of these structures have served as homesteads that never quite survived the struggles of early settlers. One sight I found somehow soothing was fruit trees, often apple, blooming in the spring in a place otherwise showing no human touch.

I must confess to readers that while I certainly enjoy the eastern forests, they are not my favorite destinations. Simply stated, I have a "sameness problem." Ten minutes into a hike on Thursday I ask myself, "Didn't I just do this hike yesterday?" This may be completely unfair, but it is my reaction. My judgment is reflected in my ratings. I have given no five-star ratings and only a few four-star ratings.

Many eastern wilderness areas have no trails. Depending on the terrain, hiking can be very difficult. Some areas are much better seen by watercraft than by hiking. There will be some areas I rate as two stars because I was trying to hike in a place nature never meant for hiking. An exception for me was the Okefenokee, which I did visit by boat with a guide. The Okefenokee ended up with four stars, probably more than it would have received had I been on foot (nearly impossible).

The vast majority of my eastern wilderness area visits have been day hikes. I maintain that one can get a good sense of these small areas in a one-day visit. Many of the smaller areas can be covered in just half a day.

Hunting and fishing regulations, Cohutta Wilderness, Georgia

Joyce Kilmer-Slickrock

★ ★ ★ ★

Citico Creek

★ ★ ★ ★

JOYCE KILMER-SLICKROCK	**Size:** 17,394 acres	**Year Designated:** 1975	**Responsible Agency:** USFS
CITICO CREEK	**Size:** 16,226 acres	**Year Designated:** 1984	**Responsible Agency:** USFS

These two areas are described together because they are contiguous and I hiked both on the same day. The Citico Creek Wilderness is entirely in Tennessee and is in the Cherokee National Forest. The Joyce Kilmer-Slickrock Wilderness is partly in Tennessee and partly in North Carolina in the Nantahala National Forest. The areas are west of US Highway 129 and north of State Highway 165 and west of the town of Robbinsville. At the time of my visit there was a National Geographic Trails Illustrated map 781, Cherokee National Forest, that included these two areas.

The Joyce Kilmer-Slickrock Wilderness provides protection to one of the last stands of virgin forest in the southern Appalachian Mountains. In the mid-1930s, after much of the forests had been essentially removed, the USFS decided to purchase 13,055 acres of the remaining intact forest to preserve the old growth. Some of the trees are now as much as 450 years old, including tulip poplars one hundred feet tall and more than six feet in diameter.

MY VISIT: October 15, 2006

This was a magnificent day with perfect weather and pretty much peak fall foliage color. My hike began at a trailhead for the Cowdry Branch Trail at the western Citico Creek Wilderness boundary. My trail took me to the eastern Citico boundary, then south along a ridge and into the Joyce Kilm-er-Slickrock area in the Slickrock Creek drainage. The route was through classic southern Appalachian forest with lots of big deciduous trees, an occasional pine or hemlock, and some granite outcroppings. Slickrock Creek was quite lovely. There were other hikers about, including some backpackers on a perfect autumn day. The photo is from the Joyce Kilmer-Slickrock and I cannot think of a more appropriate image. These areas would make an excellent destination for hikers new to the Appalachians. The hiking is easy.

Joyce Kilmer's trees

Congaree National Park

★ ★ ★ ★

Size: 15,010 acres | **Year Designated:** 1988 | **Responsible Agency:** USNPS

Most of Congaree National Park Wilderness is designated wilderness. The park and wilderness protect some of the last remaining old-growth bottomland hardwood forest in the United States. In the prerevolutionary United States there were about fifty-two *million* acres of these bottomland forests. Now the park's fifteen *thousand* acres are all that remain. That means that only 0.027 percent of the original forests remain. Why did so much of this forest type disappear? Because the hardwood trees were excellent for construction lumber and because the forests were easy to access by water—no need to build roads or railroads. Some of the trees in Congaree hold size records for their species. Almost all the park is part of a floodplain. My first visit to the park was in 2009 and most of the trails were closed because of flooding. On another trip in 2016 the entire park was closed because of a recent hurricane.

MY VISIT: April 13–14, 2018

My overnight backpack began at the park visitor center (permit required for overnight stay). I hiked boardwalk trails to the wilderness boundary, then on the Oakridge Trail to the Kingsnake Trail. This route included an oxbow lake from Cedar Creek. I found a campsite south of the Kingsnake Trail surrounded by the park's iconic bald cypress trees. One of the park's champion trees is a cypress over 27 feet in circumference. The next day I finished a loop back to the visitor center going past a champion loblolly pine tree with a height of 167 feet and a circumference of 15 feet. Other tree species included oak, ash, sweetgum, and holly in well-drained soils. Congaree has one of the most diverse forests in North America.

This trip was neither long nor arduous, but certainly opened my eyes to a new type of landscape. I was quite impressed. I recommend this wilderness to just about anybody.

My backpack at the champion loblolly pine, Congaree National Park Wilderness

Okefenokee

★ ★ ★ ★

Size: 353,981 acres | **Year Designated:** 1974 | **Responsible Agency:** USFWS

Most of the Okefenokee National Wildlife Refuge is designated wilderness. The refuge is located west of US Highway 1 and west of the town of Folkston. The main entrance to the refuge is via State Highway 121, which runs west from US Highway 1.

MY VISIT: April 12, 2018

I looked at the map showing the wilderness portion of the refuge. It was quite clear that I was not going to see the wilderness on foot. I wanted to see it, so I took a boat tour. Sometimes it takes me a while to do the obvious, most logical thing. As it turned out, the law designating the Okefenokee Wilderness allowed for motorized boats with motors less than 10 horsepower. The boat operators all use Honda motors of 9.9 horsepower.

April 12 was "low season" at the refuge and I had the boat and guide to myself. This worked out well and I got a truly grand tour with a very knowledgeable guide. He was clearly well informed about the biology and ecology of the swamp, and by the end of the tour we were even dissecting plants.

The refuge is clearly set up for people with boats. There are established routes (trails) with signs and several places where boaters can camp on dry land with shelters. We did see a group of four people in two canoes on their way in for a multi-day trip. Otherwise we saw nobody.

It is hard for me to describe the area. A large fraction of the surface was water, but water almost completely covered with vegetation. Lots of aquatic plants were in bloom, including fragrant water lily, golden club, hooded pitcher plant, and wild iris. We had to stop often to clean the boat propeller of ensnared plants. There were islands, called houses, where trees had established themselves. Some were very small, some quite large. There were large expanses of water called prairies.

There were birds everywhere, especially red-shouldered hawks and several barred owls and pileated woodpeckers, great egrets, and one male prothonotary warbler, the brilliant yellow "swamp canary." There were, of course, alligators everywhere including babies with their mammas.

For me, this trip ended too soon. If I were to return (unlikely), I would try to reserve a spot for an overnight stay at one of the shelters. I heartily recommend this area to just about anybody interested in the natural world in North America.

*Chesser Prairie,
Okefenokee Wilderness*

Cumberland Island

Size: 9,886 acres | **Year Designated:** 1982 | **Responsible Agency:** USNPS

A significant fraction of the Cumberland Island National Seashore is designated wilderness. The seashore is just off the Georgia coast east of Interstate Highway 95 and northeast of the town of St. Marys. Access for most visitors is via ferry from St. Marys where there is also a visitor center. Basically, all visitors will need reservations for the ferry and, if staying overnight, they will need reservations for a campsite. There are campgrounds in both the wilderness and nonwilderness portions of the seashore.

MY VISIT: April 9–11, 2018

This three-day backpack began at the seashore visitor center in St. Marys where I obtained my ferry ticket and my wilderness camping permit. I and lots of other folks boarded a ferry for a short ride to the island. There was an extensive network of both trails and roads on the island. The wilderness was fragmented by roads, many going to private inholdings left over from before the designation as a national seashore. There was also a concessionaire that offered van-based tours of the island.

Once away from the ferry dock, I hiked north on the Parallel Trail (I think parallel to a road) to the Hickory Hill wilderness campsite. I had the place to myself. It was nice enough, but some previous visitors had left an unconscionable amount of trash behind. One thing I must mention is that I knew before leaving home that potable water could be a problem here. This was reinforced in a conversation with a park ranger in St. Marys. So I carried water for my three-day trip. It turned out there was a water tap maybe a mile from the camp site, but the water was foul smelling with sulfur. This worked for me because the weather was cool and I did not need a lot of water. As an aside, the Hickory Hill campsite was not on a hill and, as nearly as I could see, had no hickory trees.

After setting up my camp I took the Willow Pond Trail east to the Atlantic Coast. This was a cool, cloudy day with a *heavy* wind. Heavy as in I was blasted by windborne sand. With reluctance, I took out my camera to get a photo. I was hoping to see some shorebirds, but conditions were not the best. There were some sanderlings poking in the surf but not much more. Most notable, however, was the local ecosystem, something I had never really seen before. The dominant species were huge live oak trees and the omnipresent palmetto. The oaks were draped in Spanish moss and the branches provided homes for a variety of other plants, especially ferns. That night at Hickory Hill there was some rain and a little thunder and lightning.

The second day was devoted to a day hike to the north. This took me on the Kings Bottom Trail, the Table Point Trail, and the Ashley Pond Trail to some extensive wetlands along the western side of the island. Some of this route included walking along a road. Without exception I saw tour vans on the road, and the drivers always stopped to ask me if I knew where I was and if I was OK. I got back to my Hickory Hill camp with time to spare and made a second trip to the Atlantic beach. It was much the same as the previous day with a heavy, sand-carrying wind. There were more migrating birds this day. I seemed to scare up big flocks of several species, especially ibis. The Willow Pond Trail skirts around some brackish ponds inland of the beach. One pond was home to a very large alligator.

My third day was pretty much devoted to hiking back to the dock for my ride back to St. Marys. The major sight along the route was of wild horses. I heard a couple of different explanations for the presence of horses, but it seems like they were escapees from now-departed private landowners.

Like Okefenokee, this area was something of a revelation for me—new ecosystems with great presence and beauty. This was not the wildest wilderness, but I certainly recommend it as a destination for the curious hiker who may not be familiar with the southeast US coast.

Trail through live oak and palmetto, Cumberland Island Wilderness

Boundary Waters Canoe Area

★ ★ ★

Size: 809,772 acres | **Year Designated:** 1964 | **Responsible Agency:** USFS

The Boundary Waters Canoe Area Wilderness is located in the Superior National Forest south of the Canadian border, west of the town of Grand Marais, north of the town of Ely, and east of the town of International Falls. State Highway 61 runs parallel to the eastern boundary and State Highway 1 runs parallel to the southern boundary. At the time of my visit there was a set of maps of the area published by the W.A. Fisher Company.

MY VISIT: October 31–November 2, 2007

There is a cautionary tale attached to this visit. I needed a map for this trip. I first stopped at the USFS ranger station in Ely. I told them I wanted to do a backpack *on land* and to get a required permit. The office did not have a map for hiking but did give me a permit and suggested a canoe outfitter who should have a map. As part of this discussion I was told (warned) that hiking might be difficult because of extensive deadfall on trails due to severe storms a few years earlier. I just nodded and went looking for the outfitter. I found him and he did indeed have a map that I purchased. He also mentioned that I could be in for a difficult hike as there was a lot of deadfall on the trails due to severe storms a few years ago. Again, I filed this away in my head and went to a trailhead for the Snowbank Trail to begin this three-day backpack. My route took me past Parent Lake on a trail with only modest deadfall, but thereafter conditions quickly became much worse. First, it was a cold, windy day with spitting snow, not surprising for the end of October in northern Minnesota. I went south of Disappointment Lake, then to Moiyaka Lake where there was an established USFS campsite. The USFS wants visitors to use established campsites. They consist of a fire pit and a latrine, and are usually sited in scenic spots. Unfortunately, the trail conditions were such that I got to this site well after dark. No, it was not fun trying to slither through deadfall with a headlamp.

Day two took me west across Disappointment Peak through a miserable tangle of deadfall that made for very slow going. Late in the day I got to Boot Lake where I intended to cross the outlet, but it was way too difficult, so I went south to the shore of Snowbank Lake and another official campsite. Again, I got there in the dark and just did a hasty bivouac. It was another cold, windy day but with some sun. Day three was still cold but had more sun and there were good views. I went south past Birdseye Lake and back to Parent Lake and completed my loop hike.

This trip covered few miles but required a lot of energy. As a note to readers (and to myself), this is the Boundary Waters *Canoe* Area. My conclusion is that if you want to visit, bring a canoe. I did meet two canoeists this day and they said that in all their years in this area I was the first on-foot backpacker they had ever seen. They were confident that more than 99 percent of visitors use watercraft.

Having said all that, was this a nice area? Yes, definitely. Rather flat with dense forest, both coniferous and deciduous, and a lot of water. I recommend it to hikers but with a serious push to getting a canoe.

Island in Moiyaka Lake, Boundary Waters Canoe Area Wilderness

Gaylord Nelson

★ ★ ★

Size: 33,500 acres **Year Designated:** 2004
Responsible Agency: USNPS

Most of the Apostle Islands National Lakeshore is designated wilderness. The islands sit in Lake Superior a few miles off the Wisconsin shore north of the town of Ashland. Gaylord Nelson was a governor of Wisconsin and later a US senator from Wisconsin. He was an unapologetic environmentalist and the founder of Earth Day.

MY VISIT: Memorial Day Weekend, 1976

One of my first jobs was in the Chicago suburbs where access to the "serious" outdoors was difficult. I was also new to the Midwest. To get some insights into that part of the country I joined the Sierra Club, which had an outings group. In what I remember, in 1976 the group planned a trip to northern Wisconsin where one could pretty much get away from human domination. The trip was to be a backpack in the Chequamegon National Forest. We drove most of the night to get close to Ashland, where we camped near a trailhead. Upon waking the next morning, the dominant sound outside the tent was mosquitoes. Upon emerging from our tents, it was clear this was going to be a heavy-duty bug day. The trip leader made a wise management decision to cancel the Chequamegon trip and instead find a boat to take us to one of the Apostle Islands in hopes that a Lake Superior breeze would reduce the mosquito impact. We got to one of the smaller islands whose name I cannot remember and had a very enjoyable couple of days. There were not a lot of miles to hike due to the island's small size, but it was a pleasant place, rocky with both evergreen and deciduous trees. Mosquitoes were not a problem. I have little more memory of the trip other than I enjoyed it. There are certainly no surviving photographs.

Sylvania

★ ★ ★

Size: 18,327 acres **Year Designated:** 1987
Responsible Agency: USFS

The Sylvania Wilderness is located in the Ottawa National Forest south of US Highway 2, just across the border with Wisconsin, and southwest of the town of Watersmeet. At the time of my visit there was a USFS map dedicated to this area.

MY VISIT: October 22, 2007

My day hike began at an unsigned trailhead on the western edge of the wilderness. The trail went east to the quite large Whitefish Lake and ended. Being optimistic, I bushwhacked around the lake until I found another trail also heading east. After a short way I got to Hay Lake. Here there was a sign for canoeists informing them that Whitefish Lake was 159 *rods* to the west. This was the first and still only time I have ever encountered a sign giving distance in rods. A bit farther along there was a trail junction and I took the north-leading trail to Clark Lake, also quite large. Here I stopped and turned around. The terrain was pretty flat with dense forest including large maples and hemlocks. A pleasant place, but the weather was not good, gray and cold with poor light, so I took no photos. I still recommend it.

Sturgeon River Gorge

★ ★ ★

Size: 14,500 acres   **Year Designated:** 1987
Responsible Agency: USFS

The Sturgeon River Gorge Wilderness is located in the Ottawa National Forest north of State Highway 28 and north of the community of Sidnaw. At the time of my visit there was a USFS map devoted to this and the McCormick Wilderness areas.

MY VISIT: October 23, 2007

This day hike began at a trailhead for what my map called the Sidnaw Creek Trail. I saw what looked like two trails but my map only showed one. I tried *both* trails, but neither seemed to go anywhere. I ultimately dropped into Woo Creek and decided to just bushwhack northeast along the creek to where the map showed it joining the Sturgeon River. While this was slow, it was also successful. I was impressed by the river—fast, deep, and dark. The terrain was mostly flat and the forest moderately dense with hemlock, maple, and birch. This was another day with some sun early, then becoming gray with some rain. Nonetheless, I found this a worthwhile day and recommend the area.

Sturgeon River, Sturgeon River Gorge Wilderness

McCormick

★ ★ ★

Size: 16,850 acres   **Year Designated:** 1987
Responsible Agency: USFS

The McCormick Wilderness is located in the Ottawa National Forest north of US Highway 41 and between the towns of Michigamme and Ishpeming. At the time of my visit there was a USFS map devoted to this and the Sturgeon River Gorge Wilderness areas. This part of the national forest had been owned by the family of Cyrus McCormick of reaper fame. A descendent of Cyrus willed the land to the US Forest Service.

MY VISIT: October 24, 2007

This day hike began at a trailhead for the Deer Lake Trail off County Road 607. As was the case the previous few days, the weather was cold and gray with snow showers. The trail followed the Pechechee River, another fast, deep, and dark stream. The forest was relatively flat with the normal Upper Peninsula birch, hemlock, and maple trees. There were a number of rock knobs and outcrops. The trail ended at Deer Lake where the foundations of the old McCormick vacation home were still visible. They chose a great spot. I turned around here and on my way back took a side trail to Lower Baraga Lake. While this was not a day of great weather it was clearly a nice area and I recommend it. I took a few photos, but the cover for my camera lens did not open completely and the images were very poor.

MICHIGAN

Rock River Canyon

★ ★ ★

Size: 4,640 acres   **Year Designated:** 1987
Responsible Agency: USFS

The Rock River Canyon Wilderness is located in the Hiawatha National Forest between State Highways 94 in the south and 28 in the north, west of the town of Munising, and a few miles south of the Lake Superior shore. At the time of my visit there was a USFS two-page handout for the wilderness that included a map of marginal use, but did include driving directions.

MY VISIT: October 25, 2007

This day hike began at a trailhead for a trail along the Rock River in the southeast part of the wilderness. Calling the route a trail was an exaggeration. It was an old roadbed that had not been cleared in a long time. I eventually got to Silver Creek and the road improved as it got to higher ground. It did not take long for the trail to disappear completely. I turned south and back to the Silver Creek Canyon, but this ended up going nowhere. I went back up to the original road and dropped down into Rock Canyon, stumbling on Ginpole Lake. This lake was very nice and remote, and it was hosting swans! They were tundra swans and it turned out they winter here. From the lake I returned to the trailhead. This was a nice area on a nice weather day and a destination that I recommend.

Southern shore of Lake Superior, Beaver Basin Wilderness

MICHIGAN

Big Island Lake

★ ★ ★

Size: 5,856 acres   **Year Designated:** 1987
Responsible Agency: USFS

The Big Island Lake Wilderness is located in the Hiawatha National Forest west of State Highway 94 and between the towns of Munising to the northwest and Manistique to the southeast. It is about halfway between Lake Superior to the north and Lake Michigan to the south. At the time of my visit there was a USFS map dedicated to this area.

MY VISIT: October 26, 2007

For this day hike I started on the western wilderness boundary, hiking east to Twilight Lake, then north to Vance Lake, southeast to Byers Lake, and east to a trailhead on the eastern wilderness boundary. These were very nice lakes surrounded by nice wetlands and standard Upper Peninsula forest with open areas around the lakes. Back at my western trailhead I drove a bit north and hiked from the road east into the wilderness a short way to Ned's Lake. This sounds like a lot of hiking, but this was a very small area and I had a lot of time left over, enough to visit a second nearby wilderness (Horseshoe Bay, a two-star area described later). This was a nice day in a pleasant if not exciting area.

Tundra swans on Ginpole Lake, Rock River Canyon Wilderness

Beaver Basin

★ ★ ★

Size: 11,740 acres **Year Designated:** 2009
Responsible Agency: USNPS

Approximately half of the Pictured Rocks National Lakeshore is designated wilderness. The area is located on the northern shore of Michigan's Upper Peninsula (southern shore of Lake Superior) northeast of the town of Munising. Access is via County Road H58 to the south.

MY VISIT: September 13, 2015

This day hike began at a trailhead at the Beaver Basin Overlook. The trail was an old roadbed and I took it down to Trappers Lake through rather dense forest and then to the Lake Superior shore. The trail ran through mostly forest above the lakeshore, but with good views of the shore. I had lunch overlooking Beaver Lake, then continued west to Little Beaver Lake before closing a loop back to the trailhead. This was typical southern Lake Superior shore with a mix of coniferous and deciduous forest with almost constant views of the lake. What was different here from other Upper Peninsula areas was the presence of exposed sandstone ledges above the lakeshore. I was east of the better-known pictured rocks, but it was still a nice shoreline. This was a day of good weather and nice scenery, and I recommend the hike to anyone interested in seeing a relatively undisturbed piece of the southern Lake Superior shore.

Round Island

★ ★ ★

Size: 378 acres **Year Designated:** 1987
Responsible Agency: USFS

The Round Island Wilderness is part of the Hiawatha National Forest. It is located where Lake Michigan and Lake Huron merge, a few miles east of the northern point of Michigan's lower peninsula near the town of Mackinaw City. One acre of the island is not designated wilderness and is occupied by a now-inactive lighthouse.

MY VISIT: September 12, 2015

I was not sure I would ever be able to visit this little wilderness because it requires a boat. The USFS office in St. Ignace could not offer any suggestions for getting there. Finally, I called some fishing boat operators and found someone who was willing to take me there. We were supposed to go on September 11, but there were high winds and the boat captain strongly recommended waiting until the next day. We did wait and departed Mackinaw City on September 12. The fishing boat's draft would not allow it to go directly to shore, so the boat operator rented (for a case of beer) a rubber dingy. The trip to the island was short and the boat's mate rowed me and a friend to the island. It did not take long to see the 378-acre wilderness. My friend and I hiked the whole circumference of this elliptical-shaped island. It was heavily forested with some large pine trees and deciduous shrubs. Because it was close to the mainland, there was quite a bit of trash along the shore. When we returned to our landing spot the fishing boat and dingy picked us up and took us back to Mackinaw City. This area did not get high marks for wildness. The water was very busy with boats of all sizes and descriptions. The sights and sounds of civilization were always present. Still, I am willing to give this area three stars for no other reason than its uniqueness and what I considered a very scenic lighthouse.

Round Island Lighthouse,
Round Island Wilderness

Sleeping Bear Dunes

★ ★ ★

Size: 32,557 acres   **Year Designated:** 2014
Responsible Agency: USNPS

Much of Sleeping Bear National Lakeshore is designated wilderness. The wilderness is made up of four separate parcels along the eastern shore of Lake Michigan and two islands, North Manitou and South Manitou, just off the Lake Michigan shore. The lakeshore is located west of US Highway 31 and northwest of Traverse City.

MY VISIT: September 14, 2015

This day hike began at a parking area at the northeastern-most part of the wilderness at Good Harbor Bay. My route was just to walk the beach to the west with occasional excursions into the adjacent forest. The forest was pleasant and dominated by large eastern white pine trees and some deciduous shrubs. In the forest I stumbled onto an old road and hiked it until reaching a still-used road where I turned around. This was a nice weather day and definitely a nice sand beach with forest just inland. It would be an ideal hike for someone not already familiar with Great Lakes landscapes.

Nordhouse Dunes

★ ★ ★

Size: 3,450 acres   **Year Designated:** 1987
Responsible Agency: USFS

The Nordhouse Dunes Wilderness is located in the Huron-Manistee National Forest on the eastern shore of Lake Michigan, west of US Highway 31, and between the towns of Manistee in the north and Ludington in the south. The southern wilderness boundary is the northern boundary of Ludington State Park. At the time of my visit there was a USFS handout with a map showing the location of the wilderness and its trail system.

MY VISIT: October 29, 2007

This hike began on a very nice day at a parking area and trailhead at the northern edge of the wilderness. There were a few other hikers about. I mostly hiked the beach with occasional excursions inland. There were, of course, the dunes, and the inland forest contained jack pine, dwarf juniper, and hemlock along with oak, maple, and beech. The leaf color peak was past, but the trees still retained many of their leaves. Findings along the beach included a dead fox, a very large number of ladybugs, and wintering snow buntings. I continued along the beach to the southern wilderness boundary where I turned around.

Grass, dunes, and forest, Nordhouse Dunes Wilderness

Breadloaf

★ ★ ★

Size: 25,237 acres   **Year Designated:** 1984
Responsible Agency: USFS

The Breadloaf Wilderness is located in the Green Mountain National Forest between State Highway 100 to the east and State Highway 116 to the west and east of the city of Middlebury. At the time of my visit the USFS put out a series of brochures called *The Wilderness Times* that included information about and maps of wilderness areas, including one dedicated to Breadloaf.

MY VISIT: September 24, 2009

This day hike began at a trailhead near Lincoln Gap at the northern wilderness boundary where I had camped the previous night. I hiked south from here on the Long Trail, which runs north-south the length of Vermont. The morning was sunny but cool. The trail ran through heavy forest with occasional views. Here the fall color had not yet peaked although the birch trees had already lost most of their leaves. One viewpoint was called the Sunset Ledges. The next stop was the summit of Mount Grant (3,623 feet). My intention was to get to Mount Cleveland, but I decided to turn around at a shelter on the Long Trail. Several backpackers were also on the trail and I got the impression that the trail was quite popular. This was certainly a pleasant day in a very typical northern New England setting. I enjoyed the day and recommend the trail to other hikers.

Wild River

★ ★ ★

Size: 23,700 acres   **Year Designated:** 2004
Responsible Agency: USFS

The Wild River Wilderness is located in the White Mountain National Forest between State Highways 113 to the east and 16 to the west and south of US Highway 2. The nearest town is Gorham to the north. At the time of my visit there was a Map Adventures map dedicated to the White Mountains that covered the national forest wilderness areas in New Hampshire and Maine.

MY VISIT: September 18, 2009

My day hike began at a trailhead for the High-Water Trail at the end of the Wild River Road. The trail soon crossed the Wild River on a suspension bridge. This was the beginning of the Moriah Brook Trail following Moriah Brook to the northwest. The brook was pretty with occasional cascades and small falls with pools big enough for swimming on a warm day (but not this day). I kept going northwest to the western wilderness boundary, which followed some high ridges. The weather came in here, and while there were open granite ridges there were no views in the fog. I turned around and retraced my steps. The weather improved on the way down. Somewhere on the return I scared up a *big* bull moose. This was a nice route up a nice stream in a nice area, and I recommend it to other hikers.

Great Gulf

★ ★ ★

Size: 5,522 acres   **Year Designated:** 1964
Responsible Agency: USFS

The Great Gulf Wilderness is located in the White Mountain National Forest south of US Highway 2, west of State Highway 16, and southwest of the town of Gorham. Mount Washington is just to the south. This area was shown on the Map Adventures White Mountains map. The term "Gulf" here refers to a valley surrounded by steep mountains.

MY VISIT: September 19, 2009

This day hike began at a trailhead for the Great Gulf Trail just off State Highway 16 on the eastern side of the wilderness. The trail followed the west branch of the Peabody River to a junction with the Madison Gulf Trail that took off to the north toward Mount Madison, whose summit was my goal for the day. The day was windy and chilly with the nearby summits in fog. The Madison Gulf Trail was *very steep* and I was very slow. I got to about 4,300 feet, well below the summit, and it was getting late so I had to turn around. I was not expecting a trail this difficult, so I was humbled in New Hampshire. Still, this was a nice route in a nice area and I certainly recommend it to others.

Ridge of the Presidential Range from Mount Isolation, Presidential Range-Dry River Wilderness

Presidential Range-Dry River

★ ★ ★

Size: 27,380 acres   **Year Designated:** 1975
Responsible Agency: USFS

The Presidential Range-Dry River Wilderness is located in the White Mountain National Forest east of US Highway 302, west of State Highway 16, and north of the community of Bartlett. This area was shown on the Map Adventures White Mountains map. Mount Washington is just to the north, outside the wilderness.

MY VISIT: September 20, 2009

This day hike began at a parking area off State Highway 16 near the northeast wilderness boundary. It was perfect weather, cloudless, mild, and very little wind. The trail was clearly popular with lots of backpackers coming out and other day hikers going in. The goal this day was the summit of Mount Isolation. It was a fifteen-mile round-trip with about a 3,600-foot vertical gain. Most of the route was through dense forest, but near the summit (4,003 feet) the trees gave way to open terrain. The views were marvelous, including of Mount Washington. In the photo one can see the open, bald granite ridgetops and peaks above the densely forested valleys.

I quite enjoyed this day. It would be a great introductory hike for anyone interested in seeing what mountains are like in New England. I recommend it.

Sandwich Range

★ ★ ★

Size: 35,303 acres   **Year Designated:** 1984
Responsible Agency: USFS

The Sandwich Range Wilderness is located in the White Mountain National Forest south of State Highway 112 and southeast of State Highway 49. The town of Lincoln is to the northwest. The area was shown on the Map Adventures White Mountains map.

MY VISIT: September 21, 2009

This day hike began at a trailhead for the Oliverian Brook Trail off State Highway 112. The trail went south to a junction with the Passaconaway Cutoff Trail, which when combined with short stretches of other trails led me to the summit of Mount Passaconaway (4,043 feet). Most of this route was in heavy forest, but there were occasional views from rocky outcrops. The summit was forested. By now, the New England mountain scene was becoming familiar, and this hike was very much like the preceding few hikes. It was another day of perfect hiking weather. This was a worthwhile destination.

Pemigewasset

★ ★ ★

Size: 45,809 acres   **Year Designated:** 1984
Responsible Agency: USFS

The Pemigewasset Wilderness is located in the White Mountain National Forest south and west of US Highway 302, east of Interstate Highway 93, and northeast of the town of Lincoln. The area was shown on the Map Adventures White Mountains map.

MY VISIT: September 22, 2009

This day hike began at a trailhead in a parking area for the East Side Trail at the Lincoln Woods Visitor Center. The parking area was a beehive of activity. In addition to the normal mix of day hikers, backpackers, and trail runners there was a big crew of USFS employees getting ready to hike up the trail to dismantle an old suspension bridge in the wilderness. Apparently, this was not going to be a small task, and the crew was determined to do the job with hand tools only. Someone told me that if they had asked, they would have received permission to use power tools, but they wanted to demonstrate that power tools were not needed.

The East Side Trail went north along the East Branch of the Pemigewasset River three miles to the wilderness boundary, then east until it became the Wilderness Trail. I kept going east until I had used up half of my daylight and stopped where the trail crossed Crystal Brook. Compared to other recent hikes, this day was easy in relatively flat terrain. My memory is that the route was pretty much all in forested terrain with both deciduous and evergreen trees. I saw many other hikers and backpackers on this weekday, telling me this is a popular area. There was some fall color, but rather subdued.

Caribou-Speckled Mountain

★ ★ ★

Size: 11,236 acres   **Year Designated:** 1990
Responsible Agency: USFS

The Caribou-Speckled Mountain Wilderness is located in the White Mountain National Forest just east of the New Hampshire state line. It is south of US Highway 2, east of State Highway 113, and northeast of the town of North Chatham, New Hampshire. This area was covered by the Map Adventures White Mountains map.

MY VISIT: September 17, 2009

This was my first ever day in Maine. I did not start early, but my map said I could probably get to the summit of Speckled Mountain with the remaining daylight. The hike began at a parking area off State Highway 113 where there was a trailhead for the Spruce Hill Trail. I took this trail south and east through forest to the Bickford Brook Trail and then the Ridge Trail to the summit of Speckled Mountain (2,906 feet). There were excellent views from this summit. One difference from some other New England areas was that the summit views showed many fewer signs of civilization, just big expanses of forest. The forest here seemed to have more evergreen trees than other New England areas I visited.

There were three other hikers on the summit, and I went back down with them. It turned out that one was a USFS employee, and we talked at some length about wilderness areas.

While I understand that a lot of time has passed, my memory is that this may have been my favorite New England hike. I recommend it.

View north from the summit of Speckled Mountain, Caribou-Speckled Mountain Wilderness

Burden Falls

★ ★ ★

Size: 3,671 acres   **Year Designated:** 1990
Responsible Agency: USFS

The Burden Falls Wilderness is located in the Shawnee National Forest southeast of US Highway 45, west of State Highway 145, and southwest of the city of Harrisburg. At the time of my visit there was a USFS handout map for this wilderness.

MY VISIT: October 25, 2005

My day hike began at a trailhead for Burden Falls on Burden Creek at the southern wilderness boundary. The falls were dry, but the area around it was quite lovely with some fall color and limestone cliffs. My map showed no trail, but there was a flagged route that went north. There was also a group of equestrians getting ready to go up the trail with their horses and mules. The route was in closed, mostly deciduous forest with occasional views of limestone cliffs. Like some other eastern wilderness areas, this one had remnants of earlier human activity, including an old, rusted truss bridge. The route continued north to Sand Hill and I went almost to the northern wilderness boundary. This was a very enjoyable day in a truly nice place and I recommend it.

Garden of the Gods

★ ★ ★

Size: 3,990 acres   **Year Designated:** 1990
Responsible Agency: USFS

The Garden of the Gods Wilderness is located in the Shawnee National Forest east of State Highway 34 and southeast of the city of Harrisburg. At the time of my visit there was a USFS handout map for this wilderness.

MY VISIT: October 27, 2005

I really did two hikes on this day from a trailhead on the western wilderness boundary. The first was on the "Blue Loop," which wound around through colorful hardwood forest along marvelous little eroded sandstone bluffs. The second was on the River to River Trail (Ohio to Mississippi). I took this trail to what I think was the western wilderness boundary and turned around.

On my way west on the River to River Trail, what did I see in the middle of the trail but a money clip. With lots of money. After a small hesitation I decided to pick it up. In addition to money, it also contained a business card with the name and address of the owner. The address was for a nearby community and I vowed to return it. As I neared the trailhead, I could hear horses (as it turned out, mules) behind me. Riding the lead mule was the money's owner. He knew he had lost it and was hoping to find it. It turned out that some of the riders were the same ones I had seen two days earlier at the trailhead for Burden Falls. We all had a good laugh.

Like Burden Falls, this was a very nice area on a day of perfect weather. I recommend it.

Eroded sandstone and autumn leaves, Garden of the Gods Wilderness

Allegheny Islands

★ ★ ★

Size: 372 acres **Year Designated:** 1984
Responsible Agency: USFS

The Allegheny Islands Wilderness is made up of seven islands in the Allegheny River in the Allegheny National Forest. At the time of my visit I relied on a map for the Middle Allegheny River Water Trail prepared by a consortium of agencies including the USFS.

MY VISIT: September 17, 2015

For once, I was able to get outside my comfort zone. To get to this wilderness, one must negotiate water. In this case, a canoe was perfect. I did this trip with my friend Maya who did have canoe experience. We rented a canoe from a local outfitter and were taken to a put-in called West Hickory along US Highway 62 near river mile 158. It was a nice day, and as advertised this stretch of river was very easy with water temperature about 70 degrees F and river depth about 3.5 feet (river flow was controlled by an upstream dam). The first wilderness island we came to was King at thirty-six acres. This island, like all the others, was heavily forested, with oak, maple, hickory, and sycamore. Some islands had suffered heavy loss of trees because of tornadoes in the 1980s. We rummaged around the island a bit, then continued downstream. Our second stop was on the small (ten-acre) No Name Island where we wandered around a bit, then walked, sometimes in shallow water, to the larger (sixty-seven-acre) Baker Island, which had more big trees and not much understory with some grass and wildflowers. After lunch on Baker Island we went back to the canoe and paddled down to the village of Tionesta where we took out at our outfitter's facility.

This was a day of nice weather, ideal river conditions, and pleasant forested islands. What this day was not was a wilderness experience. The river was probably never more than two hundred yards from US Highway 62, which had lots of traffic, most of it audible to anyone in a canoe. More than that, the highway was experiencing construction, so there was more noise than one might expect. Also, we passed private homes on the west bank. I have struggled to come up with a rating for this trip and have settled on three stars, mostly because of the unique nature of the islands. They appeared to be in pristine condition.

*Canoe along Allegheny River,
Allegheny Islands Wilderness*

Dolly Sods

★ ★ ★

Size: 17,371 acres   **Year Designated:** 1975
Responsible Agency: USFS

The Dolly Sods Wilderness is located in the Monongahela National Forest east of State Highway 32, west of State Highway 28, and west of the town of Petersburg. At the time of my visit there was a USFS pamphlet describing the area and its trails, including a map.

MY VISIT: May 22, 2008

My day hike began at a trailhead for the Wildlife Trail on the eastern side of the wilderness, then I took the Rohrbaugh Trail to the Fisher Spring Run Trail to Red Creek. This route went through mostly hardwood forest with some hemlock and some open areas. Somewhere I saw a definition of "sods" as open, grassy areas surrounded by forest. What I can't remember is whether or not the open areas were natural or cleared by humans in the past. The photo shows a typical mix of forest and grassy surroundings. There were areas of exposed granite, and the high, flat areas had stunted trees and shrubs and tended to be wind scoured. It had been raining and Red Creek was running high and the trails were muddy. This was a genuinely nice area and I recommend it.

Big Draft

★ ★ ★

Size: 5,144 acres   **Year Designated:** 2009
Responsible Agency: USFS

After the 2008 presidential election, Congress passed an omnibus public lands bill that designated three wilderness areas in the Monongahela National Forest. One of these was the Big Draft Wilderness, located west of State Highway 92, north of Interstate Highway 64, and north of the city of White Sulfur Springs. At the time of my visit the USFS had a small map showing the wilderness boundaries.

MY VISIT: May 7, 2010

This day hike began at a trailhead for the Blue Bend Loop next to the Blue Bend Campground. This trail was pretty much the only trail giving access to the interior of the wilderness. The trail first crossed the very pleasant Anthony Creek, then ran through a rather thick forest with a few rock outcrops. The trail then went to the summit of Round Mountain (2,495 feet) and back down to close the loop. There were no real views from the dense forest on the summit. While there was nothing unique or especially noteworthy about this area, it was still a nice hike in a nice area.

Sod and forest, Dolly Sods Wilderness

Roaring Plains West

★ ★ ★

Size: 6,792 acres   **Year Designated:** 2009
Responsible Agency: USFS

The roaring Plains West Wilderness is another Monongahela National Forest area designated in the 2009 omnibus public lands bill. It is located just southwest of the Dolly Sods Wilderness, west and south of State Highway 55, and east of the town of Harmon.

MY VISIT: May 8, 2010

I did not have any map that showed the wilderness boundaries for this area, so I stopped at the Seneca Rocks Visitor Center to ask directions. I was directed to a parking area (signed) for the Flatrock Run Trail. The first mile of trail went through private property and had a sign urging hikers not to feed the horses hanging out nearby. Once past the wilderness boundary the trail climbed along the run with its small waterfalls and cascades, then climbed more steeply to a junction with the Roaring Plains Trail. Here the forest changed character, becoming more open with rock outcrops. With still more elevation gain the terrain became relatively flat and wind scoured with lots of rock, huckleberries, shrubs, and grasses and only occasional pine trees. This was hard, spare country on a chilly, windy, gray day. The elevation was, I think, just under 5,000 feet. This was a nice hiking day with a good introduction to a harsh version of an eastern forest. I recommend this area.

Cranberry

★ ★ ★

Size: 47,815 acres   **Year Designated:** 1983
Responsible Agency: USFS

The Cranberry Wilderness is located in the Monongahela National Forest west of State Highway 150, north of State Highway 55, and west of the town of Marlinton.

MY VISIT: May 23, 2008

This day hike began at a trailhead along State Highway 150 for the North South Trail. (Note: this trail ran almost exactly east-west.) This was a ridge-top trail running just under 4,500 feet. My notes for this hike are sparse, but I did note that there were a lot of pine trees early then a transition to mostly hardwoods with lots of rhododendron. I took this trail to a junction with the Tumbling Rock Trail where I turned around. Cranberries can be found in these mountains, but I would probably not be able to identify a cranberry plant in spring. I admit I don't remember much of anything from this trip, but on the day I did the hike, I called it a three-star area, so I will let that stand.

Ramseys Draft

★ ★ ★

Size: 6,518 acres   **Year Designated:** 1984
Responsible Agency: USFS

The Ramseys Draft Wilderness is located in the George Washington National Forest north of US Highway 250 and west of the city of Harrisonburg.

This wilderness is known for its stands of virgin timber, very rare in Virginia. My day hike began at a trailhead for the Ramseys Draft Trail at the southwest wilderness boundary. I took it as a good omen that there was an eastern phoebe nest on the trailhead signboard. The trail followed Ramseys Draft (the creek) to the northeastern wilderness boundary through truly impressive, huge oak and pine trees. The trail crossed the creek often, but the crossings were easy. The scenery, aside from the big trees, was pretty standard Appalachian hardwood forest, pleasant but with few noteworthy features. Once close to the northeast wilderness boundary I just turned around and retraced my steps.

VIRGINIA

Rough Mountain

★ ★ ★

Size: 9,300 acres   **Year Designated:** 1988
Responsible Agency: USFS

The Rough Mountain Wilderness is located in the George Washington National Forest north of US Highway 60, east of State Highway 42, and northeast of the town of Clifton Forge. The CSX Railway runs along the eastern wilderness boundary. Although I did not have it at the time of my visit there is a National Geographic Trails Illustrated map number 788, Covington Allegheny Highlands, that includes the wilderness. For my visit I used an old USFS map of the George Washington National Forest.

MY VISIT: April 28, 2010

I had a very hard time finding this area. The George Washington National Forest map I was using was simply wrong about the roads near this wilderness. After asking for directions multiple times with no success, I just started driving down roads that looked promising. I finally found a prospective track, but it was filled with large mud puddles. Fortunately, two locals came by and said the road was OK and described how to get to the location of the supposed trail shown on my map. I followed their directions and got to and crossed the CSX tracks, and there, lo and behold, was a sign for the Crane Trail. The only problem was that there was no trail. I looked and looked but never saw a hint of trail, so I just got out my trusty GPS and started climbing the ridge of Rough Mountain, which runs northeast-southwest the length of the wilderness. This was a good choice as the forest was quite open and pleasant. The many dogwood trees were at their peak of bloom. I got to the summit of the ridge at about an elevation of 2,500 feet. I had lunch there among some pine trees and then followed my GPS (mandatory here) back to the "trailhead." Despite the early frustrations, this turned out to be a good hiking day.

VIRGINIA

Saint Marys

★ ★ ★

Size: 9,835 acres   **Year Designated:** 1984
Responsible Agency: USFS

The Saint Marys Wilderness is located in the George Washington National Forest east of US Highway 11; the Blue Ridge Parkway runs just south of the wilderness. The closest town is Waynesboro to the northeast. At the time of my visit there was a National Geographic Trails Illustrated map number 789, Lexington Blue Ridge Mountains, that included this wilderness.

MY VISIT: May 1, 2010

This day hike began at a trailhead on the western wilderness boundary for the Saint Marys Trail. The route was east along the river with a side trip to some waterfalls. This was clearly a popular area as I passed lots of folks including groups of up to ten people. I went as far upstream as a junction with the Mine Bank Trail where I turned around. There once had been an old manganese mine. Essentially all the hike was in forest, the standard middle Appalachian hardwoods. The nicest features along the route were the stream and waterfalls (pictured). The old mine was at least a little interesting if only because I had never seen a manganese mine. I could not identify any manganese.

Falls, Saint Marys River,
Saint Marys Wilderness

Stone Mountain

★ ★ ★

Size: 3,270 acres   **Year Designated:** 2009
Responsible Agency: USFS

The Stone Mountain Wilderness is located in the Jefferson National Forest north of State Road 621 and northeast of the town of Pennington Gap. The area's designation was part of the 2009 omnibus public lands bill.

MY VISIT: May 5, 2010

Because wilderness designation was very recent, I had no map that showed the wilderness boundaries. I was able to find a USFS employee in the Wise Ranger Station who made a copy of some other map and marked where I could find a trailhead for the Stone Mountain Trail within the Cave Springs Recreation Area. When I arrived, the recreation area was not yet open to the public, so I parked by State Road 621 and walked up to the trailhead. The trail went approximately north to the top of the Stone Mountain ridge. The area was forest with oak, maple, and tulip poplar. Parts of the trail were quite difficult because of severe blowdown. Near the summit were sandstone cliffs, boulders, and overhangs. Along the trail I even found a pink lady slipper orchid! Once on the summit I walked the ridge trail to the east a way before turning around. While never spectacular, I found this a nice hike.

Hunting Camp Creek

★ ★ ★

Size: 8,470 acres   **Year Designated:** 2009
Responsible Agency: USFS

The Hunting Camp Creek Wilderness is located in the Jefferson National Forest west of Interstate Highway 77, north of State Highway 42, and northwest of the town of Wytheville. The Appalachian Trail runs through the wilderness. The Garden Mountain Wilderness is just to the west. Although the wilderness boundaries are not shown, the National Geographic Trails Illustrated map 787 for Blacksburg New River Valley includes what is now the wilderness.

MY VISIT: April 25, 2010

This day hike began at a parking area for the Appalachian Trail (AT) off State Route 623. The hike began as a nice ridge walk on the AT, then the trail dropped steeply to Hunting Camp Creek where I turned around. This was about a ten-mile day through standard oak, maple, and tulip poplar forest with lots of rhododendron at lower elevation and pine and hemlock at higher elevation. Nothing spectacular or unusual, but still a nice hike in a pleasant forest.

James River Face

★ ★ ★

Size: 8,866 acres   **Year Designated:** 1975
Responsible Agency: USFS

The James River Face Wilderness is located in the Jefferson National Forest south of US Highway 501, just north of the Blue Ridge Parkway, and south of the town of Glasgow. At the time of my visit there was a USFS handout for the wilderness and the wilderness is also shown on National Geographic Trails Illustrated map 789, Lexington Blue Ridge Mountains. The Appalachian Trail goes through the area.

MY VISIT: April 29, 2010

This day hike began at a parking area for the Appalachian Trail (AT) just off the Blue Ridge Parkway. I hiked the AT north until I got to an overlook with a great view of the James River and then turned around. I went over Highcock Knob, at 3,073 feet the highest point in the wilderness. The forest had not yet fully leafed out, so there were some pretty good views, especially down to the James River. This being the AT, there were quite a few other hikers. The weather was good, the forest pleasant, and the views good, so an all-around nice day. I recommend this area.

James River from the Appalachian Trail, James River Face Wilderness

Brush Mountain East

★ ★ ★

Size: 3,743 acres   **Year Designated:** 2009
Responsible Agency: USFS

The Brush Mountain East Wilderness is located in the Jefferson National Forest north of State Route 624, south of State Route 621, and northeast of the city of Blacksburg. Because of the recent wilderness designation, I did not have a map showing wilderness boundaries, but the area is shown on National Geographic Trails Illustrated map 787, Blacksburg New River Valley.

MY VISIT: April 26, 2010

This day hike began at a parking area for the Appalachian Trail (AT) off State Route 621. I hiked the AT south along mostly ridgetops to a memorial for Audie Murphy (just off the AT). This was a nice route on a gray, breezy day. The forest was by now a very familiar mix of hardwood and pine with a few shrubs beginning to blossom. Again, nothing spectacular or of special interest, but still enough variation to not be boring. It was a worthwhile day.

Mountain Lake

★ ★ ★

Size: 16,511 acres   **Year Designated:** 1984
Responsible Agency: USFS

The Mountain Lake Wilderness is located in the Jefferson National Forest north of US Highway 460 and north of the city of Blacksburg. This area is shown on the National Geographic Trails Illustrated map 787, Blacksburg New River Valley. Most of the wilderness is in Virginia, but the northern portion is in West Virginia. Mountain Lake itself is outside the wilderness area.

MY VISIT: May 24, 2008

My day hike began at a trailhead for the War Spur Loop Trail off State Route 613 along the western wilderness boundary. I hiked the short loop first. After finishing the loop, I took a trail that connected to the Appalachian Trail. I then hiked the AT north (compass direction) to the summit of Lone Pine Peak at 4,054 feet. Here I turned around. The AT was quite busy with lots of backpackers and one USFS employee. Azaleas were in bloom. I also saw some of the year's first blooming rhododendron. This was a nice day in a nice area and I recommend it.

Little Wilson Creek

★ ★ ★

Size: 5,458 acres   **Year Designated:** 1984
Responsible Agency: USFS

The Little Wilson Creek Wilderness is located in the Jefferson National Forest and within the Mount Rogers National Recreation Area. It is north of US Highway 50, west of State Highway 16, and south of the city of Marion. The National Geographic Trails Illustrated map 786, Mount Rogers, covers this area. The Appalachian Trail runs through the wilderness.

MY VISIT: May 28, 2008

This day hike began at a parking area for the Jackie Street Trail off State Route 739. Almost all of the hike was in the rain. The trail went south through standard Appalachian forest, ultimately to the summit of First Peak, then I retraced a bit and took a trail north to Second Peak at 4,857 feet. Both First and Second Peaks were open on their summits with a variety of shrubs and wildflowers, some in bloom. Second Peak was wrapped in fog. Even on a rainy day, this was a nice hike in a nice area and I recommend it.

Wilderness boundary sign on a foggy day

Lewis Fork

★ ★ ★

Size: 5,926 acres   **Year Designated:** 1984
Responsible Agency: USFS

The Lewis Fork Wilderness is located in the Jefferson National Forest and is within the Mount Rogers National Recreation Area. It is just west of the Little Wilson Creek Wilderness, north of US Highway 58, west of State Highway 16, and south of the city of Marion. The National Geographic Trails Illustrated map 786, Mount Rogers, covers this area.

MY VISIT: May 29, 2008

My day hike began at the Appalachian Trail trailhead Elk Garden, off State Route 600 on the west side of the wilderness. The AT ran a few miles east along Elk Garden Ridge, then to a spur trail to the summit of Mount Rogers. The day was overcast but dry. The first part of the trail was in open, meadow-like terrain. Somewhere I saw a sign telling hikers that these openings were cleared by early settlers.

Farther along, the trail went back into dense forest. There were a few more open areas near the Mount Rogers trail junction, but the summit itself, at 5,729 feet (highest in Virginia), was still in dense forest with no views. I had lunch at the summit with some Canadian hikers. The clearings near the AT were then free of fog and I got at least one photo of the neighborhood. This was another day in a nice place and I recommend it.

Shenandoah

★ ★ ★

Size: 79,579 acres   **Year Designated:** 1976
Responsible Agency: USNPS

A significant portion of Shenandoah National Park is designated wilderness. The park is located in northern Virginia south of Interstate Highway 66, east of Interstate Highway 81, and north of Interstate Highway 64. Washington DC is to the northeast and the city of Harrisonburg is to the west. The 79,579 acres of wilderness is somewhat misleading because these acres are divided into eleven pieces separated by roads.

MY VISIT: October 17–19, 2016

This visit consisted of three consecutive day hikes. The first day hike began at a parking area along the famous Skyline Drive. I took the Corbin Cutoff Trail down to two cabins on the Hughes River, one restored and locked, the other somewhat restored but still rustic. There was a note on the door of the locked cabin warning visitors to be aware that a copperhead (a venomous snake) liked to hang out around the chimney. I then continued south on the Indian Run Trail to its junction with the Corbin Mountain Trail where I turned around. This time of year was very close to the peak of fall color and it was a nice day for hiking. This route had several other hikers.

The second day hike began at the Two-Mile Run turnout along Skyline Drive. Here I did a balloon-shaped route on the Rocky Mount and Gap Run Trails, a somewhat more ambitious hike. The terrain here was a bit more open than the previous day, with views of ridges and from ridges and again a lot of fall color. From the summit of Rocky Mount itself (2,741 feet) there were partial views to the west into the Shenandoah Valley with its ever-so-modern industrial trappings. This was another pretty nice day. I saw three backpackers.

The third day I just did a short hike toward the southern end of the park on the Turk Mountain Trail beginning again at a turnout along Skyline Drive. The trail went to the summit of Turk Mountain, made up of exposed granite blocks with views of nearby ridges and again views into the very developed Shenandoah Valley.

All in all, this was a worthwhile three days of hiking, although always within sight and sound of civilization. Still, if a hiker is in the area this could be a good destination.

Corbin Cabin, Shenandoah Wilderness

Upper Buffalo

★ ★ ★

Size: 12,018 acres   **Year Designated:** 1975
Responsible Agency: USFS

The Upper Buffalo Wilderness is located in the Ozark National Forest north and west of State Highway 21 and east of the city of Fayetteville. At the time of my visit there was a USFS map available for this area. The wilderness includes the headwaters of the Buffalo River.

The main reason people visit this area is to see the Hawksbill Crag, a rock outcrop at the edge of a deep valley. Officially there are no trails in the wilderness, but the path to the crag is well worn. On the morning of my first visit I was the first person to arrive, but several other visitors were close behind me. The view from the crag was good and it was a nice spot. A more recent map now calls this Whitaker Point, accessed by the Whitaker Point Trail.

Twelve years later I was in the neighborhood again and wanted to show a friend the crag. We got there around midday and the place was mobbed with people. There was even a bus and it was hard to find a place to park. I figured there must be some sort of special event, so hung out near the trailhead. Streams of vehicles kept coming. After a while I just decided we should join the parade. It took awhile to get a photo with nobody else on the crag. This is a nice area, but hikers wanting solitude might want to look for another destination or just keep going beyond the crag.

Hawksbill Crag, now Whitaker Point, Upper Buffalo Wilderness

Richland Creek

★ ★ ★

Size: 11,801 acres   **Year Designated:** 1984
Responsible Agency: USFS

The Richland Creek Wilderness is located in the Ozark National Forest east of State Highway 123, north of State Highway 16, and south of the town of Harrison. Forest Road 1200 and its branches wrap around most of the wilderness. At the time of my visits there was a USFS map dedicated to this area.

MY VISITS: November 3, 2004 and October 10, 2016

I remember well my first visit. It rained the entire time, sometimes very heavy. All the streams were high, bordering on flooding. Nonetheless, hike I did, beginning along Forest Road 1200 on the east side of the wilderness just north of the Richland Creek Campground. By pure chance I quickly found an old road grade and was able to hike along it to the Devils Fork of Richland Creek. I hiked upstream to some falls, not very tall but carrying a lot of water. The forest itself was nice, with typical Arkansas oak and hickory. I turned around at the falls and on my way back happened to see, huddled under some bushes, my very first woodcock. The second visit in 2016 was rather brief, just following the creek upstream a way. I think most hikers would like this area even without any formal trails. Both the forest and streams are quite nice.

Black Fork Mountain

★ ★ ★

Size: 13,199 acres   **Year Designated:** 1984
Responsible Agency: USFS

The Black Fork Mountain Wilderness is located in the Ouachita National Forest just north of US Highway 59/270 and northwest of the town of Mena. The eastern portion of the wilderness is in Arkansas and the western portion in Oklahoma. At the time of my visits there was a USFS handout for this wilderness.

MY VISITS: October 27, 2004 and April 6, 2018 and April 16, 2018

Was I stubborn? Or persistent? There was only one trail, the Black Fork Mountain Trail. My first attempt in 2004 was thwarted by some of the heaviest rainfall I have ever experienced. I tried finding shelter under big trees and rock overhangs, but nothing helped. Ultimately, the rain eased off a bit and I got most of the way up the trail in fog and gnarled oak trees almost expecting some three-foot-tall old man with a beard down to his knees to come out and ask where I was going. The forest looked intriguing and I wanted to come back.

Fourteen years later I made a second attempt. After two minutes on the trail it began to rain, although not too heavy. Then came the thunder and lightning. Close. I decided that discretion would be the better part and stopped climbing, going back instead to my truck at the trailhead along US Highway 59/270. A second time denied. Ten days later I made my third try. This day was clear, cool, and perfect for hiking. It was early spring and trees and shrubs were leafing out. The forest was rather open with some shrubs but mostly oak with some hickory, maple, and pine. The trail went up to the top of the ridge of Black Fork Mountain and then continued along the ridge until I turned around. There were some good views from my lunch spot on top of the ridge. One unusual name that I have seen associated with this area is the Ozark's early settlers' idea of "glaciers." These are slopes of forest with pale rocks covering the hillsides.

While this wilderness may not have been worth three trips, it was still a nice day in a nice area and I recommend it to anyone new to the greater Ozarks.

Buffalo National River

★ ★ ★

Size: 34,933 acres   **Year Designated:** 1978
Responsible Agency: USNPS

Parts of the Buffalo National River are designated wilderness. There are three segments to the wilderness: the Upper Buffalo (see earlier, but administered by the NPS) at the upstream end, the Ponca in the central portion and the Lower Buffalo, which is contiguous with the USFS Leatherwood Wilderness at the downstream end. The area is accessed by State Highways 21 in the west, 43 west of the Ponca, and 14 in the east. The closest towns are Harrison to the north and Jasper to the south. At the time of my visit there was a National Geographic Trails Illustrated map 232, Buffalo National River West, that covered the area of my trip.

MY VISIT: October 9–10, 2016

This overnight backpack began at a parking area for the Centerpoint Trailhead along State Highway 43. I did this trip with a friend and we descended to the river and the River Trail, along which we set up our camp. We had lots of time so we decided to cross the river twice near Horseshoe Bend and then went up a trail to the waterfall at Hemmed-in Hollow. There was not a lot of water falling, but the spot was superb. We could see little packets of water catching the sun as they fell over the edge. In the photo, see if you can find my companion near the bottom to provide some sense of scale. This was a big drop.

I made a major mistake that evening. It was warm and calm and I decided to stay outside the tent, sitting against a pine tree, to read. The next morning I felt pretty itchy, and as I got out of my sleeping bag, I realized that I was covered in bites—in this case chiggers. Those bites plagued me for a long time.

This was a nice trip in a nice place. The river and forest were pleasant and the cliffs were impressive. It was probably my favorite Arkansas area and I can easily recommend it to other hikers.

Pond Mountain

★ ★ ★

Size: 6,890 acres   **Year Designated:** 1986
Responsible Agency: USFS

The Pond Mountain Wilderness is located in the Cherokee National Forest south of State Highway 67, east and north of State Highway 37, and southeast of the city of Elizabethton. At the time of my visit this wilderness was shown on National Geographic Trails Illustrated map 783, Cherokee and Pisgah National Forests.

MY VISIT: October 13, 2006

This day hike began at a parking area for the Appalachian Trail near Dennis Cove. I hiked the AT northeast over Potato Top (2,540 feet), past the quite lovely Laurel Falls, then past an AT shelter and on to the High-Water Trail, then and up a ridge for lunch where I turned around. This hike was almost all in forest, dominated by oak with colored leaves but with other hardwoods and pines and vines, some with bright red berries. It was a brilliantly clear day with cool temperatures—a great day to be hiking in a forest. I recommend this area.

Falls, Hemmed-in Hollow, Buffalo National River Wilderness

Laurel Falls, Pond Mountain Wilderness

Big Frog

★ ★ ★

Size: 8,082 acres   **Year Designated:** 1984
Responsible Agency: USFS

The Big Frog Wilderness is located in the Cherokee National Forest south of US Highway 74/64 and west of the town of Duck Town. The southern wilderness boundary is the Georgia state line and the northern boundary is the Cohutta Wilderness. At the time of my visit this wilderness was shown on National Geographic Trails Illustrated map 781, Cherokee National Forest.

MY VISIT: October 18, 2006

My day hike began at a trailhead for the Big Frog Trail at Low Gap. This trail went across the wilderness from the northern boundary to Big Frog Mountain on the southwestern boundary, 5.5 miles one-way according to my map. After a day of intense rain, this day was dry with some sun. The trail stayed high, most of the way near the top of the ridge. I was mainly in oak forest with good color. From the summit of Big Frog Mountain (4,220 feet) I took the Hemp Top Trail a bit to the east before turning around and retracing my steps. On my way out, I spotted, to my surprise, a coyote. This was a nice ridgetop hike, which I liked and recommend to others.

Shining Rock

★ ★ ★

Size: 18,483 acres   **Year Designated:** 1964
Responsible Agency: USFS

The Shining Rock Wilderness is located in the Pisgah National Forest west of US Highway 276, east of State Highway 215, north of the Blue Ridge Parkway, and southeast of the city of Waynesville. At the time of my visit there was a USFS map devoted to this area and the nearby Middle Prong Wilderness.

MY VISIT: October 30, 2006

I had read the book *Cold Mountain* and quite liked it, so I could not resist doing my hike in this area to the Cold Mountain summit. I encountered a hunter near the trailhead and he told me that there were still members of the Inman family (name of the book's main character) in the neighborhood. The hike began at a parking area with a trailhead for the Art Loeb Trail. I climbed up this trail to an intersection with the Cold Mountain Trail and took it to the 6,030-foot summit. This was a glorious day, crystal clear and still the last of the fall color. There were no completely clear views from the timbered summit, but views were still good. I wanted to have my lunch on the summit, but I was not alone there. Hanging out were two hunting hounds with radio collars and they were very hungry. As soon as I sat down and pulled out food, they were all over it. I did not see or hear any sign of another human, but to have peace I went back down the trail a little way for lunch.

I have a memory that near the Art Loeb-Cold Mountain Trail junction there was an ancient apple tree with some seriously over-ripe fruit hanging on.

Ellicott Rock

★ ★ ★

Size: 8,274 acres **Year Designated:** 1975
Responsible Agency: USFS

The Ellicott Rock Wilderness is located in the Nantahala National Forest west of State Highway 107, east of State Highway 83, and southwest of the town of Brevard. While described here with North Carolina, this wilderness is also in South Carolina and Georgia. To the best of my knowledge, this is the only three-state wilderness.

MY VISIT: October 29, 2006

This day hike began in an obviously wealthy neighborhood of fancy homes and vehicles such as BMW, Mercedes, Volvo, Lexus, etc. I found a trailhead off Bull Run Road for the Ellicott Rock Trail. I hiked this trail south and east down an old road grade to the Chattooga Wild and Scenic River. The trail ran through colorful forest with hardwoods and white pine. The river was quite lovely. The trail forded the river, but I was reluctant to cross, so turned around without actually seeing Ellicott Rock. This was a very nice day in a nice area and I recommend it.

Black Creek

★ ★ ★

Size: 5,052 acres **Year Designated:** 1984
Responsible Agency: USFS

The Black Creek Wilderness is located in the De Soto National Forest east of State Highway 29, west of County Road 301, and northeast of the town of De Soto.

MY VISIT: March 17, 2009

This was not a long visit. I parked at a trailhead along State Highway 29 on the western boundary of the wilderness. I had picked up a rudimentary map at a nearby ranger station that stated that the Black Creek Trail was closed because of remaining damage from Hurricane Katrina. When I arrived at the trailhead there was a big sign that read "Closed to all Human Uses. Violators Will Be Prosecuted." That meant me. The ranger station was close by. On the other hand, this was likely to be my only time driving to Mississippi (that turned out to be untrue). I swallowed hard and decided to take at least a short hike. There was a trail, obviously recently cleared and in places rerouted around massive blowdown debris. There were no obstacles on the reworked trail that I saw, but I did not go the entire length of the trail before turning around. The terrain was nearly flat. Black Creek itself was pleasant and there were some early blooming shrubs. The forest was thick and I have no memory of tree or shrub species. I do remember seeing few if any birds, surprising for this time of year. I left with the impression that this was a pretty nice area and probably a good place to visit to get a sense of what the ecosystem is like here in the Mississippi lowlands.

Spring blossoms, Black Creek Wilderness

Gulf Islands

★ ★ ★

Size: 4,080 acres   **Year Designated:** 1978
Responsible Agency: USNPS

Two islands in the Gulf Islands National Seashore are designated wilderness. These islands are Horn and Petit Bois, about ten miles off the coast of Mississippi. The closest city is Pascagoula. The only access is by boat.

MY VISIT: October 12–13, 2016

This overnight backpack began in Gautier, Mississippi, at a dock where a friend and I had hired a boat operator to take us to Horn Island. Horn Island is a classic barrier island protecting the main Gulf Coast from storms. The passage to the island was easy in a jon boat. This bit of the Gulf of Mexico is very busy with ships large and small and a huge Ingalls Shipbuilding facility on the mainland, and also a liquified natural gas terminal under construction nearby. We carried all our water with us as fresh water could not be reliably found on the island.

Gulf Coast and dunes, Horn Island, Gulf Islands Wilderness

The island was a fascinating place, mostly vegetated sand dunes with some live oaks, wildflowers, and grasses. There were some ponds of brackish water and lots of birds including many brown pelicans, some least sandpipers, and the almost inevitable sanderlings making their forays into and out of the surf. On one of my strolls along the beach I saw an old, partially submerged oak stump with a bunch of old crustacean shells attached. I stared at it for a bit and realized that it was wriggling. The shells were inhabited by hermit crabs.

In our two days we saw no other humans, but the human activities off the island were always within sight and hearing. A wild island in a sea (gulf) of human activity. My friend and I were glad we made this trip and I recommend it to others who are looking to experience the real (mostly), natural Gulf Coast.

Cheaha

★ ★ ★

Size: 7,245 acres   **Year Designated:** 1983
Responsible Agency: USFS

The Cheaha Wilderness is located in the Talladega National Forest west of State Highway 49, east of State Highway 281, and south of the town of Oxford.

MY VISIT: April 10, 2009

This day hike began at a trailhead off State Highway 281 for the Chinnabee Silent Trail. The morning was gray, warm, and raining. I climbed southeast, sweating in my rain gear, to a ridge where I went southwest on the Pinhoti Trail. When on the ridge, the rain stopped and there was partial clearing with some nice views from rocky outcrops. The forest was pleasant

Dogwood and red bud, Cheaha Wilderness

and the dogwood just about at its prime. This hike was a good introduction to the southern end of the Appalachians, still mostly hardwood forest but more gentle terrain than areas farther north.

The day's excitement really began when I got back to my truck. I began driving toward my next destination as the rain returned and quickly became heavy. I was listening to the radio and warnings came on about possible tornadoes. Warnings were for specific areas, but I did not know any of the names. I looked at a map, and the warnings were for exactly where I was. Soon I could hear the warning sirens. As I drove into villages the siren sounds would wax, then wane, then begin again as I approached the next village. I have one clear memory of driving past a volunteer fire station. One door was open exposing a fire truck with a man sitting in a lawn chair in front of the truck, arms folded, waiting for a call.

Sandstone grotto, Sipsey Wilderness

Sipsey

★ ★ ★

Size: 24,922 acres **Year Designated:** 1975
Responsible Agency: USFS

The Sipsey Wilderness is located in the William B. Bankhead National Forest just west of State Highway 33 and south of the town of Moulton.

MY VISIT: April 12, 2009

This was one area for which I had no map, including how to get there. While driving around the Bankhead National Forest I spied State Highway 33, suggestively called the Wilderness Parkway. There were lots of signs, some with maps, and I took a cherry-stem road to a trailhead for Borden Creek. This was a lucky guess. I hiked up Borden Creek, a pretty stream through mostly deciduous forest including some very large trees. Ultimately, I got to a beautiful grotto with sandstone cliffs with waterfalls. A wonderful spot. I kept going and came upon other spots with cliffs and waterfalls. To make an even better day I was able to spot a Kentucky warbler and a broad-winged hawk.

This area has been discovered and there were lots of hikers around. Also, I was never very far from a road. Still though, this was a nice day in a very nice place. I recommend it.

Little Wambaw Swamp

★ ★ ★

Size: 5,047 acres   **Year Designated:** 1980
Responsible Agency: USFS

The Little Wambaw Swamp Wilderness is located in the Francis Marion National Forest west of US Highway 17 and southwest of the town of McClellanville. The area is just southeast of the Wambaw Swamp Wilderness.

MY VISIT: April 4, 2009

This day hike began at the northern wilderness boundary where what I thought was an old railroad grade entered the wilderness. It was a nice, cool, bright day and the early hiking was deceptively easy. However, after a bit, the old route became very overgrown and progress was slow and difficult. It got worse—after thrashing around in the undergrowth the route dipped into the water and everything was submerged. I went a bit farther but felt I needed to turn around. This was my nicest day in the South Carolina swamps, and this was probably the nicest area I visited.

Saint Marks

★ ★ ★

Size: 17,350 acres   **Year Designated:** 1975
Responsible Agency: USFWS

Much of the Saint Marks National Wildlife Refuge is designated wilderness. The refuge is located south of US Highway 98, east of US Highway 319, and south of the city of Tallahassee. State Highway 363 provides access to the refuge visitor center. The shore of Apalachee Bay is the southern refuge and wilderness boundary.

MY VISIT: March 22, 2009

My (birth)day hike began near the refuge visitor center where I was advised that the best birding in the wilderness would be along the salt marshes north of the lighthouse near the end of the paved road. I went there, but there was an unmistakable sign saying that the salt marshes were closed to "all human entry." I was disappointed, but there was a trail along a dike running northwest from the road, so this is where I hiked until the trail and dike stopped and I had to turn around. This was a day of perfect weather and other visitors were out in good numbers. I spoke with some fishermen who told me that they had actually seen a Florida panther along the dike. I was not so fortunate. In all, this was an excellent day in a very nice area and I recommend this wilderness and, indeed, the entire refuge to other hikers.

Little Lake George

★ ★ ★

Size: 2,833 acres **Year Designated:** 1984
Responsible Agency: USFS

The Little Lake George Wilderness is located in the Ocala National Forest on the western shore of Little Lake George, east of State Highway 19 and north of the town of Salt Springs. The Saint Johns River begins at the outlet of Little Lake George. There are no trails.

MY VISIT: March 23, 2009

I began this visit along the western wilderness boundary on Forest Road 74. I spied a very dim old path and began hiking east into the wilderness. This was a neat bit of forest, starting near the western edge with pine and palmetto, but then becoming palm, oak, gum, and cypress hardwood. Here it was wet, a swamp. Again, perhaps only because it was new, I found this an appealing place. I wandered almost at random until it started to rain when I turned around and, using my GPS, found my way back to my truck. A pleasant and pretty interesting place.

Marjory Stoneman Douglas

★ ★ ★

Size: 1,296,500 acres **Year Designated:** 1978
Responsible Agency: USNPS

Most of Everglades National Park is designated wilderness. The park occupies most of the southern tip of the Florida mainland south of US Highway 41, west of US Highway 1, and west of the town of Homestead. Marjory Stoneman Douglas was a conservationist and longtime supporter of preserving the Everglades in a natural state as opposed to their draining and development for housing and agriculture.

MY VISIT: March 27, 2009 and March 28, 2009

The terrain in this wilderness was not meant for hiking. Well, I am a hiker so I tried to do what I could. Both these day hikes began at or near the campground by the Flamingo Visitor Center. The first hike was to greater Bear Lake. My notes are almost silent on what I did or saw there. The second hike was to Clubhouse Beach via the Coastal Prairie Trail. Coastal prairie was one of the park's main ecosystems. Near the end of the trail I encountered the mangrove ecosystem. I did a little beachcombing and then just turned around.

Clearly, the visitor that really wants to see this park must use some sort of watercraft. I did not have such a craft, so was very limited in where I could go.

Two-Star Areas

WISCONSIN

Headwaters 6,583 acres, designated 1984, located in the Chequamegon-Nicolet National Forest west of State Highway 55, north of State Highway 32, and south of State Highway 70. The town of Eagle River is to the northwest. The wilderness is divided into three sections separated by USFS roads. The area contains the headwaters of the Pine River. On October 20, 2007 I did a short hike in each of the three wilderness units. The first unit visited was the Shelp Lake Unit and its two-mile-long Giant Pine Loop Trail, the only trail in the wilderness. The trail circled a bog and there were indeed some tall pine trees. It was hunting season and I saw two hunters and heard some shots. The second hike was in the Kimball Creek Unit. I hiked north from USFS Road 2182 through a bog to Kimball Creek itself. The third hike was in the Headwaters of the Pine Unit and I found a hint of an old logging road south from USFS Road 2182. I followed this until it disappeared. I needed my GPS to get back to my starting point.

Porcupine Lake 4,292 acres, designated 1984, located in the Chequamegon-Nicolet National Forest southeast of US Highway 63 and southeast of the town of Iron River. The North Country National Scenic Trail runs through the wilderness. This day hike on October 18, 2007 began in the rain at the eastern wilderness boundary at a trailhead for the North Country Trail. My route was west through bogs and past lakes and fairly dense forest including tamarack in full gold color. I thought the bogs were real because they had that springy sensation as I walked on them. The area was pretty, Porcupine Lake was pretty, but nothing outstanding or especially interesting. The not-so-great weather may have impacted my opinion.

Whisker Lake 7,428 acres, designated 1978, located in the Chequamegon-Nicolet National Forest south of US Highway 2, north of State High-way 70, and southeast of the town of Iron River, Michigan. This day hike on October 21, 2007 began at a trailhead off USFS Road 2150 at the western wilderness boundary. I made a loop that included Whisker Lake, Riley Lake, and Little Riley Lake. The forest was pretty much closed in except around the lakes. Much of the trail followed either an old railroad grade or road grade. The forest was mostly hardwood, but there were pines around Whisker Lake and Riley Lake. The weather was good early, then became heavily overcast. Once more a pleasant hike but with no features of particular interest.

Blackjack Springs 5,886 acres, designated 1978, located in the Chequamegon-Nicolet National Forest north of State Highway 70, east of US Highway 45, and northeast of the town of Eagle River. My day hike on October 19, 2007 began in steady rain at a trailhead in the northeast corner of the wilderness. This trail and, apparently, other trails led to Whispering Lake. This part of the hike was in dense forest except around Whispering Lake. I wanted to get to some small lakes near Blackjack Springs, but had a hard time finding a trail that went anywhere other than to Whispering Lake. Finally, I found a different trailhead whose trail took me to the other small lakes. The forest here was somewhat open, but still did not have any features of particular interest. I think I hiked every foot of trail here, every foot of it in rain.

Rainbow Lake 6,583 acres, designated 1975, located in the Chequamegon-Nicolet National Forest south of US Highway 2 and northwest of US Highway 63. The town of Iron River is to the northwest. The North Country National Scenic Trail runs through the wilderness. This day hike on October 17, 2007 began at a trailhead for the North Country Trail at the northwest corner of the wilderness. The trail ran southeast through mostly dense forest of birch, maple, and oak, very similar to other areas in Wisconsin. I went past Tower Lake, then Rainbow Lake, and finally Bofu Lake where a beaver was cruising about slapping his tail. The day was mostly gray with occasional rain.

Riley Lake, Whisker Lake Wilderness

MICHIGAN

Horseshoe Bay 3,790 acres, designated 1987, located in the Hiawatha National Forest on the western shore of Lake Huron, just east of Interstate Highway 75, and north of the town of Saint Ignace. This day hike on October 26, 2007 began at a trailhead near the Foley Creek Campground near the southern end of the wilderness. The trail wandered through dense forest to the shore of Lake Huron, then I continued north along the shore until I started running out of daylight (I got a late start). The forest was mostly cedar and hemlock with some pine and deciduous trees and shrubs. I must confess to having very little enthusiasm for this area, in part because of the ever-present noise from traffic on I-75, a not-very-inviting forest, and obvious buildings and human activity just south of the wilderness.

Mackinac 12,230 acres, designated 1987, located in the Hiawatha National Forest west of Interstate Highway 75, east of State Highway 123, and northwest of the town of Saint Ignace. The Horseshoe Bay Wilderness is nearby to the southeast. This day hike on October 27, 2007 began at a canoe put-in for the Carp River Canoe Trail. There was more or less of a foot trail parallel to the river. The trail followed an old roadbed through dense forest with beaver ponds and marshes, very closed in. After about 2.5 miles the trail crossed a northern branch of the Carp River. The trail might have

crossed, but I would not. The river was too wide and too deep for me. I tried to bushwhack up the northern branch, but was blocked by dense vegetation. Oh, and yes, this day was dark and gray with a light rain. I found this area to be neither pleasant nor interesting but will give it a second star anyway. I promise not to return.

VERMONT

Bristol Cliffs 3,738 acres, designated 1975, located in the Green Mountain National Forest east of State Highway 116, south of State Highway 17, and just southeast of the town of Bristol. There were no trails. This day hike on September 16, 2009 began late in the day at the far northeast corner of the wilderness where there was a parking area and what my White Mountain National Forest map called a Wilderness Entry Point. There were a couple of dim paths and the first one I took soon reached private property. The second was visible for probably less than one mile before it disappeared. I tried bushwhacking through pretty dense forest with lots of understory. I decided to turn around because I had no destination in mind and I did not find the surroundings either especially pleasant and certainly not interesting.

Big Branch 6,767 acres, designated 1984, located in the Green Mountain National Forest just east of US Highway 7 and northeast of the town of Manchester Center. The Peru Peak Wilderness is just to the east. The Appalachian Trail runs through the wilderness. This day hike on September 13, 2009 began at a parking area and trailhead for the AT in the northwest corner of the wilderness along USFS Road 10. I hiked south through dense forest to Baker Peak. There was an opening here with rocks and some views, but nothing of particular interest or scenic value.

Peru Peak 7,672 acres, designated 1984, located in the Green Mountain National Forest just east of the Big Branch Wilderness, east of US Highway 7 and northeast of the town of Manchester Center. The Appalachian Trail runs through the southern portion of the wilderness. My day hike on

September 14, 2009 began at a trailhead for the Appalachian Trail at Mad Tom Notch at the southern wilderness boundary. There was no sign of Mad Tom. I climbed north on the AT to Styles Peak (3,392 feet) where there was a view to the east, then continued down and back up to Peru Peak (3,429 feet) where there was no view. I continued north a bit, but no more views appeared so I turned around. I stopped for lunch back on the Peru Peak summit. I could hear voices. As the voices got closer, I heard a great crashing noise behind me. The voices had scared up a big bull moose that had not been disturbed by my quiet lunch. The moose crossed the trail just ahead of the other hikers. We had a good laugh. This being the AT I also saw some other hikers. I cannot call this an area of special interest.

George D. Aiken 5,060 acres, designated 1984, located in the Green Mountain National Forest south of State Highway 9, west of State Highway 8, and east of the town of Bennington. There were no trails. George D. Aiken was a governor of Vermont and a long-serving (thirty-four years) US senator from Vermont. He was a supporter of wilderness and was instrumental in obtaining wilderness status for areas in the eastern United States. At the time of my visit there was a USFS *Wilderness Times* map and brochure for this area. This not-very-long morning hike on September 16, 2009 began at the end of USFS Road 74. I decided to walk south-southwest toward where some ponds were shown on my map. The going was difficult through heavy undergrowth. I ended up in wetlands including beaver ponds, but I saw nothing of interest and decided to turn around and go back to my truck and look for a different hike for the afternoon (which turned out to be the Bristol Cliffs area described above).

Lye Brook 17,841 acres, designated 1975, located in the Green Mountain National Forest just east of US Highway 7 and south of the town of Manchester. At the time of my visit there was an issue of the USFS *Wilderness Times* dedicated to this area. My day hike on September 12, 2009 began at a parking area and trailhead for the Bourn Pond Trail. This was a dark, gray, and rainy day and everything underfoot was soggy. I hiked northeast to Bourn Pond, then west on the Lye Brook Trail. This trail was an old railroad grade back when the forest was logged in the early twentieth century. Like most of the eastern forests, Vermont was pretty much clear-cut to bare earth. The terrain was essentially flat and the forest dense with openings around ponds and wetlands. Somewhere I saw a reference to a waterfall off the Lye Brook Trail, but I ran out of daylight before I got there.

Glastonbury 22,425 acres, designated 2006, located in the Green Mountain National Forest just east of US Highway 7, north of State Highway 9, and east of the town of Bennington. This wilderness was designated as part of a 2006 New England wilderness bill that also designated the Joseph Battell Wilderness and added land to several other existing areas. The Appalachian Trail goes through the Glastonbury Wilderness. This day hike on September 15, 2009 began along State Highway 9 at a parking area and trailhead for the Appalachian Trail. I climbed steeply, then leveled off and made a slight drop to Hell Hollow Brook, then went to a spot with a view of Little Pond and then toward Little Pond Mountain. It looked like there would be no view from Little Pond Mountain, so I just turned around. The terrain on this hike was essentially identical to other Vermont AT segments that I hiked.

Joseph Battell 12,333 acres, designated 2006, located in the Green Mountain National Forest north of State Highway 73, south of State Highway 125, and northeast of the town of Brandon. The Long National Recreation Trail goes through the wilderness. Joseph Battell was a philanthropist and a supporter of preserving Vermont forests. This day hike on September 25, 2009 began along State Highway 73 at a parking area and trailhead for the Long Trail. I took a side trail to the Great Cliff. Hardly great, but OK. Then back to the Long Trail and to the summit of Mount Horrid (3,216 feet), then Gillespie Peak at 3,366 feet, then Romance Mountain at 3,125 feet, and down almost to Sucker Brook for lunch where I turned around. It was another day of hiking in dense forest with every mile looking like every other mile.

Paddy Creek 7,019 acres, designated 1983, located in the Mark Twain National Forest north of State Highway 32, west of US Highway 63, and southwest of the city of Rolla. At the time of my visit there was a USFS brochure for this wilderness including a map showing trails and trailheads. The wilderness was named after Sylvester Paddy, an early settler who ran a logging operation in what is now the wilderness. My day hike on October 18, 2005 began at a trailhead near the Paddy Creek Campground for the southern portion of the Big Piney Trail. I did not complete the loop, but did go along the southern portion of the trail for about 5.5 miles before turning around and retracing my steps. The terrain was closed-in forest of mostly oak and hickory with some short-leaf pine. There was some fall color, but the oaks were mostly still green. The map identified an area as a "scenic overlook," but there were only a few bluffs barely visible through the trees. I encountered a rather large group of backpackers, mostly young people, on a "rehabilitation" trip accompanied by State of Missouri adults.

Bell Mountain 9,027 acres, designated 1980, located in the Mark Twain National Forest south of State Highway 32, east of Highway A, and southwest of the town of Farmington. At the time of my visit there was a USFS brochure for this wilderness including a map showing trails and trailheads. This day hike on October 23, 2005 began at a trailhead along Highway A for the Ozark Trail at the western wilderness boundary. The trail went south to a junction where I took a trail to the east that made a loop along the Bell Mountain ridge, dropping into Joes Creek, then south and west back to the Ozark Trail. This area was more open than some, with granite outcrops and even some walking on granite slabs. I saw a few backpackers along the trail. There were some views, but on this cold, gray day I did not take any photos.

Rock Pile Mountain 4,069 acres, designated 1980, located in the Mark Twain National Forest west of US Highway 67, and south of the town of Farmington. At the time of my visit there was a USFS brochure for this wilderness including a map showing trails and trailheads. This day hike on October 24, 2005 began at a trailhead in the northeast corner of the wilderness. The trail led almost due south to the summit of Rock Pile Mountain (1,270 feet). There was indeed not a pile of rocks but an ancient stone circle made of modest-size granite boulders. The trail to the mountain was through mostly closed-in forest of oak, hickory, and pine. The area around the Rock Pile was relatively open and sort of pretty. I never saw anything offering a hint about just how "ancient" the circle was, whether it is thought to be decades or millennia.

Irish 16,227 acres, designated 1984, located in the Mark Twain National Forest north of US Highway 160, east of State Highway 19, and northwest of the town of Doniphan. At the time of my visit there was a USFS brochure for this wilderness including a map showing trails and trailheads. The wilderness name came from a community organized by a Catholic priest where Irish immigrants could find an escape from sinful St. Louis. His timing was

Cave, Irish Wilderness

bad. Shortly after the community was formed, the Civil War broke out and Missouri was plagued by raiding parties from both the Union and Confederate sides. When the war was over, the community had simply vanished. This community and the Irish Wilderness are mentioned in the novel *Enemy Women* by Paulette Jiles, which is about the Civil War in Missouri.

My day hike on October 22, 2005 began at a trailhead at the northeast corner of the wilderness for the White's Creek Trail. I did an out-and-back hike on the southern leg of the trail to the Eleven Point River, about fourteen miles round-trip. Almost the entire route was in dense forest with the only opening at the river. The only noteworthy feature was the White's Creek Cave. This was karst terrain with caves and sinkholes. The cave entrance was closed by a metal-bar gate to prevent human entry to avoid disturbing the endangered Indiana bat. I saw some other hikers and also several equestrians and deer.

Hercules Glades 12,314 acres, designated 1976, located in the Mark Twain National Forest north of US Highway 160, west of State Highway 125, and east of the country music mecca of Branson. At the time of my visit there was a USFS brochure for this wilderness including a map showing trails and trailheads. My notes for this hike are pretty thin. I think I started at a trailhead along the eastern wilderness boundary and hiked due west to Long Creek. I then climbed up on a long ridge, probably just above Long Creek to the south. I was hoping for some views, but there was not much to see. The terrain here was different from other hikes in the Mark Twain. Here the soil was rather thin, and instead of forest there was more prairie grass. I think these grassy openings are the "glades." There were some limestone cliffs and even some stretches of trail where I was hiking on bare limestone. My notes do tell me that this was a very gray and dark day, difficult for photos.

Piney Creek 8,112 acres, designated 1980, located in the Mark Twain National Forest north and west of State Highway 76 and west of the famous country music town of Branson. The Table Rock Reservoir is just east of the wilderness. At the time of my visit there was a USFS brochure for this wilderness including a map showing trails and trailheads. The area was extensively logged in the late nineteenth century, followed by farmers, some growing strawberries and tomatoes. Human activity declined after the 1930s and the last human residents were gone by 1960. This day hike on October 20, 2005 began at a trailhead at the northern wilderness boundary. The trail took me south to Piney Creek, dry on this day. I then went east on a trail that ended at an arm of Table Rock Reservoir where I turned around.

Devils Backbone 6,595 acres, designated 1980, located in the Mark Twain National Forest north of US Highway 160, east of State Highway 181, and west of the town of West Plains. At the time of my visit there was a USFS brochure for this wilderness including a map showing trails and trailheads. My day hike on October 19, 2005 began at an equestrian trailhead near the northeast corner of the wilderness. I took the Mary Hollow Trail south, then southwest to the Devils Backbone, a hogback limestone ridge. Fall colors were good along this mostly closed-in forest. This area also gets a mention in Paulette Jiles' novel *Enemy Women*. I saw exactly one other hiker. This was probably my favorite Missouri hike.

Limestone ledge,
Devils Backbone Wilderness

Bay Creek 2,866 acres, designated 1990, located in the Shawnee National Forest west of State Highway 145, southeast of US Highway 45, and south of the city of Harrisburg. The Burden Falls Wilderness is just to the north. At the time of my visit there was a USFS handout map of the wilderness. This day hike on October 26, 2005 began at a trailhead near the Teal Pond Campground along the western wilderness boundary. The trail wound almost aimlessly through closed-in forest, ultimately getting to Bay Creek. My recollection is that the trails here may have been old roads. After crossing Bay Creek, the trail wandered aimlessly on the eastern side.

Lusk Creek 6,838 acres, designated 1990, located in the Shawnee National Forest southeast of the Bay Creek Wilderness, east of State Highway 145, and south of the city of Harrisburg. My day hike on October 28, 2005 began at the western wilderness boundary. My intention was to hike east on the River-to-River Trail to the eastern boundary. Once in the wilderness, there were many side trails with no signs and I quickly got off-route. There were equestrians about and I asked them for directions, but their answers were as confused as the nest of trails. I gave up and just blundered about, ultimately finding the Saltpeter Cave and a nearby natural bridge. Eventually, I got tired of blundering around and went back to my truck. I did not find this area to be particularly rewarding.

Bald Knob 5,973 acres, designated 1990
Clear Springs 4,730 acres, designated 1990

I describe these two areas together because they are contiguous and I hiked both on the same day. These two areas are located in the Shawnee National Forest east of State Highway 3, west of State Highway 127, north of State Highway 146, and south of the city of Murphysboro. The western boundary of the Bald Knob Wilderness is the eastern boundary of the Clear Springs Wilderness. At the time of my visit there were USFS handouts with hard-to-read maps for these areas. The River-to-River Trail goes through both areas.

My notes are a bit sparse for these two areas that I visited on October 30, 2005. I know I started on the western boundary of Clear Springs Wilderness and went up to Inspiration Point where I had a good view of the Big Muddy River, some of the areas adjacent to the Mississippi River, and maybe just a glimpse of the Mississippi itself. I continued east and a bit south and crossed into the Bald Knob Wilderness. I think I walked to the eastern boundary of the Bald Knob before turning around. I encountered at least two other hikers and some equestrians.

Panther Den 821 acres, designated 1990
Crab Orchard 4,050 acres, designated 1976

As with the two areas described together above, I will do likewise for these two areas because they are contiguous and I hiked both on the same day. The southernmost part of the Crab Orchard National Wildlife Refuge is designated wilderness (managed by the USFWS). The two areas are east of US Highway 51, west of Interstate Highway 57, south of State Highway 13, and southeast of the city of Carbondale. My USFS Shawnee National Forest map showed a road accessing the southern boundary of the Panther Den (managed by the USFS), but a huge sign at that road announced that the road was private. As I sat contemplating my next move, the landowner came by and told me the only legal entry was through the Crab Orchard and told me how to find the parking area and trailhead. I followed his directions. I would have never found the trailhead without them.

My day hike on October 29, 2005 began at a trailhead for the River-to-River Trail along the Rocky Comfort Road. I went east into the Crab Orchard. As nearly as I could tell, the trail wound between the two areas. I did side trips up the two arms of Devils Kitchen Lake in the refuge. On my way back west, I ran into two backpackers and we discussed what we had seen. Apparently, I had just missed the Panther Den itself. Not the wilderness area, but the den with its supposedly well-known Fat Man's Squeeze.

INDIANA

Charles Deam 12,946 acres, designated 1982, located in the Hoosier National Forest north of US Highway 50, south of State Highway 46, just east of Highway 446, and southeast of the city of Bloomington. Much of the northern wilderness boundary is Monroe Lake. At the time of my visit there was a USFS handout for the wilderness with a map showing trails and trailheads. Charles Deam was the first state forester for Indiana. In the early twentieth century when Indiana had lost 93 percent of its forests to logging, Deam suggested that perhaps sustainable forestry might be a better way to go.

This day hike on October 29, 2009 began at a trailhead for the Grub Ridge Trail just off the Tower Ridge Road. The trail went northwest to a junction with the Peninsula Trail, which took me to the shore of Monroe Lake. The route was through closed-in hardwood forest almost devoid of color even at this late date. There was a surprising number of folks around, including a big group of kids and adults from a Bible camp and a few other day hikers. I saw nothing of interest here.

PENNSYLVANIA

Hickory Creek 8,663 acres, designated 1984, located in the Allegheny National Forest south of US Highway 6, east of US Highway 62, and southwest of the town of Warren. At the time of my visit there was a USFS handout including a map and driving directions for this wilderness. There is only one trail in this wilderness, the Hickory Creek Trail, with a trailhead near the Heart's Content Recreation Area. On September 27, 2009 I hiked this twelve-mile loop on a dark, gray, rainy day. The terrain was familiar from my childhood, gentle with some granite boulders and a mostly open forest of deciduous trees with a sprinkling of white pine and hemlock. There was some fall color. There were a few fern-filled meadows and some wetlands along creeks. There were also some ATV tracks in the mud. I saw one other hiker, someone who appeared completely out of place. He was soaked, bedraggled, and carrying lots of irrelevant stuff. He was out of water and I gave him most of mine.

KENTUCKY

Beaver Creek 4,753 acres, designated 1975, located in the Daniel Boone National Forest just about a mile south of the Cumberland River, west of Interstate Highway 75, east of US Highway 27, and west of the town of Corbin. For my visit on April 22, 2010 I only had a map of the southern Daniel Boone National Forest. The boundary of the wilderness area looked like an example of a fractal one would find in a mathematics book, tiny changes in direction at very small intervals. My only guess as how this came about was that the wilderness was tightly confined to small creek drainages.

My day hike began at a trailhead for the Three Forks of the Beaver Trail. The trail was fine for a short distance, but then turned into an impossible jumble of fallen trees left over from a severe ice storm (I had seen other damage driving through this part of Kentucky). I had to give up, go back to my truck, and go to a different trailhead, this for the Bowman Ridge Trail. This was an old road grade that descended to Beaver Creek, then ascended to another trailhead at Swain Ridge. Because of the peculiar wilderness boundaries almost all the trails were short. This being spring, there were some flowering trees, the dogwood past its peak and the redbud near peak. Spring can also bring out ticks, and I spent some time removing several from my skin and clothes.

Clifty 13,344 acres, designated 1985, located in the Daniel Boone National Forest north of State Highway 15, east of State Highway 715, and southeast of the city of Lexington. At the time of my visit there was a USFS brochure for the wilderness and the adjacent Red River Gorge that included a map showing trails and trailheads. My day hike on April 21, 2010 began at a trailhead for the Osborn Bend Loop Trail, listed on my map as seven miles plus two more along State Highway 715 to get back to my truck. As I drove to the trailhead I was impressed with the area's geology with arches and bridges and cliffs and the pretty Red River. Unfortunately, the terrain in the wilderness area was not as interesting as that outside it. This was very unusual in my wilderness hiking experience. Here again I was in closed-in hardwood forest with few interesting features. One thing that I did notice was the density of cigarette butts on the trail. Kentucky is a very tobacco-intensive state.

WEST VIRGINIA

Laurel Fork North 6,055 acres, designated 1983
Laurel Fork South 5,997 acres, designated 1983

These two wilderness areas are described together because they are separated only by a dirt road and because I hiked both on the same day. These areas are located in the Monongahela National Forest south of US Highway 33, north of US Highway 250, and southeast of the city of Elkins. At the time of my visit there was a USFS brochure for these areas including a map showing trails and trailheads. My day hike on May 21, 2008 began at a trailhead for the Laurel River Trail, which followed the river through both the north and south wilderness areas. I went first to the south. The day was gray, windy, and chilly and not good for photography. The terrain was nice if not spectacular. I haven't seen much bear scat on eastern wilderness trails, but there was some here today. What was most noteworthy, though, was the number and variety of birds. It was one of my best birding days in recent years. I must have been close to a nest as the bird was scolding and escorting me out of its territory. One other nice sight was old apple trees in bloom. This area had seen a lot of human activity in the past. Once back at the trailhead I headed into the northern wilderness. This part of the hike did not go very far. The trail forded the creek and, due to recent rains, I was not willing to attempt the ford.

Spice Run 6,030 acres, designated 2009, located in the Monongahela National Forest east of US Highway 219, west of State Highway 92, and north of the town of White Sulfur Spring. At the time of my visit there was a USFS handout page showing the boundaries of this newly designated wilderness.

The Greenbrier River forms part of the western wilderness boundary. There were no trails. This day hike on May 7, 2010 began along a dirt road that ran past the eastern wilderness boundary. One article I had seen on this area claimed it was the wildest and most difficult to get to of all the West Virginia wilderness areas. That was probably correct. I parked by a USFS sign announcing the newly designated area. Not knowing much about the area, I just hiked a westerly compass bearing and blundered around roughly following Spice Run itself. Much of the area around the creek was pine with traditional hardwoods on the hillsides. I soon found what was almost certainly an old road and the walking got easier. There were occasional openings, probably human created, and some apple trees in bloom. I followed the road until it disappeared, then a bit farther until I was maybe two miles from my truck when I turned around. I saw an old survey marker from 1920. The terrain here was not especially interesting and similar to what I had already seen in West Virginia.

The interesting part of this day occurred after I got back to my truck. As I fiddled with my gear, a no-longer-young man pulled up in his no-longer-young pickup truck, saw my license plate, and stopped. He got out and introduced himself. He had spent his life close to here. He spoke of relatives and other local folks, living and dead, and rummaged in a toolbox and came out with a photo album. He was on his way down the road to a nearby hunting camp he owned. He wanted to show it to me, so off we went in his truck, with a hunting rifle between us. He showed me ginseng growing wild and a huge, ancient oak tree and more apple trees in a very nice setting. Here was a man who had a close, personal relationship to this place. It was part of him and he was part of it. For me it was a fascinating, rewarding meeting.

Otter Creek 20,698 acres, designated 1975, located in the Monongahela National Forest north of US Highway 33, southwest of State Highway 72, and east of the city of Elkins. At the time of my visit there was a USFS brochure that included a map showing trails and trailheads. According to the brochure, the first logging here was by the Otter Creek Boom and Lumber

Company (a great name) from 1897 to 1917. Homesteading also occurred in these years. More logging occurred between 1968 and 1972. So the forest one sees here today is third generation, now finally protected.

My day hike on May 20, 2008 started with a whimper. I found the Condon Run Trailhead at the southern wilderness boundary, but before I could start hiking it began to pour rain. I hung out in the truck until it slowed, then started hiking up the Otter Creek Trail. It remained an ugly day with a cold rain and wind. The trail was an old road and very sloppy. I crossed Yellow Creek and went farther north through completely closed-in forest of mixed hardwoods, hemlock, and rhododendron. No, I was not having fun, so I turned around. It may not be wise to make judgments about an area on a cold, rainy day, but I did not see anything interesting or scenic here.

VIRGINIA

Peters Mountain 4,531 acres, designated 1984, located in the Jefferson National Forest just south of the West Virginia state line, south of US Highway 219, north of US Highway 460, and northeast of the town of Pearisburg. For my visit I used the National Geographic Trails Illustrated map 787, Blacksburg New River Valley. The Appalachian Trail runs through the area. The Mountain Lake Wilderness is to the east. This half-day hike on May 24, 2008 began at a trailhead for the AT off USFS Road 734 at the southern wilderness boundary. I hiked the AT north to the northern wilderness boundary (a little over two miles and at the West Virginia state line) and turned around. The trail was busy with other hikers. The terrain was standard Virginia hardwoods and there were some blooming azalea and rhododendron, but nothing to distinguish this area from any of the others nearby.

Little Dry Run 2,858 acres, designated 1984, located in the Mount Rodgers National Recreation Area within the Jefferson National Forest, south of Interstate Highway 81, west of US Highway 21, and southwest of the town of Wytheville. For my visit I used the National Geographic Trails Illustrated map 786, Mount Rogers. There is only one trail in this area, the Little Dry Run Trail, and I hiked it twice, once from the southeast boundary to the southwestern boundary, then the reverse. It was a nice weather day and there were blooming azalea and rhododendron, and I was able to identify a spectacular hooded warbler. There were also three equestrians. Otherwise, nothing to distinguish this area from any of the numerous other areas in this part of Virginia.

Shawvers Run 5,686 acres, designated 1988, located in the Jefferson National Forest south of State Highway 18, north of State Highway 311, and north of the town of New Castle. At the time of my visit this area was shown on the National Geographic Trails Illustrated map 788, Covington Allegheny Highlands. This wilderness had only one trail and I hiked all 0.7 mile of it on April 27, 2010. The hike began at a trailhead for the Hanging Rock Trail in the southeast corner of the wilderness. It was a gray, chilly, windy day and the trail ran along a ridgetop through gnarled oak trees ending at Hanging Rock, a bare rock outcrop with a fine view of the rest of the wilderness to the north. It was a pretty nice spot by Appalachian standards.

Beartown 5,609 acres, designated 1984, located in the Jefferson National Forest north of State Highway 42, south of State Highway 61, southwest of the town of Bluefield, and northwest of the town of Wytheville. The Garden Mountain and Hunting Camp Creek Wilderness areas are to the east. There was a USFS brochure for this area and it is also shown on the National Geographic Trails Illustrated map 787, Blacksburg New River Valley. The closest trail access, according to my map, was from USFS Road 631. This road was in poor condition and I elected to park and walk to the trailhead. This trail was the Roaring Fork Trail and it began at the southern wilderness boundary. It was the only trail in the wilderness. The trail descended to Roaring Fork Creek. On my way down, I met three fishermen coming up. (My map showed a little fish symbol at Roaring Fork.) They assured me that the area was full of bears, although I did not see any. The trail ended about 2.5 miles from the official trailhead (my trip was longer). The creek and its surroundings were pretty. The area overall, however, suffers from the problem that it looks like all the other areas I have visited in this part of Virginia. I did this day hike on May 27, 2008.

Kimberling Creek 5,805 acres, designated 1984, located in the Jefferson National Forest east of Interstate Highway 77, north of State Highway 42, and southeast of the town of Bluefield. There was a USFS brochure for this wilderness and it was also shown on National Geographic Trails Illustrated map 787, Blacksburg New River Valley. There were no trails. My day hike on May 30, 2008 began at a USFS road that ran along the southwest wilderness boundary. My nominal goal was to reach Kimberling Springs. The hiking was very difficult due to the density of forest (the usual mix of hardwoods and pine) and understory (mostly rhododendron, dogwood, and laurel), deadfall, and steep terrain. I made multiple sorties into the forest, including trying to follow streams, with no success at finding the springs. At the end of the day, I saw nothing interesting here and I do not recommend the area to other hikers.

Raccoon Branch 4,223 acres, designated 2009, located in the Jefferson National Forest west of state Highway 16, south of Interstate Highway 81, and south of the town of Marion. The Lewis Fork and Little Wilson Creek Wilderness areas are to the south. For my visit I relied on the National Geographic Trails Illustrated map 786, Mount Rogers, plus a USFS person showing me on my map where the new wilderness area boundaries were. The Appalachian Trail goes through the wilderness. My day hike on April 23, 2010 began in light rain at a trailhead for the Virginia Highlands Trail at the Raccoon Branch Campground off State Highway 16. I took this trail west to Bobby's Trail, then to the AT. There I took the AT north (compass direction) to the Timpi Shelter where I turned around. The terrain was typical for this part of Virginia: pine, hardwood, and rhododendron down low, then mostly hardwood on the ridges. Spring was late along the ridges, almost wintry looking. My return trip was mostly in sun.

Garden Mountain 3,291 acres, designated 2009, located in the Jefferson National Forest northwest of State Highway 42, west of Interstate Highway 77, and northwest of the town of Wytheville. The Appalachian Trail runs along the northern wilderness boundary. This was a frustrating day in which I wasted time and gasoline trying to find what my map said was a trail going through this newly designated wilderness (my idea of the wilderness boundary came from the wilderness.net website). I never did find the elusive Lick Creek Trail. Instead, I found an obscure closed road off State Road 623 going west. I parked and followed this old road into what I believed to be the wilderness. I was somewhere north of Lick Creek and south of the AT. The old road became a trail that I eventually lost. This was standard Virginia forest of hardwood and a few pines and a lot of rhododendron and laurel thickets. After I left the trail, the going was very slow in these thickets. Fortunately, I had my GPS to get me back to my truck. I did this hike on April 24, 2010.

Brush Mountain 4,794 acres, designated 2009, located in the Jefferson National Forest south of State Highway 42, north of State Route 624, and northeast of the city of Blacksburg. The Brush Mountain East Wilderness is, well, just to the east. There were no trails. I did my day hike on April 26, 2010. I was relying on my National Geographic Trails Illustrated map 787, Blacksburg New River Valley, even though it did not show the wilderness boundaries. I had made pencil marks based on a map on the wilderness. net website. My day hike began on USFS Road 114 along what I believed to be the southern wilderness boundary. There were several signs noting wilderness and private property boundaries. I made a few sorties into the wilderness where hiking was difficult in steep, trailless terrain. I saw nothing of interest or to distinguish this area from others nearby. Hikers would do better visiting the Brush Mountain East Wilderness.

Barbour's Creek 5,382 acres, designated 1988, located in the George Washington National Forest north of State Highway 311, south of State Highway 18 and north of the town of New Castle. For my visit I used the National

Geographic Trails Illustrated map Covington Allegheny Highlands. There was only one trail in this wilderness, the Lipes Trail, and I hiked it twice, southeast to northwest and then the reverse. The trailhead was near the USFS Pines Campground. The trail climbed northwest through dense forest of hardwood and pine with thick understory to the summit ridge of Potts Mountain, which was the northern wilderness boundary. Just outside the wilderness was an old orchard in full bloom. I did this day hike on April 27, 2010.

Rich Hole 6,450 acres, designated 1988, located in the George Washington National Forest northwest of US Highway 60 and Interstate Highway 64 and northeast of the town of Clifton Forge. The Rough Mountain Wilderness is a few miles to the northwest. At the time of my visit I used the National Geographic Trails Illustrated map 788, Covington Allegheny Highlands. This day hike on April 28, 2010 began at a trailhead along the southeastern wilderness boundary just off US Highway 60 (also State Highway 850 according to my map). The trail, the only trail in the wilderness, climbed steeply to the north to a saddle. Standing in the saddle were two black bears, glossy in the sunshine. They were most likely a mother with a yearling cub. They watched me for a bit, then disappeared. There was a lot of traffic noise from the nearby I-64. I continued descending on the trail first to the north, then to the southwest, until I was about halfway to the southwestern end of the trail. I turned around there and went back to my truck. This was standard Virginia hardwood forest, looking pretty much like all the other areas in the neighborhood, with the exception of the bears.

Thunder Ridge 2,344 acres, designated 1984, located in the Jefferson National Forest. The Blue Ridge Parkway runs along the eastern and southern wilderness boundaries. The James River Face Wilderness is just to the north. The closest town is Glasgow to the north. The Appalachian Trail goes through the area. For my visit I used the National Geographic Trails Illustrated map 789, Lexington Blue Ridge Mountains. My day hike on April 30, 2010 began along the Blue Ridge Parkway at Petites Gap. I took the AT south a few miles until it came back to the Blue Ridge Park-

way where I turned around. There was lots of traffic noise. While there was little of scenic or other interest, the birding was good. I saw several Tennessee warblers, a female worm-eating warbler at her ground nest, and an American redstart.

Priest 5,963 acres, designated 2000, located in the George Washington National Forest south and west of State Highway 56 and southwest of the town of Waynesboro. The Appalachian Trail runs through the area. For my visit I used the National Geographic Trails Illustrated map 789, Lexington Blue Ridge Mountains. This day hike on May 2, 2010 began at a parking area and trailhead for the AT in the northeastern corner of the wilderness. This day's weather conditions were one reason I moved to the western United States; it was hot and humid with biting flies being a nuisance. The AT here required a major climb to a pretty nice ridge with views to the west. I hiked the entire length of the AT in this wilderness, making this something of a long day. There were quite a few other hikers, this being a Sunday and the AT.

Three Ridges 4,606 acres, designated 2000, located in the George Washington National Forest southeast of the Blue Ridge Parkway, northeast of State Highway 56, and southwest of the town of Waynesboro. The Appalachian Trail goes through the area. For my visit I used the National Geographic Trails Illustrated map 789, Lexington Blue Ridge Mountains. My day hike on May 3, 2010 began at a parking area and trailhead for the AT. I hiked about 1.6 miles to the northern wilderness boundary, then south on the AT over Bee Mountain (3,034 feet), and then to the base of Three Ridges Mountain where I turned around. My notes tell me that I thought that this might be my last day on the AT and that I would not miss it.

OKLAHOMA

Upper Kiamichi River 9,754 acres, designated 1988, located in the Ouachita National Forest just west of the Arkansas state line. I know, I have put Oklahoma in with the Great Plains, but this wilderness is not part of any grasslands. It is an extension of the eastern forests of Arkansas. The Oklahoma portion of the Black Fork Mountain Wilderness is just to the north. Oklahoma State Highway 1 runs along the northern wilderness boundary and State Highway 63 is to the south. The closest major town is Mena, Arkansas. My day hike on October 26, 2004 began at the northeastern corner of the wilderness at a trailhead for the Ouachita National Recreation Trail. I hiked this trail west and a bit south to the southern wilderness boundary and then turned around. The trail followed the Kiamichi River, which was dry on this day. The terrain was standard Arkansas hardwood forest with some pine and an understory of various shrubs.

ARKANSAS

Caney Creek 14,460 acres, designated 1975, located in the Ouachita National Forest north of State Highway 246, south of State Highway 375, and southeast of the town of Mena. My day hike on October 28, 2004 began at the East Caney Creek Trailhead. I made the Caney Creek-Buckeye loop. The previous day had seen heavy rain and creeks were high. My boots were already wet, so I just made creek crossings in my boots. I took no photos because my camera did not work, probably because it got wet the previous day. The hike was pleasant but without anything particularly interesting, standard Arkansas terrain with mostly hardwood forest with some pine and undergrowth. I did see a red-bellied woodpecker and a lot of ticks. I probably removed fifty ticks from my clothes, but none made it to my skin.

Poteau Mountain 11,299 acres, designated 1984, located in the Ouachita National Forest north of State Highway 28, south of State Highway 378, and northwest of the town of Waldron. The wilderness is in two sections, east and west, separated by about three miles. USFS Road 158 runs along the southern wilderness boundaries of both sections. There were no trails. My day hike was on October 29, 2004 and my notes on this day are very sparse. I am not even certain which wilderness section I hiked, al-

though I think it was the western. I began where a very old logging road took off from USFS Road 158. I followed this old road about three miles before it disappeared. My only recollection of this hike is that the terrain was indistinguishable from most other Arkansas areas with no particularly interesting features. If I took any photos, none survive.

Dry Creek 6,310 acres, designated 1984, located in the Ouachita National Forest north of State Highway 80, south of State Highway 10, and southeast of the town of Booneville. There were no trails shown on the Ouachita National Forest map, but the wilderness.net website said there was a trail. I did my day hike on October 30, 2004. My notes from this hike are sparse, but clear enough that I know I did not hike on any trail. My notes do say that I started at Harvey Cemetery (probably off USFS Road 51) on a very dim old road that soon disappeared. I then hiked a compass bearing to Dry Creek where I hiked the creek upstream until I got tired of fighting the deadfall and brush and used my GPS to get me back out. I saw nothing of interest here.

Flatside 9,507 acres, designated 1984, located in the Ouachita National Forest east of State highway 7, south of State Highway 60, and southwest of the town of Perryville. The Ouachita National Recreation Trail runs through the area. My only map was for the whole Ouachita National Forest. Again, my notes are very sparse for this hike on October 31, 2004, although they do tell me that I started on the southern wilderness boundary, which means I hiked the Ouachita National Scenic Trail, probably to the east, staying close to the road for a considerable way. I have no recollection of this hike other than the day was gray and foggy and all the creeks were running high because of recent rains. It is also my recollection that this area was indistinguishable from others in Arkansas.

East Fork 10,688 acres, designated 1984, located in the Ozark-St. Francis National Forest north of Interstate Highway 40, west of US Highway 65, east of State Highway 27, and northeast of the town of Russellville. I did this day hike on a very rainy November 1, 2004. I drove to a trailhead on the western wilderness boundary off State Highway 27 and sat in my truck until the downpour slowed. I began hiking on an old road grade along a ridge for a couple of miles, then descended to the East Fork of the Illinois Bayou (hence the name of the wilderness). This stream was raging. The route crossed the stream, but there was no way I was going into that water. I wandered around somewhat aimlessly but was not able to continue on the route, so I just turned around and went back to my truck. The forest here was pretty much like the forests farther south, oak and hickory with an understory of maple, dogwood, redbud, and sumac.

Hurricane Creek 15,307 acres, designated 1984, located in the Ozark-St. Francis National Forest west of State Highway 7, north of State Highway 123, and north of the town of Russellville. For my visit I used a USFS map and a brochure dedicated to this wilderness. The Ozark Highlands National Recreation Trail runs through the area. My day hike on November 2, 2004 began at a trailhead for the Ozark National Recreation Trail at the southwest corner of the wilderness. This day was dark and overcast, but at least not raining. The streams, however, were still raging and very high. The Ozark Trail had two routes: one for low Hurricane Creek water and one for high water. I took the high-water route, which allowed me to take a side trip to the Wheeler Cemetery with gravestones dating back to the 1880s. Much of the trail here was on an old road grade. This wilderness and the East Fork Wilderness had human occupation in the past and old homesites remained. By taking the high-water route I missed a natural bridge shown on the map. This was a pleasant area, but the most interesting feature was the cemetery. If I took any photos, none survive.

Leatherwood 16,838 acres, designated 1984, located in the Ozark-St. Francis National Forest north of State Highway 14, west of State Highway 341, and south of the town of Mountain Home. For my visit I used a USFS map and brochure dedicated to this wilderness. The western wilderness border is the eastern border of the Lower Buffalo Wilderness, managed by the USNPS as part of the Buffalo National River. The name of the wilderness is the name of a shrub found in the Ozarks.

My day hike on November 4, 2004 began at a parking area off State Highway 341 at the eastern wilderness boundary. My route followed an old road grade west to the boundary with the Buffalo National River and a view of the river. The route ran through some private property inholdings including what appeared to be an abandoned farm. The day was dark with heavy overcast and if I took any photos, none survive. My recommendation to hikers is that better opportunities are to be found in the Buffalo National River.

TENNESSEE

Sampson Mountain 7,991 acres, designated 1986, located in the Cherokee National Forest west of Interstate Highway 26, south of State Highway 107, and west of the town of Erwin. For my hike I used the National Geographic Trails Illustrated map 782, Cherokee and Pisgah National Forests. My day hike on October 11, 2006 began at a trailhead at the extreme western wilderness boundary in the Horse Creek Recreation Area. There was a sign that told me I would not see many trail signs here because it was, after all, a wilderness. My intention was to take a loop trail, but I could not find the first turn in the loop, so I just hiked the Squibb Creek Trail first along the creek and then along the Middle Spring Ridge until I got to the southern wilderness boundary where I turned around. This was a classic southern Appalachian dense hardwood forest. I saw no other humans and nothing of interest.

Big Laurel Branch 6,332 acres, designated 1986, located in the Cherokee National Forest north of US Highway 321, southeast of State Highway 91, and east of the town of Elizabethton. For my hike I used the National Geographic Trails Illustrated map 783, Cherokee and Pisgah National Forests. The Appalachian Trail runs through the wilderness. This day hike on October 12, 2006 began at a trailhead for the AT off Lookout Road. I hiked the AT north for at least five miles before turning around. This was a true ridge walk. The autumn color was good and there was some exposed granite. I saw only two other hikers. This was classic southern Appalachian hardwood forest and I had my classic Appalachian reaction of "Didn't I just do this hike yesterday?"

Unaka Mountain 4,496 acres, designated 1986, located in the Cherokee National Forest south and west of State Highway 107, east of State Highway 395, and east of the town of Erwin. The Appalachian Trail runs along some of the southwestern wilderness boundary. My day hike on October 14, 2006 began at the Rock Creek Recreation Area at a trailhead for the Rattlesnake Trail. I hiked this trail from the northwestern wilderness boundary to the southeastern wilderness boundary in only a few miles. I saw two other hikers on the trail, but saw nothing of interest. It was a nice weather day and I did get a good photo of the high Smokies in their autumn color.

Bald River Gorge 3,721 acres, designated 1984, located in the Cherokee National Forest south and west of State Highway 165, east of State Highway 68, and southeast of the town of Tellico Plains. For this area I used the National Geographic Trails Illustrated map 781, Cherokee National Forest. My day hike on October 16, 2006 began at a trailhead for the Bald River Trail off USFS Road 210. The trailhead was at the northern wilderness boundary and the trail followed the river for 5.6 miles south to the southern wilderness boundary. I hiked this whole route both ways. It was a dark, gray, drippy day. The river was pretty and there were falls along the way. As I hiked the trail, I speculated that the trail was an old railroad grade as it was elevated above its surroundings. This area closely resembled all the other nearby areas.

NORTH CAROLINA

Linville Gorge 11,786 acres, designated 1964, located in the Pisgah National Forest east of US Highway 221, south of the Blue Ridge Highway, and south of the town of Linville. The Linville River runs the length of the wilderness. Pisgah was the name of the mountain from whose summit Moses could see the Promised Land. This day, October 27, 2006, was spent hiking in the rain. I began at a trailhead for the Spence Ridge Trail. There were lots of vehicles at the trailhead, surprising to me since the road getting here was bad. My guess was that it was bear hunting season. There were signs at the trailhead requesting that people not pick up dogs (used for bear hunting), not mess with their radio collars (!), and wear a red hat. I complied with all three requests.

The forest was pleasant with lots of fall color. The trail dropped to the river and then crossed on a bridge. The gorge was certainly steep and the river scenic with water cascading over large boulders. The heavy cloud cover prevented seeing very far and the steady rain limited photo opportunities. I might be judging this area unfairly with a two-star rating, but I thought it appropriate at the time. Maybe it was the rain.

Birkhead Mountains 5,025 acres, designated 1984, located in the Uwharrie National Forest west of US Highway 220, south of State Highway 49, and southwest of the city of Asheboro. My day hike on October 28, 2006 began near the western wilderness boundary at a trailhead for the Robbins Branch Trail. There were lots of other vehicles at the trailhead and there were hunters. They said they were after squirrels. I wore my orange hat. The trail went a little more than three miles to the northeast to the Birkhead Mountain Trail, which continued north along Coolers Knob Mountain to the northern wilderness boundary. I turned around before getting to the boundary. The terrain was rather level, this being east of the more mountainous country. Otherwise standard eastern hardwood forest with little of interest.

Southern Nantahala 23,473 acres, designated 1984, located in the Chattahoochee and Nantahala National Forests in North Carolina and Georgia. Here I include the area with North Carolina because my hike was in the North Carolina portion. The area is south and east of US Highway 64, west of US Highway 23, north of US Highway 76, and southwest of the town of Franklin. For my hike on October 26, 2006 I used a USFS map dedicated to the Southern Nantahala Wilderness and the Standing Indian Basin. The Appalachian Trail runs through the area. My day hike began at Deep Gap in a parking area and trailhead for the AT. I took the AT north (compass southeast) to Coleman Gap (about six miles) where I turned around. The route went over Standing Indian Mountain (5,499 feet) with good views, and through Beech Gap. The forest was standard southern Appalachian with good fall color. It was a nice day and a nice route. The only drawback was the usual this-looks-like-all-the-other-areas complaint.

Pocosin 11,709 acres, designated 1984, located in the Croatan National Forest west of US Highway 70, north of State Highway 24, east of State Highway 58, and west of the town of Moorhead City. According to a USFS handout, the term *pocosin* comes from a Native American word for "swamp on a hill." Another term is "raised bog." As is normal for bogs, the area is spongy and saturated with water around slowly decaying vegetation. It has low oxygen content so plant diversity is small and growth rates are slow. This has implications for hikers. One type of plant one finds is vines, especially greenbrier.

There were no trails in this area. That is somewhat of an understatement. In fact, it was almost impossible to move about on foot in this wilderness. My first attempt, on April 7, 2009, was along USFS Road 617 near the southwestern wilderness boundary. After blundering around for a while, I saw a dim path into the very dense vegetation. It was all muck (a USFS term) underfoot. It was not physically possible to deviate from this tiny path. Progress was painfully slow. I did see pitcher plants and even some orchids. The terrain was absolutely flat. One reason the vegetation was so impenetrable was that it was stitched together by the very thorny greenbrier. I have no idea how far I went, but it was not far before being forced to give up. I made a second attempt to enter the wilderness along the northwest boundary, but this was worse than the previous spot. For a third attempt I drove to the northern wilderness boundary along a railroad track. There was sort of a path, but it was parallel to the track and probably not in the wilderness. At this point I gave up. I do not recommend this area to hikers. Botanists, maybe. Hikers, no.

Big Slough 3,455 acres, designated 1984, located in the Davy Crockett National Forest southeast of State Highway 21, north of State Highway 7, and north of the town of Ratcliff. The Neches River runs along the eastern wilderness boundary. My morning of February 16, 2007 began in a USFS campground with a temperature of 19 degrees F, probably not a normal morning for southeast Texas. The day remained very much on the cool side. My day hike began at a trailhead off USFS Road 517 along the western wilderness boundary. The trail was the Four C National Recreation Trail (no, I don't know what Four C represents). My route was south on a real, maintained trail to the southern wilderness boundary where I turned around. This was not a long hike, so I went a bit farther north and took a different trail to the Big Slough itself. This was a new terrain type to me. I felt no attraction to this area and do not intend to return.

Little Lake Creek 3,855 acres, designated 1984, located in the Sam Houston National Forest west and south of Farm to Market Road 149 and southwest of the town of Huntsville. This was a beautiful, crisp, clear day and lots of folks were set to do some outside activities, especially an enthusiastic group of Girl Scouts getting ready for a backpacking trip. My day hike on February 17, 2007 began at a trailhead in the northwest corner of the wilderness. I went south and then east on the Lone Star Hiking Trail, exiting the wilderness on its eastern boundary, then north and west back into the wilderness making a loop. I have no recollection of what the terrain was like and there are no surviving photos. The terrain was flat with, if I remember, mixed coniferous and deciduous forest. I do remember having no desire to return.

LOUISIANA

Kisatchie Hills 8,679 acres, designated 1980, located in the Kisatchie National Forest (and the Kisatchie Ranger District) southwest of Interstate Highway 49, west of State Highway 119, and south of the city of Natchitoches. I used a USFS handout map showing the wilderness trails. My day hike on February 22, 2007 began at a trailhead for the Backbone Trail at the western wilderness boundary. I went east to a junction with another trail heading south, then went back west to the Longleaf Trail Scenic Byway (a road) and made a loop by walking back along the road. The terrain was a mix of hardwood and longleaf pine, pleasant but not very interesting. I did get to see my first pine warbler. After my hike I wandered around the old part of Natchitoches, which was more interesting than the wilderness.

MISSISSIPPI

Leaf 994 acres, designated 1984, located in the De Soto National Forest southwest of US Highway 98, north of State Highway 26, and south of the town of McLain. The wilderness lies in the floodplain of the Leaf River. This was a rather short visit. The area was officially closed because of damage from Hurricane Katrina. On March 17, 2009 I found an old trailhead off State Highway 57 where a dim trail led to an old signboard buried in storm debris. A writeup of this area said there was a 1.5-mile boardwalk through the wilderness, but there was no sign of any boardwalk. I began to wander about in the shallow water of this forested floodplain, seeing lots of oak, cypress, gum, and some pine, but the storm damage was severe and walking was difficult. I turned around, admitting defeat. This could be an interesting hike in better conditions.

ALABAMA

Dugger Mountain 9,200 acres, designated 1999, located in the Talladega National Forest east of State Highway 9, north of Forest Road 55, and southeast of the town of Piedmont. After a previous night's tornado excitement, the next day dawned gray and chilly and on April 11, 2009 I began a day hike on the Pinhoti Trail again, but this time the starting point was the Pink E. Burns Trailhead. I hiked north a few miles along a ridge with occasional rock outcrops, almost identical to the previous day. At some point I decided I had seen what this neighborhood had to offer and I turned around. My notes say that I took no photos. Still, this was a pleasant place and I think many hikers might enjoy it.

GEORGIA

Cohutta 6,977 acres, designated 1975, located in the Chattahoochee National Forest east of US Highway 411, north of State Highway 52, just south of the Tennessee state line, and west of the town of Blue Ridge. The southern boundary of the Big Frog Wilderness in Tennessee is the northern boundary of the Cohutta. My day hike on October 20, 2006 began at a trailhead at Dally Gap on the eastern wilderness boundary. This was a ridge hike by design because recent heavy rains had made creek and river crossings difficult. It was a gray day with a fair bit of mist along the ridges. My route was north into Tennessee and the Lick Log Trail where I had halted on a previous hike. Here I just turned around. I met three backpackers and a hunter on this day. The whole hike was in forest, standard southern Appalachian hardwood with some pine. While certainly pleasant, this day had no especially interesting or scenic features.

Brasstown 12,896 acres, designated 1986, located in the Chattahoochee National Forest southeast of US Highway 76, northwest of State Highway 180, and east of the town of Blairsville. My day hike on October 21, 2006 began at the Trackrock Gap Trailhead for the Arkaquah Trail near the western wilderness boundary. It was a day of beautiful weather, a Saturday; the fall colors were good and people were out in force. The trail climbed out of the gap heading east to Brasstown Bald, the highest point in Georgia. There were lots of other folks on the trail (5.5 miles one-way): a dozen day hikers, four backpackers, and one trail runner. I had intended to go up the tower that marks the high point, but when I got to the parking area there was an ant parade of people heading to the tower, so I just turned around and went back down. Nice enough place, but just like all the other Georgia areas.

Raven Cliffs 9,115 acres, designated 1986, located in the Chattahoochee National Forest southeast of State Highway 348, east of US Highway 19/129, and southeast of the town of Blairsville. The Appalachian Trail runs through the area. My day hike on October 22, 2006 began at a trailhead for the AT in Neels Gap on US Highway 19/129. I took the AT north (compass east) on a ridge route. It was another nice day with good fall color, and lots of people were out. The sound of Harleys charging up and down the highway lingered a long time. I went close to the eastern wilderness boundary where there were some views of what I thought were the Raven Cliffs and turned around. Another nice enough area indistinguishable from other nearby areas.

Blood Mountain 7,800 acres, designated 1991, located in the Chattahoochee National Forest just west of US Highway 19/129, south of State Highway 180, and south of the town of Blairsville. The Raven Cliffs Wilderness is to the east. The Appalachian Trail runs through the wilderness. Like the preceding day, my day hike on October 23, 2006 began at a trailhead for the AT in Neels Gap on US Highway 19/129. This day I took the AT south (compass west) on a ridge route. The trail climbed steeply to the summit of Blood Mountain where there were good views on a windy, chilly day with sun early, then clouds. After Blood Mountain, the AT turned southwest and I followed it through uninteresting hardwood forest terrain to Woody Gap where I turned around.

Mark Trail 16,400 acres, designated 1991, located in the Chattahoochee National Forest east of State Highway 180, south of State Highway 66, and southeast of the town of Blairsville. The Appalachian Trail runs through the wilderness. My old Chattahoochee National Forest map did not show the boundaries of this "recently" designated wilderness, but I had spoken with some locals who told me where it was and where the AT went through it. My hike on October 24, 2006 began at Jacks Gap at a trailhead for the AT. I did not go very far before encountering six members of an "old folks" hikers' group who invited me to accompany them on their outing. I accepted their invita-tion and we followed the AT south as far as a shelter at Low Gap. I learned quite a bit about the mountains of Georgia and their plants. One thing I learned was that chestnut trees are still around and they pointed one out to me. The blight that virtually wiped them out still allows some new trees to get started, but they never mature. I turned around at Low Gap, but cannot remember whether or not the group accompanied me.

Tray Mountain 9,702 acres, designated 1986, located in the Chattahoochee National Forest south of US Highway 76, east of State Highway 17/75, north of State Highway 356, and southeast of the town of Hiawassee. The Appalachian Trail runs through the area. My day hike on October 25, 2006 began at a trailhead at Tray Gap at the western wilderness boundary. I took the AT north over the summit of Tray Mountain to Addis Gap on the northern wilderness boundary. It was a nice, sunny if chilly day for a stroll through standard Georgia mountain forest with lots of old, gnarled oak trees.

SOUTH CAROLINA

Wambaw Swamp 4,815 acres, designated 1980, located in the Francis Marion National Forest east of State Highway 96 S, and north of State Highway 133 S, and northwest of the town of McClellanville. The Little Wambaw Swamp Wilderness is just to the southeast and the Wambaw Creek Wilderness is to the northeast. There were no trails. This area was very easy to find on April 1, 2009, with considerable road frontage. I basically circumnavigated the wilderness without finding any inviting entry point, so I stopped at an uninviting spot along the northeast wilderness boundary. This place was utterly trackless. It was wet, almost every step in had at least a little water. The forest was moderately dense with a mix of pine, cypress, and other hardwoods. There was some brush and lots of greenbrier near the edges, but it was more open in the interior. I wandered around almost aimlessly and just as I decided to stop and turn around, I heard a loud grunt. Was it an alligator? A loud frog? After a few seconds looking around there was a very loud thrashing and splashing as a whole herd of feral hogs ran away from me.

One beast stayed behind as the others ran. He had big, nasty-looking tusks and did not leave until the others were safely away. This was quite a sight, my first of feral hogs, which I later learned were a real problem in much of the southeast lowlands.

The wilderness.net website for this area said that it might be the least visited place in South Carolina. I believe it. Still, if a hiker is looking for solitude and wants to see well-preserved (except for the exotic wildlife) swamp, this might be an interesting destination. If you go, a GPS is essential. I gave myself a test here. Without a GPS, could I remember the direction back to my truck? The challenge was that in every direction, I saw exactly the same view. There were *no* landmarks. The answer was no, I could not find my back to the road without aid.

Wambaw Creek 1,825 acres, designated 1980, located in the Francis Marion National Forest west of US Highway 17, just south of the Santee River, and northwest of the town of McClellanville. The Wambaw Swamp and Little Wambaw Swamp Wilderness areas are nearby to the southwest. There were no trails. On April 1, 2009, the same day as the Wambaw Swamp Wilderness hike, I attempted the Wambaw Creek Wilderness. The areas were close and neither hike was long. The first attempted hike here was at a boat launch point at the far northern end of the wilderness. I walked the east creek bank a short way, but was blocked by a deep side channel. The forest was mostly cypress and other hardwoods with a dense understory. Hiking was always difficult and every step was in water. The creek itself was big, flat and lazy. After about an hour I gave up and went back to my truck. I drove upstream a bit and found another wilderness entry point. The hiking here was a bit easier with less understory. However, after not any great distance I was again stopped by a deep side channel.

Like the Wambaw Swamp Wilderness, no hiker should go here without a GPS, or in this case a compass would do. Unlike the Wambaw Swamp, this area could probably be attempted with a watercraft (from what I saw, the Wambaw Swamp would not be navigable by watercraft). I do not recommend it as a hiking destination.

Hell Hole Bay 2,125 acres, designated 1980, located in the Francis Marion National Forest southeast of State Highway 41, west of State Highway 45, and northwest of the town of McClellanville. There were no trails. My day hike on April 2, 2009 began along USFS Road 158, which ran along the northwestern wilderness boundary. I found a spot where a small bridge crossed a ditch next to the road. First, I put on my brand-new chest waters, because all of the wilderness forest is covered in water. A creek ran out of the wilderness here and I decided to walk up the creek to avoid dense undergrowth. The water was sometimes a little over waist high. After a bit I decided I was being really foolish because I could not get out of the creek with its steep banks if I had to because of water depth, a snake, or an alligator. I also realized that the bridge over the ditch was intended for people putting a canoe into the creek. Indeed, a canoe was probably the only sensible way to see this area.

Back at the road, I tried a second entry point, this one more open with less undergrowth. A barred owl watched me closely. The depth of water here was between a few inches and knee deep. There was a fair bit of grass and the forest was a mix of pine and hardwood including maple and cypress. While this area was unusual for me, it was clearly not a great hiking destination. Hikers should go elsewhere.

Later that evening, in a nearby USFS campground, I was telling some other campers, all locals, about my day's activities and was soundly scolded for using chest waders because of possible bad outcomes should one unwittingly step into deep water.

FLORIDA

Bradwell Bay 24,602 acres, designated 1975, located in the Apalachicola National Forest west of US Highway 319, north of State Highway 375, south of State Highway 267, and southwest of the city of Tallahassee. The Florida National Scenic Trail runs through the wilderness. My day hike on March 20, 2009 began at a trailhead for the Florida National Scenic Trail on the eastern wilderness boundary. The terrain was essentially flat with mostly pine trees, recently burned, with palmetto and huckleberry understory. There were occasional wet areas surrounded by thick brush. Some of the wet areas hosted alligators. The whole area was filled with birds, many migrating. I was able to identify a palm warbler, Bachman's sparrow, and Swainson's warbler. I continued on the trail west until I had used up half of my daylight, then turned around. Another case of, well, OK, but not much of a hiking destination.

Mud Swamp-New River 8,075 acres, designated 1984, located in the Apalachicola National Forest east of State Highway 65, north of County Road 22, and northwest of the town of Sumatra. The New River flows through the area. There were no trails. Access to this area was easy as it was almost surrounded by Forest Service roads. My visit on March 19, 2009 consisted of three short day hikes. The first, from Forest Road 114, was along the western wilderness boundary. The wilderness area here was very narrow. I hiked through dense forest to the New River, but did not attempt to cross. Back to the road, I drove south, still along the western wilderness boundary but now in the wider portion of the wilderness. Here I saw what looked like an old two-track. I took this east through burned forest of palmetto and other brush. Ultimately, the brush became impenetrable and I was forced to turn around. I went back north a bit and found another two-track heading east into the narrow neck of the wilderness. The hiking was easier here and I got to a pleasant bend in the river. I walked upstream a way, but was again blocked by dense brush. This was not much of a hiking destination. Someone new to Florida may find it interesting.

Big Gum Swamp 13,660 acres, designated 1984, located in the Osceola National Forest north of Interstate Highway 10, east of US Highway 441, and northeast of the town of Lake City. I did two birthday hikes in this wilderness on March 22, 2009. My map showed a trailhead on the eastern wilderness boundary near the intersection of State Highway 250 and USFS Road 235. There was an indistinct trail here that passed through very recently burned forest with lots of undergrowth. This

burned brush completely coated my trousers with fine charcoal. After a short way, the trail just disappeared into dense, green vegetation growing in a couple of inches of water. I backtracked a bit and tried another dim trail that similarly died in dense green brush. I thrashed on anyway until I gave up, in part because there did not appear to be anything interesting in this thicket. On my way out, I became badly tangled in brush and vines and ended up having my spectacles stripped from my face. I never found them. Bummer, although I always carry a spare.

My map also showed a loop trail in the northwestern part of the wilderness. Here I found a real trail, even marked with white paint blazes. Here also was flat terrain with pine and palmetto and other undergrowth. I completed the loop by walking up USFS Road 232. I was tempted to give this area only one star because I certainly did not find my day pleasant, but I have relented and included this wilderness with the two-star areas. No, I am not coming back.

Juniper Prairie 14,277 acres, designated 1984, located in the Ocala National Forest just north of State Highway 40, just west of State Highway 19, and east of the town of Ocala. The Florida National Scenic Trail runs through the wilderness. This wilderness presented me with a problem. I was here and not likely to return, but the wilderness area and all its trails were closed because of a very recent fire. I decided to ignore the closure. I parked about a mile away from the formal trailhead for the Florida National Scenic Trail and hiked to the northern wilderness boundary. To my surprise there was a fire truck there with two firefighters. I figured I was busted, but they were contract firefighters who had been checking conditions and told me the area was safe. We made a deal. If some official found me, I had never spoken with them, and if they saw an official, they had never seen me. This worked out as well as could be expected. The whole of my route this day was completely safe. My route on March 24, 2009 was south on the Florida National Scenic Trail until I used up half of my daylight, when I turned around and went back north. There was some fire damage, but it had burned in a mosaic pattern with no large expanses of burned vegetation. The terrain was not very interesting, just flat, sandy ground with undergrowth, some stands of pine, some stands of oak, and some shallow ponds for wetlands. Some wetlands had alligators.

One-Star Areas

★

MICHIGAN

Delirium 11,870 acres, designated 1987, located in the Hiawatha National Forest west of Interstate Highway 75, east of State Highway 123, south of State Highway 28, and southwest of the town of Sault Ste. Marie. My day hike on October 28, 2007 began near the end of USFS Road 3130 near the northeast wilderness boundary where my map showed a trail taking off across the wilderness. There were an astonishing number of folks here because it was hunting *and* trapping season. One hunter had been here before and pointed me to the trail that nominally goes across the wilderness. This so-called trail follows an old road or railroad grade and, as the hunter warned me, becomes progressively overgrown. The terrain was a dead-flat wetland with tamarack, spruce, hemlock, birch, and, worst of all, alder. I was forced to twist, duck, push, and turn my way through. I finally gave up when the route went into water. I was maybe just a bit more than halfway across the wilderness. Upon my return to the "trailhead" some trappers were there with their catch. They had lots of corpses, mostly muskrats but two beavers, two minks and one river otter. The trappers were at least legitimate, putting state tags on the animals. I cannot pretend to have enjoyed this hiking day. I do not recommend the area.

TENNESSEE

Gee Creek 2,493 acres, designated 1975, located in the Cherokee National Forest east of US Highway 141, west of State Highway 315, north of State Highway 30, and south of the town of Etowah. For my visit I used the National Geographic Trails Illustrated map 781, Cherokee National Forest.

It really had been a dark and stormy night. I had spent it in a USFS equestrian campground (the only occupant) and my truck was buffeted by wind and rain and falling tree branches. The morning featured utility workers restoring power after the night's storm damage. I drove a short way to the end of USFS Road 2013 where there was a trailhead for the Gee Creek Trail. My map said this trail was 1.8 miles long and was rated "difficult." It was still raining and windy, but the real issue was stream crossings. I managed one or two, but was stopped at one before the end of the trail. I gave up and turned around. Aside from the weather, what I saw hiking along this creek looked exactly like every other creekside trail in the southern Appalachians. I did this hike on October 17, 2006.

Little Frog Mountain 4,668 acres, designated 1986, located in the Cherokee National Forest north of US Highway 64/74, west of State Highway 68, and northwest of the town of Ducktown. For my visit I used the National Geographic Trails Illustrated map 781, Cherokee National Forest. This area has one trail, the Rock Creek, and I hiked half of it on October 19, 2006. It was a gray and rainy day and the sounds of traffic from US Highway 64/74 lasted a long time. The terrain and forest were indistinguishable from other hikes in this neighborhood. There are better hiking destinations in this area (like Big Frog).

Catfish Lake South 8,530 acres, designated 1984
Pond Pine 1,665 acres, designated 1984
Sheep Ridge 9,297 acres, designated 1984

These three areas are presented together because they are close together and I visited all of them in the same two-day period, April 6 and 7, 2009. All three are one-star areas. All three areas are in the Croatan National Forest west of US Highway 70, east of State Highway 58, north of State Highway 24, and west of the town of Havelock. There was not even the pretense of a trail in these areas.

April 6 was a day of thunderstorms. I had a hard time finding the areas because the wilderness boundaries were not posted. I finally found a spot off USFS Road 606 along the western boundary of the Catfish Lake South Wilderness. I was able to cross the roadside ditch on a culvert and found a very dim path that led east. The vegetation was super dense, but I was able to go maybe one route mile before getting totally tangled and stopped dead in my tracks. The terrain here was wet and spongy underfoot in a forest of hardwood and pine with a lot of undergrowth. My hard work of pushing into this area was not rewarded with anything of interest. This was a thrash, not a hike. My advice to any other hiker is to stay away.

Looking to next visit the Pond Pine Wilderness, I drove to the end of USFS Road 126, which runs along the western wilderness boundary. There were some off-duty marines fishing and they warned me about alligators. I went back down the road a bit and saw a relatively open area and charged in. I was soon stopped by a veritable wall of vegetation. I backed up and charged again in a different direction but with the same result. There was not so much as a gap or crease in the wall. I gave up. This was another thrash, not a hike.

April 7 was at least a nice weather day. This was my day to attempt the Sheep Ridge Wilderness. The area is bounded on the north by the USFS Catfish Lake Road and on the northeast by the gated USFS Road 121-3. I parked by the gate and walked down Forest Road 121-3 looking for an entry point into the wilderness. I made a couple of attempts but in each case I was blocked by impenetrable masses of vegetation, especially greenbrier.

Later I went back to Catfish Lake Road and found a hint of an opening and went south for a small fraction of a mile before being blocked yet again. I took zero photos. These areas might be of some interest to botanists, but not to hikers. Crowds will not be a problem.

Middle Prong 7,460 acres, designated 1984, located in the Pisgah National Forest east and south of the Blue Ridge Parkway, west of State Highway 215, and south of the town of Waynesville. The Shining Rock Wilderness is just to the east. For this hike I used a USFS map for the Middle Prong and Shining Rock areas. My day hike on October 31, 2006 began at a locked gate on USFS Road 97 near the Sunburst Campground where I had spent the previous night. I hiked the road south to a trailhead for the Haywood Gap Trail, then took that trail to the wilderness boundary. Here the trail crossed the stream, but for some reason I did not want to cross and instead followed an old road to the Big Beartrap Branch. I hiked up the Beartrap Branch. This may not have been a good choice as the route was steep with lots of tangles of laurel and greenbrier. I gave up this route well before getting to Reinhart Gap. I basically just walked back to my truck. I may have missed some trails, but I certainly did not see trails that corresponded to what I saw on my map. This was a frustrating day in an area that looked a lot like all the other areas in this neighborhood. In my opinion, hikers would be better off in the nearby Shining Rock Wilderness.

Indian Mounds 12,369 acres, designated 1984, located in the Sabine National Forest on the west shore of the Toledo Bend Reservoir, south of Farm-to-Market Road 83, east of State Highway 87, and east of the town of Hemphill. The wilderness is divided by roads and a pipeline into six segments. My notes from this day are sparse. I know I hiked on a trail, but did not note in which segment. The "trail" was an old road, mostly overgrown. Hiking off the road was nearly impossible because of dense, thorny undergrowth. My notes are quite specific about my finding this area overtly unpleasant and uninteresting. I did this hike on February 13, 2007. I took no photos.

Turkey Hill 5,473 acres, designated 1984, located in the Angelina National Forest southeast of State Highway 147, north of Farm-to-Market Road 83, west of Farm-to-Market Road 705, and southwest of the town of San Augustine. According to my Angelina National Forest map there were no trails in this area, but the wilderness.net website said there was a trail off USFS Road 307. It took me awhile, but I found a parking area (no signs) off this road where there was a flagged route that went through brush and shortleaf pine until it made a dead end. I went beyond the trail's end until I saw traffic on a road and turned around. No doubt about it, this hike was neither pleasant nor interesting. I did this hike on February 14, 2007.

Upland Island 13,331 acres, designated 1984, located in the Angelina National Forest east of US Highway 69, south of State Highway 63, and southeast of the town of Zavalla. Here again, my Angelina National Forest map showed no trails, but a USFS employee told me that I might find a trail off USFS Road 314. I tried this and found a parking area and with more searching found an old road that looked like it might go somewhere. The hiking was OK for a little while, but deteriorated as brush had reclaimed the road. In fact, the hiking was easier in the forest than on the old road. It did not take very long and I was tired of the thrashing, so I just turned around and finished another not very pleasant day in a totally uninteresting area. I left southeast Texas with no regrets.

GEORGIA

Rich Mountain 9,476 acres, designated 1986, located in the Chattahoochee National Forest southeast of US Highway 76, northeast of State Highway 52, and northeast of the town of Ellijay. Somehow, I had been led to believe that this area was hard to access. It was. After an unreasonably long time blundering around, I found myself at the northern wilderness boundary at Indian Grave Gap. There was a sort of trail that led me to what my notes call a "bridge to nowhere." I could not understand the reason for the bridge. It took me awhile to find the trail on the other side. Not much later, still blundering around, I was running out of daylight so I went back to my truck. This was a frustrating day in an area devoid of anything interesting. There are much better hiking areas in Georgia.

FLORIDA

Billies Bay 3,092 acres, designated 1984, located in the Ocala National Forest east of State Highway 19, west and north of Highway 445, and southwest of the town of Astor Park. Prior to this day I had asked some locals about how to gain access to this wilderness without a boat (a sizeable creek flows through the wilderness). Nobody could make any suggestions. I scouted the area on USFS roads but did not see anything promising. Finally, I just parked at the northwest corner of the wilderness and dove into the brush, hoping to go southeast to the creek. I did not get far. The vegetation was very dense with vines wrapped around vines. It was impenetrable. My notes say that this is one of my worst hikes ever. If anyone wants to visit, do it by boat. I did this hike on March 25, 2009.

Alexander Springs 7,941 acres, designated 1984, managed by the Ocala National Forest west of US Highway 17, north of State Highway 42, and west of the town of DeLand. The Lake Woodruff National Wildlife Refuge is to the east across the Saint Johns River. There were no trails. Forest Roads 552 and 552-A ran along parts of the western wilderness boundary. On March 25, 2009 I picked a spot where an old two-track entered the wilderness and began a day hike. The two-track dissolved into several branches, all of which disappeared into heavy undergrowth. The forest was nice with palm and oak and other hardwoods. I went back to my truck and drove north to the end of Forest Road 552-A and took another dive into dense undergrowth. There was a slough here with at least one resident alligator. I wandered around aimlessly for a while and then went back to my truck.

Cinder cones in the main crater from the Sliding Sands Trail,
Haleakala Wilderness, Hawaii

Tropical Rainforest, Hawaii

Readers do not need me to tell them what a tropical rainforest is, but I will nonetheless give a brief description. First, it is warm year-round, or at least never cold (with a few exceptions for very high elevations). It rains pretty much all year. There is a lot of vegetation, often dense, and trees can be quite large. Species diversity tends to be high. The United States has only three designated wilderness areas in tropical rainforest. Two are in the state of Hawaii and one in the territory of Puerto Rico. I have only visited the two in Hawaii. Indeed, the El Toro Wilderness in Puerto Rico is the *only* USFS wilderness that I have not visited, in part because I only learned of its existence in 2014 and also because it has been closed to the public for much of the subsequent time, now mostly due to hurricane damage.

Hawaii Volcanoes

★ ★ ★ ★

Size: 130,790 acres · **Year Designated:** 1978 · **Responsible Agency:** USNPS

The Hawaii Volcanoes Wilderness is located in the southern part of the "Big" Island of Hawaii. Access is by State Highway 11. There are four parts of the wilderness—Mauna Loa, Ka'u Desert, East Rift, and Ola'a Forest.

MY VISIT: May 9–11, 2015 and May 13, 2015

I made this trip with a friend and we visited the four wilderness segments on four separate day hikes. The first day we took the Mauna Loa Trail from the end of the Mauna Loa Road. It was a steady climb with good views of the Kilauea Crater sending up a modest column of smoke. The weather was not the best, hiking mostly in mist. We were impressed with the pink lava along the trail. There was some forest, everything was new to us, and there were lots of birds. Once away from the trailhead we saw no other hikers.

Our second day hike was on the Napau Trail from the Chain of Craters Road. This was in the East Rift section of the wilderness. The hike began as a pure lava hike winding through old flows and following a chain of cairns. Soon, wind and rain descended and we came to the Makaopuhi Crater with some smoke and steam and then entered a real jungle. The trail became progressively more narrow and wet and we turned around before getting to my nominal objective of the Napau Crater. Again, once away from the trailhead we saw no other hikers.

The third day hike was to the Ka'u Desert section of the wilderness. We began at a trailhead off State Highway 11. We climbed to the top of the Maunaiki Volcano, then went west through the desert through fascinating old lava flows and cinder cones until it was time to turn around.

The fourth wilderness segment is the Ola'a Forest. My understanding was that the Park Service did not want people in this protected intact segment, but when driving along the western boundary we saw no signs telling people to keep out, so I did a quick solo excursion into the jungle. It certainly gave me the impression of an honest, genuine, undisturbed bit of jungle. I had no idea what plant species I was seeing. All these hikes were in fascinating, lovely terrain. I highly recommend anyone visiting the island to do some hiking here.

Pink lava flow along the Mauna Loa Trail, Hawaii Volcanoes Wilderness

Haleakala

★ ★ ★ ★

Size: 24,719 acres   **Year Designated:** 1976
Responsible Agency: USNPS

The Haleakala Wilderness is located in the southeast portion of the island of Maui. Access is by State Highway 378.

MY VISIT: May 15, 2015 and May 16, 2015

The first of two day hikes began at the visitor center at the southwest corner of the park. We took the Sliding Sands Trail east, descending from the crater rim through fields of lava and cinder cones sticking up through the main crater. This was a fascinating journey through a quintessential volcanic landscape. We went to the Kapalaoa Cabin where we had lunch. As soon as we arrived a contingent of nene, a remnant population of geese, surrounded us hoping to be fed. We resisted. After lunch we turned around and retraced our steps.

The second hike I did by myself. I began at a trailhead for the Halemau'u Trail. The trail descended thorough dramatic volcanic cliffs and into the main crater. The route was through much more vegetation than the previous day. Again, there were lava flows and cinder cones inside the main crater. I went past the Holua Cabin, then around the Silversword Loop where I turned around. Both of these hikes were marvelous, always in interesting and highly scenic terrain. There were lots of other hikers on both days.

Acknowledgments

I have had some remarkable mentors in my early days of hiking and backpacking. While this list is long, two people who stand out are Paul McCarthy and Kord Smith.

Also, I would never have been able to travel as easily and with as much confidence in Alaska without the expertise of very knowledgeable bush pilots. These include Michelle Masden with Island Wings in Ketchikan, Drake Olsen in Haines, the pilots and crew of Harris Aircraft Services in Sitka, the pilots and crew of Brooks Range Aviation in Bettles, and Steller Air Service in Homer. Also, thanks to Dave Metz for generously sharing his photographic expertise. Many thanks to you all.

Waterfall above Leduc Lake, Misty Fiords Wilderness, Alaska

Wilderness Areas Visited, by Number of Stars

★ ★ ★ ★ ★

Alaska
Coronation Island (USFS), p. 12
Gates of the Arctic (USNPS), p. 5
Misty Fiords (USFS), p. 7
South Etolin (USFS), p. 8
Tracy Arm-Fords Terror (USFS), p. 11
West Chichagov-Yakobi (USFS), p. 10
Wrangell-Saint Elias (USNPS), p. 4

California
Ansel Adams (USFS), p. 59
Hoover (USFS), p. 60
John Muir (USFS), p. 61
Phillip Burton (USNPS), p. 64
Sequoia-Kings Canyon (USNPS). p. 63
Trinity Alps (USFS), p. 58
Yosemite (USNPS), p. 61

Colorado
Maroon Bells (USFS), p. 113

Idaho
Sawtooth (USFS), p. 104

Montana
Absaroka-Beartooth (USFS, also Wyoming). p. 105

Oregon
Three Sisters (USFS), p. 19

Utah
Zion (USNPS), p. 114

Washington
Alpine Lakes (USFS), p. 18
Daniel J. Evans (USNPS), p. 13
Glacier Peak (USFS), p. 15
Mount Rainer (USNPS), p. 15
Pasayten (USFS), p. 16
Stephen Mather (USNPS), p. 14

Wyoming
Bridger (USFS), p. 107
Fitzpatrick (USFS), p. 107
Gros Ventre (USFS), p. 109
Jedediah Smith (USFS), p. 111
Popo Agie (USFS), p. 107
Washakie (USFS), p. 110

★ ★ ★ ★

Alaska
Chuck River (USFS), p. 21
Denali (USNPS), p. 25
Glacier Bay (USNPS), p. 22
Lake Clark (USNPS), p. 23
Noatak (USNPS), p. 24
Stikine-LeConte (USFS), p. 20

Arizona
Aravaipa Canyon (BLM), p. 196
Chiricahua National Monument (USNPS), p. 195
Kofa Refuge (USFWS), p. 197
Superstition (USFS), p. 194

California
Joshua Tree (USNPS), p. 67
Lassen Volcanic (USNPS), p. 65
Mokelumne (USFS), p. 66
San Mateo Canyon (USFS), p. 67
Siskiyou (USFS), p. 64

Colorado
Black Ridge Canyons (BLM), p. 128
Collegiate Peaks (USFS), p. 123
Eagle's Nest (USFS), p. 125
Holy Cross (USFS), p. 124
Hunter-Fryingpan (USFS), p. 124
Rocky Mountain National Park (USNPS), p. 127
Weminuche (USFS), p. 126
West Elk (USFS), p. 127

Georgia
Cumberland Island (USNPS), p. 244
Okefenokee (USFWS), p. 243

Hawaii
Haleakala (USNPS), p. 301
Hawaii Volcanoes (USNPS), p. 300

Idaho
Cecil D. Andrus-White Clouds (USFS), p. 118
Craters of the Moon (USNPS), p. 199
Frank Church-River of No Return (USFS), p. 117
Selway-Bitterroot (also Montana, USFS), p. 115

Montana
Anaconda-Pintler (USFS), p. 120
Cabinet Mountains (USFS), p. 120

Nevada
Jarbidge (USFS), p. 132
Muddy Mountains (USNPS/BLM), p. 134
Ruby Mountains (USFS), p. 133

New Mexico
Bisti/De-Ne-Zin (BLM), p. 199
Pecos (USFS), p. 198

Oregon
Eagle Cap (USFS), p. 28

South Carolina
Congaree National Park (USNPS), p. 242

South Dakota
Badlands (USNPS), p. 234

Tennessee
Joyce Kilmer-Slickrock/Citico Creek (USFS), p. 241

Utah
Ashdown Gorge (USFS), p. 129
Dark Canyon (USFS), p. 130
High Uinta (USFS), p. 131
Mount Timpanogos (USFS), p. 132

Washington
Goat Rocks (USFS), p. 27
Mount Baker (USFS), p. 26

Wyoming
Cloud Peak (USFS), p. 121
Teton (USFS), p. 122

★ ★ ★

Alabama
Cheaha (USFS), p. 272
Sipsey (USFS), p. 273

Alaska
Karta River (USFS), p. 30
Katmai (USNPS), p. 32
Kenai (USFWS), p. 32

Unaware Goat (top), Aware Goat (bottom), Misty Fiords, Wilderness, Alaska

Arctic Poppy, Gates of the Arctic Wilderness, Alaska

 ★ ★

Wilderness Areas Visited, by State

Fang Mountain, Denali Wilderness, Alaska

Between obstacles, Misty Fiords Wilderness, Alaska

Tundra and Caribou Antlers, Continental Divide, Gates of the Arctic Wilderness, Alaska

Moss Campion, Denali Wilderness, Alaska